Wild Experiment

Duke University Press
Durham and London 2022

WILD EXPERIMENT
FEELING SCIENCE AND SECULARISM AFTER DARWIN

Donovan O. Schaefer

© 2022 DUKE UNIVERSITY PRESS
All rights reserved
Designed by A. Mattson Gallagher
Typeset in Garamond Premier Pro, ITC Clearface Std,
and ITC Franklin Gothic Std by Westchester Publishing Services

Library of Congress Cataloging-in-Publication Data
Names: Schaefer, Donovan O., [date] author.
Title: Wild experiment : feeling science and secularism after Darwin / Donovan O. Schaefer.
Description: Durham : Duke University Press, 2022. | Includes bibliographical references and index.
Identifiers: LCCN 2021033004 (print)
LCCN 2021033005 (ebook)
ISBN 9781478015628 (hardcover)
ISBN 9781478018254 (paperback)
ISBN 9781478022879 (ebook)
Subjects: LCSH: Religion and science. | Secularism. | Atheism. | Knowledge, Theory of. | Emotions (Philosophy) | Science—Social aspects. | BISAC: RELIGION / Religion & Science | PHILOSOPHY / Religious
Classification: LCC BL240.3 .S3443 2022 (print) | LCC BL240.3 (ebook) | DDC 201/.65—dc23/eng/20211008
LC record available at https://lccn.loc.gov/2021033004
LC ebook record available at https://lccn.loc.gov/2021033005

Cover art: Barbara Takenaga, *Atmosphere L and R* (detail), 2017. Acrylic on linen, 72 × 72 inches (overall). Private collection. Courtesy of the artist and DC Moore Gallery, New York.

For Allison

Our passions do not live apart in locked chambers, but, dressed in their small wardrobe of notions, bring their provisions to a common table and mess together, feeding out of the common store according to their appetite.
—George Eliot, *Middlemarch*

How far is truth susceptible of embodiment?—that is the question, that is the experiment.
—Friedrich Nietzsche, *The Joyful Wisdom*

Contents

Introduction. COGENCY THEORY 1
An Essay on Our Intellectual Affects

Part I Cogency Theory

1. THE LONGING TO BELIEVE 33
Philosophers on Conspiracy Theory and the Sense of Science

2. SENSUALIZED EPISTEMOLOGY 57
Affect Theory on How Reason Gets Racialized

3. SCIENCE AS AN INTOXICATION 80
Secularism Studies on Enchantment and Critique

4. FEELING IS BELIEVING 107
The Triune Brain, Mere Exposure, and Cogency

Part II Feeling Science and Secularism

5. ONLY BETTER BEASTS 137
Darwin, Huxley, and the Sense of Science

6. THE SECULAR CIRCUS 169
Science and Racialized Reason in the Scopes Trial

7. THE FOUR HORSEMEN 200
New Atheism as Secular Conspiracy Theory

Epilogue. FROM CREATIONISM TO CLIMATE DENIALISM 230

Acknowledgments 239
Notes 243
Bibliography 281
Index 309

INTRODUCTION
COGENCY THEORY
AN ESSAY ON
OUR INTELLECTUAL
AFFECTS

Thinking Feeling

In the early spring of 1863, Charles Darwin wrote to a botanist at London's Kew Gardens asking for specimens of lichens or mosses. "For love of heaven," he pleaded, "favour my madness & have some scraped off & sent to me. I am like a gambler, & love a wild experiment."[1] Darwin's son, Francis Darwin, confirmed this strange self-description, writing that "love of experiment was very strong in him, and I can remember the way he would say, 'I shan't be easy till I have tried it,' as if an outside force were driving him."[2] Janet Browne, Darwin's preeminent contemporary biographer, describes how Darwin found research to be a sort of compulsion. He was "stirred by the excitement of hard scientific thought."[3]

This exhilarating sense of science shows up again in Evelyn Fox Keller's biography of Nobel Prize winner Barbara McClintock, whose research on corn genetics revolutionized her field. She accomplished this through what Keller calls a *feeling for the organism*. "I start with the seedling," McClintock told her, "and I don't want to leave it. I don't feel I really know the story if I don't watch the plant all the way along. So I know every plant in the field. I know them intimately, and I find it a great pleasure to know them."[4] This vivid joy in detail, in mapping the subtleties of a living landscape of information—the length of the stalks, the tint of the leaves, the jostling rows of kernels—was the driver of McClintock's vision.

Keller likens McClintock to Albert Einstein—an Einstein of the ear of corn. Although Einstein's science was numbers and particles rather than beautiful things like plants and animals, he, too, was convinced that science comes from emotion. Common sense says numbers work is quintessentially boring—exactly the thing you do *without* feeling. But that conventional wisdom doesn't hold up. Mathematicians describe their work as richly emotional, likening it to music, mysticism, or poetry. Mathematician Srinivasa Ramanujan may have had something like this in mind when he famously told a colleague, "An equation has no meaning for me unless it expresses a thought of God."[5]

Einstein—said to have put the finishing touches on his theory of general relativity by sitting down at a piano—wrote in 1930 that science demands "strength of the emotion."[6] Like his hero Spinoza, he rejected the claim that emotion and reason were in conflict. Instead, he insisted that the emotional taproot of science was *identical* with the motivating force driving religion. They were one and the same, a compulsion he called *cosmic religious feeling*. As Einstein's protégé Michael Polanyi wrote, the "inarticulate coefficient by which we understand and assent to mathematics" is not a dry, mechanical function. It's a *longing*, a need, a "passion for intellectual beauty."[7]

It's not just scientists who feel the life of the mind. The rich work of historians, philosophers, anthropologists, and other scholars of the humanities is joyful too. The ecstasy of the historian is the deep dive in the archives, finding connections, tracing the contours of a story—maybe even making a discovery that breaks ground. David Hume called philosophy "the ruling Passion of my Life and the Great Source of my Enjoyments."[8] Narrative pleasure, all the pieces of a story coming together—Chekhov's loaded rifle on the wall in chapter 1 becoming murder weapon in chapter 3—is the same kind of stuff, a *clicking-into-place*. Bad writing—plot hole, weakly drawn character, abrupt deus ex machina—breaks the spell because it interrupts this stream of pleasure, as astringent as a wrong note in a song. The electric charge of *thinking-learning-knowing* is the lifeblood of teaching, too, planting students in their seats, temples tightening, shoulders shifting forward, hands fluttering, then shooting up, just like it keeps us, their teachers, wedded to our archives, our consultants, our laboratories, our calculations, our classrooms, our blackboards, our books, generation after generation. Even the grammar nerd, secretly correcting typos in library books, is playing with language, mining joy from the arcana of structured rules and subtly mutating conventions.

We can take this further. This isn't just a theory of nerding out; it sets out to explain all our everyday pleasures of exploration and interaction. Like wikiholes, the hypnosis of the encyclopedia sending us scrambling up trellises of fascination, ruining disciplined bedtimes. Or puzzles—crosswords, jigsaws, Tetris—all designed to draw us into a pleasurized sphere of *playing by thinking*, organizing a maze of noise into a tidy whole. We find it in gossip, the piecing together of secrets. It's in the love of devices and contraptions and things that work in weird ways. And the joy of a good mystery. If, as affect theorist Lauren Berlant writes, literary genres are delivery systems for different emotional flavors—horror, romance, adventure—the emotional tone of the detective story has something to do with *neatness*, the way it wraps up the elements of a plot in a satisfying *click*.[9] We thrill to the immaculate resolution, a symphony of details in sudden alignment. A bad detective story overpromises and underdelivers, setting up a dizzying mystery around so many glittering plot points, only to collapse in a screeching mess of forced revelations and junk red herrings.

In bringing all these examples together, my suggestion is this: as diverse as they might seem at first glance, they all draw on the same emotional aquifer. The strange hothouses in which researchers make knowledge—study, archive, seminar room, laboratory, observatory—are just highly structured venues for channeling and focusing something we experience all the time: the way thinking feels. They're the macro forms of a micrological process that's with us every moment of the day, sometimes above, sometimes below, the watery threshold of awareness. Math, science, history, philosophy, and all other forms of formalized knowledge-making are scaled-up versions of this micro-level delight in the subtle click of things coming together. And that's what it really is. *Click*: the feeling that drives us to learn about the world. Click is how it feels when pieces of information coalesce. A phone book is pure information, but it doesn't click. A letter in a shoebox handed down by your ancestors, now crumbling in your basement, may be dull to you, but to a historian immersed in its time and place, for whom the letter solves a puzzle—or changes how the story is told—it's radiant.

With all that said, the emotions that move thought don't just deliver better history books, sharper equations, and more effective medicines. This is the golden age of misinformation—of conspiracy theory, climate denialism, and self-serving selective belief. We have yet to escape from the droning refrain of those who benefit from slanted regimes of knowledge naming their own thoughts *reason* and dismissing everything else as *emotion*. Discredited race science keeps getting dug up from its shallow grave and retrofitted to contemporary formations of white supremacy. What I'm going to call *cogency theory* sees knowledge-making (from monograph, laboratory, and archive to group text, Reddit thread, and people-watching at a café) as defined by pleasure. But that knowledge includes both truth and error. Feeling makes science work, but it also leads to the *collapse* of good knowledge—the giddy downward spiral of conspiracism or the intoxicated self-confirmations of racialized reason. There's no way out of this dynamic of risk and opportunity. But studying how rationality works by feeling its way along offers our best chance to name and cultivate the habits and dispositions that make up the sense of science and veer away from the traps set by our own sweet tooth.

The conventional wisdom is that thinking and feeling are opposites. *Be reasonable*, we're told. *Don't be ruled by your emotions*. It's the standard maneuver deployed after a crisis—environmental disaster, racist police brutality, senseless gun violence—to fortify the status quo. Even in academic conversations, the divide between feeling and thinking is mostly taken for granted. Although science and technology studies (STS) has spent half a century showing that science isn't just what's in our heads—that knowledge production is always practical, social, and embodied—almost no work has been dedicated to exploring the relationship between knowledge-making and *feeling*.[10] STS pioneer Bruno Latour, for instance, for all his sophisticated accounts of how science is made by coalitions of human bodies and nonhuman actants, still argues that science is *emotionally inert*.[11] Even affect theory (the scene of some of the most interesting contemporary conversations about feeling) often seems to offer a funhouse mirror of common sense, recapitulating the assumption that feeling is separate from thinking.[12]

This thinking/feeling binary is also integral to the self-understanding of many modern visions of secularism. The story of secularization as the slow but steady fade-out of religion depicts rationality floating above the world and guiding history, immune to the local, the particular, the bodily, and—especially—the emotional. As we'll see, cogency theory is by no means antisecular, but it rejects the mythology of superlunary rationality that sees reason as destined to straighten everything out (a view that, incidentally, also has no shortage of religious advocates). Cogency theory shines a light on the secular not as the gleaming fortress of reason, but as a humming network of tastes, dispositions, and moods laying down the rhythm that enables our memories, ideas, concepts, and beliefs.

There are, however, academic conversations where the thinking/feeling binary is being challenged. Bringing some of these conversations together is the project of part I of this book. My focus will be on eighteenth- and nineteenth-century philosophy in the prelude and aftermath of Darwin (chapter 1), affect theory (chapter 2), recent research on secularism and what's being called the postcritical turn (chapter 3), neuroscience, and experimental psychology (chapter 4). But disruptions of the feeling/thinking binary have been put forward by many others not considered at length here, including ancient Stoics and their contemporary interpreters,[13] premodern Christians,[14] philosophers like Spinoza and Alfred North Whitehead,[15] French Enlightenment *philosophes*,[16] the New Formalists in literary studies,[17] phenomenologists,[18] Black studies thinkers,[19] moral psychologists,[20] and other lineages of affect theory.[21] And those are just the Western outlooks. These conversations are already happening in Islamic thought, Indian philosophy, and Indigenous philosophy in the Americas, among other places.[22]

This book's goal in pulling these conversations together is to challenge the ambient belief that feeling and thinking are separate. I go further than some others who have advanced this challenge in contending, for instance, that knowledge-making is not just *entangled* with feeling, as some claim (*Feeling* can *shape how we think, under certain circumstances*), but encompassed by it (*Feeling is* necessary *for thinking; there is no thinking that is not feeling*). Moreover, some existing work uses *affect* to indicate the intellect's *affectability*, as susceptible to the world around it.[23] I go further in suggesting that tangible *feelings* make thinking happen. (As we'll see in chapter 1, naming many specific intellectual emotions is vital for understanding how science is made by feelings in tension.) This book also sets out to connect studies of reason and feeling with STS. In particular, a main concern of STS is *methodological symmetry*: explaining *both* good and bad knowledge—both truth and error—with the same theory. The goal of the first half of this book, then, is to link up a landscape of dispersed conversations about the relationship between feeling and thinking, and to place that relationship at the center of a new understanding of truth, persuasion, reason, secularism, and science itself.

This is a first step rather than a detailed schematic, so one feature of this book will be a light-touch approach to some central vocabulary, including terms like *feeling* and *cognition*. *Feeling* is used loosely as a rough-and-ready synonym for kin words like *affect* and *emotion*, shelving, for now, technical senses of those terms developed in fields like emotion psychology and affect theory.[24] *Cognition* will be used as a catchall to include many kinds of thought like *reasoning, knowing, recalling, discovering,* and *learning*. Similarly, I'm going to use *knowledge production* and *knowledge-making* as master terms that include science and the humanities as well as the informal, everyday ways bodies watch, learn from, and think about the world. *Science* comes down from its pedestal, too, and should be heard as any organized system of knowledge production, including the human, social, and natural sciences, but also folding in modes of knowledge-making happening outside formal settings. Finally, I won't go deep into debates about *secularism, secularity,* and *the secular*. I'll note where different thinkers pose these words in different ways, but my own use will tend to run them together.

Cogency Theory: Two Arguments

This book makes a small argument and a big one. The small argument is that the reason/emotion binary is a mistake. Thinking feels. There's no thinking that doesn't feel, and nothing that we know that we don't know through feeling. In keeping with STS scholars' interest in methodological symmetry, this approach addresses *both* how science succeeds *and* how it fails.[25] If our bodies can feel their way to truth, how do we stumble into error? And if knowledge is only ever made by riding the current of our feelings, how could it *ever* be true? The small argument maps the feeling of thinking with an eye to understanding how science still works after we've untethered it from the myth of icy reason. New knowledge *feels true* to us because it lands on our existing landscape of understanding in a way that fits. It clicks with the terrain already in place. If the landscape is skewed—if it's out of alignment with the way the world actually is—then the knowledge that clicks with it will all be twisted, too.

The small argument of this book is engaged with a concept still viewed with suspicion in some camps of the humanities: scientific rationality. It's the suspicion of those who have in full view the abuses of natural science—long histories of scientific racism, sexism, homophobia, and transphobia, for instance. It's why Michel Foucault, in the preface to *The Order of Things*, insists that scientific development is not progress, but a randomly guided intellectual shapeshift, the same history of oppression donning new masks and parading on a loop.[26]

When we read Foucault together, my students are often skeptical toward these passages. How can knowledge not get better, they ask? Don't we *know more* now than we did a hundred or a thousand years ago? But when Foucault put pen to paper in the mid-1960s, even though France had not had antisodomy laws since the revolution in 1791, there was no forgetting that gay sex was under permanent siege by psychiatry, medicine, and law. For all he knew, the scientific establishment that had medicalized homosexuality in Britain (where the punishment for those convicted of "gross indecency," like Alan Turing just ten years earlier, was chemical castration) would take hold in France.

And meanwhile, France and other colonial powers were only recently letting go of their overseas claims, often with ferocious violence. Anticolonial thinkers like Frantz Fanon—born in the colonies and daily victims of their cruelty—knew that the European intellectual apparatus of their time was rigged against them. "When someone else strives and strains to prove to me that black men are as intelligent as white men," he wrote in 1952, "I say that intelligence has never saved anyone; and that is true, for, if philosophy and intelligence are invoked to proclaim the equality of men, they have also been employed to justify the extermination of men."[27] That same apparatus defined their race as the biological basis of their oppression. Science (not to mention the humanities) was used to reinforce racist, sexist, and heterosexist hierarchies. So why trust science?

Even though the scientific establishment has today abandoned these positions, the evergreen interest in pseudoscience—like the racial intelligence hierarchies still in common currency in the right-wing mediaverse—puts science under a permanent shroud of suspicion in the eyes of many humanities scholars. There's justification for this wariness. But it's dangerous to cut off contact with science. It ignores the diligent work of antiracist, feminist, and antiheterosexist scientists to mobilize science as a weapon against oppression. It cedes too much ground in the public conversation, allowing science to be picked up and distorted by oppressive power. And it overlooks the vital contributions offered by science to interrupting climate catastrophe, misinformation, and pandemics, not to mention burying the oppressive ideas it once shielded. This leads to a lost opportunity to understand science, learn its limits and possibilities, engage and ally with it. Thinking about science as feeling helps to set up this dialogue.

This brings us to the big argument of the book: if thinking isn't the unfolding of pure reason, then the fact that cognition feels is what makes it work *and* what leaves it open to error. If reason feels, then it's *susceptible*, rather than immune, to the other emotions swirling around it. This includes emotions wrapped up with self-interest, prejudice, or confirmation bias. Feminist STS scholars Rebecca Jordan-Young and Katrina Karzakis call this the *Mulder effect*, after the motto of fictional conspiracy theorist Fox Mulder: I WANT TO BELIEVE.[28]

Wanting to believe is not limited to scientists. The feeling/reason binary makes it impossible to see that all kinds of knowledge production are defined by structures of feeling—sprawling grids of emotion that make our existing prejudices *feel like* neutral reason. Philosopher Imani Perry, for instance, has suggested that the conventional understanding of racism as *intentional*—something we're aware of, something we think and say—is inadequate. She proposes, instead, that we think of racism as something shaped by "visceral responses to assumptions that operate *within* the process of reason and analysis."[29] These visceral responses produce a landscape of thought on which racist logic *feels right*.[30] They're in direct contact with the emotional machinery of scientific knowledge production. That intimacy is exactly what threatens to pull science off course.

Mary Ann Evans—the British polymath who saloned with scientists, translated Spinoza, and helped build nineteenth-century secularism through the novels and essays she published under her pen name, George Eliot—was a shrewd observer of this process. She put it this way: "Our passions do not live apart in locked chambers, but, dressed in their small wardrobe of notions, bring their provisions to a common table and *mess together*."[31] *Messing together* is the big argument of this book in a nutshell. If reason is itself a passion, then it *messes together* with the other feelings that define our lives. It eats (*messes*) at the same table with them, and it sloshes around (*messes*) in the same cup, creating a strange brew of felt intuitions from which thought emerges, dripping. This is how the argument that thinking feels transacts with a set of implications for studying science and secularism.

To understand science, reason, secularism, and our everyday ways of thinking about the world, we need to see them not as cloistered speculation but as rubbing elbows with the other passions of our embodied lives. Science as a felt process that registers the way things are in the world produces good knowledge, but it's also susceptible to contamination. It messes together with the other emotions that give form to our social, embodied lives. A racist society will tend to produce racist science not just because of bad data but because the coordinates of interpretation of that data—of *what feels true*—are disfigured. Science also has a powerful engine of self-correction, though: our felt desire to *get things right*. The struggle—the agonism—between these tendencies is what an affective account of knowledge-making sets out to diagram.

This is the framework of cogency theory. Why *cogency*? To say an argument is *cogent* doesn't mean, exactly, that it's *true*. It means *it appeals*, or *it's compelling*. It means it *feels* true. It has a *pull*—a weight. *Cogency* takes knowledge-making out of a binary frame, in which sovereign reason sizes up a situation, strokes its chin, and then judiciously flicks the switch to YES or NO. It suggests, instead, knowledge-making as an ongoing *process*—a contest of forces—and specifically as a constant measuring and remeasuring of the *felt* weight of facts. Cogency lights up the way our spectrum of confidence and conviction is always constituted by feeling. New information that tips the balance *adds weight*. Changing our minds means changing how we feel.

Cogency, at first glance, looks to be related to the Latin *cogito*—the *I think* part of René Descartes's *cogito ergo sum*—and modern English words like *cogitate*. But *cogent* isn't related to *cogito* at all. It comes from the Latin roots *co-*, meaning "together," and *agō*, meaning "drive" or "act." Its descendants are English words like *agent* or *action*. The related Greek root *ágō* gives the further sense of a "guide" or "duct" and enters English in words like the *agonism* of dramatic action, or the *pedagogy* of guiding the young, or *axiom*—a thing found to be weighty. Cogency as *cō + agō* corrals all these meanings. This *confluence and contest of forces* is *agonism*, a struggle of different priorities. To say something is *cogent* is not the self-evident testimony of truth to an abstract intellect. It spotlights forces streaming together, creating a tangible *feeling of truth* measured by the body. These forces interact on the microregister of feeling. *Believing* means one of these struggling currents of feeling has prevailed. It has, for now, been found *cogent*.

Cogitation pictures rationality as a grid of abacus beads that we carefully arrange to produce a binary YES/NO belief. It obscures the cascade of affective forces that are the real drivers of reasoning, thinking, and believing. Like a light switch, cogitation is either on or off. Cogency is scalar; we feel *more* or *less* convinced. Affect theorist Eve Kosofsky Sedgwick gets at this when she names the fatal defect of so much Western epistemology as the *threshold model* of knowing: "Once you've *learned* it you *know* it, and then you will always know it until you *forget* it. ... In this model," she points out, "learning the same thing again makes as much sense as getting the same pizza delivered twice."[32] It's knowing like a computer knows, since hard drives either contain information or they don't. But nothing we know actually follows this template. We're always in states of varying degrees of conviction. No one believes anything absolutely—even if some beliefs are strong enough to die for. This goes for science, too. Rather than thinking of it as an abstract truth machine, centering cogency allows us to study how scientific rationality is built, how it tests and explores, how it inculcates confidence or gets impaled by prejudice, how it succeeds or falls. Cogency theory is a collection of perspectives on how thinking is made by feeling.[33]

Why a theory? As philosopher of science Thomas Kuhn proposed, a *theory* is a map of what matters for answering a question. A theory of combustion needs to look at both the makeup of the combustible substance and the composition of the surrounding air. If a theory looks at the wrong data points (if we've figured out the importance of substance, say, but not of air), it will produce inconsistent results (like failing to explain why a candle is snuffed out when placed under a glass). Cogitation is our theory of knowledge production in the West—in most academic conversations and at the level of common sense. It starts with a thinking/feeling binary and concludes that we can understand how knowledge is produced by looking only at the intellectual side of the ledger. Cogency theory challenges this. As a theory, it says we'll understand knowledge production, in its successes and its failures, not only by examining feeling, but highlighting how feeling and thinking are a single process.

Of course, no epistemology is total, and most people have already figured out that the cogitation framework is missing something. Things we say all the time like *You only believe what you want to believe* or *He just likes simple answers* reflect our awareness that cognition and emotion are part of the same cat's cradle. The Mulder effect is the same. These are the kinds of intuitions that cogitation can't explain but that cogency theory sets out to organize and develop into a full-spectrum understanding of thinking and feeling.

The Intellectual Passions: From Kuhn to Polanyi

The interdisciplinary field of science and technology studies has always been concerned with representing science in its full complexity—as made not only by minds but also by bodies, communities, and material objects. Steven Shapin and Christopher Lawrence, for instance, argue that one flaw of the approach to rationality championed by early modern philosophers like Descartes (Mr. Cogitation himself) was its total exclusion of the body.[34] Science in the STS picture is historically contingent—on community, on access to resources, on facilities, instruments, and laboratories. Capital-S *Science* comes down from its pedestal and rubs elbows with other everyday modes of knowledge production. Britt Rusert's concept of *fugitive science* or Katherine McKittrick's reframing of Black thought as *scientia*, for instance, are blends of formal and informal knowledge-making that mount a powerful intellectual counterattack against racism. What makes science *science* is the way it brings together a whole ensemble of mundane practices in strange ways. Lorraine Daston and Peter Galison propose that *objectivity* needs to be thought of "in shirtsleeves"—a set of epistemological virtues cultivated from the bottom up through bodily training.[35] Collectively, STS has tracked the way science emerges as *lived science* rather than a mystical freeway to truth.

This is important for pushing back on cogitation. But there's been very little attention in the STS literature to the shaping role of feeling in knowledge production. Reframing knowledge production as emotional brings us back to the big argument of this book. If cognition is felt, it's susceptible to the affective ecology from which it emerges. Knowledge production is emotional, so it's always at risk of messing together with the other spreading inkblots of feeling making up our embodied lives. (The Mulder effect, all the self-serving reasons we might *want to believe*.) This is how powerful prejudices seep into our intellectual bedrock. Cogency theory follows STS in thinking about scientific rationality in shirtsleeves. However, it goes further in picturing science in a feeling body—science with a pulse. This allows it to draw textured, detailed maps of the liquid landscapes of emotion that define our thinking and track the ways wheeling matrixes of feeling lure us to misbegotten beliefs.

But *mistakes* are only half of what cogency theory sets out to explain. From the perspective of cogency theory, good knowledge, too, is made by emotions. It's precisely *because we feel* that knowledge works in the first place. Bruno Latour writes that the project of STS "was never to get *away* from facts but *closer* to them, not fighting empiricism but, on the contrary, renewing empiricism."[36] Cogency theory, putting affect theory and STS in conversation, has the same goal. The feeling of thinking is what guides us to good knowledge. Understanding *how knowledge is made by feeling* is a way of showing our work. It strengthens knowledge claims rather than undermining them.

Good knowledge isn't knowledge that has been drained of feeling. It's knowledge that reflects a working, durable relationship with the things around us, a relationship resolutely defined by emotion. It's the product of complicated operations of feeling—an agonism, an invisible clash of forces holding our desire to know the world in tension and trying to outmaneuver other felt priorities that might muddy the waters. This *sense of science* isn't a forensic tool for calculating absolute truth. Instead, it's a cultivated contraption for feeling our way toward truth (objectivity in shirtsleeves) without the anticipation of certainty. Collapsing the binary of reason and emotion doesn't leave us adrift. It shines a light on the carefully staged agonism of intellectual feelings that is the real driver of good knowledge. (We'll explore this in detail in chapter 1.)

The contours of STS came into focus in the mid-twentieth century with an increasingly sharp challenge to *logical positivism*—the view that science, by deriving theory from a steadily expanding research base, makes linear progress. Enter Thomas Kuhn, the chain-smoking, hard-driving theoretical physicist turned philosopher of science. Kuhn's 1962 volume *The Structure of Scientific Revolutions* was a watershed moment in overturning positivism. His insight was that the philosophy of science of his day was a cartoonish misrepresentation of how science actually played out on the ground. To solve this problem he created a new genre: a *descriptive* philosophy of science—attached to a rich historical sensibility—detailing science's limitations, rather than a *prescriptive* philosophy that rhapsodized its infinite horizons.

Kuhn argued that science is best understood not as a straight line but as an unsteady cascade of separate periods of *normal science* linked by interludes of radical transformation—*revolutions*. Normal science is governed by a *paradigm*, a set of mostly interlocking theories that organize available data. During normal science, the day-to-day activity of scientists is pretty low-key, amounting to what Kuhn calls *puzzle solving*—plugging new data points into existing theories. In the process, scattered data points emerge—anomalies—that don't fit the paradigm. These anomalies loom outside the paradigm, building pressure. As the anomalies accumulate, the pressure bears down, eventually crashing the paradigm and triggering a revolution. Finally, a new paradigm is assembled from the anomalies stacked in the smoking ruins of its predecessor.[37]

At the heart of Kuhn's picture of science as a cycle was a skepticism—resonant with Foucault—toward the idea that science was getting better. Kuhn saw scientific paradigms as a string of separate intellectual bubbles. His keyword was *incommensurability*: incompatible standards of measurement;

different "ways of seeing the world and of practicing science in it."[38] A paradigm change is not just a theory change. It often goes along with a fundamental reconsideration of *how scientific work is done*. The world looks different after a revolution. The scientist in the new paradigm finds that the ground has shifted so much beneath her feet she can't even talk to the old paradigm.[39] Rather than linear progress, science is a sequence of self-enclosed whirlpools.

The science-skeptical overtone of Kuhn's work has become the template for a lot of the thinking about science done by the humanities in the half century since.[40] The aftershocks of Kuhn's project rumbled through the strong programme in the 1970s and poststructuralism in the 1980s and are still powerfully present in the humanities today. In the early 1990s, Bruno Latour was confronted on the sidelines of a conference by a flustered scientist who demanded to know: *"Do you believe in reality?"*[41] Latour's answer, he assures his readers, is *Yes*—but he can hardly pretend he doesn't know the source of the concern.

Kuhn's science-skepticism won him no friends among hard realists and positivists. They flat-out rejected the new model of science as shaky and uneven. But feminist STS scholars of the past two decades have presented a more textured response. They have called for an approach to science that maps its limitations *and* its successes, allowing new, productive points of contact with the humanities.[42] Stacey Alaimo and Susan Hekman, for instance, point out that the Kuhnian approach to science found in some corners of the humanities has gone so far in the direction of skepticism that it actively "excludes lived experience, corporeal practice, and biological substance from consideration" and "makes it nearly impossible for feminism to engage with medicine or science in innovative, productive, or affirmative ways."[43] Feminist science historians have become similarly concerned with the inability of the humanities to put up a fight against capitalist institutions muddying the waters around, for instance, climate change science.[44] Latour in recent decades has developed a similar anxiety. He and other thinkers have tried to advance a *postcritical* turn, rethinking the default adversarial posture taken by some humanities scholarship toward the natural sciences.[45]

This is where Latour's project of *renewing empiricism* comes in. But these sophisticated responses to Kuhn and the science-skeptical attitude he sponsored still tend to overlook the role of feeling in scientific rationality. Knowledge production may be contingent, historical, social, material, and even embodied, but it is still, in the words of philosopher of science Alison Jaggar, susceptible to "the myth of dispassionate investigation."[46] This means that they still accept the basic map offered by Kuhn, of a science defined, at heart, by the play of concepts.

To remap science as emotional, cogency theory winds back the clock. Rather than starting with Kuhn, it looks to Michael Polanyi, and specifically his work on *intellectual passions*. Polanyi, the Hungarian Jewish chemist who turned to philosophy after fleeing Nazi Germany and taking refuge in Manchester, published his book *Personal Knowledge* in 1958, four years before *Structure*. Studying the Kuhn-Polanyi relationship is already a cottage industry for historians and philosophers of science.[47] Kuhn himself—though he at first championed Polanyi's ideas—later disavowed the association, announcing late in his life that he saw Polanyi's position as hopelessly misguided. He especially disdained Polanyi's reliance on "something very like ESP" as the motor of scientific discovery.[48] Polanyi, for his part, came to believe that Kuhn plagiarized several of his key concepts, while at the same time mutating them into "nonsense."[49]

But that came later. The historians agree that, early on, Kuhn was aware of, and may well have adapted, Polanyi's idea of *tacit knowledge*, the repertoire of unspoken background coordinates—absorbed through experience rather than language—that powerfully shape scientific knowledge production.[50] Although Kuhn initially neglected him completely, between the first and second editions of *Structure* he added two references to Polanyi in his footnotes.[51] And similarly, Polanyi welcomed Kuhn's appearance on the battlefield, seeing him as an indispensable ally in his solo assault against positivism.[52] Like Kuhn, Polanyi didn't think science advanced on a linear, upward trajectory.[53] Both saw the unfurling of science as jagged and fragmentary rather than an open road.

This has led to a long tradition of reading Kuhn and Polanyi as basically saying the same thing. But as philosopher Maben Poirier shows, this is a mistake. The arch-relativist Kuhn of *Structure* writes in a very different vein from Polanyi, who has a more nuanced take on science's capacity to make good knowledge. "Polanyi may not be an empiricist," writes Poirier, "but he is by no means a relativist either, radical or otherwise." Instead, Polanyi "repeatedly makes it very clear that natural scientists investigate what is real—what exists independently of themselves, in the world beyond their minds—and not some subjective entity which is a construction of their minds."[54] Polanyi says good science is driven by "the feeling of making contact with reality." His hero is Copernicus, who saw through the grand error of his age, grasped the truth behind the veil, and patiently drew it into view.[55] It wasn't just a new paradigm, destined to be overthrown in the next revolution. It was truth, or at least closer to it than what came before. And it was built by feeling.[56]

The widespread failure to grasp what Polanyi was really saying about science has even led to a tendency (and this on the part of Polanyi's admirers) to read him as a sort of Neoplatonic mystic, who discovered in science a divine resonance between human minds and truth.[57] But Polanyi's theory of science is anything but mystical. It's just that it's organized around, in his words, the *intellectual passions*—and these have been so badly neglected in Western philosophy that they look, to some, like ethereal intuitions rather than extensions of our embodied life. Our received picture of science as pure cogitation totally obscures the real reason why Polanyi rejects the hard relativism of incommensurable paradigms: his conviction that science works through feeling.

Polanyi sees science everywhere. It's down from its pedestal, fully continuous with our everyday ways of making knowledge in the world—and even with what other animals and infants do all the time. "As far down the scale of life as the worms and even perhaps the amoeba," he writes, "we meet a *general alertness of animals*, not directed towards any specific satisfaction, but merely exploring what is there."[58] The mystical reading of Polanyi falls apart when we see how committed he is to a Darwinian frame. If pleasure is a rough-and-ready (though far from perfect) mechanism by which animals are guided to flourishing (the delight of eating good food, the dread of meeting a dangerous predator), then it makes sense that animals would find pleasure in learning about their environments. "These intellectual tastes of the animal prefigure, no doubt," he writes, "the joys of discovery which our articulate powers can attain for man."[59]

We see this same budding intellectual passion in the curiosity and playfulness of infants. These feelings are the precursors to grown-up rationality. "A game of chess creates its own pleasures," Polanyi contends, "but could not do so if babies could not play with rattles."[60] Babies and their games with shapes, words, dolls, blocks, faces, gestures, and toys are already learning to revel in click. Rationality isn't either/or, you have it or you don't—the surreal claim of all the royalized self-portraits in which humans become magically *reasonable* when we cross some secret threshold of development. (This idea, the *black monolith myth*, is discussed below.) All animals and all humans are *rational* in the sense of desiring, considering, and more or less effectively arranging information about our environments. This is because all animals have intellectual feelings, in different combinations and in varying degrees. What gets called rationality is really a combination of intellectual passions nudging us to know the world.

Polanyi runs down a few of these intellectual passions. There's *interest*—a felt sense of what matters. Only through interest do we get a sense of how to prioritize some pieces of information in the environment over others. Without interest and *intuition* (a felt sense of what *might* be useful in the future), all our science "would inevitably spread out into a desert of trivialities"—a library of phone books.[61] Then there's what Polanyi calls the *persuasive passion*—the desire to convince others.[62] Persuasive passion pulls us into conversation with others. It's what makes science social.

But the overriding intellectual passion, the urge driving the whole ensemble, is the *love of elegance*, or *beauty*. What Polanyi calls *the feeling of making contact with reality* is click, the subtle joy of pieces of information snapping together. "The affirmation of a great scientific theory is," Polanyi proposes, "in part an expression of delight. The theory has an inarticulate component acclaiming its beauty, and this is essential to the belief that the theory is true."[63] This means that the objects held up by intellectual passions are not just holograms projected by artificial paradigms. They can accurately "be said to be right or wrong."[64] Rather than being trapped in our own private intellectual whirlpools, our body's intuitions about how truth feels drive discovery forward. Our persuasive passions scale this up, building good knowledge in community.

Although trained as a chemist, Polanyi holds up math as the ideal of this passion for intellectual beauty, envisioning it as an endless garden of neatly fitted pieces of information. "Nowhere is intellectual beauty so deeply felt and fastidiously appreciated in its various grades and qualities as in mathematics," he writes. "It is by satisfying his intellectual passions that mathematics fascinates the mathematician and compels him to pursue it in his thoughts and give it his assent."[65] Math isn't limited by having to check in with the material world. Like an endless game of polychromatic abstract shapes clicking into place, it pulls us forward as far as we can physically follow it.

That said, throughout the sciences (and, of course, all the other forms of rationality, from babies playing with blocks to giddy proofreaders picking out mistakes in a text), this felt desire to know the world is the propulsive mechanism at the heart of thinking. We aren't directed by abstract certainty. We feel our way to the most satisfying theory, the conclusion that turns the most tumblers. For Polanyi, we feel the click of information coalescing with what we already know. The domain of *what-we-already-know* can be tacit, an accumulation of experiences, no less powerful for being unsaid, or explicit, conveyed by language and available to our conscious self-inspection. But either way, *intellectual beauty* for Polanyi is the felt admiration for a solution that clicks.

This definition of science as a contraption of intellectual passions is what leaves Kuhn sputtering with fury at Polanyi for centering science on "something very like ESP."[66] Kuhn is so in hock to a picture of science as cogitation—the myth that all knowledge-making is, at its heartless heart, a language-like system, a cipher of words and ideas—that a theory of scientific knowledge production as driven by feeling rather than concepts (and more concepts, all the way down) looks, to him, like gnomes dancing under a toadstool. It just doesn't make sense. Science in Kuhn's eyes is a murmuration of concepts, so it follows that it would amount to nothing more than a maze of speculation—with no mechanism for making contact with reality. Kuhn has no avenue for seeing science as defined by feeling—let alone the possibility that feeling might be the very thing that moves science forward.

My suspicion is that the selection of Kuhn rather than Polanyi as the anointed gadfly of science is a big part of why the feeling/thinking binary still has the power that it does in the humanities (and is also why we're still spiraling in a bottomless pit of debates about relativism). Like a robot that only sees in black-and-white, Kuhn can't wrap his head around the possibility that science could draw on the matrix of our *felt* encounters with the world—the living archive of all our tacit experiences—and that these intuitions could break through our conceptual carapaces.[67] But for Polanyi, intellectual *passions* are melded together into an alloy that creates the canopy of science. The reason/emotion binary collapses. As psychologist Lisa Feldman Barrett (discussed further in chapter 4) writes, "The human brain is anatomically structured so that no decision or action can be free of interoception and affect, no matter what fiction people tell themselves about how rational they are."[68] This landscape of cognitive feeling is the matrix that guides our knowledge production, pursuing the pleasure of a thought that clicks.

We'll hear the pleasure that attaches to knowledge-making called by many names in this book—*the feeling of making contact with reality* for

Polanyi, but also the *sentiment of rationality* for William James, *interest* for Silvan Tomkins, and the *passion for reason* for Antonio Damasio. What they share is a sense that knowledge clicks with us, and that click is *felt*. There are obvious moments where knowledge production is emotional—the *Eureka!* over an astonishing discovery or the quiet spreading sense of awe when everything falls gently into place. Cogency theory proposes that these obvious moments are only the most extreme, most visible manifestations of a much larger network of affects driving knowledge production, the macro version of a process that is always occurring at the micro level. *Eureka!*, in this view, is a monsoon of droplets of feeling coalescing into an emotion. But those droplets are always there, forming a sticky dew on everything around us, subtly guiding belief. And without them, belief would dry up and disappear.

This cognitive-affective intuition (sometimes above, sometimes below the threshold of conscious awareness) is an imperfectly effective means for tracking what works in the world. It's also an evolutionary necessity. Without it, extremely complicated organisms requiring highly specialized resource streams to survive and reproduce—animals like us—would be phylogenetic dead ends. We have to be tuned in to the world in a way that allows us—even compels us—to be right about it often enough to continue living.[69] This grounds both our felt sense of pleasure in things clicking together and our sense of dissonance, frustration, and discomfort when information grates or jars with what we think we know. Yes, we believe what we want to believe. But *one of the things* we want to believe is the way things actually are.

By expanding Polanyi's inventory of intellectual passions, cogency theory lights up knowledge-making as more than just the con job of indoctrination or an endless chain of language games. We know things—and we know them well. We feel the force of truth. At the same time, cogency theory frees truth from the impossible expectation of invincibility. Knowledge emerges in our real-time, fluid, felt relationships with the world around us. It's always susceptible to being pulled off course or landing awkwardly on a skewed surface. But so, too, is it capable of rumbling under the surface, steadily gathering force, and shattering a falsehood. (Anyone who has ever escaped a society, a community, or a relationship defined by the repetition of lies knows this well.) Cogency is our felt sense of the *force* of what we've learned. *I feel that.*

The Black Monolith Myth: Feeling Secularism

A few months after Darwin's 1863 letter, an ambitious British member of Parliament, Benjamin Disraeli, delivered a fist-pumping political speech at Oxford's Sheldonian Theatre. He saluted the political unity of the Church of England and the British nation by taking square aim at Darwinian theory itself. In the final minutes, Disraeli spoke the lines that would make the speech famous, later reprinted in a pamphlet like this:

> What is the highest nature? Man is the highest nature. But I must say that when I compare the interpretation of the highest nature by the most advanced, the most fashionable and modish school of modern science, with some other teachings with which we are familiar, I am not prepared to say that the lecture-room is more scientific than the Church (cheers). What is the question now placed before society with a glib assurance the most astounding? The question is this—Is man an ape or an angel? (loud laughter.) My lord, I am on the side of the angels (laughter and cheering).[70]

In my first book, *Religious Affects*, I looked at this speech as part of a study of the emotional dimension of embodied life. In particular, I argued that seeing humans as continuous with other animals—rather than as angels—allowed us to focus on how affect and emotion are foundational to subjectivity.

My interpretation of affect theory is that affect is essentially *power*, understood not as an external, oppressive force but, following Michel Foucault, as fundamentally productive.[71] Power is *what makes bodies move* (or binds them). *Affect* is a word for processes—beneath, beside, and within cognition—that register in awareness as feelings, emotions, and moods.[72] At heart, power is affect, affect is power. Everything we do emerges out of an agonism of feelings. There's a fully fleshed-out continuum from the micro to the macro, from the cyclone of small, felt pulses splashing across us all the time—a tug of longing, a pinprick of annoyance, a pang of grief—to thoughts, actions, decisions, moods, words.

In *Religious Affects* I argued that it's a mistake to make feeling into a sideshow far from the main stage of the operations of power. This mistake is the *linguistic fallacy*—the idea that humans are basically thinking, reasoning beings, that what makes us tick is a sedimentation of words and ideas. Language is important, of course—it's a highly sophisticated bodily tool that can circulate and distribute affects with amazing precision (see chapter 2).

But affect theory suggests that to understand how bodies fit into messy contraptions of power, we have to look past words themselves. It's the affects carried by words—as well as by all the other wordless things enfolding our bodies—that add up to make subjectivity.

The book also had a blind spot. In zeroing in on how the affective dimensions of subjectivity shaped religion, it implicitly suggested *religion* was *uniquely* affective—as if only religion was tethered to emotion, while science and the secular peered down from orbit. Cogency theory is designed to correct this oversight. It asserts that *everything* we do as bodies is affective. That includes even the domains of life we imagine to be the most heady, the most angelic—reason, science, secularism. They, too, are saturated with feeling.

This brings us back to Disraeli's speech. Disraeli is on the side of cogitation, likening man (and *man* is the right word here—there were no women in the Sheldonian that day) to angels—those beings Thomas Aquinas described as pure intellect, "quite separated from bodies."[73] But what's even more interesting, for our purposes, is the response to the speech, not spoken by Disraeli but recorded in the pamphlet text: "Laughter and cheering." Why do the attendees laugh and cheer when Disraeli speaks? And what does the reaction to the answer tell us about the question itself? What do we learn about the kind of creatures we are, ape or angel, that we laugh and cheer when we are faced with what we take to be truth? Where *Religious Affects* proposed that affect determines *where bodies go*, this book studies how thoughts, discourses, conversations, arguments, calculations, science, and reason itself are *also* controlled by affective tides. There is, then, no facet of being human in which we are angels. Cogency theory sets out to animalize cognition, language, and rationality. It highlights the ways science and secularism, like religion, are continuous with animal lifeways, the surging emotional ground of our bodies. The laughter and cheering at the Sheldonian in 1863 illustrate this perfectly. The ideas that click are cogent, which means they trigger an emotional response. We believe because it *feels right*.

In his atheist manifesto *The God Delusion*, Richard Dawkins advises us to "be clear, in any particular conversation, what we are talking about: feelings, or truth. Both may be important, but they are not the same thing."[74] For Dawkins, to furnish the house of truth is to declutter it of the emotional relics of religion. Science alone makes truth uncontaminated by emotion. That's what makes secularism inevitable. Elsewhere, though, Dawkins seems to know about a link between feeling and truth. His book *Unweaving the Rainbow*, for instance, is a tactical response to the accusation that science, by draining off feeling, *disenchants* the world. It's a common technique among some secular partisans who argue that science gives us new figures of beauty and wonder.[75]

But Dawkins's strategy is to shine the spotlight on the extravagance of *discoveries*: the wonder of distant galaxies, our fabulously intricate cells, or the architecture of DNA.[76] The emotionality of science is, in this view, an aftereffect. It's the prize at the end of the race. This science brings beautiful things into our field of view—nebulas and geothermal fauna and teeming canopies—but *knowledge-making is not itself affective*. To see science as *made of emotion* would crash the wall of separation between feeling and truth, locating the scientific method too close to the ambiguities of being a body. So even when Dawkins affiliates emotion and science, he reasserts that science itself is cogitation. Scientific rationality and the secular order that rests on top of it are truth-machines built by eliminating feeling.[77] Cogency theory, by contrast, views thought—all thought—as saturated with feeling. Science never gets outside of the emotional coordinates of our bodies. Affects are the pulse of reason. This is both why science succeeds and why it fails.

These same contemporary forms of atheism also take on the mantle of Darwinism. They hold up Darwin as an ideal of scientific dispassion. Darwin's biographers tell a different story, as we'll see in chapter 5, but even more importantly, Darwin's *own work* contradicts the idea that cognition is feelingless.[78] Darwin was a scientist, and he was sympathetic enough to the secular project to call himself an agnostic. But Darwin was dedicated to defending what he saw as his most urgent contribution to human knowledge—the fact of our continuity with other animals. This meant, for him, a sensitivity to the emotional contours of science as part of the project of understanding where we come from.

If Darwin's portrait of human continuity with animals is our starting point, we should be suspicious of any attempt to place *reason* on a separate plane from the rest of our embodied life. Stanley Kubrick's 1968 film *2001: A Space Odyssey* illustrates this mistake nicely. The opening sequence, "The Dawn of Man," presents a mythic picture of the emergence of humanity. After the appearance of a mysterious black monolith on a primitive savannah, a group of violent apes abruptly discovers how to use tools. In an interview with *Playboy*, Kubrick said this was just the beginning of "progress[ion] from biological species, which are fragile shells for the mind at best, into immortal machine entities."[79] The monolith is a bolt from the blue that jump-starts reason and pushes humans over a metaphysical threshold to become *Man*, in Sylvia Wynter's sense—the secular "Rational Self."[80] The animal falls, Man stands up. Rationality cleaves us from animals in a single stroke, producing something abrupt and unforeseen.

But *2001*'s story was obsolete before it even came out. In 1960, Jane Goodall had already watched the chimpanzees of Gombe National Park both using and fashioning tools. She built her method from the ground up, relying on a feeling for animals rather than the prevailing scientific wisdom that chimpanzees were furry robots.[81] This was what allowed her to rapidly upend a long-held scientific and philosophical consensus that human tool use was unique. Not only that, but the "Dawn of Man" story also invoked the popular misconception that evolution is a teleological process—a trajectory of improvement directed at a goal (Man) rather than a random set of motions in response to changing geologic landscapes.[82] What *2001* illustrates, then, is what I'll call the *black monolith myth*. The black monolith myth claims there is a wall of separation between humans and animals, minds and bodies, thinking and feeling. It sees Man as standing above the world, rather than living as part of it. Darwin had no time for that mistake and spent half a lifetime trying to overturn it. Cogency theory follows suit.

This brings us back to the secular. Because despite their claim to follow Darwin, many modern visions of secularism fall for the black monolith myth. Secularism's autobiography tells a story of sober philosophers and scientists grinding down religious superstition and revealing humanity's emotionless, rational core. They miss Darwin's insistence that because humans are continuous with other animals, reason must be integrated with feeling. Cogency theory uses the Darwinian insight—that thought itself is animal—to ask, instead, the question posed by scholars of secularism like Janet Jakobsen and Ann Pellegrini: "What does secularism 'feel' like?"[83] The secular isn't the extraction of emotion and the injection of feelingless science. Nor is it an abrupt break with the histories that came before it as reason comes rushing in. It is, instead, no more and no less than an effort to build new formations of feeling—in part by fashioning new modes of knowing. Considering how scientific secularisms build these new structures of feeling is the project of the second half of this book.

The emerging field of *secularism studies* tends not to focus on science. Several early architects of the secularization thesis, such as Karl Marx and Max Weber, did not see science as the driver of religious disbelief. For Marx, the twilight of religion was predicated on the transformation of economic systems, not new science. For Weber, the "iron cage of modernity" was an elaborate mousetrap triggered by the Protestant Reformation centuries earlier.[84] These sociopolitical concerns set the template for much of today's secularism studies literature, which has primarily focused on secularism as a political project that combines with race, identity, law, and the public sphere. Some other work in this field sees secularism as a metaphysical system, a set of philosophical assumptions to be dug up and examined. Where science is engaged, it's often done with an eye to studying how science comes to be a sort of simulacrum of religious devotion.[85]

But this misses a key part of the picture. Philosopher Charles Taylor writes that secularism transforms religion by making religious belief *one option among many*.[86] Even when it doesn't become an *explicit* reason for departing from faith, the stunning success, reach, and prestige of the programmatic reconstruction of human knowledge achieved by science have totally rebuilt this backdrop of belief. So the eighteenth-century French *philosophes* saw science as the bedrock of their new vision of a churchless society (and influenced Hume's philosophy along the same lines).[87] In the nineteenth century, Percy Bysshe Shelley and Auguste Comte viewed the rise of science as precipitating religion's decline.[88] This was the seed of the science-religion *conflict thesis* in the latter half of the nineteenth century and was a driving force of the X Club, cofounded by Thomas Henry Huxley, the man who called himself *Darwin's bulldog*.[89] "No, our science is no illusion," Sigmund Freud wrote in the final lines of *The Future of an Illusion*, in 1927. "But an illusion it would be to suppose that what science cannot give us we can get elsewhere."[90] And, of course, a zero-sum war between science and religion is the message of New Atheism in the twenty-first century. This book, then, tries to flesh out this relationship between science and secularism and expand the conversation between secularism studies and STS.

Plan of the Book

To push beyond the reason/emotion binary, this book considers three interrelated key concepts: the *sense of science, conspiracy theory*, and *racialized reason*. The *sense of science* is a new way of understanding science as a method. It proposes that rather than seeing the success of science as driven by emotionless cogitation, science works by cultivating an agonism of affects, a permanent struggle between the excitement of click and countervailing pressures—like fear or shame—about getting things wrong. The sense of science is a kind of ascetic discipline, harnessing click but striving, however imperfectly, not to let it distort the search for good knowledge.

It might seem that click is the feeling of truth. But the reality is more complicated, as we can see by considering conspiracy theory. Click is necessary for knowledge. Our bodies are truth-chasers only because of our capacity to feel it. But click can also totally derail the search for truth, licensing our prejudices as what *feels true*, sanctifying what we think we know and rendering it immune to challenge. And without guardrails, click will multiply exciting connections, producing the lurid string figures of conspiracy theory. Conspiracy theory creates what we might call a *simplex system*—an artificial flattening of the complexity of the world in order to make it more enjoyable (see chapter 1). Click fascination leads to an endless pursuit of interesting ideas with no checks and balances—a corrupt, broken-mirror version of the sense of science. There are lots of reasons conspiracy theory has managed to get our public conversation in a chokehold. But macro-level explanations—dire racial and economic inequality, for instance—need to be fleshed out by a detailed account of conspiracism's emotional structure. That's cogency theory's task.

Conspiracy theory is closely related to *racialized reason*. (As we'll see, it's no accident that conspiracy theory so often comes along with racist stories.) *Racialized reason* is the skin of thought that forms around racist feelings. It's another way of naming what critical race scholars have been saying for decades—namely, that racism isn't just a set of explicit *beliefs*, but a whole topography of ways of thinking.[91] What cogency theory highlights is that racialized reason is itself created by feeling. Rather than a set of propositional claims about who's up and who's down, racism is sunk deep into the bodies of both its agents and its victims. As Perry and others point out, it tinges the way we think about things in ways we don't expect—and that arguably become even harder to detect once we've persuaded ourselves that our thoughts are unaffected by feeling.[92]

Race and racialization come up again and again in the study of secularism, it seems, because secularism creates a canopy of obliviousness to its own affective determination—the way felt lines of continuity bolt secularists to histories, desires, and structures of violence from the past, even when the metaphysical proper nouns have all been changed. Denise Ferreira da Silva goes so far as to argue that the racial order of Euro-American modernity rests on exactly this denial of its own affective influences.[93] Secularism, repeating the black monolith myth, often offers itself as the transformative irruption of rationality remaking the world. But the concept of *racialized reason* maps how old feelings stick to the new words and the new ideas hawked by modernity, gluing them into grimly familiar shapes.

Cogency theory connects conversations happening across the humanities, social sciences, and natural sciences. There's no shortage of material, and this book will consider only a handful of approaches.[94] The first part of the book surveys four resources for cogency theory: eighteenth- and nineteenth-century philosophy, affect theory, secularism studies, and contemporary psychology. The second part turns to the history of scientific secularism to consider how cogency shapes styles of disbelief—and responds to the question *How does secularism feel?*

Chapter 1 looks at three philosophers whose writings point to the inseparability of emotion and cognition. These philosophers—David Hume, Friedrich Nietzsche, William James—bookend one of the central figures in the story of cogency theory: Darwin. Hume dies before Darwin is born, but Darwin is strongly influenced by Hume's effort to imagine human thought as a feature of the natural world (rather than the shadow cast by a black monolith). Nietzsche, writing almost a century later, responds in complex ways to the challenge to human exceptionalism put down by Darwin. He locates morality, aesthetics, and reason itself inside bodies, though his elitism ultimately leads him to a warped picture of science. William James continues this line of development, building on Darwinian insights in ways that make feeling central for belief. Crucially, these thinkers point to a need to think about philosophy, science, and rationality as made up not just of *one* emotion, but of plural emotional priorities placed in tension. That's the sense of science. These same philosophical resources also help us better understand conspiracy theory—sham knowledge that superficially resembles science, but is built using a skewed emotional palette.

Chapter 2 turns to contemporary affect theory and the theme of racialized reason. Affect theory emerges out of a tradition that runs through Nietzsche (by way of French thinkers like Michel Foucault and Gilles Deleuze), queer theory, and feminism but is also shaped by psychology—both psychoanalysis and academic psychology from James and Darwin to Silvan Tomkins. Tomkins is especially relevant for moving beyond cogitation. His proposal to develop what he called *the psychology of knowledge* was rooted in his conviction that the components of cognition, such as the felt register of *interest*, could all be understood as affects, the matrix of motivation in animal bodies. This gets picked up by Sedgwick, who develops it into what Lauren Berlant has called a *sensualized epistemology*—a theory of knowledge in full communion with feeling.

Queer theorists who have examined the relationship between affect and race make another vital contribution to cogency theory. Racialization, they show, is quickened by feeling. Racism, in this view, is not just a set of beliefs. Instead, the ideas and concepts that form the surface topography of racism are animated by an underlying emotional configuration. This includes a felt desire for racial others, what Sharon Patricia Holland calls racism's *erotic* aspect. *Racialized reason* names the way racism—both explicit racist beliefs and subtler forms of racist color-blind policy—becomes cogent *by feeling true*.

Chapter 3 considers the interdisciplinary field of secularism studies. It starts with Weber and traces his complex theory of *disenchantment* in the early twentieth century. The peak of the secularization thesis came in the late 1960s and 1970s—when the imminent vanishing of religion from the world was taken as given. But the same theoretical tools that predicted secularization also led to the overturning of the secularization thesis, because secular reason *itself* was increasingly seen as a parochial outlook on the world. Talal Asad, for instance, provides a genealogy of secular reason, analyzing how tendentious priorities, preferences, and concerns are embedded within self-avowedly neutral intellectual traditions. For Asad, this tracks the way secularism constitutes not just an analytic posture but also dispositions and habits—the *secular body*.

This chapter explores how secularism studies has developed two lines of interest relevant to cogency theory: disenchantment and critique. It reassesses Weber's consideration of science as a *vocation*—an emotionally urgent outcropping of the affective landscape of secular bodies—to argue that disenchantment has been misunderstood. For Weber, it wasn't the erasure of feeling; it was the emergence of *new kinds of feeling* as epistemological coordinates shift beneath our feet. The chapter then examines how Asad and Saba Mahmood have challenged the presumptive neutrality of *secular critique*, connecting their work to recent research in what has been called the *postcritical turn* in the work of Sedgwick, Latour, and Rita Felski. Both lines flesh out the question of *how secularism feels* in conjunction with changing horizons of knowledge. This is illustrated through the example of the Sheldonian Theatre itself, constructed in the early modern period, I argue, to architecturally separate secular and religious affects.

The final chapter of part I turns to contemporary psychology, a field in which the rejection of a divide between emotion and reason has been decisive. This consensus was articulated in Antonio Damasio's 1994 volume *Descartes' Error*, but the resources for cogency theory in psychology are extensive. As neuroscientists such as Lisa Feldman Barrett, Luiz Pessoa, and Elizabeth Phelps have pointed out, the integration of reason and emotion is evidenced by the structure of the brain. Neural tissue is so densely interconnected that the metaphysical categories we've inherited to separate *cognition* and *emotion* just don't line up. This chapter considers how contemporary neuroscience has pushed back on the twentieth-century *triune brain hypothesis* of Paul MacLean, which stressed the phylogenetic distinctiveness of the emotional and intellectual faculties. It then turns to experimental psychology, zooming in on the literature surrounding the *mere exposure effect* first examined by Robert Zajonc in the 1960s for another perspective on the relationship between emotion, cognition, and racialization.

Part II, "Feeling Science and Secularism," switches tracks. In light of the reconsideration of the relationship between emotion and cognition, it sets out to retell the story of scientific secularism. The guiding question here is something like this: If reason is felt, how does that change our understanding of the signal moments in Western intellectual history where evolutionary science and secularism seem to march hand in hand? It shows that just as scientific rationality is formed out of an alloy of feelings, so, too, are formations of the secular.

Each of the three chapters of part II reexamines a moment in science history in tandem with one of the book's key concepts. Chapter 5 considers the *sense of science* by looking at Darwin himself, who works at a turning point in the Western understanding of what it means to be human. But the focus will not be on Darwin's discoveries, exactly. Instead, the chapter considers how Darwin's own sense of science intersects with his approach to religious belief and disbelief. Darwin's story becomes even more interesting when we crosscut it with the attitude toward religion of one of his closest allies, Thomas Henry Huxley. Huxley, too, has a clear emotional signature on his science. But whereas for Darwin this leads to shy absorption in his studies, Huxley's science is vividly *social*—and often adversarial. The love of science, for Huxley, messes together with a love of fight. The different affective alloys undergirding the way they do science lines up with their divergence in how they feel their way to secularism.

Chapter 6 looks at the links between scientific secularism and *racialized reason* by reexamining the reception of Darwinism in the United States in the early twentieth century. Although many nineteenth-century American Protestants had found it easy to reconcile Darwinism and Christianity, the emergence of the fundamentalist movement in the 1910s set the stage for one of the most significant case studies in the history of science-religion interaction: the Scopes Trial of 1925. The tendency of scientific affects to mess together with a range of other secular feelings—including the felt component of racialized reason—is on full display in this case. This is particularly well illustrated by the contrast between two of the trial's main figures: William Jennings Bryan, the failed presidential candidate and fundamentalist ally who joined the prosecution, and H. L. Mencken, the eugenics-obsessed journalist who reported on the trial for the *Baltimore Sun*.

Chapter 7 moves to a final case study in scientific secularism: the contemporary New Atheist movement championed by scientists such as Richard Dawkins, Daniel Dennett, and Sam Harris. The chapter argues that the New Atheists are secularism's modern bulldogs, aggressively pushing a version of scientific secularism with more than a passing resemblance to conspiracy theory. As with Huxley and Mencken, their commitment to science messes together with a zeal for combat. This often glides into racialization, especially Islamophobic racism. It's paralleled by a sort of conspiracy theory version of evolutionary biology—adaptationist sociobiology, a simplex system strongly associated with the principal New Atheist writers. But this isn't the only version of secularism on offer. The chapter concludes by considering three atheists writing in the wake of the New Atheism—Sikivu Hutchinson, Anthony Pinn, and Chris Stedman—who are actively trying to rebuild atheism, in part by subjecting secular rationality *itself* to scrutiny. This leads to a sophisticated sensitivity to how racialization seeps through the walls of reason. These thinkers offer their own experiments in composing formations of the secular using feeling. The book's epilogue considers how cogency theory can help us understand contemporary climate denialism.

This book makes two specific arguments. The first is that there is no divide between emotion and reason. The reeling mass of information in our heads is not a grid of ones and zeroes. Thinking and feeling aren't just intertwined—that suggests they could be disentangled. They're a unity, but with distinct profiles when viewed from different angles, like architectural drawings showing two-dimensional aspects of a three-dimensional building.

Thinking *is* feeling. The second argument is that this reframing has consequences for how we think about things like science and secularism. If knowledge is felt, it is always in intimate proximity to *other* things we feel—things we want—including our secretly savored prejudices.

Cogency theory is not exactly new. Thinkers have been making versions of these arguments for centuries. But at the same time, the argument that reason itself is made by feeling is deeply unsettling to liberal common sense and its vision of Man as sovereign, self-lawed creature controlled by a rational soul. It intensifies what Shapin and Lawrence call "the shock value of speaking about scientific knowledge-making in relation to the body," spotlighting the unsteady ground on which the dangerously tilted monolith of secular triumphalism has been raised.[95] It changes our big-picture understandings of science, reason, and secularism itself, not to mention the everyday, embodied ways of knowledge-making from which they're built.

Part I
Cogency Theory

1.
THE LONGING TO BELIEVE
PHILOSOPHERS ON CONSPIRACY THEORY AND THE SENSE OF SCIENCE

> I have discovered for myself that the old humanity and animality, yea, the collective primeval age, and the past of all sentient being, continues to meditate, love, hate, and reason in me.... among all these dreamers, I also, the "thinker," dance my dance. —Nietzsche, *The Joyful Wisdom*

Introduction: The Paranoid Style

Lecturing at Oxford the day before the assassination of President Kennedy in 1963, the historian Richard Hofstadter described what he called the *paranoid style* in American politics, a heady bouquet of "heated exaggeration, suspiciousness, and conspiratorial fantasy."[1] This style stretched all the way back to the eighteenth century, with the panic kicked off by the 1797 volume *Proofs of a Conspiracy against All the Religions and Governments of Europe, Carried On in the Secret Meetings of Free Masons, Illuminati, and Reading Societies.* And it continued to his own moment with the diehard conspiracy-mongering—what we might call *conspiracism*—of Red Scares, Goldwater conservatism, and the John Birch Society. And that was before the shots heard around the world from Dealey Plaza.

But it's hard to deny that the twenty-first century is shaping up to be the golden age of conspiracism. The Cold War, the culture wars, and the premillennium tension of the 1990s were just warm-ups for the present moment, when the most urgent problems facing the globe are pulled into arenas of lurid speculation. Political parties are consumed by fictions about pedophilia and Satanic rites. Protests against racist violence and police brutality are dismissed as the work of paid agents. Scientists are called on to defend research with planetary implications against the claim they're fabricating their findings for profit. Public figures are forced to respond to laughable accusations. People die of diseases they don't believe exist.

Hofstadter saw the flowering of conspiracism as the effect of a broken public conversation, the result of a political disagreement that seemed closed to compromise. This became the pattern for a lot of the contemporary literature on conspiracy theory, which continues to focus on its *epistemological* backdrop, as a question of what and how we know.[2] In other words, much of the speculation about conspiracy theory has seen it as a problem of cogitation. But scholars working on affect have also taken an interest in conspiracy theory and have concluded that a strictly epistemological approach doesn't go far enough.[3] They start with conspiracism's most salient feature: the fact that once it has taken root, it's extremely difficult to dislodge—even to the point of near-immunity to contradictory facts. Cogency theory builds directly on these insights. From the cogency theory perspective, conspiracism is less a hypothesis that tries to understand the world than a way of setting the mood. It uses contorted architectures of information to *make the world feel a certain way*. Conspiracy theory doesn't try to explain. It aims to electrify the world with significance, saturating it with click.

There's no hard-and-fast rule for distinguishing conspiracy theory from legitimate questioning, criticism, or even science. Cogency theory can't solve this problem. But setting up conspiracism as a limit case—as the far end of a spectrum of intellectual procedures—highlights how good science operates when it's working well. Science, like conspiracism, is driven by intellectual affects. As this chapter argues, the *sense of science* is not about pursuit of a single cognitive emotion. It is, instead, a dynamic of multiple intellectual affects held in tension. Without this countervailing emotional pressure, knowledge production spirals up into an over-the-top tapestry of correlations, everything clicking with everything else. In the limelight of conspiracism, the links shimmer and glide around us. It feels so good it *has* to be true.

This chapter explores these themes—cogency, conspiracy, and the sense of science—from the perspective of European philosophy, especially of the eighteenth and nineteenth centuries. Western philosophy has wrestled with the link between feeling and knowing from its beginnings. "All men naturally desire knowledge," Aristotle wrote in the opening line of *Metaphysics*.[4] Augustine warned of the *libido sciendi*—the "lust for experimenting and knowing"—that must be purged to purify focus on God.[5] Spinoza suggested that we find the discovery of order in nature pleasing to our senses and speculated that the desire for the world to be a simple, orderly thing—what we'll call a simplex system—entices us into error.[6] ("Men have been so mad as to believe that God is pleased by harmony," he mused, and some have even "persuaded themselves that the motions of the heavens produce a harmony.")[7] The French Enlightenment *philosophes* developed a remarkable body of work about the relationship between knowing and feeling. Nicolas de Condorcet wrote that the self-serving superstitions imposed by religious authorities would all someday be overthrown by the unerring force of "the love of truth."[8]

In the twentieth century, Karl Popper concurred with Einstein that "every discovery contains an irrational element," an "intellectual feeling" that is necessary for its creation.[9] Philosophers have continued to develop these ideas over the past couple decades. Thinkers like Giovanna Colombetti, Michelle Maiese, and John Protevi have built on research into 4E cognition (that is, cognition that is *e*mbodied, *e*mbedded in its context, *e*xtended through its environment, and *e*nacted in practice) by adding the dimension of affect, which they understood as openness to—or the capacity to be *affected by*—the surrounding world.[10] Martha Nussbaum has sought to develop a neo-Stoic account of feeling that compels us to take emotion into account when making moral or political decisions.[11]

Paul Thagard's book *Hot Thought*—also taking cues from classical philosophy—exemplifies this foundational work toward a theory of cogency. Thagard recognizes emotional cognition as a major source of scientific discovery. He analyzes dozens of biographies and manuals written by scientists and determines that they almost unfailingly mention joy and exhilaration as guidelines of scientific method, like the neuroscientist Santiago Roman y Cajalo, who, echoing Darwin and McClintock, called discovery an "indescribable pleasure—which pales the rest of life's joys."[12] But Thagard stops short of fully enmeshing cognition in feeling, insisting that feeling only sometimes leads to good knowledge and so needs to be checked by "cold judgments."[13] Cogency theory reworks this. Rather than keeping the reason/emotion divide intact while shrinking the domain of reason, it abandons the binary altogether. It says the dynamic agonism that leads to the sense of science is not between feeling and nonfeeling, but between *different forms of feeling*.

This chapter only looks at one short span of this long philosophical trajectory (and sidesteps other important conversations happening outside the Western tradition). It studies three thinkers who influenced or were influenced by the naturalizing thought of Charles Darwin—David Hume, Friedrich Nietzsche, and William James—and considers their relevance for cogency theory. In each, we see the little argument of this book playing out: rationality is made of feeling. For Hume, rationality was fully subordinate to the passions, an exciting pursuit no different from hunting or gambling. For Nietzsche, science shrank beside his vision of a noble, prancing philosophy—but both were made from complex combinations of emotion. And for James, knowledge production was entirely motivated by what he called *the sentiment of rationality*. We believe and disbelieve, he insisted, not through innocent deduction but by riding the riptides of feeling.

Crucially, though, these philosophers offered ideas about knowledge production in which the exhilarating *desire to know* was tempered. They suggested that reason, philosophy, and science work only when they have *both* exhilaration *and* feelings that check and channel that excitement, what Hume called *cool passions* and James called *nervousness* about error. These countervailing forces, too, were emotions. In this picture, scientific rationality—the *sense of science*—is not the binary opposite of emotion but a carefully constructed amalgam of feelings in tension. The final section of this chapter turns to conspiracy theory as an illustration of how knowledge production collapses when this emotional agonism is removed. Conspiracism eliminates the nervous dimension of science, doubling down on the feeling of click but doing very little to produce good knowledge. And as we'll see in chapter 2, this pleasure of conspiracism is intensified by adding racializing affects.

David Hume on Reason as a Passion

David Hume's naturalistic philosophy was extremely influential on Darwin. As much as Darwin's thought was a turning point, it emerged from an intellectual ecosystem that had already set the stage for his findings. The early evolutionary theories of Darwin's grandfather Erasmus Darwin (who knew Hume's work well) and Jean-Baptiste Lamarck emerged a few decades after Hume's death and were well studied by Darwin. And Hume was a major influence on Darwin directly, in part through Darwin's interest in Hume's speculations about the rationality of animals as emerging from instinct.[14] Hume's philosophy emboldened Darwin's willingness to challenge the black monolith myth and connect human and animal cognition through an evolutionary genealogy.[15]

Although he is mostly studied today for his contributions to a tradition of empiricism, Hume's work consistently returned to the relationship between feeling and knowing. Reason, Hume was convinced, is always plugged into the grid of our emotions. In *Enquiry concerning Human Understanding* he depicted scientific knowledge-making as unhooked from objective certainty. This is the famous critique of causality that has left so many undergraduates agape. *How do we know what we know?*, Hume asked. *How do we know the leaves will fall, the moon will change phases, and water will quench our thirst?* His answer was disarming. We don't. We know *what has happened* well enough. The moon has changed phases many times during our lives and, to the best of our knowledge, for many lifetimes before ours. Yet Hume showed we can't *know with certainty* that it will change phase again.[16]

But Hume didn't see this sabotage of certainty as a way of undoing the effectiveness of knowledge. His point was that everything we know has its source in experience rather than abstract deductions. The battle was against causality, but the real war was against *rationalism*, the belief that good knowledge is always built on a stack of bulletproof deductions. In Hume's eyes, if reason couldn't conclusively demonstrate something as basic as cause and effect, what little could it offer by way of raw material for science? "*What is the foundation of all our reasonings and conclusions concerning that relation [of cause and effect]?*" Hume asked. "It may be replied in one word, EXPERIENCE."[17] The contents of our minds are furnished through the impressions left by the world in our bodies.[18]

This is the Hume we all know from Philosophy 101. But there's more to the story. Because Hume *was* confident that our mind *does* make causal links—even in the absence of certainty.[19] Immanuel Kant's solution to this problem a generation later is the one most often cited. He believed the mind casts a sort of net over the objects of sense experience, automatically arranging them into causal relations.[20] Hume's solution was similar but much less well known. For Hume, the mind figures out causality by *feeling*. "If I see a billiard-ball moving towards another," he wrote, "I can easily *conceive* it to stop upon contact. This conception implies no contradiction; but still *it feels* very differently from that conception, by which I represent to myself the impulse, and the communication of motion from one ball to another."[21] Imagining a range of possible scenarios—including absurd ones, like billiard balls colliding and staying still—we assess their plausibility by how they feel. So for Hume, the mechanism that makes knowledge about the world possible is feeling. We don't *know* that a causal relationship is in effect through a line of rationally deduced propositions. Our *emotional response* guides us to the right understanding.

That's just the beginning. Hume scaled this up into an even more spectacular claim that *all knowledge* is gauged by this truth-discerning emotion. For example, he wrote, "the difference between *fiction* and *belief* lies in some sentiment or feeling, which is annexed to the latter, not to the former."[22] In other words, we distinguish *true* from *false* by feeling, not through the calculus of detached reason. This is Hume's big play. He contended that the thinking/feeling divide has obscured our sense—available to us in every moment—that cognition is predicated on emotion. "BELIEF is the true and proper name of this feeling," he affirmed, "and no one is ever at a loss to know the meaning of that term; because every man is every moment conscious of the sentiment represented by it."[23] It's a radical proposal, an uncompromising refutation of rationalism in favor of a model of knowledge organized around affects. Belief is a sentiment. We suss truth and falsity by feeling our way.

Hume's *A Treatise of Human Nature* developed an even more strident statement of the total dependency of reason on feeling. Even though reason can illuminate the relationships between pieces of information, Hume wrote, reason is inert when it comes to actual decision-making. This is because reason can't discern *value*. It can draw connections between pieces of information and between actions and outcomes. But it can't dictate which outcomes will or should matter to us.[24] Reason can only supply the information that will then be arranged by the magnetic field of desire into meaningful actions. This is where Hume offers one of his most trenchant and controversial lines: "Reason is and ought only to be," he wrote, "the slave of the passions, and can never pretend to any other office than to serve and obey them."[25] As part of the broadside against rationalism, Hume insisted that reason is totally dependent on emotion for direction and motivation, always riding the tectonic plates of the passions beneath the surface. What we think, Hume insisted, follows what we feel.[26]

This isn't to say that we can't reason. It's just that what gets called *rationality* is, for Hume, *actually a passion*. In fact, it's a configuration of what he labels *calm passions*. "What we call strength of mind," he proposed, "implies the prevalence of the calm passions above the violent."[27] The calm passions—passions that fixate on distant rewards or pleasures rather than immediate ones—are arrayed in such a way as to discipline and outmaneuver the violent passions. Even tranquility is not the absence of feeling, but a specific emotional posture that allows us to patiently explore a problem, listening attentively for the soft click of real discovery. "By *reason* we mean affections," Hume concluded, "but such as operate more calmly, and cause no disorder in the temper: Which tranquility leads us into a mistake concerning them, and causes us to regard them as conclusions only of our intellectual faculties."[28] The calm passions compose themselves into an alloy that makes scientific knowledge production possible. Science is not the progressive supremacy of reason over passion, but a way of feeling in tension.

Hunting, Gambling, Philosophy

Hume didn't just overthrow the thinking/feeling binary. He also gave us a map of how feelings are organized to make science. The status of what we would now call *science* for Hume was ambiguous—in part because Hume's word *science* meant something different for him than it does for us now. (As Peter Harrison points out, a range of concepts like *natural philosophy* and *natural history* were only brought together under the unifying term *science* in the nineteenth century.)[29] But we can get a sense of what Hume might say about science today by studying what he said about philosophy. This starts with a picture of philosophy as not only organized by feeling but driven by it. In a chapter of the *Treatise* titled "Of Curiosity, or the Love of Truth," Hume pointed out that "many philosophers have consum'd their time, have destroy'd their health, and neglected their fortune, in the search of such truths, as they esteem'd important."[30] Although he didn't name it, Hume was vividly aware that reason is suffused with desire. The click that comes along with knowledge-making produces intoxicating pleasure—a pleasure so vivid it can lead to self-destruction.

Although Hume cast the spotlight on calm passions in explaining the emotional machinery of knowledge-making, there's another element—drawn from the violent passions—that also seems to be part of the emotional alchemy of philosophy. Hume identified this as *surprise*. The thrill of discovery is what drives this process forward: "Every thing, that is new, is most affecting," Hume wrote.[31] Surprise adds the dimension of intensity to the landscape of knowledge production, making us pursue it all the more zealously. It's why philosophy is associated, for Hume, with two other pastimes: hunting and gambling. "There cannot be two passions more nearly resembling each other," he mused, "than those of hunting and philosophy."[32] A page later, he added gambling.[33] What brings these three activities together is their *affective* congruence. Each one is about the pleasurable navigation of a field of information occasionally punctuated by sharp spikes of discovery. It's like a slot machine that spits out rewards at random intervals, always leaving us on the edge of our seats.[34] It is, in short, the feeling of a wild experiment. Just as a gambler can become addicted to the dice, the roulette wheel, the first glance at a fresh hand of cards, so scientists and philosophers can become addicted to the flush of making knowledge.

Like Polanyi, Hume turned to mathematics as the epitome of philosophy's emotional pull.[35] Math offers us the pleasure of a satisfying click, but only when it crosses the threshold of real interest. So Hume noted that "in an arithmetical operation, where both the truth and the assurance are of the same nature, as in the most profound algebraical problem, the pleasure is very inconsiderable, if rather it does not degenerate into pain."[36] There's a subtle but vital point embedded in this statement. The truth of a mathematical explanation is not enough to be pleasurable; it also has to match the level of sophistication of our understanding (neither too simple nor too complex). Children find joy in playing with simple toys or blocks, but different bodies have different scales of taste. A library of phone books may be pure information, but it doesn't land at the right register of complexity to produce click.

Hume's model of knowledge production, then, is very different from the approach taken by scientific secularists like Richard Dawkins who find the treasures unearthed by science wondrous to behold.[37] For them, the pursuit of truth has no *internal* emotional structure. But Hume saw knowledge-making *itself* as emotionally saturated. For Hume, the thinking/feeling binary has collapsed in on itself. Philosophy and reason are offshoots of feeling, not a domain above. We're pulled by the excitement of our expanding comprehension of the world, a desire in tension with cooling affects that dampen our enthusiasm and increase our precision. Science is born out of an agonism of contesting feelings.

Nietzsche on the Animality of Reason

Hume wrote in the prelude to Darwinism, Nietzsche in its aftermath. (Daniel Dennett sees the two as pursuing the same ideas, though Nietzsche was able to go farther thanks to the Darwinian sea change.)[38] Yet Nietzsche's relationship to Darwinism was far from straightforward.[39] In a comprehensive study of Nietzsche's influences from biology, intellectual historian Gregory Moore proposes that even when Nietzsche tried to separate himself from Darwinism, his attitude toward biology was deeply embedded in conversations about evolution and human continuity with animals happening around him.[40] As philosopher Vanessa Lemm writes, the animal "stands at the center of Nietzsche's renewal of the practice and meaning of philosophy itself."[41] Nietzsche might have declared himself in opposition to Darwin, but he never got away from Darwinism.

His efforts to understand humanity inside an animal frame led Nietzsche to abandon the thinking/feeling binary. In the preface to the second edition of *The Joyful Wisdom*, he wrote that all philosophy is "merely an interpretation of the body"—and often "a misunderstanding of the body."[42] "Consciousness," he insisted later, is a by-product of a chain of evolutionary accidents, "the last and latest development of the organic, and consequently also the most unfinished and least powerful of these developments."[43] The Darwinian frame is exactly what allowed Nietzsche to relink philosophy to physiology. For Nietzsche, all modes of knowledge "depend for their conceptual origins on the body and its forces."[44] Nietzsche would have it no other way. Philosophy, he insisted, is worthwhile only when it moves with our bodies. The nearer philosophy is to our passions, the stronger it becomes. This is why in *The Joyful Wisdom*—a book dedicated to sweeping away the distinction between philosophy and poetry—Nietzsche wrote, "We must discover the hero, and likewise the fool, that is hidden in our *passion for knowledge*; we must now and then be joyful in our folly, that we may continue to be joyful in our wisdom!"[45] For both Nietzsche and Hume, philosophy is not just knowledge. It's a kind of dance.[46]

What does it mean to have a *passion for knowledge*—and to embrace this love of knowledge that makes us fools? It means we can fall in love with philosophy in a way that exceeds any kind of calculation, let alone usefulness. The broad trellis of ideas, experiences, and conversations that is the history of philosophy is not just a repository of knowledge, for Nietzsche. It relinks us to the most ancient story of animal life: the struggle to find joy. "I have discovered for myself that the old humanity and animality," Nietzsche announced, "the collective primeval age, and the past of all sentient being, continues to meditate, love, hate, and reason in me," before declaring, "Among all these dreamers, I also, the 'thinker,' dance my dance."[47]

All the same, philosophical truth is not solitary. "I am overburdened with my wisdom," Zarathustra proclaims. "Like the bee that has gathered too much honey, I need hands outstretched to receive it."[48] Hume's analogies are the concentration-oriented pleasures of hunting and gaming, but Nietzsche makes philosophy social. As with Polanyi's *persuasive passion*, to philosophize, for Nietzsche, is pleasurable in part because of the way it presses us outward into conversation with others. It's why holding one's tongue is so viscerally frustrating. When restrained from truth telling, Nietzsche warned, philosophers seethe: "They emerge from their cave wearing a terrifying aspect; their words and deeds are then explosions and it is possible for them to perish by their own hand."[49] In Nietzsche's version of cogency theory, truth isn't a fragile object to be admired on a shelf. It's a force demanding to crash into the world.

Tepid Science

But whereas for Hume philosophy and mathematics ran together in a continuous playground of exhilarating discovery, *science* earned no applause from Nietzsche. Instead, he poured out scorn on this lesser variety of intellectual action. Nietzsche's word was *Wissenschaft*—"knowledge making"—a broad term that includes all academic disciplines, from the humanities to the emerging natural and experimental sciences.[50] Hume was friendly toward science (which he never programmatically separated from philosophy). But Nietzsche blasted science for being trivial—more like dithering than *thinking*. As early as *The Birth of Tragedy*, he mocked what he saw as the pathetic error of Socrates, "the imperturbable belief that thought, as it follows the thread of causality, reaches down into the deepest abysses of being."[51] Now, he insisted, it's science that carries the torch of this misbegotten approach to life. For Nietzsche, it's all dreck. Only philosophy stands above and apart.

One of Nietzsche's most extraordinary condemnations of science came in his early essay "Schopenhauer as Educator," which contains a long overview of science's laughable failures. "Science is related to wisdom as virtuousness is related to holiness," Nietzsche admonished. "It is cold and dry, it has not love and knows nothing of a deep feeling of inadequacy and longing."[52] Science stands accused of "translating every experience into a dialectical question-and-answer game and into an affair purely of the head," wasting its practitioners down to "almost nothing but bones."[53] Nietzsche could only speculate how anyone could be enticed by this adventure of "skeletons." "It can hardly originate in any supposed 'desire for truth,'" he mused, "for how could there exist any desire at all for cold, pure, inconsequential knowledge!"[54]

Sounds like cogitation, right? But then Nietzsche made a stunning move. Far from saying that science is *unfeeling*, he affirmed that it is, in fact, made of passions. It's just that science, unlike philosophy, is made of *lesser feelings*. What are these tepid emotions of science? "First of all," he announced, taking a deep breath,

> there is a strong and ever more intense curiosity, the search for adventures in the domain of knowledge, the constant stimulation exercised by the new and rare in contrast to the old and tedious. Then there is a certain drive to dialectical investigation, the huntsman's joy in following the sly fox's path in the realm of thought, so that it is not really truth that is sought but the seeking itself, and the main pleasure consists in the cunning tracking, encircling, and correct killing. Now add to this the impulse to contradiction, the personality wanting to be aware of itself and to make itself felt in opposition to all others; the struggle becomes a pleasure and the goal is personal victory, the struggle for truth being only a pretext. Then, the man of learning is to a great extent also motivated by the discovery of *certain* "truths," motivated that is by his subjection to certain ruling persons, castes, opinions, churches, governments: he feels it is to his advantage to bring "truth" over to their side.[55]

Like Hume, Nietzsche painted a picture of science as an alloy of feelings, a mass of contending impulses that motivate the scholarly life. He even reinvented Hume's analogy to hunting.

The difference is that Nietzsche placed these passions in an idiosyncratic hierarchy. This single paragraph continues unbroken for another *four pages*.

In a piercing monologue, Nietzsche counted off the feckless motives driving scientists (thirteen by his tally) from their contemptible "sobriety and conventionality" to their horrid "low self-esteem" to their worthless delight in "looking for tangles in the sciences and unravelling them."[56] A version of the same list of indictments came a decade later in *Beyond Good and Evil*. Nietzsche settled, there, for merely observing that "compared to a genius, which is to say: compared to a being that either *begets* or *gives birth* ... the scholar, the average man of science, is somewhat like an old maid. Like her, he has no expertise in the two most valuable acts performed by humanity."[57] This leads into another proclamation of the shabbiness of the scientist: weak, shy, focused on usefulness rather than glory.[58] The scientist allows herself to become diverted with trivialities rather than meditating on the depths of her soul.[59] Nietzsche was just as committed to cogency theory as Hume—just as confident that science and philosophy are made by artfully arranging our animal passions. The only difference lies in Nietzsche's insistence that some passions are superior to others. Science isn't *dispassionate*, for Nietzsche; it just doesn't comprise the *right* passions. Like Socrates, it meagerly feels for *truth* at the expense of poetry.

But Nietzsche's view of science is ultimately a contradiction, or at least a framework that can stand only if we accept his shrill hierarchy. Nietzsche insisted, "There is cheerfulness only where there is a victory; and this applies to the works of true thinkers just as much as it does to any work of art."[60] So why aren't science's victories a source of cheer? Nietzsche's answer is that science is puppet-mastered by a deeper metaphysical commitment: the error of Socrates again—the belief that thought is up to the task of getting to the bottom of things. "Why not deceive?" he wondered. "Why not allow oneself to be deceived?"[61] He concluded that this conviction rests on nothing more than an abstract *moral* commitment, the enemy of the noble pursuit of our impulses.[62] In *On the Genealogy of Morality*, he claimed that those scions of modernity who "demand intellectual rigor" have failed to truly emancipate themselves, because their "unconditional will to truth, is *faith in the ascetic ideal itself* ... the faith in a *metaphysical* value, a *value as such of truth* as vouched for and confirmed by that ideal alone."[63]

This is the core mistake in Nietzsche's understanding of science. He assumed that it had meaning only by virtue of being suspended from a metaphysical ceiling—an abstract moral commitment to absolute truth. But this imagined too much. It misrepresented the science of his time, which was already having robust conversations about the limits of certainty.[64] More dangerously, it assumed that science was meaningful only in anticipation of some sort of final, far-distant end. It overlooked what Nietzsche's *own* insistence on the emotional richness of exploring the world would seem to indicate—that science could itself be affectively dynamic. Throwing science a bone, Nietzsche wrote, "There is a profound and fundamental satisfaction in the fact that science ascertains things that *hold their ground*, and again furnish the basis for new researches."[65] But he failed to see how his own philosophy illuminated the joy and delight in science's discovery of these small, sturdy things.

Nietzsche insisted that science was a sort of asceticism—a mode of self-denial leading to "the impoverishment of life—the emotions cooled, the tempo slackened, dialectics in place of instinct, *solemnity* stamped on faces and gestures."[66] But really, what Nietzsche identified was the *sense of science* as an agonism of emotions. Nietzsche realized—in concert with Hume—that the cool emotions are actually choreographed alongside other passions to create the scientific disposition. The question was not whether science emerged from emotional agonism; Nietzsche knew it did. He just didn't like which emotions won out in the scientific struggle.

The premise that cognition is fully embedded within the body is foundational to everything Nietzsche wrote. This is why he was convinced that philosophy in its purest form is animal joy. And it's why he recognized even science as a conglomerate of feelings fashioned into an engine for knowledge production. But Nietzsche refused to see how similar to the scientists he actually was. Catching his work in a different light, however, cogency theory finds in it a detailed portrait of how knowledge production works. Knowledge-making is a *felt* process because it coalesces from the bottom up—out of our animal impulses and instincts—rather than being dropped from above like the black monolith.

James on the Sentiment of Rationality

William James was born two years before Nietzsche but outlived him by a decade. Trained in medicine but with a strong philosophical bent, he went from department to department—anatomy to philosophy to psychology and back to philosophy—during his long career at Harvard. He was as comfortable talking about Darwin as about Kant. At the intersection of philosophy and biology, James shored up the foundations of the modern discipline of psychology, paying particular attention to the relationship between emotion and cognition.[67] James once wrote that Nietzsche's books "remind one, half the time, of the sick shriekings of … dying rats."[68] This is mean, but it's a useful window onto James's bigger argument: all philosophical states of mind, he insisted, start from a foundation of *feeling*.

For James, the way we think is always emotional. And to pursue truth *is itself pleasurable*, dancing with what he called the *sentiment of rationality*. As Gail Hamner writes, for James, thinking "is not pure, cold reason, but the intoxication of personal purpose."[69] Although the philosophical movement he helped found was dubbed *pragmatism*, James was happy to place himself solidly in the lineage of Hume. He explicitly referred to his method as *radical empiricism*, and wrote, with a modesty that would be unimaginable in Nietzsche, that there was nothing in his pragmatism that hadn't been done already by Socrates, Aristotle, Locke, Berkeley, and Hume.[70] Like Hume, he emphasized the priority of experience, rather than reflection, as the ground of knowledge production. And like Hume, James's epistemology made emotional agonism central to doing science.

James's work on religion is a good starting point, especially his analysis of Pascal's wager. In *Will to Believe*, James reviews Blaise Pascal's famous thought experiment, in which the French thinker proposed that because we can't know whether immortal life continues after physical death, it has the structure of a *bet*. For Pascal, confronted with these terms, it's only reasonable to bet on salvation: the prospect of gaining an infinite reward always justifies the low initial stake of faith. For Hume and Darwin, gambling was exhilarating, but James found nothing in this wager to celebrate. Instead, he saw it as a joyless settling of accounts. "We feel," he wrote, "that a faith in masses and holy water adopted willfully after such a mechanical calculation, would lack the inner soul of faith's reality."[71] This analytic solution to a philosophical puzzle, for James, didn't qualify as *real faith*. James was sure that belief matters only when it springs from feeling.

James didn't just think Pascal's faith was stale, though. He also said that to deduce religious belief from arithmetic is absurd. "It is evident," he insisted, "that unless there be some pre-existing tendency to believe in masses and holy water, the option offered to the will by Pascal is not a living option."[72] The *logical* channel that Pascal opened for us can't possibly be enough to instill conviction in the Catholic faith (which is why, James notes, no Muslim and no Protestant was ever persuaded by it).[73] What makes a particular set of beliefs *cogent* has to be more than a series of abstract propositions—especially when the apologist tries to authorize the trappings of a whole tradition using a few scraps of syllogistic machinery.[74]

Religion emerges not from arithmetic, James contended, but from our deep-running affective currents. So he wrote that religion is the result of a "craving of the heart to believe that behind nature there is a spirit."[75] Religious ideas aren't reached through deduction; they're motivated by *felt* urgency. Theology, he elaborated in *The Varieties of Religious Experience*, is not conceptual machinery that leads to the rich felt register of faith. It's exactly the opposite—an attempt to *dress religious feeling* in conceptual vestments. We start with the feeling, then surround it with elaborate architectures of belief. "In a world in which no religious feeling had ever existed," James reflected, "I doubt whether any philosophic theology could ever have been framed."[76] Pascal's wager was misguided precisely because it tried to flatten religion to computation. Believing, James insisted, buds from feeling.

But crucially, it's not only religious belief that is driven by feeling. *All kinds of belief*—whether religious or secular—have their sources in emotion. In *Varieties* James proposed that when an organ (such as the liver) "alters in one way the blood that percolates it, we get the methodist, when in another way, we get the atheist form of mind. So of all our raptures and our drynesses, our longings and pantings. They are equally organically founded, be they religious or of non-religious content."[77] Nonreligious beliefs are no different from religious beliefs in their point of origin: the felt impulses of the body. Although reason has been cast in the starring role in the secular drama, James was convinced that feelings are the real drivers of the plot. Or, more precisely, *the way we reason* is an organic extension of our foundational feeling, no different from a hand extending from the end of an arm. As René Rosfort and Giovanni Stanghellini put it, for James, "feelings motivate, orient, and sustain our rational thinking about the world, other people, and ourselves, and it is not possible to separate thinking and feeling in an actual human life."[78] This is why James asserted in his pragmatism lectures that rather than a contest of ideas, philosophical debate is, in the main, a "clash of human temperaments."[79] The battle of ideas is a proxy war between rival dispositions, the real substrate of thought.

This leads to one of James's key concepts, what he called the *sentiment of rationality*.[80] As far back as his 1884 article "What Is an Emotion?," James explored *how it feels* to reason through a problem. "Certain sequences of ideas charm us as much as others tire us," he observed. "It is a real intellectual delight to get a problem solved, and a real intellectual torment to have to leave it unfinished."[81] James developed this in detail in his later essay "The Sentiment of Rationality," in which he observed, "Transition from a state of puzzle and perplexity to rational comprehension is full of lively relief and pleasure."[82] James's fellow pragmatist Charles Peirce came at the same problem from another direction, describing intellectual inquiry as motivated by the affective need to neutralize the "irritation of doubt."[83] Like Hume and Nietzsche, James asserted that knowledge is produced by emotion rather than cogitation. And even more specifically, he *named* the pleasure of making knowledge—the *sentiment of rationality*. There's a feeling of excitement that comes from solving a puzzle, James insisted. The sentiment of rationality is the emotion generated by the act of correlating pieces of information. The felt cogency of an idea lies in the way it clicks with what's around it.

Nervous Science

The scientific method, for James, rests on this feeling of click but isn't exhausted by it. Much as Hume noted that what we call reason is actually a configuration of cool and hot affects in tension (and Nietzsche rebuked scientists for being too quick to tamp down their own electric enthusiasm for discovery in order to arrive at truth), James thought science is made by balancing "eager interest" with "equally keen nervousness lest [we] become deceived."[84] This nervousness could be the product of a horror at falsehood, but it could also be an anxiety about being embarrassed in front of one's professional colleagues, putting a new spin on theories of science as social. Either way, rather than a clash between feeling and reason, science is born in an agonism of *different emotions.*

What James saw is that we need the oscillation between excitement and frustration. The dynamic of expansion and contraction, growth and pruning, sculpts our ideas into effective actors in the world. Too much anxiety and you lock down, never even venturing a guess. Too much excitement and you end up with an overgrowth of silliness, a proliferation of connections that feel good but fail to represent the world. Of course, this does nothing to guarantee that what *feels* true *is* true. "Biologically considered," James noted, anticipating methodological symmetry, "our minds are as ready to grind out falsehood as veracity."[85]

As with Hume and Nietzsche, philosophy itself, in James's framing, becomes an emotional task, what contemporary pragmatists call a *strenuous mood*.[86] Pragmatism is a philosophy that embraces the full spectrum of cognitive affects—from frustration to delight. It channels the cooling passion of humility by reconciling itself to the inability of our finite, physical minds to attain objective certainty. The "Jamesian strenuous mood"—the emotional template of pragmatic philosophy—"requires the pragmatist to live without the comfort of an Absolute that ultimately guarantees ultimate truth and harmonizes all conflict and difference."[87] This is how James came to think of his philosophy as *tough-mindedness*.[88] The spirit of pragmatist philosophy is exhilaration tempered by humility. At the intersection of these horizons emerges the affective profile of scientific inquiry.

Pascal tried to reduce faith to a coin flip. But James showed that belief and disbelief are, of necessity, much more than this: they open onto a glittering casino of games of chance calling our names. "The split between the intellectual and the affective," writes the literary critic George Levine, "does not operate for James, since all intellection is involved in the whole person thinking."[89] We're pulled in many directions—toward many ways of feeling and knowing the world. In this vortex of forces, we find ourselves believing in ways both religious and nonreligious, both scientific and philosophical. James rejected knowing *anything* meaningful by unfeeling reason. This goes not only for God but for all beliefs, all knowledge—including science and secularism.

Conspiracy Theory and the Sense of Science

The philosophical perspectives we've considered here are all part of the project of taking apart the reason/emotion binary. But they also offer a nuanced account of how specific cognitive feelings converge to create what gets called rationality. This involves optimistic intellectual passions like the sentiment of rationality, but also countervailing affects—nervousness, fear, shame—to control and channel the exhilaration of discovery. This dynamic is the sense of science, an emotional recipe for producing reliable knowledge. Precisely because knowledge that clicks is exciting, we need to be ever-vigilant that our own preferences and predilections don't eclipse the feeling tone of making contact with reality. We can gain an even better understanding of the sense of science, though, by studying how it malfunctions. Conspiracy theory is a perfect illustration of this. It's a mutation of the scientific method that operates by deleting the checks and balances of the sense of science and hypertrophying the pleasure of click.

Conspiracism does this by producing what we could call a *simplex system*. A simplex system is an information system that has been artificially simplified to produce more click. Anyone who's ever accused someone of *liking simple answers* has already encountered a simplex system, but really, they're everywhere. Puzzles and games use simplicity to create fields in which we can find pleasure by moving pieces of information around. Narrative entertainment—novels, plays, biographies, movies—isolates a sequence of details in order to produce the most emotionally satisfying story, veering away from the freewheeling, seldom-satisfying open-endedness of real life. In all these cases, details are carefully curated to allow a small number of elements to combine in satisfying ways.

Conspiracism takes this recreational technique and transposes it to reality, imagining every detail to be saturated with narrative importance. Let's start with a few examples. The Pizzagate conspiracy that engulfed the presidential campaign of Hillary Clinton and its aftermath was triggered after the release of a cache of stolen emails in the autumn of 2016. These emails became a sort of information playground for conspiracists, with every line scrutinized for layers of hidden meaning. Messages between campaign workers and a Washington, DC, pizzeria became the focus of an obsession with the phrase *cheese pizza*, which is code, on the dark web, for "child pornography." Rhetoric scholar Jenny Rice mentions a conspiracist who elaborated this even further, advising his readers that "*cheese* is code for *little girl,* while *pasta* is code for *little boy*" and instructing them to comb the email archives for these keywords.[90] Four years later, the conspiracist obsession with Clinton was still running strong. When Donald Trump announced he had contracted the COVID-19 virus in October 2020, he tweeted, "We will get through this TOGETHER!" QAnon followers zeroed in on the word *together*, breaking it down into the component parts *to/get/her*. Trump was signaling to his followers that his diagnosis was all part of a master plan to catch Clinton.[91]

In the summer of 2020, users on the Reddit forum R/conspiracy claimed that an online furniture company was using highly priced merchandise to traffic children for sexual abuse.[92] The theory began with an anomaly: several items on the store were weirdly overpriced—pillows and generic storage cabinets running over $10,000 apiece. This oddity of the algorithm then became a magnetic field, drawing in additional conspiracist data points. Many of the cabinets had been given stylized female names, for instance. Some pillows had labels that corresponded to the names of missing children, like

"Dunning." Googling the numeric item codes turned up pornographic images. One observer noticed that a picture of one item was placed near a book about Bill and Hillary Clinton.[93]

At the capillary level, these tiny, thrilling moments of click weave conspiracy theories into being and cement them in our minds. A leaked email here, a blurry photograph there, a world-rocking clue tucked away in a speech or webpage. Conspiracism elevates these flecks of information into a constellation of acute relevance, telling a vast drama of hidden power, stunning exploitation, and terrifying violence—just out of sight. It's often suggested that conspiracy theory is motivated by a scarcity of evidence.[94] But it's the opposite—conspiracism is obsessed with evidence. Hofstadter points us to Joseph McCarthy's ninety-six-page pamphlet *McCarthyism*, with its 313 footnotes.[95] Rice talks about how conversations with committed conspiracists left her "overwhelmed by sheer abundance, buried beneath a textual landslide."[96] There are data points for conspiracies, just as there were data points for phrenology, for the historical reality of the biblical flood, and for ether as the medium of space within which stars and planets float. The issue is not a lack of evidence. The issue is how our intellectual affects organize that evidence. Conspiracy theory picks and chooses from a broad field of possible clues (names, numbers, codes, puzzles, metaphors, puns) and finds the most *thrilling* way of arranging them. The goal is to maximize the excitement of click. You're gambling in a game you can't lose.

Conspiracism reconstructs the world as a sort of live-action mystery in which a string of plot points have been carefully orchestrated for the highest possible enjoyment. "The paranoid mind is *far more* coherent than the real world," Hofstadter writes.[97] The clues present themselves generously, eagerly waiting to be picked up. Political scientist Michael Barkun argues that one of the central organizing principles of conspiracy theory is a rejection of accident.[98] It demands a world of total intelligibility, maximizing the pleasure of moving from ambiguity to clarity in every instant. Nothing is noise. Everything clicks together with everything else. Conspiracy theory sugarcoats the world, hypercharging every act, event, and word with relevance. It's a jigsaw puzzle where all the pieces are squares.

Conspiracism isn't about understanding the world, then. It's about chasing a feeling *through* a particular configuration of knowledge. It decorates the world, rendering it dazzlingly interesting. Anthropologist Susan Lepselter proposes that conspiracy theories, UFO encounters, and paranormal experiences are united by an affective template, what she calls *apophenia*, the feeling that seemingly unconnected objects have a hidden vital correspondence."⁹⁹ Apophenia manifests, for instance, in the "feeling of a hidden 'deep structure'" drawing in "an omniscient colluding government, or omniscient aliens, or a sense that an inexplicable synchronicity underlies seemingly random coincidences."¹⁰⁰ In other words, it's the feeling of building knowledge that clicks.

Lepselter proposes that apophenia isn't an "error" so much as a way of cultivating dispositions that allow connections to come to the surface.¹⁰¹ But this misses the fact that in tuning our cognitive affects, we can go too far in the direction of sensitivity to connections. So even though it distantly resembles science, ordinary science is hated by conspiracy theorists—and climate change deniers, antivaxxers, GMO skeptics, and creationists—because science requires that all knowledge be put to the test. Knowledge production guided by the sense of science is wary of generously splashing the world with promising connections. Scientists get suspicious if you strike gold every time. Programmatic science is organized around struggle, the agonism of disciplined knowledge-making, chasing the exhilaration of click while subjecting it to constant pressure. There's a continuous exchange between hot and cold passions. Conspiracy theory deletes these safeguards, flooding knowledge with the pure pleasure of finding *significance* in everything. Everything is code, everything is a clue.

Ironically, this means the ability of conspiracy theorists to detect *actual* abuses of power is severely clipped. As the authors of the *Conspiracy Theory Handbook* point out, real conspiracies are pretty much always "discovered through conventional thinking—healthy skepticism of official accounts while carefully considering available evidence and being committed to internal consistency."¹⁰² Conspiracism hunts for child abusers on a furniture website while the climate crisis intensifies, for-profit incarceration sprawls, police brutality boils over, and oligarchs shred ecosystems and public life.

This is why it's just about impossible to persuade conspiracists that things might be dull, that power might be sloppy and clumsy rather than ruthless and operatic. Affect theorist Kathleen Stewart writes: "There's pleasure in conspiracy theory. An intimate knowledge of secret collusions, clandestine activities, and little collaborative worlds of an 'us' tracking what 'they' are doing. There are the small, inventive interpretive practices ... the moment of the 'Ah ha! *That's* what this is all about!'"¹⁰³ Conspiracy theories drench the world in narrative pleasure. And because they have anchors in a carefully winnowed dossier of data, they're extremely difficult to dislodge.

The sense of science, with its tentativeness and its oscillation between pleasure and frustration, loses to the desire for a world dripping with interest. Whereas James and Hume soberly throw their lot in with science, Nietzsche, weirdly, is a sort of conspiracy theory philosopher. He refuses exactly the parts of science that make it an effective engine for knowledge production, demanding that the excitement of philosophy remain untrammeled. (A similar technique underpins New Atheism, as we'll see in chapter 7.) For conspiracists, the unquestioning masses are *sheeple*, lulled into a state of uncritical complacency. Everyone who doesn't get it is a dupe. But what if this is exactly the way the unbridled pleasure of click gets its hooks in us? What if the permanent posture of suspicion is itself a kind of opium dream?

The relevance of thinking about conspiracy theory here is not that it gives us, as the logical positivists wanted, an ironclad rule for dividing science from nonscience. Instead, it leads us to the fundamental ambiguity of science. Science has reliable—but not infallible—mechanisms for recovering truths. We don't just *think* our way to scientific truth—we feel it. Science itself, as an institution, has evolved to not only tune in to the feeling of things clicking into place, but also use skepticism to try to dissolve that very same feeling, to probe it as rigorously as possible. This is what James means by *nervousness about getting things wrong* and Hume means by *cool passions*. It dovetails with historian of science Naomi Oreskes's emphasis on the importance of *humility* in scientific communities.[104] This tension makes scientific discovery effective. Conspiracy theory, by removing these dampening mechanisms, is like a cigarette with the filter snipped off, maxing out the hit you get from studying the world, leaving you dizzy. It steps away from the sense of science as a struggle of forces and ramps up the feeling of click—often, as we'll see, with a hit of racism thrown in to spike the high. Conspiracy theories throw our longing to believe into high relief. They feel so good they have to be true.

But still, sometimes the rogue scientist with a brazen hunch is right. Sometimes the anomaly that bucks the paradigm has to be chased down. Sometimes they really are out to get you. Just as conspiracy theories can never really be disproven (and sometimes contain flashes of truth), there is no mechanism within science for manufacturing certainty, only a carefully constructed arena for staging the contest of forces. The sense of science, as Hume and James show, fumbles for cogency, then tests it as rigorously as it can, always in fear and trembling that it's succumbing to its own unseen urges. Cogency theory, driven by the feeling of click, maps the path to durable knowledge.

But we can't ever be *certain* that it isn't a changeling. This is why James's resolute conclusion is that all we can do is mind our intellectual desires, cultivating a new *temperament* for knowledge production—a tolerance for ambiguity rather than a zeal for order, a willingness to engage with the frustration of encountering the world in its messiness.[105]

Conclusion: The Affects of Objectivity

"How far is truth susceptible of embodiment?" Nietzsche asked, before affirming, "That is the question, that is the experiment."[106] Reading Nietzsche in concert with Hume and James adds their work to the conversation around cogency theory, breaking down the feeling/thinking binary and connecting knowledge production, thought, and rationality to emotion. In an essay exploring Nietzsche's idea of philosophy as dance, feminist theorist Kimerer LaMothe describes how scholarly research itself is guided by feeling. "The sensory patterns that guide our study can be subtle indeed," she writes. "A tingle of awe in response to a text or ritual or event impels us to learn more. A wrinkle of confusion troubles us to revisit a mark that remains and ask new questions, gather more data, consult other experts. A surge of excitement pushes us on as pieces of our research start falling into shapes of understanding we have learned to recognize. A sense of ease lets us know that our interpretations are objective or empathetic enough, or will be well received."[107] LaMothe uses Nietzsche to chart the affective seams that guide our practices of knowledge-making. This is the choreography of the sense of science—how we feel our way to knowing via a rich agonism of pleasure and frustration.

LaMothe, like other feminist commentators, insists that we shake off Nietzsche's teenagerish hierarchy of tastes—the sneering rank-ordering of joys—in favor of a focused explication of how *all* knowledge production transacts with feeling.[108] But to simply say science is *affective* isn't enough. We need the specific definition that goes along with naming our differently patterned feelings. The *sentiment of rationality* alone isn't enough to map the sense of science. For science to get off the ground, it needs to be blended with other emotional priorities—Hume's *cool passions* or James's *nervousness* (and shame?) that we will be deceived.[109] This is not an erasure of the emotional dimension of reason, but a way of making reason *from* emotion. The sense of science is composed of these elements. Cogency theory's rejection of the reason/emotion binary is predicated on the recognition that feeling is foundational to every aspect of thought.

STS has always been concerned with exactly this problem of how science fails to live up to the logical positivist fantasy that truth is hailed, immediately and enthusiastically, by our all-too-rational minds. As Kuhn points out, normal science "often suppresses fundamental novelties because they are necessarily subversive of its basic commitments."[110] Scientific rationality as a carefully calibrated configuration of intellectual passions in tension is always susceptible to a conservative tilt that can obscure truth, but is also—when it works—responsive to new evidence. Science succeeds to the extent that it's able to effectively maintain its immune system while still remaining sensitive to the paradigm-shaking click. This separates it from its superficial alter ego, conspiracy theory.

There's a strong link here to the work historians of science Lorraine Daston and Peter Galison have done tracing the historical development of *objectivity* in the sciences. Objectivity, they note, is not the same as truth—or even reason. Instead, it's best understood as a historically embedded *epistemic virtue,* assuming different configurations in different moments, each with a different emphasis on how to convert observations of nature into truth.[111] And crucially, for Daston and Galison, objectivity needs to be understood from the bottom up—as a cultivated attitude, a set of practices shaped by bodily training, rather than a mental switch that activates truthmaking. It's the asceticism so loathed by Nietzsche, a dispositional framework built through self-discipline and self-cultivation.[112] It requires many affective strands—"the humility of the seeker, the wonder of the psalmist who praises creation, the asceticism of the saint."[113]

Scientific objectivity is built by sculpting these affects, creating a tensed, mobile apparatus that sifts information, filters it through a contraption of feeling, and builds reliable knowledge. Peter Harrison's work, calling our attention to how we might rethink science as *scientia*—a cultivated set of virtues—fits in here as well.[114] Depedestaling science means that arrangements like this are actually much less special than we might expect. Whether we're standing in a chemistry laboratory, a noisy pub, an operating room, or a wheat field, we all think from this state of tension, alternately exhilarated by what clicks for us and wary of our own joy where it seems liable to expose us to the shame or frustration of being wrong. The complete failure of these checks and balances is a rarity.

But balance out of whack—like the click addiction we see in conspiracism—is a predictable effect of a tilt in the matrix of our intellectual desires. There are lots of answers to the question of how conspiracism gets its hooks in us, including social, political, and economic factors, not to mention powerful amplifiers like racialized reason, as we'll see in the next chapter. But we can no more afford to ignore the internal emotional anatomy of conspiracy theory than we can the structural isomorphism of endorphin molecules and heroin. Conspiracism hangs on tightly because it's so good at winning the agonism of knowledge production. It makes the entire world a simplex system, the easiest possible game with the highest possible stakes. It feels so good it has to be true.

These philosophers contribute to the little argument of this book, offering concentric templates for tracing the relationship between emotion and knowledge-making. This draws out a detailed theory of science in which we feel our way to knowledge, not just through the passion for reason but by dampening emotions like fear of error. Collectively, their approach offers a new way of doing the genealogy of reason. Scientific rationality is made not only through discourses but also in the unfurling of feeling.

2.
SENSUALIZED EPISTEMOLOGY
AFFECT THEORY ON HOW REASON GETS RACIALIZED

This is an essay about a love affair with an idea.
—Silvan Tomkins, "The Quest for Primary Motives"

Racism can also be described as the emotional lifeblood of race; it is the "feeling" that articulates and keeps the flawed logic of race in its place.
—Sharon Patricia Holland, *The Erotic Life of Racism*

Introduction: The Speaker's Benefit

In the opening pages of his 1976 book, *The History of Sexuality: An Introduction,* the French philosopher Michel Foucault tells the story of the *repressive hypothesis.* According to the repressive hypothesis, good sex was extinguished by the moralism of nineteenth-century Western society. Our task is to restore it to its state of natural happiness. But Foucault is nakedly contemptuous of this view. Take psychoanalysis, he says. It claims that sexual repression is the root of our modern malaise, yet it resembles nothing more than a confession booth, where sex, rather than being banished, has a million private showings every hour. We haven't killed sex, Foucault counters; we've diffused it into the atmosphere. Now it clings to everything.

So why is the repressive hypothesis so powerful? Why claim, over and over, that sex is gone, when in fact it's always with us? "There may be another reason that makes it *so gratifying*" to fight against repression, he writes, "something that one might call the *speaker's benefit*.... A person who holds forth in such language places himself to a certain extent outside the reach of power; he upsets established law; he somehow anticipates the coming freedom. This explains the *solemnity* with which one speaks of sex nowadays."[1] Foucault says that in this proclamation "that smacks of revolt, of promised freedom, of the coming age of a different law ... the ancient functions of prophecy are reactivated."[2] Rather than a truth, the repressive hypothesis is an idea that brings pleasure.

In a series of books from the 1960s and early 1970s, Foucault had charted the intimate relationship between *power* and *knowledge*—the many ways systems of discourse, classification, and naming shape our lives.[3] They were so close, Foucault suggested, that they could be brought together under a single formula: *power-knowledge*, a continuum of relationships of force running between bodies, institutions, and ideas.[4] But in the first volume of *The History of Sexuality*, Foucault modifies this frame. Now he's concerned not just with power and knowledge, but with the way power and knowledge *feel*— "the regime of power-knowledge-pleasure"—or what we might think of as *power-knowledge-affect*.[5]

This is exactly what Foucault points to with *the speaker's benefit*. Power-knowledge isn't just a booklet of ideas running the hardware of repression. It's saturated with feeling. Foucault takes the French title of his book—*La volonté de savoir*, "the will to know"—from Nietzsche. Much as Nietzsche saw reason as continuous with our animal emotions, Foucault suggests that ideas are pursued by bodies under a canopy of feelings: with solemnity, with excitement, with the electricity of prophecy. Action within the supposedly neutral field of knowledge-making is driven by affects. In other words, volume 1 of *The History of Sexuality* is where Foucault transforms the analytics of power-knowledge into an analytics of feeling. *We think* that prophecy— whether religious or secular—is clear-eyed truth-telling. But it's actually a field of desire, a swishing play of incitements to induce pleasure within a net of ideas.

Foucault is not just suspicious, then, in the way Paul Ricoeur wrote that Marx, Nietzsche, and Freud are—the *masters of suspicion*, architects of the *hermeneutic of suspicion* that seeks to pull off the mask of the insidious systems around us.[6] He is suspicious, but he's also *suspicious of suspicion*. Suspicion, he realizes, is not a neutral stance. It's configured by feeling, perching its acolytes high in the cathedral of truth, looming over everyone else. The game of suspicion—the game Foucault had mastered earlier in his career, devout apprentice of Nietzsche that he was—is *pleasurized*, just one more string of the cat's cradle of power-knowledge-affect.

This chapter takes a closer look at cogency theory's relationship with affect theory, a subfield drawing on queer theory, poststructuralist philosophy, feminism, postcolonial studies, and psychoanalysis. Affect theory comes in a few different flavors, but the one I'll focus on is particularly relevant for building a theory of cogency.[7] This kind of affect theory suggests that feeling is the foundation of our embodied lives: relationships, actions, thoughts, and decisions at the micro level, history, culture, politics, and society at the macro level. It proposes that everything we do as humans—as with all animals—emerges from an agonism of feelings. This includes knowledge-making. Affect theorist Eve Kosofsky Sedgwick writes that she sees her task as linking J. L. Austin's theory of performatives, Foucault's analytics of power, Silvan Tomkins's affect theory, and queer theory.[8] The first part of this chapter will consider each of these elements and how they add to the cogency theory approach. Taken together, they show that knowledge production, too, emerges out of multilayered tissues of feeling. Power doesn't just order us to think and believe. It both compels and entices through a vast, jumbled conjunction of force, feeling, and thought.

The chapter then turns to scholars of race and affect like Mel Chen, Sharon Patricia Holland, and José Esteban Muñoz to build a theory of *racialized reason*. Racialized reason names the processes by which racist ideas are mobilized and held in place by underlying racialized feelings. Racialized feelings mess together with other affects, and the cognitive skin that forms around this raw mix is racialized reason—a set of intellectual coordinates that make racist ideas feel true. It's through the affective force of racism that racialized reason gains such a firm grip, a perspective echoed in recent analyses of structural racism. The chapter closes by turning again to conspiracy theory, demonstrating that part of the pleasure of conspiracy theory lies in the way it is entangled with racialized reason.

From Foucault to Affect Theory

Although Foucault doesn't use the vocabulary of affect, affect theory takes many of its cues from his work. Foucault's early writings in the 1960s focused on the way power is directed by regimes of knowledge. But by the

1970s, Foucault's sights had shifted from the epistemic to the somatic. His 1975 book *Discipline and Punish* illustrates this well. Although Foucault was an antiprison activist in the early 1970s, working to raise awareness about the grim conditions of the French penal system, his argument in *Discipline and Punish* focuses on creating a philosophical account of how prisons make subjects. For Foucault, the transformative effect of prison on the prisoner is not reducible to a cognitive change. His most famous example of this—the panopticon, the prison where prisoners worry they're under constant surveillance, a paranoia machine—is designed to make prisoners *feel* and *act* differently.

The panopticon, Foucault explains, reorganizes a body's dispositions. This transformation isn't about changing minds. The prisoners aren't there to read books, attend lectures, debate, and reflect on their past decisions. Instead, the panopticon works by, in Foucault's words, "composing forces" within bodies.[9] It reshapes subjects by shuffling the tangle of forces running through them, reconstructing the matrix from which thoughts and actions emerge. Foucault calls it an "art of the human body."[10] Though he seldom uses the word, Foucault had already modeled how to think about embodied subjectivity within a frame of *affects*. His shift to thinking about bodies rather than words as the scene of power relations led to direct consideration of the forces that make up subjectivity within, beside, and beneath words and concepts.

It's this attention to the body as a node of power, knowledge, and feeling that Foucault extends in volume 1 of *The History of Sexuality*. And it's this same model of forces making bodies that becomes one of the main conceptual engines of affect theory. In her 2004 essay "Affective Economies," Sara Ahmed argues that power doesn't only draw force from systems of knowledge. It also shapes and is shaped by *affects*. Emotions, she proposes, are not cosmetic, the frilly by-products of systems of power. Rather than the surface, they're the substance of how power moves bodies. In affective economies, Ahmed writes, "emotions *do things*, and they align individuals with communities—or bodily space with social space—through the very intensity of their attachments."[11]

Similarly, Lauren Berlant writes that affect is "sensual matter that is elsewhere to sovereign consciousness but that has historical significance in domains of subjectivity."[12] In other words, we can feel our affects, but rather than being under the thumb of our reason or will, they're structuring our decisions upstream of the *I*. For affect theorists, the question of how power guides bodies is answered by exploring these affective attachments.[13] In the early work of Foucault, knowledge was power. But affect theory, taking its cues from Foucault's later work, proposes a new formula: *feeling is power*. A body's action is evoked only when primed by an underlying affective grid. Everything happens for a feeling.

Illocutionary Force: Affect Theory and Performativity

Affect is a tricky word, in part because it's been used in so many ways and so many different contexts—from early modern philosophy to clinical psychology to the everyday dictionary definition of "facial expression" (think *flat affect*). Readers dipping into affect theory for the first time are often understandably put off by the blitz of meanings packed into this single term. To try to clarify things, affect theorists have noted the existence of two different *dialects* of affect theory—one guided by the philosopher Gilles Deleuze, the other by queer theory and feminism.[14]

This classification is useful but, as the editors of *The Affect Theory Reader* note, a bit too pat.[15] Many who use affect theory end up applying *affect* in more or less ad hoc or hybrid ways.[16] However, in its purer strains, the Deleuzian version of affect theory has a strong tendency to frame affect as fundamentally separate from cognition, seeing it instead as the vector of novelty in the world (*becoming*, in Deleuze's vocabulary) that makes change possible.[17] Cogency theory veers away from this, affiliating with the less technical definition of affect current in what Ahmed calls "feminist cultural studies of emotion and affect."[18] This leads to a casual (and capacious) use of the word *affect* as more or less synonymous with *feeling* and *emotion*.[19] This branch of affect theory is, at its heart, a theory of what makes bodies do what they do. That's why it's also a theory of power.[20] Thought and language are not separate from affect, in this view. They're in full communion with it. To say that affect theory is about what bodies do means it's also about what bodies say, think, and believe.

Sedgwick's interest in the mid-twentieth-century philosopher J. L. Austin helps shade in why this emphasis is important, not only for affect theory but also for a theory of cogency. For Austin, language is not just the dictionary-bound meaning of words. Instead, language is also always an effort to *do* something—what he calls a *speech act*. His 1960 lecture collection *How to Do Things with Words* begins by abandoning the binary of *words that say* (constative) and *words that do* (performatives).[21] Austin says we need a more textured account of the relationship between words and actions.

To explore this relationship, he introduces the concept of *illocutionary force*—the capacity of an utterance to *trigger an effect*. A performative speech act, for instance, is authorized by power.[22] But power is never absolute. It has zones of control as well as gaps and fissures. A soldier receiving an order might obey, but might not. Why does power work in some situations and not in others? Similarly, what Austin calls a *perlocution* is an effort to persuade a listener. But persuasion is hard! Most of the words that bump against us over the course of a day have very little impact on how we think. So why do some words *work* and others stall? What's the substance of persuasion? The answer to all of these questions, Austin concludes, is *illocutionary force*. Yet Austin himself admits, in the final lecture, that he's failed to explain what illocutionary force actually is. He never gets a chance to return to the topic.[23]

This is where affect theory steps up. Affect theory is interested in exactly this question of whether and how a speech act *works*—and how this relates to affect and power. Does my statement *I love you* make your heart sing, or awkwardly slide down the surface of our conversation? Does my statement *I hereby excommunicate you* leave you reeling with horror or gently perplexed? From the perspective of affect theory, that success or failure isn't determined by the propositional content of the statement itself. Instead, it's decided by the affects surrounding it. The circuit of feeling running between and through our bodies, objects, and institutions makes up the force field guiding the currents of illocutionary force, determining whether words succeed or fall flat.

Historian of emotions William Reddy has also adapted Austin's framework in developing his theory of *emotives*—statements about the emotional state of the speaker.[24] Like performatives—words at work—emotives change the state of the self and the relationships we have with others around us.[25] But affect theory goes even further than this. For one thing, emotives seem in Reddy's work to be exclusively matters of speech. Affect theory, by contrast, is interested in a whole range of ways of emitting feeling: from facial expressions, like the racialized ways of emoting José Esteban Muñoz calls *national affect*, to material things, like the vibrant objects brought together in queer rituals of remembrance described by Ann Cvetkovich.[26] Everything in this living, moment-to-moment panorama needs to be considered as part of the field of feeling making a space. Every aspect of our world is shaping how we feel, and we feel the world in ways that are configured by our distinct affective histories. It's this deep field of feeling that shapes how words strike us, blocking or triggering illocutionary force.

Affect theory, then, is designed to break us out of the *linguistic fallacy*—the claim that the *only way* to do things is with words.[27] A theory of linguistic meaning isn't sufficient, as Austin shows. We're surrounded by words. They follow us around like an electrical storm. But which ones seize us, and which ones bounce lightly off our skin? Affect theory's proposal is that we can only answer the question of whether words connect with us by considering the interaction between the landscapes of feeling bodies and the affective charge of words themselves. Affect is the illocutionary force that makes words work—not to mention all the other, nonlinguistic vessels of feeling that surround us in our daily lives.

Affective Agonism: Reading Silvan Tomkins Queerly

Sedgwick connects Foucault not only to Austin but also to Silvan Tomkins. Tomkins is a psychologist, but, like James (his intellectual hero), he can look like either a scientist or a philosopher depending on the angle.[28] His life's work was a multidecade, four-volume magnum opus titled *Affect Imagery Consciousness*, which Sedgwick reworked as the 1995 edited volume *Shame and Its Sisters*.[29] Why Tomkins? By the early 1990s, Sedgwick had become convinced that Freudian psychoanalysis was totally heterosexist—that it would never be able to give up a central image of a libido that is fundamentally about *men wanting women* or *women wanting men*.[30] Sedgwick turned to Tomkins as a way of affirming desires and pleasures beyond this rigid, teleological frame. This became the path to affect theory.

Tomkins defines his project in part as a reaction against the drive model of motivation devised by Freud.[31] For Freud, the drives—especially sex—quicken us to respond to fixed, predetermined features of the world (food, phallus, everything in between). When the drives are frustrated by the absence of their fixed objects, they're *sublimated* into strange forms. That's the source of the variety of human interests. But Tomkins points out that drives are actually only *weak* forms of desire. Sex is powerful, of course. But sex can also be knocked off balance—surrounded by so much confusion or pain that it collapses. Freud's id is "a paper tiger," Tomkins writes, "since sexuality, as he best knew, was the most finicky of drives, easily rendered impotent by shame or anxiety or boredom or rage."[32] The problem comes when we start with drives and use them to model *all* feeling, leading to a reduction of the whole theater of human activity to *sublimation*.[33] Tomkins saw the drive theory as making a whole range of wants—art, poetry, music, political ambition—into clumsy offshoots of staunched drive force. There's no room to understand those wants on their own terms. Every non(hetero) sexual urge becomes a twisted side effect of a broken psychosexual dynamic.

Tomkins argues that subordinating the panorama of our desires to drive is not just wrong, but backward. The affect system orchestrates the drives, he contends, rather than the other way around. The drives are more like dormant machines that need injections of *affect* to wake up. As Adam Frank and Elizabeth Wilson put it, Tomkins sees drives as "surprisingly weak motivators of action; they provide information about motivation but very little impetus to actually move."[34] Affect, rather than drive, is the primary motivational system for bodies. A drive is an arm that reaches out and grabs a fixed object in the environment. These drives may well be essential for reproduction and survival, but they can only operate when fueled by affect. Sex draws on the aquifer of feeling, the real wellspring of our actions.[35]

Centering the motivational force of affect produces a model of subjectivity that veers away from psychoanalysis. But it also cuts against our commonsense ideas about how people work. In the conventional wisdom, we're thinking beings that size up the world and select goals through rational deliberation. Feeling is an afterthought—a by-product of actions, which are themselves created by thoughts. But Tomkins flips this. He insists we start with a baseline of feeling, from which emerge all of our wants and intentions. Feeling isn't a by-product of achieving a goal. Goals are *means to the end* of feeling affects. Affect, he writes, "is the bottom line for thought as well as perception and behavior."[36] Feeling is a dictatorship of joy, rage, fascination, excitement, and all the other emotions that pull our strings. For Tomkins, affects are "the primitive gods within the individual."[37] Sedgwick gives this a twist, calling affects the pantheon of "queer little gods" that create the wordless, intransigent matrix of our wants, thoughts, and acts.[38] In Sedgwick's term, affects are *autotelic*.[39] That is, they're ends in themselves, the elemental substance of what we want.[40]

This doesn't mean we can overlook language, ideology, discourse, or propositional thinking. Part of what makes language so extraordinary (and why the study of discourse can pass itself off as a full-fledged theory of power in weak light) is its precision. Words are instruments for the evocation of affect—and can do so with far more precision than, say, hand gestures or facial expressions. But this precision is still nothing without affect. Without affect, words lack the illocutionary force necessary to catch us. As Lauren Berlant writes, "Affect theory is another phase in the history of ideology theory," an approach that brings us back "to the encounter of what is sensed with what is known and what has impact."[41] Language happens to be an extremely powerful technology for the distribution of focused affects. But the error of standard ideology critique is to assume that the story starts and ends with ideas, that the language itself dictates the parameters of transmission and reception. Affect theory contends that it's the affects running behind and through words that are doing the real work of linking them to our bodies.

This portrait of a multilayered self is consistent with the way affect theory sees feeling as a continuum—from micro to macro—stretching both within and below our field of awareness. Tomkins arranges emotion words into pairs representing opposite ends of a range. *Interest* is actually just the little version of *excitement, shame* the little version of *humiliation, distress* the little version of *anguish*. Small feelings—often so small they slip through the net of our awareness—are of the same *kind* as the big feelings we point to when we announce "I'm happy" or "I'm upset." *Anger* is a condensation of droplets of smaller affective elements that have grown big enough to command our attention. But we'd still be *angry-ish* if we were a bit *less* angry. And we can be *angry-ish* and *happy-ish* and a dozen other tones and tints at the same time. We usually are. These different affective elements mess together in our bodies, a cauldron of felt ingredients fusing into our dispositions, actions, and thoughts. Picturing this dynamic model of struggling motivations and contending priorities, Foucault writes, "There is always within each of us something that fights something else."[42] For affect theorists, our subjectivity is determined, from top to bottom, by an agonism of feelings.

The affects, Tomkins says, are like the letters in the alphabet, available for configuration into all kinds of emotional compounds.[43] These forces motivate the core drives, but can also outmatch them. A carefully staged disciplining of the emotions, Tomkins tells us, "can frighten the soldier out of cowardice by making him more afraid of cowardice than death."[44] This quality of affective combinability creates the endless gallery of human behavior. It also sets the parameters for how we encounter language. As the currency of the illocutionary force theorized by Austin, it's what makes words work or short circuit. Affect theory, then, is a theory of how emotional agonism produces subjectivity, both conducting and resisting the formations of power that enmesh us.

The Psychology of Knowledge

This model of how power laces bodies, societies, institutions, and objects together is ambitious. It's designed to totally invert our commonsense understanding of ourselves, inherited from liberal philosophies of the sovereign self, as well as structuralist and poststructuralist approaches that make language central for subjectivity. Rather than a contraption of thoughts and words commanding bodies, a *subject* is really a sort of hypercomplicated sensitive surface responding to the force fields of feeling running through us. This continuum of feeling includes all the places where we would expect to find emotions at work—culture, history, relationships, politics. But it also contains the zone of knowledge-making itself. As far back as the 1960s, Tomkins was exploring what he named the *psychology of knowledge*—a set of questions about how underlying grids of feeling organize our ideas, what he calls *ideo-affective resonance*. Belief, he proposes, is gelled by the force of feeling.

An experiment Tomkins runs in the early 1960s suggests what this intersection of affect and knowledge might mean. His hypothesis is that our affects pull ideas into specific shapes, like scattered iron filings arranging themselves in a hidden magnetic field. The binding force of these thoughts is feeling, not the propositional content of the ideas themselves. This means, Tomkins suggests, that the underlying affective mechanisms create predictable patterns across *totally unrelated topics*: "If one knows what an individual believes about the nature of literature," Tomkins claims, "one would also know what he would believe about the nature of mathematics if he were to be confronted with mathematical problems."[45] Even if the subject had *no opinion whatsoever* about math, if we knew her dispositions in another field (say, politics), we could reliably predict where she would land in this new subject area.[46]

Tomkins calls this the *basic left-right polarity* of the psyche, where *left* is something like Protagoras's maxim "Man is the measure of all things," and *right* is something like Plato's "There are eternal constants that should define our values."[47] The rough contours of the argument between progressives (*Let's organize society around what's best for people*) and conservatives (*Tradition has innate value*) are just one iteration of this. Exploring what initially attracted mathematicians to their work, Tomkins writes that he finds "a polarization between right-wing mathematicians, who were attracted as children by its certainty and discipline, by the possibility of knowing what the right answer was and whether they had attained it," and "left-wing mathematicians," who "were attracted by its novelty and promise of excitement and its 'wild, unaccountable spaces.'"[48]

Tomkins sets out to test this, interviewing hundreds of subjects from many walks of life. He asks them to choose between statements arranged in a series of pairs like

> Imagination frees people from the dull routines of life.
> *and* Imagination leads people into self deception and delusions.

Or...

> The fact that people once believed the world was flat is just one in a long series of errors which shows how much progress human beings have made and will continue to make.
> *and* The fact that people once believed the world was flat is just one in a long series of errors which show how foolish human beings have been and will continue to be.[49]

Just as he thought, there's a pattern of correlations between viewpoints across disparate topics.[50] In other words, there's a *right-wing* science and a *right-wing* math and a *right-wing* approach to child-rearing that all correlate. (Not a one-to-one correlation, of course, but a statistically significant correlation that suggests something more than random noise.)[51] The underlying mechanism of this correlation is, Tomkins proposes, a polarity of emotional dispositions. It's an underdeveloped line of inquiry (and Tomkins, to my knowledge, never comes back to it after the 1960s), but it's suggestive for thinking about cogency. Tomkins was beginning to explore how affective infrastructure organizes cognition from below, like a piece of furniture shaping a draped sheet.[52]

Tomkins's strongest contribution to a theory of cogency comes later, when he links cognition to a specific affect: *interest*. Tomkins is an advocate of what psychologists now call the basic emotions hypothesis, the controversial view (many supporters, many detractors) that humans have a fixed number of biologically ingrained emotions.[53] Tomkins's inventory runs up to nine by the end of his career, including what he calls *interest-excitement*—the continuum that runs from the faint flecks of *interest* at the small end to the pulse-pounding crescendo of *excitement* on the other.

For Tomkins, *interest* is a sort of master switch of thinking. It's the animating force that moves minds through the world by guiding our attention to some things rather than others. It's like what Jaak Panksepp called the mammalian brain's SEEKING system and what Lisa Feldman Barrett calls *arousal*.[54] As Tomkins writes, "The interrelationships between the affect of interest and the functions of thought and memory are so extensive that absence of the affective support of interest would jeopardize intellectual development no less than destruction of brain tissue. To think, as to engage in any other human activity, one must care, one must be excited, must be continually rewarded."[55] From the micro to the macro, from our everyday modes of exploring and interacting with the world to wild experiments, we're guided by this system. "No matter how reasonable," writes one of Tomkins's students, "the engine of analysis is engaged and focused where aimed and sent by emotion; human thought is never dispassionate."[56] Although Tomkins endorses a version of Robert Zajonc's model of affect and cognition as two systems (which, as we'll see in chapter 4, still affirmed the priority of feeling in defining thinking), it's clear that he sees these systems as totally interwoven. "Reason without affect," he says, "would be impotent, affect without reason would be blind."[57]

The interest surging through information is also, for Tomkins, why thinking itself is a source of pleasure. Even in our most subtle cognitive capacities, Tomkins tells us, "varying perception and thinking is ... combined with varying shades of interest and excitement."[58] Or, to put it another way, even though "mathematics and sexuality are different, the excitement that amplifies either cognitive activity or drive is identical."[59] We don't make knowledge for knowledge's sake. On a core level, the driver of knowledge production is the *pleasure* of running our fingertips over textures of facts and ideas.[60] Study is a playground of information within which we pursue the feeling of click.

Tomkins is also clear that the pleasure of *interest* is not the whole story of knowledge production. Like other theorists of cogency we've looked at, he proposes that thinking is a struggle of feelings. Although Tomkins doesn't have a comprehensive theory of the sense of science as a tensed agonism of passions (like Hume or James), he gives us a prototype in his thoughts on child-rearing. For Tomkins, raising children means shaping what they find interesting in the world.[61] This can mean admonishing them to keep away from the bank of a river or pointing out an exciting plant or animal. Some interests are rewarded and nourished, others are obstructed and shamed (with all the splotchy, uneven results that shame delivers) by imposing "barriers to interest or enjoyment."[62] Pedagogy, for Tomkins, is about shaping intellectual affects.

A statement like "That's interesting" has a very specific meaning. It describes your emotional response to something in front of you. It's the same kind of statement as "That's sad" or "That's annoying." From a *mild tug of attention* to *fascination* to *awe*, the scale of *interest* is the amplitude of click. It's what you feel when you draw the right card in a hand of poker—which is why philosophy, for Hume, is as addictive as gambling. One could even say that the Deleuzian version of *affect*—in its focus on the production of newness—is actually just a name for the exhilarating feelings that came along with discovery. It's a crude approximation of *interest-excitement*, what Tomkins calls our "affect for novelty."[63] Still, Deleuzian affect theory misses the importance of disciplining interest, of creating an agonism in which our felt sense of excitement in discovery is tempered by an insistence that our discoveries make contact with reality.

Sedgwick, too, is entranced by the idea of *interest*. She narrates her own path to what she calls *perverse reading* as beginning in her childhood, when "the ability to attach intently to a few cultural objects, objects of high or popular culture or both, objects whose meaning seemed mysterious, excessive, or oblique in relation to the codes most readily available to us, became a prime resource for survival."[64] Our weird intellectual passions aren't a twisted sublimation of straight sex, as the hardcore Freudians thought. They have their own domain and need to be studied on their own terms. So she sneaks Tomkins in the side door of the humanities. The possibility of thinking about reading as an emotional currency with its own texture, its own riveting fascination, and its own healing force seduces Sedgwick to Tomkins's way of thinking.

This displacement of the thinking/feeling binary is explored by other affect theorists, too. Ahmed also sees affect as the foundation of subjectivity. Everything makes an emotional impression on our bodies, she writes, defining our relationship with the world—and redefining us in the process.[65] Building on the work of phenomenologist Martin Heidegger, for whom we are always *in a mood*, Ahmed points out that bodies "never arrive in neutral," and this quality of being always emotional, always in motion, can't help but shape the way we feel our way through our experiences.[66]

This extends to the way we encounter information. Whether literature, philosophy, or science, reading means splashing around in what she calls *the emotionality of texts*—the way words summon an emotional labyrinth and entice us in.[67] Carolyn Pedwell expands on this in an essay on the relationship between theory and mood. Readers and texts, she points out, are always wrapped up in a dynamic swirl of feeling. Not only do readers always start in a mood that shapes our encounter with texts, "texts themselves exude their 'own' moods, linked to the affective atmospheres of their production and circulation."[68] Sianne Ngai's own theory of interest fits nicely with Tomkins's. She defines it as "the relatively small surprise of information or variation from an existing norm," marking "a tension between the unknown and the already known, and ... generally bound up with a desire to know and document reality."[69] All these approaches express the shared goal of affect theory and cogency theory: collapsing the black monolith myth and tracing the bonds linking thought and emotion.

Sedgwick tells us in the opening pages of *Touching Feeling* that she sees her work—and the whole project of queer theory—as moving toward thinking nondualistically, wearing down the black monolith by disrupting barriers between mind and body, thought and act, emotion and reason.[70] Berlant follows this cue in her call for a history of *sensualized epistemologies*—the way protocols of knowledge acceptance and transmission are structured by emotional contours.[71] But in a way, *sensualized epistemology* is backward. We don't start with knowledge and then add feeling. We begin with sensuality—the deep, resonant hum of our embodied life—and knowledge climbs, dripping, from the waves. It's *epistemologized sensuality*, the way knowledge production emerges, in the long, untellable history of bodies, as one of many ways we find the world vibrant and exciting. "Cognition," Berlant reminds us, "follows the affects."[72]

Racialized Reason

Affect theory doesn't take us to the other side of reason. It lights up the interior of reason. It shows us the anatomy of rationality as pulsing with desire. We weigh up the world by feeling our way. And because rationality is affective, it's susceptible to contamination by the other emotional inkblots surrounding it. For affect theorists, racialization is one of these forms of thought totally wrapped up in feeling. It seeps into our bodies—often below the threshold of conscious awareness—and shapes how we think. Already in the 1960s, Tomkins realized that the psychology of knowledge framework helped explain the intransigence of American anti-Black racism.[73]

But the most important work defining the dynamic between racialization and feeling has been done by queer of color scholars studying affect over the past few decades. They've filled in the details of how affect makes up the invisible landscape of *racialized reason*. Race is something we feel, what James Baldwin calls a "labyrinth of attitudes."[74] When racialized affects mess together with our other intellectual emotions, they shape the way we think. Racialized reason is the skin that forms around racialized feelings. Racism passes itself off as objective by *feeling true*. And just as important, these scholars have explored how racism gets its hooks into us by bringing along its own kind of pleasure.

In the early 1980s, Audre Lorde (a major influence on later affect theorists like Ahmed and Holland) developed a theory of the relationship between affect, cognition, and race. What Lorde called the "European mode of thought"—in which "we rely solely upon our ideas to make us free"—has to be rejected.[75] Feeling, she argued, is the real foundation of thinking. Poetry, for instance, is a sort of reactive agent, coaxing our emotional substrata to blossom into thoughts.[76] And racism is not just about attacking the mental self-understanding of the oppressed; it also wreaks havoc on their sense of cohesive feeling, and disrupts their capacity for pleasure. This is what Lorde calls *the erotic*: "the nurturer or nursemaid of all our deepest knowledge."[77] The way we think, for Lorde, emerges from how we feel, with significant consequences for diagnosing and fighting racism.

More recent affect theorists have brought the affective dynamics of racialized reason into even sharper focus. They've done this by diagramming how affective regimes produce oppressive effects by setting up *what feels neutral*. José Esteban Muñoz, who studied with Sedgwick, has a particular interest in how race, rationality, and feeling connect. Writing about the conservative backlash against Supreme Court justice Sonia Sotomayor's advocacy of Latina judges, he talks about how the conservative arguments were based on contempt for "empathy and experience, the realm of the affective," privileging instead unfeeling rationality.[78] Sotomayor's critics baptized their own selective empathy as neutral reason. Crucially, though, Muñoz insists that the way to respond to these accusations is not to expunge feeling from thinking, but to topple the thinking/feeling binary entirely. "The simple rejection of reason as a majoritarian project seems too easy and indeed counterproductive," he writes, calling instead for a reconceptualization of reason and affect as a single, reciprocally shaping field.[79]

This new outlook, Muñoz shows, has significant consequences for thinking about race. It recasts dominant racial norms as not just known, but *felt*. "Whiteness," he says, "can be understood as an affective code that positions itself as the law."[80] The force of racism hammers down on bodies who fail to match this affectively configured standard masquerading as objectivity.[81] The template of identification and disidentification is infused with feeling, creating a *national affect* undetectable to those on the inside, but felt as constant friction by everybody beyond the pale.[82] Affect constructs an inertial frame in which a particular racialized logic comes to feel like standing still—but only for those it benefits. Latino/a affect in the United States, for instance, is *off* compared to the background tone of whiteness.[83] Jasbir Puar follows the same track, arguing that *racialization* is built by affect. Racialization, as Puar understands it, is a process that *can* draw on race as phenotype, but is also ample enough to include nonbiological categories like religion or citizenship.[84] We make races through a procedure that is both affective and cognitive, creating categories and then giving them urgency by charging them with feeling.[85]

Mel Chen, trained in cognitive linguistics, adds to this picture, exploring how languages encode *animacy hierarchies*, or implicit registers by which some forms of life are afforded more value than others. As an example, Chen offers the phrase "the hikers that rocks crush," noting that it registers as viscerally wrong to English speakers because it violates our implicit preference to organize sentences around what we perceive to be *subjects* rather than *objects*.[86] This reveals the way a *felt* register of who and what matters (and who gets to count as a *who*) is woven into the seams of language.[87] Chen explicitly links this to Ahmed's theory of *affective economies*, proposing that animacy hierarchies build cognitive processes of labeling and separating out of histories of feeling.[88]

Imani Perry's postintentional theory of racism also highlights the way racialization happens in the affects upstream of words themselves. For Perry, the paradox of contemporary American racism is that it is no longer *said out loud*, but still fixes structures of thought and value—the politics of which bodies matter, which bodies are perceived as innocent or trustworthy, which bodies are granted patience, and which are judged by the harshest standard. "If articulating a deep antipathy for a people is against the rules," she writes, "not just as a matter of politeness but as an ethical norm, that doesn't mean the antipathy necessarily disappears."[89] The landscape of racialized reason is defined by submerged affective structures that are only marginally inconvenienced by being banished from the realm of What People Say. They even survive exile from What People Think Without Saying. What *seems reasonable* or objective or neutral may have no *explicitly* racist content. But the affective mechanisms configuring how knowledge is made are churning below the surface. And these do the real work of fixing racist ideas. They set the table of what feels true.

Racialization is defined by feeling. But equally vital for thinking about racialization and cogency is the way racism comes along with its own hit of pleasure. To say racialized reason is affective is not just to say that it's (sometimes) outside conscious awareness. It also names racialization as something *desired*. As Holland argues in *The Erotic Life of Racism*, racism is not so much a desire for the absence of others but a desire for intimacy with them.[90] Writing about a racist confrontation with a white woman in a parking lot, she realizes that the woman, in her words, "*wanted a connection with me.*"[91] The conventional wisdom about racism is that it's about separation or elimination of racial groups. Holland flips this. She proposes that racists *want* the thrill of contact with their racial others. It's Lorde's concept of *the erotic* as the felt foundation of thought, but rather than liberatory it's predatory; one side experiences violence, the other savors the hedonicity of hate.[92]

Racism is so tenacious because it is motivated by a felt *want* to hate other bodies or groups. It's an affective economy in which abject others are desired. Their degradation builds the racist's dignity. Lorde celebrated the erotic. But Holland points out that the erotic also drives the words and deeds of domination and violence.[93] We've all seen how cynical political actors strum racial divides to cement new political fronts, inciting laughter and cheering to power their own ambitions. The right words about the wrong people move mountains by marshalling the erotic. Racialized reason, then, isn't just a soft shell of misperceptions about other people that we hold in mind, easily dissolved by new information or gentle retraining. It has its own freestanding power source: desire. What makes it so dangerous is that although it unfurls from a thick, tangled layer of pleasure, it can quickly protect itself by putting on a featureless mask. This is how the sensualized epistemology of affect theory redraws our understanding of racialized cognition. It recasts racism as hedonic, driven by the good feelings that come along with making other people feel bad. These feelings are always ready to mess together with our intellectual affects and make racialized reason seem like the only cogent possibility.

Racialized reason is also a theme in the analysis of *structural racism*. (Though it's worth noting this term is used in different ways by different thinkers.) Marxist sociologist Eduardo Bonilla-Silva, for instance, like Perry, begins with the puzzle of how racial inequality persists—in housing, income, incarceration rates, state violence—even though the number of whites who admit to holding racist views in surveys has plummeted.[94] Bonilla-Silva's answer is that racist ideas are still there, even if they're not being said out loud. These racist ideas, he argues, are dictated by class position.[95] In a racially unequal society, the well-off find ways to justify and explain away the poverty of others.[96] The Marxist "materialist interpretation of racial matters sees the views of actors as corresponding to their systemic location."[97] Racist beliefs are still under the surface, pinned to economic rank, even if they're kept quiet.

Some approaches to structural racism lead away from the analysis of feeling. But Bonilla-Silva has argued recently that structural racism can only be understood through scrupulous attention to how emotion and class position act in concert, which includes a decisive rejection of the thinking/feeling binary.[98] "It is time for us to cease reproducing in our theories and work the modernist binaries of rationality/irrationality, objective/subjective, and so on," he writes, adding: "Material interests include the affective dimension."[99] Much like Holland and Ahmed, Bonilla-Silva is expressly interested in the way "emotional goods" are delivered through racist politics, defining racism not just in terms of the negative emotions it rains down on minority groups, but the pleasure it evokes for the powerful.[100]

From this structural perspective, as with cogency theory, class position—money, property, status, political power—shapes the way things feel, which in turn makes our ideas about how the world works seem self-evident. Racialized reason doesn't need people to say—or even think—racist words. Color-blind racism isn't just about secretly held beliefs diligently concealed from pollsters and polite conversation. It's about the way racism lives on even in sincere nonracist beliefs by making color-blind policies (those that perpetuate inequality) *feel reasonable*. The power of affect to shape cognition lies in the way it casts the spell of obviousness over a point of view. "While Whites believe the system is fair," Bonilla-Silva writes, "the racially subordinate experience the unfairness of the system, leading each group to develop emotions that match their 'perceptual segregation.'"[101] A dominant position sets itself up as unbiased reason, but its neutrality is actually made by coils of affect that feel—for those who reap its benefits—like level ground.

That said, racism isn't necessarily *for* something. Some structural analysis frames racism as a proxy for class interests, assuming people are racist because it protects their financial bottom line. There are many situations where that's exactly right. But if racialized feelings really are erotic—if they're driven by pleasure rather than simply being a tool for controlling money, property, or labor—then we should expect racialization to snake up, at least some of the time, without any clear payoff. Cogency theory unhooks us from the functionalist imperative to always explain racism as tactical or strategic, let alone smart. In Sedgwick's phrasing, the hedonic part of racism is autotelic. It isn't necessarily deployed with an instrumental purpose in mind. All these micro-level feelings form the smooth surface of racialized reason, which defines the whole spectrum from individual words and deeds to broadscale systems of abuse and violence. The core of racism, as Holland writes, is "the 'feeling' that articulates and keeps the flawed logic of race in its place."[102]

Sparking Cogency: Conspiracy Theory and Racialized Reason

The conjunction of racism and desire is why racialized reason and conspiracy theory so often seem to come joined at the hip. Cogency theory proposes that knowledge feels. And it tells us that some formations of knowledge are more seductive than others. From the perspective of cogency theory, pleasure in knowledge is a driver of belief, a pounding pulse that guides our thoughts. As we saw in the last chapter, conspiracy theory seizes this desire, crafting simplex systems that harness the affective force of click. ("The cognition of the ideologue," Tomkins tells us, "burns with a gem-like flame.")[103] In this world, interest sticks to everything. Signs and portents shimmer around us. A song on the radio or a scrap of paper on the street blazes with fateful importance. Eliminating the emotional safeguards that help to build reliable knowledge, conspiracy theories guzzle evidence in an exaggerated parody of scientific rationality.

But this isn't the whole story of conspiracy theory's manipulation of cogency. Conspiracy theories are also devoutly focused on finding enemies— enemies that always seem to melt into a shadowy supergroup. "The enemy identified by the paranoid style is clearly delineated," Richard Hofstadter writes; "he is a perfect model of malice, a kind of amoral superman— sinister, ubiquitous, powerful, cruel, sensual, luxury-loving."[104] It's a description that comes up over and over in conspiracy theory, and it's usually pinned to racial groups. Conspiracism uses racialization to consolidate its affective power.

We can see this dynamic as far back as conspiracism's obsession with Freemasonry.[105] But tracking demographic changes brought about by immigration, the American nineteenth century saw the Masons give way to the Catholics as the plotters par excellence.[106] Jesuits, in particular, played the villain. Michael Barkun picks up the story at the beginning of the twentieth century, when Illuminatist conspiracies fused with antisemitism. This link was popularized in England and gained momentum with Henry Ford's printing of half a million copies of the forged *Protocols of the Elders of Zion* in the early 1920s.[107] Hannah Arendt notes that the Nazis weaponized the global Jewish conspiracy as the "most efficient fiction" in their propaganda arsenal.[108] The "stab-in-the-back" myth created in the aftermath of World War I, for instance, built fascist power by deluding Germans into thinking that their armed forces were at full strength in 1918 and had only been tricked into surrendering by a Jewish cabal.[109] In his final testament, dictated hours before he shot himself in an underground bunker, Adolf Hitler continued to blame Jews for the entirety of World War II. The Nazis harnessed the emotional electricity of racism and conspiracism.

During the Cold War, overtly anti-Jewish conspiracy theory declined, while still holding on to antisemitic plot elements like the insidious network of "bankers" or "globalists." Still, conspiracists often saw communism and Jews as working hand in glove, even as the USSR instrumentalized its own antisemitic propaganda campaigns.[110] As late as 1991, televangelist and Republican presidential candidate Pat Robertson contended that the Illuminati organization was bankrolled by Jews.[111] George Soros is subbed in for the Rothschilds. Contemporary Western far-right movements expanded this story to claim that nonwhite groups in Europe and North America were being mobilized by a global Jewish syndicate. In Britain, the postwar British rightists "blamed the Jews for the Blacks."[112]

This paved the way for the switch-out of antisemitism for Islamophobia among twenty-first-century conspiracists—so seamless that some became flag-waving Zionists overnight. British historian Bat Ye'or's book *Eurabia: The Euro-Arab Axis*, from 2005, claimed the existence of close links between Muslims and European Union officials, all in service of an antisemitic agenda. This claim has become popular with a range of far-right figures, from English Defence League founder and Brexit booster Tommy Robinson to Norwegian mass murderer Anders Behring Breivik.[113] American conspiracy theorists, meanwhile, dreamed up a grand coalition between Muslims, Marxists, and Black and brown Democratic Party figures like Barack Obama and Huma Abedin.[114] Terms like *stealth jihad* and *creeping sharia* became codewords for a shadow campaign to bring down the United States and replace it with a new religio-racial order.

Holland's proposal is that racism, rather than being disrupted by pleasure, is actually hardened by it.[115] Racism is a thirst for the degradation of other bodies. So conspiracism turns into a high-voltage wrestling plot, using racialized reason to build up the heel of all heels. The erotic dimension of racism plugs into this narrative strategy. It spotlights not just a lone villain, but a sinister invisible nation of militant enemies.[116] The intellectual affects and the felt force of racialization mess together, producing a powerfully persuasive alliance. Sociologist Matthew Hughey writes that in the United States, "a specific ideal type of 'hegemonic whiteness' aligns with authentic citizenship."[117] The Black president isn't really an American citizen? Maybe he's even a Muslim? It feels so good to racist whites that it *has to be true*. Racialized reason accelerates the excitement of conspiracy theory, amping up its cogency. How much more thrilling—and so more cogent—the plot becomes when the new world order is racialized.

Conclusion: The Erotics of Knowledge

There are two types of discourse on sex, Foucault tells us: the *ars erotica* and the *scientia sexualis*. The *ars erotica* is lovers' talk, words of pleasure, a passed-down tradition of techniques designed to produce sensations and experiences that amplify erotic joy.[118] The *scientia sexualis* forces sex to confess, divining Truth in the secret maneuvers of desire. From the confession booth to psychoanalysis to the war on so-called repression itself, the *scientia sexualis* made it essential that "sex be inscribed not only in an economy of pleasure but in an ordered system of knowledge."[119]

But then—plot twist—*scientia sexualis* is unmasked. It was, Foucault reveals, an *ars erotica* in disguise all along. The research apparatus around sex is and always has been a vehicle of pleasure. We have only, Foucault writes, "invented a different kind of pleasure: pleasure in the truth of pleasure, the pleasure of knowing that truth, of discovering and exposing it, the fascination of seeing it and telling it, of captivating and capturing others by it, of confiding it in secret, of luring it out in the open."[120] The *scientiae sexualis* of confession, psychoanalysis, and middle-class sexual discipline were never about erasing sex. They were about plugging sex into an exhilarating device for thinking and learning—"the interplay of knowledge and pleasure"—the cat's cradle of power-knowledge-affect.[121]

STS theorists have made the case that science is embodied, material, and contingent. Cogency theory strings this insight together with affect theory. Scientific knowledge has to convince us, and this capacity to persuade depends on illocutionary force, just like any other statement that tries to catch our interest. But rather than cogitation—an affair of the rational side of the feeling/thinking binary—this illocutionary force, too, is determined by an agonism of feelings. Knowledge, reexamined through affect theory, is sparking with emotional power. It has an internal propositional structure, yes, but also an inescapable *feeling tone*. We see it when we look at a page marked up by a highlighter. The maze of color is a low-res map of our emotional response to a cascade of ideas, alternating warming and cooling interest, rising and falling click. We find it in the way our pens leap to celebrate or make war in the margins. We hear it in the way we laugh and cheer when someone recites our knowledge back to us. And it confronts us everywhere in the disturbing tilt of racialized reason, the way a felt set of racist parameters passes itself off as level ground by *just feeling right*.

Even though affect theory has been effective in pushing back on the black monolith myth—the supposed separateness of human thought from nature—it has yet to build a model of how knowledge-making works. If everything is feeling, how do we ever come up with understandings of the world that are better or worse? Are we trapped in a world of illusions projected by feeling? These concerns reflect the extent to which the feeling/thinking binary has determined the shape of our conversations. Cogency theory closes this gap. It suggests that we *feel* the fluency of a balanced, well-constructed argument that arranges the evidence surrounding us in ways that click. The world teaches us by evoking our intellectual passions. The pull of knowledge is pleasurable to us.

Feeling is the groundwater, cognition is the well. But as good as we are at making knowledge, there's no foolproof recipe for strong common sense and reliable science. The same model shows how easy it is for our thirst to find click to lead us astray. This includes the whole suite of feelings associated with the dynamic of racialization. The powerful racist affects identified by Holland and Bonilla-Silva—like desire for degraded others—seep into the emotional pulse of cognition and create formations of racialized reason that feel like neutral rationality. Much as Foucault saw the science of sex as a way of trafficking pleasure through knowledge, racism (from blog posts to political speeches, from torchlit street marches to peer-reviewed articles) is not so much a sober body of discarded knowledge as a spectacular pornography. For all that racism denies the wellspring of pleasure that powers it, the fact that racialized reason holds on so fiercely (and remains such a treasured device in the toolkit of demagogues and conspiracists) speaks to its power as a sort of public addiction.

Rhetoric theory asks, *How are emotions marshaled in the service of arguments?* But affect theory's question is the reverse: *How are arguments marshaled in the service of feeling?*[122] "What does knowledge *do*," Sedgwick wonders: "the pursuit of it, the having and exposing of it, the receiving again of knowledge of what one already knows?"[123] For affect theorists, bodies seek opportunities to study, learn, think, and explore not because we're mystical machines lured by truth but because they tickle our cogency. "Thought," write Lauren Berlant and Kathleen Stewart, "is an afterthought."[124] Pleasure is at the wheel. As we'll see in the next chapter, this line of thinking is carried over into work on *postcritique* and critical approaches to secularism.

3.
SCIENCE AS AN INTOXICATION
SECULARISM STUDIES ON ENCHANTMENT AND CRITIQUE

> Inspiration plays no less a role in science than it does in the realm of art.... Both are frenzy (in the sense of Plato's "mania") and "inspiration."
> —Max Weber, "Science as a Vocation"

Introduction: University Church

In the early seventeenth century, the academic center of Oxford was a residential square north of the High Street, now occupied by the Radcliffe Camera. To the east and west were medieval colleges; to the north, the recently completed library buildings; and to the south, the University Church of St. Mary the Virgin (SMV), its Gothic tower and spire looming above every other building in the city. Although it had the title of *University Church*, throughout the late Middle Ages, SMV was more than just the university's house of worship. It was also its "Senate House, its Divinity School, its Library, its Court-house, and its Treasury."[1] Oxford University was a federation of colleges, all with religious foundations. There was no sense that a church was an unusual centerpiece for a university, nor that a university was anything but a religious institution.

Figure 3.1 H. Toussaint. St. Mary's Church, Oxford: from the High Street with Queen's, All Souls and University Colleges, and Carfax Tower (n.d.). Wellcome Collection.

The Protestant Reformation triggered no change in this state of affairs.[2] But over the course of the sixteenth and seventeenth centuries, SMV's role in the university was totally transformed. Although it happened in the same era, this had nothing to do with the emergence of England's early modern scientists like Francis Bacon and Sir Isaac Newton in Cambridge, Robert Boyle and Robert Hooke in Oxford. The movement to cleave *the university* and *the church* into separate spheres (which would have sounded to medievals like separating *poetry* and *literature* might to us) didn't come from academics demanding a room of their own. Instead, it originated with the highest quarters of the English church itself.

William Laud became the chancellor of Oxford in 1630 and archbishop of Canterbury (the chief Anglican cleric) in 1633. He held both offices concurrently until his arrest by Puritans in 1641 during the run-up to the English Civil War. As archbishop, Laud faced a widening schism in the Church of England—the continuing echoes of the conflict between Protestant factions drawn to austere Calvinism (like the Puritans and their

Parliamentarian allies) and those drawn to a form of Protestantism that remained Catholic in its trappings—colorful ceremonies, lavish architecture, pomp and circumstance—but under the authority of the English Crown rather than Rome. Laud was in the latter camp, those we would now call *Anglo-Catholics*.

As Oxford's chancellor, Laud came in with strong opinions about ritual, dress, architecture, and worship. In 1633, for instance, he complained that the university youth were not only inappropriately dressed but were also bringing the wrong *disposition* to church: "Tho' the Masters come very duly in Caps, which I am right glad to hear of," he wrote, "yet the younger sort, which should be most in awe, are least in order, and came not ... to St. Mary's in that Form, which they ought to do."[3] Laud's mission was to change how the university felt. He focused on things like preserving the traditional Latin mass, promoting proper ceremonial attire and the proper structure of chapels and churches, and on "clearing the university's secular activities from the university church of St. Mary's."[4] The secularization of Oxford, then, was driven by an archbishop.

Laud didn't live to see the downfall of the Puritans and the return of his high church faction to power. But his legacy at Oxford was established, all the same, with the construction of Christopher Wren's Sheldonian Theatre, immediately to the north of the Bodleian Library—about a thousand feet from SMV—in 1669. A letter sent by the university to the donor, Gilbert Sheldon (himself recently appointed archbishop of Canterbury), made clear that they saw it as the completion of Laud's agenda.[5] "We have labored too much with an unlucky fate," the letter stated, "within the same walls propitiating at the same time both God and Apollo."[6] The Sheldonian became the sole venue for the performance of the Act, also known as the Comitia, or commencement ceremonies, as a special section written into the university's statutes makes clear.[7]

Why did the *secular* university functions come to be seen as out of place within the University Church of St. Mary the Virgin—and by religious leadership, at that? And how did some aspects of the university come to be seen as secular in the first place, given that the university was—as a collection of religious halls and foundations—created under the canopy of a church?[8] What does this spatial remapping of the university tell us about secularity, disenchantment, and critique? And how does all of this help us understand cogency—the way knowledge feels?

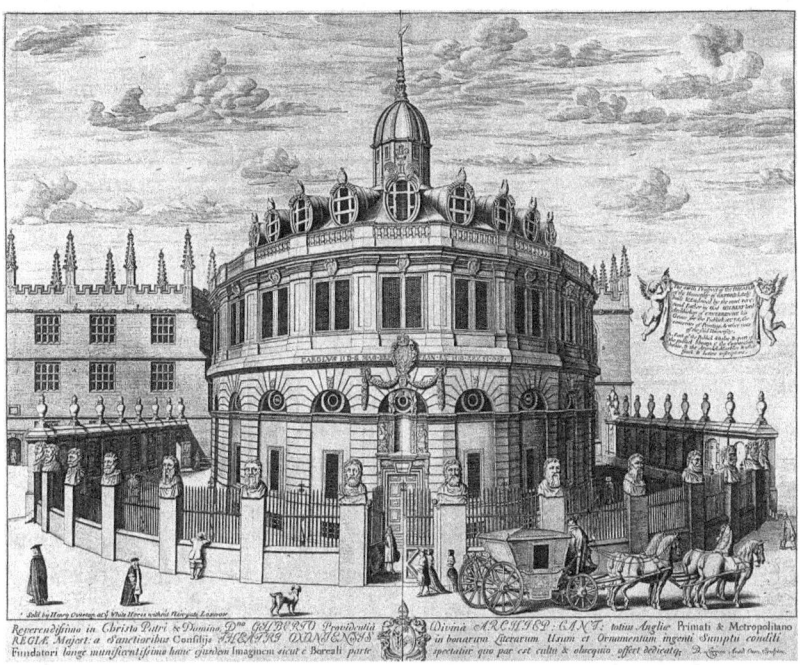

Figure 3.2 D. Loggan, after Christopher Wren. Sheldonian Theatre, Oxford: perspective view with the Bodleian Library (n.d.). Wellcome Collection.

This chapter considers these questions from the perspective of the emerging field of secularism studies. The conventional understanding of secularity locates it squarely in the realm of the intellectual, sometimes celebrating it as the triumph of universal reason, other times disdaining it as the encroachment of the emotional desert of disenchantment. But critical studies of secularity challenge both framings. A consensus is emerging that secularity is not the flat landscape left over after religion has been removed, but a *something*—a set of ways of life, habits, cultures, disciplines, and dispositions, including what scholars have identified as *secular affects*.[9] And it's not just one thing, but plural *secularisms*, what Talal Asad calls *formations of the secular*. These studies of the secular feed directly into conversations about cogency. Secular reason is not neutral. It comes along with a felt dimension. Emotions—including the felt aspects of knowledge-making—build secular bodies, secular cultures, and secular politics. Whatever secularization and disenchantment are, they're not so much the eradication of feeling as the replacement of one template of feeling by others.

At the same time, critical studies of the secular have confirmed, over and over, that the operation of secular reason—although it keeps up a mask of neutrality—can be skewed by dynamics of racialization.[10] Secular affects often get pulled into a racialized matrix, even and especially when they insist the secular has transcended emotion. This feeds into the big argument of this book: exactly because secular reason is emotionally determined, it's susceptible to *messing together* with our other desires and preferences. Formations of the secular aren't contraptions of pure reason. They are, instead, alloys of emotion.

Secularism studies scholars look at the relationships between secularism, enchantment, and critique in ways that point to the affective dimensions of reasoning. This chapter will bridge secularism studies and affect theory by considering how both have developed new frameworks for thinking about the affective profile of critique. From a secularism studies perspective, what gets called disenchantment is not the *destruction* of feeling in modernity. It's a reconfiguration. This includes a rearrangement of the intellectual passions. As the example of the Sheldonian Theatre shows, these intellectual passions came to be identified as distinctly *secular* emotions, requiring their physical separation from sacred precincts like the Church of St. Mary the Virgin.

The Common Sense of Secularization

In 1968, Peter Berger, a professor of sociology and Lutheran theologian, gave a lunchtime talk at the New School for Social Research in Manhattan. A *New York Times* write-up of the talk a few days later (headlined "A Bleak Outcome Is Seen for Religion") summed up Berger's view of the fate of faith. By the twenty-first century, he argued, religion would be nearly extinct, with believers "likely to be found only in small sects, huddled together to resist a worldwide secular culture."[11] Berger proposed that these believers would be treated like an astrologer who visits an American university—politely humored, mostly ignored.

Twenty-five years later, Berger offered a stark recantation. "The world today," he admitted, "is as furiously religious as it ever was, and in some places more so than ever."[12] Rejecting his own previous work, he admitted that "a whole body of literature written by historians and social scientists over the course of the 1950s and '60s, loosely labeled as 'secularization theory,' was essentially mistaken."[13] Berger diagnosed his misstep as a basic sampling error. The engineers of secularization theory looked most closely at who was nearest to them—an elite, highly educated global subculture of academics and professionals—and inferred on that basis that trendlines pointing to the vanishing of religion were rock-solid. But rather than the vanguard of a trend, the subculture was an aberration. And so, Berger realized, the *real* puzzle was secularity itself. "The University of Chicago," he concluded, "is a more interesting topic for the sociology of religion than are the Islamic schools of Qom."[14]

Stories about secularization in the West begin with marquee nineteenth-century thinkers like Marx, Comte, and Nietzsche. The twentieth century's most influential secularization theorist, though, was Max Weber, the German sociologist who died in 1920 after the Spanish flu epidemic, leaving behind a tantalizingly incomplete body of work. Weber, who gave us the word *disenchantment*, is central to sociological accounts of secularization, particularly influencing thinkers like Berger and the designers of the secularization thesis at its peak in the 1960s. And more importantly for cogency theory, Weber's work on secularization comes along with unexpected insights about the relationship between feeling and knowledge production.

In his 1905 volume *The Protestant Ethic and the Spirit of Capitalism*, Weber set out to explore the genealogy of capitalism. Marx had earlier proposed that capitalism resulted from modifications in the economic basis of Western society—technological shifts driving changes in the mode of production driving broadscale cultural transformation. Religion, in turn, was a toxic by-product of defective economic systems.[15] Weber's explanation was the exact opposite.[16] For Weber, far from being the soil out of which religion grew, economic systems like capitalism were the *result* of a cocktail of religious innovations. This ensemble of new beliefs, dispositions and practices, devised by the Protestant reformers, wasn't designed to produce capitalism. But it launched an explosive chain reaction leading, over centuries, to a new global economic regime.

Weber saw the driving force leading to capitalism as what he called *rationalism*, a calculated, economic obsession designed to maximize profit in every action and interaction. But rationalism, for Weber, was not just a habit of thought. It corresponded to a finely tuned system of *dispositions*.[17] The early Protestant reformers, for instance, reconfigured their emotions to craft the *Protestant ethic* of the title.[18] The story goes something like this:

in proposing, as Calvin did, that the God of Christianity was unmoved by acts like prayer, good works, and sacraments (so much so that God had already decided who was saved or damned), believers suffered "terrible inner isolation... an intolerable burden of anxiety to know whether he was one of the elect."[19] Part of Weber's innovation was to connect material and social processes to a *motivational* understanding of action.[20] History, in Weber's theory, was propelled by feeling.

It was this anxiety that motivated the Protestant obsession with what Luther had termed *calling* (*Beruf*), or vocation.[21] Whereas for Catholics vocation could only be transcendent—the priesthood, the monastery, the convent—Protestants developed a sense of calling *in the world*, measured by money.[22] This "philosophy of avarice" led to a fixation on wealth not for luxury, nor even for bare survival, but for its own sake.[23] Weber offers John Wesley's commission to his followers as the final link in this chain of developments: "We ought not to prevent people from being diligent and frugal," Wesley preached, "we must exhort all Christians to gain all they can, and to save all they can; that is, in effect, to grow rich."[24] The preoccupation with wealth evolved into the principle of rationalization.[25]

But then, golem-like, the rational disposition spawned by the Protestant prophets took on a life of its own, even to the extent of reconstructing the religious landscape from which it emerged. This brings us to the dire denouement of Weber's book, in which he introduced his readers to what he named the *iron cage of modernity*—our cage. When the religious dimension of Puritan worldly asceticism fell away like a plaster cast, Weber tells us, we were left with the "tremendous cosmos of the modern economic order."[26] So he characterized his age with a sinister epitaph: "Specialists without spirit, sensualists without heart; this nullity imagines that it has attained a level of civilization never before achieved."[27] Religious change led to economic change led to a change in our collective spirit.

Even though Weber doesn't use the word *secularization* here, it's easy to see how one might think that Weber saw the collapse of feeling and the collapse of religion in modernity as going hand in hand. (Berger certainly did; we'll turn to him in a moment.) But this founding occasion of twentieth-century secularization theory is complicated by Weber's own work toward the end of his life. Twelve years later, in the closing months of the German Empire, as the followers of Marx seized power in Russia, Weber delivered a speech, published soon after as "Science as a Vocation."[28] In this text, another portrait of secularization is painted, pinned not to Protestantism or anxiety but to scholarship. Speaking about the steady advance of science, he describes the situation of modern life as one of advanced *intellectualization*. Intellectualization is not about an increase in knowledge, but about a change in how we conceptualize knowledge. Regardless of whether we moderns actually know how things work (combustion engines, skyscrapers, Wi-Fi), Weber insists, we have "the knowledge or belief that if one but wished one *could* learn it at any time." In other words, "there are no mysterious incalculable forces that come into play, but rather that one can, in principle, master all things by calculation. This," he affirms, "means that the world is *disenchanted*."[29]

Berger's interpretation of Weber took it as given that "Science as a Vocation" continued the analysis of modernization carried out in his earlier work. This was his license to attach the vocabulary of disenchantment to a line of analysis that was much closer (though still meaningfully different) from the earlier work of *The Protestant Ethic*. Weber, it was assumed, was laying out a single *rationalization-secularization-disenchantment* complex. But the intellectual historian Jason Josephson-Storm points out that there's no reason to assume that *iron cage* and *disenchantment* in Weber are synonyms.[30] They might sound the same in English, but *rationalization* (leading to "sensualists without spirit") and *intellectualization* (leading to "disenchantment") are different processes with different drivers and different outcomes.

Later we'll revisit this split story of secularization and the crucial point of what Weber really meant by *disenchantment*. But for now, it's enough to say that the contemporary secularization thesis was built from Berger's skewed interpretation of Weber's work.[31] Berger's 1967 book *The Sacred Canopy*, for instance, identified secularism in two senses: first, the increasing division of religious and secular spheres (what philosopher Charles Taylor names *secularism 1*); and second, the reduction of the influence of religion in the world (Taylor's *secularism 2*).[32] The motor of both, Berger writes, is Protestantism. But whereas Weber's Protestant secularization drive comes from a new arrangement of emotions, Berger sees it as being about the liturgical innovations implemented by the Reformation, particularly the elimination of Catholic pomp and ceremony.[33]

By snuffing out the mystery embedded in material things—sacraments, liturgy, architecture—and forcing a stark encounter between an individual and God as the locus of faith, Berger argues, the Protestant sea change swung into motion the process of secularization.[34] For Berger, Protestantism is already a far milestone on the road to secularization because it's already an invitation to science: "A sky empty of angels," he wrote, "becomes open to the intervention of the astronomer and, eventually, of the astronaut."[35] Taylor makes an identical point, proposing that disenchantment is a by-product of the drive to *personalize* religion in Protestantism, which ends up leading to a *buffered self* that purges the world around it of influential spiritual actors.[36] This story—a subtle but distinctive mutation of Weber's, grafting the language of disenchantment onto an analysis of Protestantism—became the common sense of secularization.

Secular Bodies to Secular Affects

The classical theory of secularization as the irreversible, imminent, and inevitable decline of religion has, as Berger himself admitted, collapsed. In renouncing his previous work, Berger pointed out the insurmountable empirical evidence against him (first and foremost, powerful global revivals in Islam and Christianity). So-called secularized religions that sought to meet at a common table with modernity stumbled; traditionalism flourished.[37] As scholars such as Janet Jakobsen and Ann Pellegrini have since pointed out, this dismantling of the secular common sense gained even more force in the 2000s, with the new visibility of American Christian nationalism, global Islamic radicalism, and other religious resurgences around the world.[38]

What Berger didn't see, however, was how his own understanding of secularism was shaped by the way he defined *religion* itself. Berger called religion "the establishment, through human activity, of an all-embracing sacred order, that is, of a sacred cosmos that will be capable of maintaining itself in the ever-present face of chaos."[39] The commonsense secularization story crafted by Berger, then, blamed Protestantism for secularism. But it was also based on a definition of religion that was already basically determined by Protestantism—as exclusively focused on belief.[40] This is where postcolonial critics of the secularization thesis enter the picture.

As far back as the early 1980s, anthropologist Talal Asad had begun refashioning his field's understanding of religion. His goal was to redirect the attention of anthropology not just to the others of the West, but to the West's own categories and creations, including concepts like *religion*.[41] One of Asad's early interventions was his criticism of the anthropologist Clifford Geertz's work on religion in the 1960s and 1970s. Geertz's work is like Berger's in many ways. He was strongly influenced by an intellectualist interpretation of Weber, having studied with American sociologist Talcott Parsons at Harvard in the 1960s. "The concept of culture I espouse," Geertz writes, "is essentially a semiotic one. Believing, with Max Weber, that man is an animal suspended in webs of significance he himself has spun, I take culture to be those webs, and the analysis of it to be therefore not an experimental science in search of law but an interpretive one in search of meaning."[42] Like Berger, then, Geertz takes up what he thinks is the mantle of Weber to define religion as an arrangement of symbols and beliefs.

Asad's diagnosis of the problem with this vocabulary was that it identified religion as fundamentally about a self's private encounter with meaning.[43] This meant it could be crisply detached from politics, culture, and history.[44] This definition of religion, Asad suggests, results from immersion in a set of Protestant presuppositions about what *real* religion is.[45] In early modern Europe, he writes, religion was more and more strongly associated with *belief*, "as a set of propositions to which believers gave assent, and which could therefore be judged and compared as between different religions and as against natural science."[46] The idea of religion as the domain of private reflections designed to imbue life with meaning—the unmediated encounter of faith between God and confessor—is, Asad suggests, "a product of the only legitimate space allowed to Christianity by post-Enlightenment society, the right to individual *belief*."[47]

This designation of religion as the sphere of symbols and ideas, Asad argues, had three effects. First, Geertz (and Berger) became oblivious to how religious symbols are made meaningful through their connections to history, bodies, and power.[48] Second, *religion* was abstracted from the context that created it as a category—a modern Christian dialect that emphasizes belief—and applied to other traditions, producing contorted understandings of how religion operates in, for instance, societies formed within the cultural parameters of Islam.[49] And third, it opened the door to secularism.[50] In his subsequent book, *Formations of the Secular*, Asad points out that something distinctive happens when religion is seen as a set of private reflections that are the sincere and unique properties of the believer.[51] In the private sphere, they're purified of political implications—the Protestantized religion of symbol systems oriented to cosmic meaning—the preoccupation of Berger and Geertz.[52] This means that secularism as a doctrine, as Jakobsen and Pellegrini put it, "remains tied to a particular religion, just as the secular calendar remains tied to Christianity."[53]

Asad, then, rejects Berger's early claim that secularization erases religious weirdness and reveals a neutral terrain underneath. Instead of an unmarked worldwide secular landscape, formations of the secular "account for distinctive sensibilities, aesthetics, moralities. ... Modernity," he adds, "is not primarily a matter of cognizing the real but of living-in-the-world."[54] Weber's word *rationalization* might sound like the emergence of a universally valid set of truths about the world, but Asad's argument is that the conceptual categories created within modernity are actually keyed to distinctively modern ways of *experiencing* the world. This leads to Asad's call for an *anthropology of secularism*, an exploration of the secular as a plural field of attitudes, practices, disciplines, sensations, and discourses.[55] This approach is the defining feature of secularism studies. It starts with the assertion that the secular is not featureless, and not even singular. Different formations of the secular come along with their own strange cultures, outlooks, and priorities.

Charles Taylor calls this the myth of the *subtraction story*, the claim that secularization reveals flat ground once the strange earthworks of religion are leveled. Taylor argues that secularization is "not only loss but also remaking."[56] It's an understanding that starts from the same place as Asad's insight—that religions are fields of diverse practices, histories, and cultural forms that remake the intellectual landscape around them in multiple ways. So "changes in religion, including diminishments of religious belief or organized religious participation, cannot be mere subtractions."[57] It's why Jakobsen and Pellegrini suggest we speak of *secularisms* in the plural. The residue of history—including religion—becomes part of secular landscapes. Change is never just removal. It's always a reworking, drawing on a bricolage of existing materials.

In a sense, then, Asad agrees with Berger that the Protestant conceptual ecology leads to secularization. But Asad digs deeper: he wants an explanation of why the secularization thesis is persuasive in the first place. From Asad's perspective, the story of secularization can play out as it has only when we start with a definition of religion as private belief, something isolated and detachable. If we'd begun somewhere else—any number of non-Protestant traditions, for instance, where religion is not just a set of ideas but practices, habits, material culture, and even bodily dispositions—the subtraction story would be bizarre. There may be *formations of the secular* in which different sedimentations of what gets called religion and what gets called nonreligion layer and intersect, but the idea of a flat plain *beneath* religion would be nonsensical.

Many thinkers in secularism studies still primarily focus on the secular as fundamentally a question of what we think and how beliefs are framed.[58] As productive as this line of inquiry has been, however, I think Asad's work points to an even more expansive method. Asad argues for seeing secularity not just as a grid of ideas, but as sunk into the body. As far back as his work on the category of religion in the 1980s, he placed bodies, practices, and dispositions at center stage, reversing the Protestant image of religion as entirely within the remit of belief.[59] Invoking figures like Foucault allows Asad to reiterate the necessity of thinking about bodies and things as opposed to Geertz and Berger's shared fixation on intellectually mediated symbols.[60]

This sets the stage for Asad's bold emphasis on *bodies* in making formations of the secular. Asad's anthropology of secularism focuses on secularism not only as a political philosophy but as a network of practices, attitudes, and patterns of sensation that produce forms of life.[61] The secular, he proposes, is not simply a departure from *religion*, nor a twisted continuation of it. Secularity captures elements of what came before—ideas, yes, but also patterns of behavior, templates of sensation, dispositions, and habits—and remixes them into new forms.[62] Anthropologist Charles Hirschkind rephrases this as the question of the *secular body*.[63]

Others go even further in fully converting Asad's line of inquiry into a study of secular affects. Jakobsen and Pellegrini, for instance, ask: "What does secularism 'feel' like?"[64] Affect theorists like William Connolly, George Levine, and Jane Bennett have taken a direct interest in secularism and feeling (see below).[65] An entire literature is emerging within secularism studies on Soviet state atheism and its aftermath, with particular attention to the way the Soviet atheist propaganda network failed to meaningfully account for the need to think through the emotional dimensions of the secular/religious dynamic.[66] Asad's focus on disciplines and dispositions (and Taylor's intermittent attention to ways of life) in formations of the secular lead all the way to a set of questions about not just bodies, but the felt life of the secular.[67]

As Monique Scheer, Nadia Fadil, and Birgitte Schepelern Johansen point out, even to name *feelings* as secular is disruptive: "Those very areas which self-describe as secular (not only science, law, and medicine but scholarship generally, for example)," they write, "are typically predicated upon an exclusion of the emotional, affective, and sensorial from their operations, often relegating these aspects to domains deemed 'private' or 'subjective.'"[68] In the autobiography of secularity, emotions are out of the story. To talk about secular emotions is a contradiction in terms, an earthquake under the secular order, toppling the black monolith myth of a feeling/thinking binary.[69]

But as far as Asad and Taylor take us in bringing secular bodies and secular lifeways into the foreground, they, too, have a tendency to lapse into this way of thinking. They do this by doubling down on the narrative of disenchantment, and specifically the well-rehearsed misconception that disenchantment is about a reduction of feeling. Taylor's tableau of secularism, Bruce Robbins observes, "is full of stale *Brave New World*–style cliché about Hugh Hefner, brightly lit supermarkets, empty suburbs, and the triumph of the therapeutic."[70] Asad's most recent work associates science with what he calls *calculative reason*, or "passionless language, action, and thought."[71] To move on from the black monolith myth, we need to turn to other conversations taking place in secularism studies: a reconsideration of *disenchantment* in Weber's work and the affective anatomy of *critique*. The rest of this chapter will consider how these lines of research add to cogency theory, and in particular how they shed light on the secularization of the University Church.

The Felt Life of Disenchantment

Disenchantment, in Weber's telling, goes along with what he calls *intellectualization*—the abandonment of the belief that there are forces in the universe beyond our comprehension. But as Josephson-Storm reminds us, *disenchantment-intellectualization* doesn't line up with *secularization-rationalization* from Weber's earlier work as nicely as later interpreters thought.[72] Weber's word *disenchantment* is the German *Entzauberung*, literally "demagification." Bruce Robbins points out that this seems to be a riff on Romantic poet Friedrich Schiller's term *Entgötterung*—"de-divinization"—but with a twist.[73] So the first English-language translators of "Science as a Vocation" put the phrase *disenchantment of the world* in quotation marks: "They had decided, on the basis of what they knew, that [Weber] could not have given himself over fully to the disenchantment story."[74] The modern mythology of disenchantment as an evacuation of feeling from the world already seemed to these early translators like a misfit with Weber's views. The arc of disenchantment-intellectualization, in Weber's lecture, is about the transformation of feeling, not its eradication.[75]

"Science as a Vocation" begins with a grim scene. A professor is trying to persuade his students not to become scholars. He tells them about the poverty, the bureaucracy, the racial discrimination, and the ruthless arbitrariness of the academic life.[76] But some students ignore this advice. Doggedly following in the footsteps of their teachers, they have the vocation of science. Weber's word for *science* is *Wissenschaft*, which, as in Nietzsche's work, casts a wide net around the human, natural, and social sciences. (This means the *science* Weber is referring to in the title includes his own field of study—sociology.)[77] And Weber's word *vocation* is *Beruf*—the same term that in *The Protestant Ethic* was translated as *calling*. When it arrives as our vocation, science is "the demon," Weber writes in the final lines of the lecture, "who holds the fibers of [our] very life."[78]

Given all the frustrations of the academic life, Weber argues, only one who could somehow "come up to the idea that the fate of his soul depends upon whether or not he makes the correct conjecture at this passage of this manuscript" is suited for the scientific life.[79] There's nothing theological about this, though. Instead, the calling to science is determined by deep feeling, a "strange intoxication" with ideas.[80] That makes science much more like art than is conventionally believed: "Both are frenzy (in the sense of Plato's 'mania')," Weber tells us, "and 'inspiration.'"[81] Science and art are both sourced in the same reservoir of emotion.

It seems hard to reconcile Weber's portrait of the holy fools of science with his manifesto of disenchantment.[82] But this is only because we have mistakenly imposed a definition of disenchantment as the disintegration of feeling—a by-product of our conventional wisdom that thinking and feeling are opposites. The mainstream interpretation of Weber (repeated by Berger, Taylor, and Asad) misses that Weber's theory of disenchantment is not so much a zero-sum game of plus or minus feeling as it is a tonal shift. Disenchantment/demagification, for Weber, is an epistemological change with affective consequences, not the elimination of feeling itself.[83]

This is why Weber explicitly argues *against* those who believe that knowledge production is feelingless.[84] "Nowadays in circles of youth," he laments, "there is a widespread notion that science has become a problem in calculation, fabricated in laboratories or statistical filing systems just as 'in a factory,' a calculation involving only the cool intellect and not one's 'heart and soul.'"[85] Already in 1917, Weber was swatting down the myth that so-called calculative reason is on the other side of the river from feeling. His blueprint for disenchantment is very different. Once there were the old gods, now there is the calling to pursue knowledge-making. This change in the foundations of our knowledge has emotional consequences. We've swapped out one way of feeling our way through the world with another.

Science as calling brings disenchantment. But this is fully compatible with excitement, passion, and a kind of resolute dignity. It's the fascination of those who have "brooded at our desks and searched for answers with passionate devotion."[86] In science, the affective potential of knowledge production is streamlined, condensed, and distributed through new institutions and new practices. It's another route to the noble seriousness of the steel-eyed reformers, Weber's private obsession.[87] This isn't just a repeat of what came before—religion reborn—as Josephson-Storm claims.[88] It's part of the *new* affective signature of modernity. Disenchantment is not the elimination of feeling. It's a *transformation* of the way the world feels.

Philosopher Jane Bennett's work on Weber gets close to this understanding. She proposes that modern science is a rearrangement of fascinations, not a lapse into permanent grayness.[89] She finds in science an emotional compound—wonder, exhilaration, and sometimes even a tinge of fear.[90] The scientific encounter with the world is a way of accessing this feeling, she writes, rather than a way of nullifying it. Much like Dawkins in *Unweaving the Rainbow*, Bennett calls on us to imagine a place "where reason engenders, where faculties play, where nature gives hints, where molecules mutate, where tomatoes morph, where files zoom, where curves spiral and fields buzz, where ants swarm and vertigo reveals, and where thinking unexpectedly shouts out from the dutiful litany of thought. *That* world," she concludes, "is not disenchanted."[91]

George Levine's assessment is similar. He wants us to take seriously the possibility of *secular enchantment*—a version of the secular that makes the circulation of feeling central.[92] This includes holding up science as both a tool for making good knowledge and a source of excitement and joy, "a secular world in which science keeps its major explanatory voice, and in which the virtues of rationality are inflected with deep feeling."[93] Levine writes extensively about how Darwin emerges as a champion of this form of enchantment. Darwin, he says, "writes like a scientist *and* like a caring, loving, conventional, and reverent man whose relation to nature is intense and charged with feeling."[94]

But even though Bennett and Levine are ready to knock down the black monolith myth and rejoin science and feeling, they ultimately don't go as far as Weber himself. For one thing, they're interested in a secularism that celebrates the *discoveries* of science, rather than the emotionally laden *action* of science itself. Dawkins, with his awesome nebulas and intricate organelles, is one proponent of this way of thinking, and secularism studies researchers have turned up others—immortality-chasing transhumanists, code-happy early AI programmers, Soviet apparatchiks trying to get peasants so excited about planetariums that they would forget their old churches.[95] As we saw in the introduction, this doesn't go far enough in disrupting the feeling/thinking binary. The secular science fair implies that feeling is the prize at the end of the race rather than woven into knowledge-making itself. But even more importantly, Bennett and Levine still take it as given that *disenchantment* means feelinglessness.[96] Their goal is to reassociate science with enchantment. They miss Weber's insistence that disenchantment itself carries feeling, value, and fascination.

Taylor writes, "Everyone can agree that one of the big differences between us and our ancestors of 500 years ago is that they lived in an 'enchanted' world and we do not."[97] This may or may not be true, but what disenchantment means is a moving target. The story that disenchantment leads to the evaporation of feeling is one of the most precarious fictions advanced in the mythology of secularism (and antisecularism too, since the supposed colorlessness of secularism is a favorite weapon for religious apologetics). The cogency theory approach to secularism suggests that disenchantment is not so much the *eradication* of feeling in our understanding of the world. It remixes ways of feeling and thinking into new affective forms. This includes the emotional profile of critique itself.

The Paranoid Style of Critique

In the 2009 book *Is Critique Secular?*, Asad and anthropologist Saba Mahmood explore the idea that *critique*—intellectual work that sets out to aggressively expose the hidden moves of power lurking under every surface—is itself a feature of the affective topography of secularism.[98] In her contribution, "Religious Reason and Secular Affect," Mahmood argues that religion is defined by its *affective* relationships with signs.[99] She describes these relationships using a term from classical Greek philosophy, *schesis*—cultivated, embodied attachment.[100] Religion is about these felt connections rather than belief.[101] What's most important for our purposes, though, is that Mahmood thinks that secularism has schesis too. Its schesis is *critique*.[102]

Secular critique presents itself as feelingless knowledge-making (while portraying religion as in thrall to emotion).[103] But its fixation on squeezing secret knowledge from every piece of culture and history is itself affectively determined. "The worldly critic," Asad writes, "wants to see and hear everything: nothing is taboo, everything is subject to critical engagement."[104] There is a presumed demand, within the secular, to *know everything*. Judith Butler calls it the *sensibility* or *attitude* of modernity.[105] Foucault writes it up as the motto of the Enlightenment: *Aude sapere—dare to know*.[106] By bringing the affective dimensions of secular critique to light, these perspectives draw out the coalescence of thought and feeling.

Affect theory offers even more detail in response to the question of how critique feels, especially in its tie-ins with one of the biggest methodological conversations in the humanities over the past decade, what's been called the *postcritical turn*. Eve Kosofsky Sedgwick's essay "Paranoid Reading and Reparative Reading, or, You're So Paranoid You Probably Think This Essay Is about You" is a keystone text of this conversation.[107] Sedgwick's conclusion in this essay is that not only are our protocols of knowledge production affective, they're also *differently* affective. To take a *different approach* to an object of study is to *feel differently* about it. William James saw philosophical debates as proxy wars driven by the real differences in our secret topographies of intellectual feeling. Along similar lines, Sedgwick thinks that different modes of interpretation are defined not so much by different conceptual presuppositions as by their underlying affective configurations. These are the emotional ingredients of the pattern of secular critique.

What Sedgwick calls *paranoid reading* is marked by an insistence on slicing off the surface of an object under study in order to divine its secret intentions. Paranoid reading, she says, is a particular "cognitive/affective theoretical practice" built into method.[108] That slash between *cognitive* and *affective* identifies paranoid reading as both emotional and intellectual. This configuration of affect and knowledge is distinctive because of the way it makes knowledge feel, specifically its "extraordinary stress on the efficacy of knowledge per se—knowledge in the form of exposure."[109] Paranoid reading is about becoming the agent of unmasking, the director of surprises rather than their victim. "The first imperative of paranoia," Sedgwick writes, "is there must be no bad surprises."[110]

As one of the founders of queer theory in the storied literature program at Duke University, Sedgwick's world was what is sometimes called *high theory*—the electrifying first wave of American interpretations of poststructuralism in the 1970s and 1980s—and the inheritors of the hermeneutic of suspicion. Sedgwick's account of paranoid reading, first offered in the mid-1990s, is addressed to this world. She laments that in Theoryland, "to theorize out of anything *but* a paranoid critical stance has come to seem naïve, pious, or complaisant."[111] Lauren Berlant and Kathleen Stewart describe the same situation fifteen years later, writing that "humanist critique just keeps snapping at the world as if the whole point of being and thinking is just to catch it in a lie."[112] Literary theorist Rita Felski draws on Sedgwick in her 2015 book *The Limits of Critique*.[113] She, too, makes the link between paranoid reading and critique, a shared "attitude of vigilance, detachment, and wariness (*suspicion*)."[114] This critical mindset—a particular way of feeling/knowing things—identifies itself as the only acceptable mode of thinking and asking questions. The adoption of the paranoid stance rapidly hardens into a mandate, an emotional orthodoxy demanding exposure of the secret sins of every scrap of culture.

Neither Sedgwick nor Felski want us to abandon paranoid reading altogether, but they do ask for breathing room for alternatives. Sedgwick counterposes paranoid reading with another approach, what she calls *reparative reading*. If paranoid reading is an X-ray stare, reparative reading is eager, wide-eyed, agape. Its passion is for encountering texts in ways that anticipate nurturance, joy, and healing. It cultivates hope, strategic vulnerability, and a willingness to be surprised. "The desire of a reparative impulse," Sedgwick writes, "is additive and accretive. Its fear is that the culture surrounding it is inadequate or inimical to its nurture; it wants to assemble and confer plenitude on an object that will then have resources to offer to an inchoate self."[115] Reparative reading approaches objects of study with a different affect, hoping for an embrace rather than a brawl. Felski's version of this is what she calls *hermeneutics of restoration*, an attitude "infused with moments of wonder, reverence, exaltation, hope, epiphany, or joy."[116] Stephen Best and Sharon Marcus's call for *surface reading*, too, asks for a complex dance with the excitement of texts.[117] Whatever the term used, it's the antithesis of paranoid reading, a cultivated optimism, passionate about its own bedazzlement rather than insisting on knowing everything in advance.

What's common to these sketches is their insistence that a feeling state—a mood—is both the precondition and the structuring envelope of knowledge production. Mood "is not optional, but a prerequisite for any kind of intellectual engagement."[118] A configuration of feeling makes possible the emergence and organization of objects of knowledge as we sift through our encounters with the world. Education, in all its formal and informal modes, is about training and cultivating these intellectual dispositions. Mood "impinges on method."[119]

Sedgwick offers her main example of this in response to Judith Butler's famous analysis of drag performance, or camp.[120] Butler argued that drag inhabits extreme gender performance to parody masculinity and femininity and unmask their construction. It aims to detonate gender from within.[121] "By this account," Sedgwick writes, "the x-ray gaze of the paranoid impulse in camp sees through to an unfleshed skeleton of the culture."[122] Camp is a weapon designed to unmask ugly truths about power. Sedgwick's reparative reading of camp spins this around. Rather than seeing it as an act of sabotage, she invites us to be open to the possibility that drag performance is inflected with love, admiration, celebration, and joy.[123]

In her final book, *The Weather in Proust*, Sedgwick asks us to see camp "not in terms of parody or even wit, but with more of an eye for its visceral, operatic power: the startling outcrops of overinvested erudition; the prodigal production of alternative histories; the 'over'-attachment to fragmentary, marginal, waste, lost, or leftover cultural products; the richness of affective variety; and the irrepressible, cathartic fascination with ventriloquist forms of relation."[124] This is why Heather Love calls camp a *backward art*—a queer aesthetic of loving, accumulating, and self-adorning, gathering and celebrating abandoned objects from the past.[125] Taking a reparative approach to camp recasts it as a resource for healing and creativity rather than a concealed weapon.

How, then, has critique managed to become the monoculture of today's intellectual landscape in the secular humanities—the only game in town, with a highly effective inquisition keeping orthodoxy? Felski's response is to pay attention to the *charisma of critique*—its magnetism, the way it keeps drawing us back in. "For a generation of graduate students," she writes, "the explosion of literary theories and critical methods was irresistible. The intellectual passions of the 1980s—the Macherey reading group, the late-night discussions of Cixous or Irigaray—were intense, feverish, and palpable."[126] She draws a three-dimensional portrait of the mood of critique—*suspicion*—"an elusive and complex attitude, a secondary emotion composed out of basic affects such as fear, anger, curiosity, and repugnance."[127] These might seem like feelings we would want to avoid, but Felski argues that the cocktail of mild poisons produces something irresistible. "Critique would not be so successful," she says, "if it did not gratify and reward its practitioners."[128] It's a pattern of reflexes of reasoning. In the terms set by cogency theory, critique always finds the most suspicious, most paranoid answer to be the most cogent.

Why, Felski asks, are scholars always, in their word, *interrogating* things? Why reach for such a violent and adversarial verb to describe our intellectual practice?[129] For her, it's part of the machismo of critique—its "affective inhibition" against *yielding* to a text, which it sees as "a form of shameful abasement or ideological surrender."[130] There's a strut to critique. It's a display of indomitability, like a military parade. "Do you see now why it feels so good to be a critical mind?" Bruno Latour asks. "Why critique, this most ambiguous *pharmakon*, has become such a potent euphoric drug? You are always right! When naïve believers are clinging forcefully to their objects, claiming that they are made to do things because of their gods, their poetry, their cherished objects, you can turn all of those attachments into so many fetishes and humiliate all the believers by showing that it is nothing but their own projection, that you, yes you alone, can see."[131] Critique as a *pharmakon*—a drug—is a powerful medicine. But it also threatens to become an addiction.

The pleasure of critique, for Felski, even has a sort of literary genre. It's a crime drama—a murder mystery. Like the detective, she writes, the critic has to create a case file. Both mystery and critique "slot events into a chronological sequence, track down agents engaged in wrongdoing, and parcel out blame."[132] The detective novel, like critique, is "a plot-driven form," arousing our curiosity and then satisfying it with a sophisticated solution.[133] Every detail fits into a tautly structured narrative machine, what Felski calls a "cerebral striptease," in which "details are dangled before us, red herring piled on red herring, information doled out fragment by painstaking fragment, until the veils are finally lifted and the truth is laid bare."[134] The sophisticated marshalling of evidence that characterizes critique draws on the same kind of pleasure elicited by resolving a mystery. Both genres are effective intellectual devices for generating click.

Not only that, critique takes from the plot form of the murder mystery a crisp moral architecture of good and evil, with the detective assigned the task of pinpointing unerring blame. Critique's accounts of "literature and art," Felski writes, "are also tacit *accusations*, driven by a desire to identify fault, apportion blame, and track down wrongdoing."[135] Taken to a baroque extreme, critique morphs into conspiracy theory, making the world into a jigsaw puzzle, a field of information waiting breathlessly to be arranged into the telltale tracks of heroes and villains.

Although Sedgwick doesn't say as much, she's diagramming how paranoid reading dances with *interest*, in Tomkins's sense. But Felski makes it explicit. Suspicion, she affirms, makes the world *supremely interesting*, an intricate lattice of power rather than a pointless mess, a pulse-pounding plotline rather than a lump of stupidity. Like conspiracy theory, as both Felski and Sedgwick point out, critical suspicion runs together with a loathing of accident, insisting that every weirdness conceals a sinister secret. "Rather than an ascetic exercise in demystification," Felski notes, "suspicious reading turns out to be a style of thought infused with a range of passions and pleasures, intense engagements and eager commitment."[136]

The caricature projected on the postcritical turn by its opponents is that it's actually *anticritique*. That's the immune system of critique kicking in. It assumes that to blink even for a moment is to show weakness, demanding a full mobilization in the total war against power. (And feeling, perhaps, the sting of loss of a world in which everything under the sun can be presented as a delightfully obvious con job.)[137] But really, Sedgwick and Felski are explicit that critique does invaluable political work.[138] The postcritical lament is over what's lost when the *only* scholarly tools available to us are military hardware.

Commenting on Sedgwick's work, queer theorist Robyn Wiegman contends that reparative reading is, for Sedgwick, a way of "learning how to build small worlds of sustenance that cultivate a different present and future for the losses that one has suffered."[139] Wiegman proposes that this was one of the ways Sedgwick responded to her own terminal cancer.[140] Sedgwick, in this reading, found herself longing for something from the world of theory that it was unable to give her. Instead of an infestation of conspiracies, Sedgwick needed spaces in the humanities to trace seams of happiness and comfort. Black studies thinkers have pointed out that this is itself a political act. Stefano Harney and Fred Moten characterize critique as the paranoid defensive crouch of the settler state, transforming itself into a military camp and canceling any encounter with the transformative joy necessary for healing. "Taking down our critique," they write, "our fortifications, is self-defense alloyed with self-preservation."[141]

Sedgwick's portrait of paranoid and reparative reading as two different cognitive-affective theoretical practices reiterates the need to study the insoluble links between feeling and thinking. But this is not, as Felski writes, "to reverse the clock and be teleported back to the good old days of New Critical chitchat about irony, paradox, and ambiguity."[142] It calls us, instead, to be mindful of how scholarly inquiry is motivated by an orchestra of feelings—and to be ever wary of addiction to the monotone of denunciation and severity. Amy Hollywood echoes the same sentiment in her call for scholars to allow themselves to be, in her word, *pierced* by what we study—texts, cultures, people—to encounter positions that initially seem suspect in ways that make room for vulnerability.[143] This reparative opening of vulnerability in making knowledge is what the hardcore version of secular critique forbids.

The flat mask worn by the secular to conceal its own felt attachments has, as both Asad and Mahmood point out, another effect. It allows secularism to encrypt political priorities by making them *feel like* neutral ground.[144] One way of phrasing Asad's insight is that he's skeptical that the public/private divide secularism leans on in demanding a separation between *religious* and *secular* can ever be applied neutrally.[145] There is no process of interpretation that is detached from the coordinates of feeling, no transparent act of meaning-making. Instead, the way we read, think, study, and interpret emerges from a complex of disciplines, dispositions, habits, and practices, all of which sprawl across the washed-out border of public and private. This includes no shortage of ways of being secular, which mess together with the sexist, racializing, and colonizing projects that are also jockeying for position among formations of modernity.[146]

This leads to a focus, for some scholars, on secularism as a strategy of governance.[147] Secularism in these case studies adopts a fake neutrality, wearing the mask of evenhandedness toward all religions while actually ushering a few favorites in the side door.[148] Mahmood's study of secular rule in Egypt considers, for instance, the *Lautsi v. Italy* decision of the European Court of Human Rights, which upheld the right of Italian public schools to display the crucifix. The basis of this ruling? That the Western tradition of free subjects emerged from Christianity, so the crucifix is actually an emblem of secularism rather than religion.[149] Along similar lines, Mayanthi Fernando documents how the secular regime of *laïcité* in France morphed from a tool used to keep the Catholic faction in check during the nineteenth century into an arsenal used almost exclusively against France's Muslim minority in recent decades.[150] And Jolyon Baraka Thomas shows that the American occupation of Japan after World War II imposed a vision of *religious liberty* that locked in a Christianized template of what religion is and should be.[151] In all these cases, a racialized landscape—defined by its own affective configurations of racial supremacism and nationalism—masquerades as a flat surface. A headscarf just *feels* foreign and dangerous; a crucifix just *feels* neutral. These secular forms are tuned to this dissonant pitch.

This is Asad's point: the way secular order decides what is and isn't a valid entry into the public sphere is not a rule organized by a strict and stable division of religion from nonreligion. Instead, it builds on a felt racialized landscape that tries to predetermine whose lives matter—whose pain, whose flourishing, whose history, and whose brokenness. In a society suffused with Islamophobic rage, contempt, and scorn, these affects mess together with the intellectual feelings of critique. The result is that Islamophobia comes to feel like *being reasonable*. It feels so good it has to be true.[152] It's because *both* knowledge-making and racialized reason are organized by feeling that they can bleed into each other. As Scheer and her colleagues write, "The secular is not per se 'un-emotional' even when it is presented as adhering to the ideals of objectivity and rationality."[153]

Disputations: Science as Spectator Sport

So we return to our opening questions: Why do the secular functions of Oxford University in the early modern period need to be—in the eyes of the churchmen running the show—literally *walled off* from religion? To answer this, we can return to our microhistory of the University Church, paying special attention to how the intellectual affects circulated within its confines. By the seventeenth century, many of the exclusively academic and procedural functions of the university had already been vacated from the Church of St. Mary the Virgin.[154] What still remained was the performance of the Act or Comitia—a sort of university-wide commencement ritual for those taking master's degrees—held every summer.[155] The Act had several parts, both ceremonial and celebratory. Prayers and offerings followed the morning ringing of bells, then lectures given by professors "in scarlet capes and hoods, and caps appropriated to their degree."[156] Then came the *disputations*—or *Act-Exercises*—for the different academic faculties.

The disputations are vital for understanding how the Act circulated intellectual affects. Historian Deborah Shuger describes a disputation as a kind of semistructured debate in which a candidate was called on to state a position in response to a question.[157] A series of opponents were then presented. Each argued the opposing side, with the candidate responding in turn. Disputations were taking place constantly throughout the year—as recreation or on more formal occasions—but the Act-Exercises during the Comitia were linked to the bestowal of master's degrees. They were like a modern dissertation defense, but testing mental agility—rapidly mustering an argument and responding to challenge—rather than disciplinary expertise.

After being held in the same place—the University Church of St. Mary the Virgin—since "beyond all memory," why does Laud, as both archbishop and chancellor, conclude that the Act needs to be relocated?[158] The statutes say it was so "the Church of St. Mary the Virgin, which [had] been from time to time profaned by the tumult and licence of the Act, might thenceforth in holiness and all possible piety be subservient to the duties of sustaining religion and the ritual of God."[159] However, this was not a Puritanical (with a capital *P*) effort to throw cold water on a party. During the Protectorship, Oliver Cromwell appointed one of his cronies vice chancellor of the university. This particular Puritan attempted "not only to do away with academic habits entirely, as savouring of superstition, but also to abolish the Act itself as an occasion of frivolity."[160] This is not what Laud or his Restoration successors were after. It's not that they objected to the colors and costumes of the ceremony. Laud loved that stuff. The Act wasn't seen as wicked and needing to be abolished—the Puritan party line. But it was *in the wrong place* in a church.

The letter to Archbishop Sheldon thanking him for his donation was clear: the violation of holding the Act in SMV was not that it was bacchanalian, but because it offered "sacrifice to Apollo"—the god of the arts, poetry, and knowledge. The academic arts and letters (*literis*), the message to Sheldon complained, were both "protect[ing] the interests of the church and [oppressing] her."[161] "Religion," it added, had been "flooded by erudition" (*Religionem Literatura pessundari*).[162] The push to create a secular zone outside of the SMV was prompted, then, by a felt need to relocate the intellectual adventures of the Act to another space. It's why Wren's initial designs for the Sheldonian seem to have been specially set up to accommodate disputations, with built-in stalls for the respondent, opponents, proctors, and moderators of the Act-Exercise.[163]

The disputations were a kind of sport or theater—not just an examination technique, but a pastime. "For all that disputations were instruments of academic assessment," Shuger writes, "they were also, unlike blue-book exams, a format that university men used in their dorms or at dinner to play and wrestle with ideas."¹⁶⁴ Disputations straddled the line between work and play. They were a way to sport with intellectual affects. This is why public disputations were Queen Elizabeth's primary diversion—for hours on end—whenever she visited Oxford during her reign.¹⁶⁵ These events were held inside SMV, which one chronicler of the event described as set up like "freshly equipped wrestling grounds."¹⁶⁶

Shuger's sources describe how Elizabeth, on one of these occasions, watched a debater, swept up in passion, declare his willingness to die for his position on the superiority of elective government over hereditary monarchy. One might have expected this to annoy her, but turning to her retinue, the queen declared, "Excellent! O, excellent."¹⁶⁷ The final debate of the day, featuring professors of divinity, went on "till candles were lighted; delight devouring all weariness in the auditors."¹⁶⁸ Shuger notes that although one could be prosecuted for things said during a speech, a sermon, or even a lecture, there is no record of charges laid against a speaker for remarks made during a disputation.¹⁶⁹ Participants in disputations could take up political positions—and even heresies—for which they would never be punished. This only further underlines that the disputations were, at heart, theater. They were pleasurable, an improvised opera of click. Both disenchantment and critique were at play. But far from being affectively null, disputations were fascinating—even exhilarating.

In *The Varieties of Religious Experience*, William James writes that there "must be something solemn, serious, and tender about any attitude which we denominate religious."¹⁷⁰ The Christian theologian Rudolf Otto made the same point even more sharply several years later, characterizing the essential religious feeling as *mysterium tremendum*, an orientation to an awe-inspiring, unfathomable mystery.¹⁷¹ As we saw, Laud saw his task as guiding his subjects to be "most in awe."¹⁷² What it all adds up to is that *religion*, in this moment, came to mean not just a set of beliefs, but a *feeling tone*. Oxford historian Anthony Wood wrote that the disputations were removed so that they "might with better convenience, and according to the *dignity* of the University be celebrated; and the House of God ... might hereafter be wholly employed to sacred uses."¹⁷³ The tumult of a wild academic debate clashed with the *felt* sense of solemn sacrality in the University Church, leading to the creation of a literal wall of separation. The disputations were banished from SMV because they were *too much fun*. The emerging secular university was made by isolating the field of affects surrounding intellectualization, disenchantment, and critique, by corralling the pleasure of the play of knowledge.

Conclusion: Most in Awe

Several researchers have noted a split within secularism studies as a field.[174] On one side are scholars who are focused on *secularism* as a political ideology fixated on the management of religion, Taylor's secularism 1. Their work looks at how discourses of secularism govern religion, forcing it to conform to a set of fixed parameters. On the other are scholars interested in, to use Joseph Blankholm's term, *secular people*—the ways secularity produces communities and cultures, more like what Taylor calls *secularism 2* or *secularism 3*. Lois Lee, for instance, calls for a detailed account of the *substantial secular*: secularity not as a nullification but as a site of ongoing innovation and creativity.[175] When Berger tells us that "the University of Chicago is a more interesting topic for the sociology of religion than are the Islamic schools of Qom," this is what he has in mind.[176]

Both approaches share the understanding that there's something distinctive and interesting about formations of the secular. And each contributes to cogency theory. The former offers an entire library of studies of how our embodied dispositions mess together with our intellectual affects, producing racist and nationalist formations masquerading as sovereign reason. The latter proposes that rather than the clockwork advance of reason, secularisms are ways of living, emerging both after and alongside religion. This means there really are secular bodies, guided by alloys of feeling. Practices of knowledge production plug into these constellations of secular affects. As Ann Taves and Courtney Bender write, the secular "did not emerge as religion retreated, but rather stands alongside it with projects, ideals, and goals of its own."[177] Rather than being the purview of pure reason, a world of ideas drained of emotion, secularity is felt.

In all its forms, secularism washes over us, rewriting the parameters of how our bodies feel their way through the world. Thought—the play of ideas, concepts, reasons, and evidence—is emotionally alive, neither immune to the public domain nor detached from it. If formations of the secular have something to do with the reconfiguration of frames of knowledge, they have *everything* to do with changing how the world feels. That's disenchantment. Certain affective forms are nourished, cultivated, detailed, disciplined, refined to a level of sculptural precision. Others are left to wither and fall. Josephson-Storm writes that "we have never been disenchanted."[178] But really, the conclusion to draw is that *disenchantment*, for Weber, never meant emotional emptiness. It was a new channel of feeling-by-thinking.

The secular isn't just one thing. It's profoundly multiple, arriving from many directions and leading down many roads. Laud's remapping of Oxford, placing university and church in their own compartments, shows that secularism isn't just about suppressing or sidelining religion. A formation of separation can serve many purposes. (Plenty of individuals, organizations, and entities are eager to be classed as religion within a governing frame because of the legal, financial, or political advantages that follow that label.)[179] A religious body can be at the center of power in one formation of the secular and acutely disadvantaged in another. This means we need to focus not just on the top-down pressure of secularism as a mode of governing but also on its arterial, bottom-up structures.

These are the felt ways of navigating the world produced within secularism, including the way it organizes the pleasures of knowledge production. So secularization is not just a story of changing patterns of belief. At first the university's academic functions were seen as of a piece with its religious dimension. But over time, a process of fission separated the domains. Although this might look like a manifestly intellectual process, it was also about streaming *different affects* into different spheres, shunting the distinct emotional texture of disenchantment into its own walled garden. The intellectual affects that go along with science, critique, and even the disputations themselves are all in play in the ongoing settlement.

The goal of this chapter isn't to explain *why* this happens. But it reveals a common intuition we have, in Western modernities, about the divide between religious and secular cultures. The example of the University Church shows that when we intuitively divide the religious and the secular, we often lean on an implicit *emotional* classification: How does—or should—the secular feel? This isn't to say that there's an *essential* religious or secular emotion. There are no essentially religious or secular affects because there's no stable break between them. Yet it's telling that Laud's primary concern is to transform the sacred spaces under his care to shape a specific feeling tone—*most in awe*—and to rule other feelings out of bounds. The fluid boundaries of the map of secular and religious came to be drawn around new theaters of intellectual feeling.

4.
FEELING IS BELIEVING
THE TRIUNE BRAIN, MERE EXPOSURE, AND COGENCY

All animals feel *Wonder*, and many exhibit *Curiosity*.
—Darwin, *The Descent of Man*

Introduction: Your Secret Smile

In 2001, psychologists Piotr Winkielman and John Cacioppo wired some research subjects to an electromyograph (EMG)—a machine that measures facial muscle responses. They hooked up the EMG's sensors to each subject's cheek muscle (the zygomaticus major, for smiling) and brow muscle (the corrugator supercilii, for furrowing the brow). Previous studies had shown that emotional stimuli triggered tiny muscle responses—incipient facial expressions, like a smile or a furrowed brow—even when the face *appeared* still.[1] These aren't the better-known half-second *microexpressions* studied since the 1960s and made famous by the 2000s TV show *Lie to Me*.[2] These were responses *inside* the muscle, invisible to the naked eye. Only the EMG could pick them up.

Winkielman and Cacioppo were interested in what has been called the *mere exposure effect* (MEE), first experimentally documented by Robert Zajonc in the 1960s. The MEE is straightforward: time and again in experiments, subjects show a preference for things they recognize. New faces.

Unknown alphabets. Meaningless words. Abstract shapes. Ask them to evaluate how an otherwise neutral stimulus makes them feel and they consistently *prefer the ones they have seen before*—even just once, *even if they weren't aware they had seen it*. Scientists have long debated the implications of the MEE, with some insisting it's an affective response, others that it's no more than a change in cognitive processing speed.[3] Winkielman and Cacioppo wanted answers.

The scientists knew the MEE didn't need to be conscious. You could prime a subject for an MEE preference with an image (like an abstract shape) or a word flickered in their field of vision so fast it didn't register in their awareness. The subject would *still* prefer a matching target (a similar shape or word) displayed immediately afterward to a target they had no prime for.[4] Winkielman and Cacioppo built on this work, showing their subjects flickered priming images of sixteen milliseconds, followed, a few seconds later, by a target image of six hundred milliseconds. Sometimes the prime matched the target. This meant, as everyone in the debate agreed, that there would be an MEE present—nudging the subjects to *like* the primed target images just a little bit more. But was this an affective response, or strictly cognitive? This was where the EMG machine came in.

Winkielman and Cacioppo's gambit with facial muscle measurement paid off. In the main experiment group, they wrote, "the activity over the [cheek muscle] was greater when targets were preceded by matched primes rather than mismatched primes."[5] In other words, when subjects were shown an image they had seen before—even for a fraction of a second—a secret smile played across their faces. Winkielman and Cacioppo saw this as decisive evidence against the strictly cognitive interpretation of the MEE. They called their alternative explanation of the MEE data the *hedonic fluency* model, proposing that "processing ease is associated with positive affect."[6] Familiar visual information is pleasurable. They had documented something like the feeling of click.

This chapter explores links between psychology and cogency theory. This is a selective undertaking. There's a lot of psychological research that helps build the case against the thinking/feeling binary, not least Antonio Damasio's influential pop science book *Descartes' Error* (discussed below). Psychologists have already established an impressive consensus that the black monolith myth dividing human cognition from animal feeling is unsustainable. But even as psychology contributes to cogency theory, it also benefits from conversation with the humanities, in part because scientists so often unknowingly use the detritus of humanistic conversations—recycled into the backdrop of common sense—to organize their research. Arguably, *reason* and *emotion*, understood as autonomous categories, are just such leftovers.

The most thorough recent engagement with emotion psychology from the humanities has been Ruth Leys's 2017 volume *The Ascent of Affect*. Her book attempts to adjudicate some extraordinarily complicated debates within emotion psychology from the outside.[7] My effort here is much less ambitious. This chapter argues that many debates within psychology *already* take the basic stance of cogency theory as a given. Across the psychological sciences, affect and cognition are more and more often conceptualized as a seamless garment. This chapter sketches a consensus (not to say a unanimous opinion) found among these researchers. The consensus view is that thinking is affective. Cognition always rides a current of feeling.[8]

After a historical survey, the first half of this chapter examines why *affective neuroscientists* have found increasing cause to defend this conclusion. Research in neuroanatomy has pushed back on the mid-twentieth-century picture of the *triune brain* that claimed emotions were exclusively found in the so-called *limbic system* and cognition in the neocortex. Contemporary neuroanatomy models strike a delicate balance between brain interconnectivity and region or network specialization. Brain areas or networks seem to do certain things, but this topography doesn't map onto a reason/emotion split. This is visible in the influential *somatic marker hypothesis* of Antonio Damasio and his related concept of the *passion for reason*. Review articles surveying the field of neuroscience since the 2000s show just how widespread this rejection of the feeling/thinking binary has become.

At the same time, *experimental psychologists* working on the MEE have provided us with a set of tools for thinking about the big argument of cogency theory—how the feeling tone of information can lead us into error. As we'll see in the second half of this chapter, an ongoing series of studies on perception and familiarity have shown that perception is not a neutral sensory operation. Instead, perception itself is modified by the way we have learned to feel about the world, which in turn modifies our perceptions going forward. The MEE described above is an example of this. It's experimental evidence of click.

But rather than driving toward truth, this is click that replicates an idiosyncratic preference—a mechanism by which we *feel* more warmly toward features of the world we *recognize*, locking in existing ways of thinking and knowing, making them seem like level ground. The MEE gives us a conceptual framework for how the sedimentation of our experiences takes on a particular feeling tone. Pieces of information that click with our existing framework are more likely to be *felt to be true*—regardless of whether they actually help build good knowledge. It's part of why our opinions on things that we otherwise don't have a lot of knowledge about harden so rapidly: just a little bit of exposure makes something familiar feel right. In other words, the MEE is one channel by which the way we feel about the world messes together with other feelings—including, as some studies have shown, the felt dimension of racialization—to shape the contours of reason.

In keeping with Bruno Latour's call to understand how science is *made*, I've included as much detail as space allows to explain the setup and findings of these experiments, rather than just reporting the results.[9] I've stopped short, however, of getting into the full picture of quantitative statistical sampling carefully documented by the researchers whose work I'm summarizing. But it's important to point out that tendencies unearthed by experimental research are just that—tendencies—rather than one-to-one correlations.

Historical Approaches to Emotion and Cognition in Psychology

The relationship between emotion and cognition has been studied since the beginning of modern Western psychology in the mid-nineteenth century. Although Charles Darwin is primarily known for his contributions to evolutionary biology, his later books *The Descent of Man, and Selection in Relation to Sex* (1871) and *The Expression of the Emotions in Man and Animals* (1872) also made significant contributions to the young field of psychology. Specifically, Darwin was interested in showing that human cognition was continuous with the cognition of animals. This meant taking thought out of the realm of ethereal reason—the black monolith myth—and connecting it to feeling. In *Descent*, for instance, Darwin argued for continuity between the intellectual emotions of humans—wonder, curiosity—and those of nonhuman animals.[10]

In *Expression*, Darwin went even further. He approvingly cited the French psychologist Pierre Gratiolet's proclamation that "the senses, the imagination, and thought itself—elevated and abstract as we suppose it to be—cannot operate without arousing corresponding feeling."[11] But since Darwin's concern was with *expression*, he primarily focused on the facial display of emotions, including cognitive emotions like *meditation* and *reflection*. For Darwin, reflection literally appeared on the face. We see it on the forehead, which is smooth until the thinker "encounters some obstacle in his train of reasoning," causing it to furrow.[12] Similarly, Darwin believed that being "lost in thought" had a specific facial expression.[13] For Darwin, the fact that thinking presents on our faces showed that cognition is emotional.

William James's early essay "What Is an Emotion?" (1884), written about a decade after *Expression*, was explicit in its debt to Darwin.[14] James's objective was to explore the role of feeling in the psychophysiological system of the body.[15] Anticipating his essay "The Sentiment of Rationality" (discussed in chapter 1), James wrote that "concords of sounds, of colours, of lines, logical consistencies, teleological fitnesses, affect us with a pleasure that seems ingrained in the very form of the representation itself."[16] Education, he suggested, produces a specialized taste for this *intellectual feeling*.[17] "The 'marvels' of Science," James wrote, cater to the tastes of this highly refined intellectual-emotional palette—"'caviare' to the men in the laboratories."[18] Already, in this essay, James was sketching the relationship between the way the sentiment of rationality chases the feeling of click. His 1890 book *Principles of Psychology* went even further in exploring the necessity of emotional excitation for belief. "Speaking generally," he wrote, "the more a conceived object *excites* us, the more reality it has."[19]

In his 1919 volume *A Text-Book of Psychology*, Edward Bradford Titchener advanced James's view, writing that we "feel the difficulty of an objection, the truth of an argument, the nobility of a character, the sacredness of a belief."[20] Titchener was particularly interested in how this played out in the mechanism of recognition. He proposed a thought experiment in which, stepping onto a streetcar, you run your gaze up and down the gallery of faces in front of you. Seeing someone you recognize, you call out to them, approach them, and begin to chat. For Titchener, this is a specific cognitive feeling, what he called the *warm glow of recognition*. Its converse is a feeling of frustration when we do not encounter familiar things.[21] Like Polanyi half a century later, Titchener speculated that this evolved in early animal species to allow them to organize information in their environments into a gradient of value and risk.[22]

However, this rich attention to the interaction of affect and cognition in psychology was muted in the first half of the twentieth century with the rise of behaviorism as a research paradigm. Behaviorism set out to confine the data set of psychology to observable physical behavior, black-boxing the mental precincts as off-limits for research. As Dorothy Cheney and Robert Seyfarth write, this ramified into a divide between *methodological behaviorists* who saw behavior as the only scientifically measurable evidence in the study of animal organisms, and *radical behaviorists*, such as B. F. Skinner himself, for whom "thoughts, feelings, goals, and intentions played no role in the study of behavior because they did not, in fact, exist."[23] Both factions saw emotions as irrelevant to scientific inquiry—speculative phantasms dreamed up by earlier generations of unscientific psychologists to cover over their own failings.

With the ignition of the *cognitive revolution* in psychology, mental processes—including emotions—were back on the table as objects of study. As Noam Chomsky puts it, "Defining psychology as the science of behavior was like defining physics as the science of meter reading."[24] This set the stage for the reassertion of cognitive, neuropsychological, and affective paradigms, leading to a massive proliferation of research over the past half century.[25] These paradigms ground the research explored in the rest of this chapter, in both affective neuroscience and experimental psychology.[26]

Reintegrating the Triune Brain: Affective Neuroscience and Cogency

Neuroscience studies the brain's physical structure and operation. Though out of favor among researchers, the *triune brain* model created by twentieth-century neuroanatomist Paul MacLean is still one of the most widely known ways of thinking about brain structure. MacLean speculated that a brain region called the *limbic lobe* or *limbic system*—a set of structures in the medial region (the *limbus*, "rim") between the neocortex and the brainstem—directed the brain's sharply separate *streams* of thought and feeling.[27] His lasting impact came in formalizing this idea in an easy-to-remember diagram—the *triune brain*, first described in 1970. He divided the human brain into three parts. At the bottom, a *reptilian brain* surrounding the brainstem (so named because it was believed to be the sole brain component of nonmammalian vertebrates).[28] Above this, the *limbic system*, believed to be shared across mammalian species.[29] In MacLean's view, this was the primary brain system for nonhuman mammals. They had emotions, but not rationality. And crowning it all, the *neomammalian formation*, unique to humans, the seat of true cognition and reason. MacLean charted these borders by doing lesion experiments on a variety of animal species (monkeys, lizards, hamsters) in which their crania were opened up and parts of their brains destroyed with tools.[30] Then they were glued back together and their now-distorted behaviors studied.

MacLean developed his conceptual framework over the course of a long career, from the 1940s through the 1980s, culminating in a 1990 book, *The Triune Brain in Evolution*. This book offered the most sophisticated version of his theory, firmly engraving the divide between *emotion* (or *paleomentation*) and *thought* (or *rationality*), which he saw as emerging from "different cerebral mechanisms."[31] The reptilian brain was at work even in humans. He saw it in fads, mob violence, and "young people flocking to Woodstock [like] pigeons whose homing instinct had gone awry."[32] But the human task, according to MacLean, was to use the neomammalian brain to dominate the reptilian and emotional structures. We must, he insisted, become more fully human by "further domesticating [our] emotions" and so transcend the pitiable lives of the lesser animals—not least, one has to assume, the thousands of lesser animals mutilated and killed in his lab to provide the bedrock evidence of our moral superiority.[33]

MacLean's vocabulary had a defining impact on popular understanding of the brain, especially after authors like Arthur Koestler and Carl Sagan picked it up in the 1960s and 1970s. This is no doubt why terms like *reptilian brain* and *limbic system* still enjoy heavy trade today, applying a semiscientific polish to the idea of a brain-based emotion/reason split. It's a neurological translation of the black monolith myth. Even some academic studies in the humanities draw on it.[34] Lisa Feldman Barrett has called it a *zombie idea* that has hung on in popular language long after scientists dismissed it.[35] It sticks around, of course, because it so neatly replicates the commonsense reason/emotion binary.

But as early as the 1970s, scientists working on the brain were poking holes in MacLean's model. Neuroanatomists showed that so-called primitive animals had neocortical structures (and mental functions), even though they often were to be found in different places than corresponding features of the human brain.[36] Already, in the late 1970s, when MacLean hosted a conference on animal cognition and published the proceedings, he was pushing an idea that was contradicted by recent research on the intellectual powers of sharks and birds.[37] In 1983, Antonio Damasio and G. W. Van Hoesen reviewed the findings of this new line of research to decisively show that the stratification of brain function proposed by the triune brain model was wrong. Not only, they confirmed, does the limbic system in humans include components related to cognition—like memory and attention—but nonlimbic brain areas include emotional faculties.[38] Surveying the data, they questioned why the triune brain myth had held on for so long. "It is pertinent to ask at this point if there are any parts of the brain that are devoid of limbic system influence," they wrote, "and the answer seems decidedly negative."[39]

It wasn't just the *functional distinction* between the limbic system and other parts of the brain that didn't hold up. The *anatomical distinction* also failed. A. B. Butler, for instance, pointed out in 2009 that support for the triune brain model has completely collapsed among evolutionary comparativists.[40] The model badly short-changes the intellectual capacities of birds, which are evolutionarily similar to reptiles but cognitively on par with many mammals. This includes demonstrated capacities for forming conceptual categories (e.g., distinguishing cubist paintings from impressionist paintings); tool construction and cultural transmission of tool design; numeracy, including a zero-like concept; theory of mind; and complex nurturance behaviors toward their young.[41] These findings overturn MacLean's claim that we can localize *cognition* in a single catchment of the brain, seeing it instead as a complex of different mental functions only artificially rendered as a separate thing—*reason*. The cognition/emotion split promoted by MacLean—which has so successfully nested itself inside common sense—has to be abandoned. Rather than separate functional echelons, contemporary neuroscience presents a much more complex picture of brain function, in which cognition and emotion exist in a dynamic relationship.

Antonio Damasio's Somatic Marker Hypothesis and the Passion for Reason

This leads directly into cogency theory. And Damasio himself has been one of the most prominent contributors arguing for a turn away from the thinking/feeling binary. Much of his work was conducted with subjects who had experienced destructive brain injuries, such as a patient known as E.V.R. whose case was explored in several publications by Damasio and his colleagues. E.V.R. presented a paradox. Having suffered damage in his ventromedial prefrontal cortex (vmPFC) during surgery at age thirty-five, E.V.R. was exhibiting self-destructive behavior patterns.[42] But laboratory investigation of his cognitive capabilities using a range of memory, intellect, and other standard cognitive aptitude tests detected *no* impairment. In fact, he was cognitively exceptional, often testing in the top percentile.

Not only that, he was fully capable of *describing* the outcomes of (self-destructive) social behavior when asked.[43] The problem was that he didn't act accordingly. But not only was there no label for the physiopathology E.V.R. was exhibiting, the team noted, there was also no reliable way of testing or measuring it. The standard cognitive tests turned up nothing out of the ordinary.[44] This led the team to develop an unusual experiment designed to simulate ordinary decision-making, allowing them to isolate and measure its cognitive and emotional dimensions. This was the Iowa gambling task (IGT).

The IGT started with subjects facing four decks of cards. They were given a fund of play money to gamble with. In every turn of the game, the subject was asked to turn over a card from one of the four decks. The card awarded them a certain amount of money, but some cards also exacted a high-dollar penalty.[45] The game ended after one hundred draws and the players' remaining funds were tallied. The twist was that the decks were not identical. In decks A and B, the *penalties would exceed the awards* over time. Decks C and D had *lower* payoffs but *lighter* penalties, making them more profitable in the long run. As the researchers wrote, "It is not possible for subjects to perform an exact calculation of the net gains or losses generated from each deck as they play."[46] In essence, the experiment was designed to *control cognition as a variable* by providing a framework within which subjects were forced to make *noncognitive* decisions. It simulated the dynamism of ordinary decision-making.

The first IGT trials involved seven subjects with frontal lobe damage (including patient E.V.R.), forty-four control subjects without brain injuries, and nine control subjects with lesions in areas of the brain other than the frontal lobes. The results were consistent: all the control subjects began by sampling from all four decks, but after a few rounds, slid into a strategy of drawing almost exclusively from the smart decks C and D. E.V.R. and the other frontal lobe–damaged subjects did the opposite. They started off in the same manner, sampling from all four decks, but eventually started spending the most time with decks A and B, losing money overall when the task ended.[47]

Remember: E.V.R. was on par with the control groups across the usual cognitive tests. In interviews, he was able to articulate clearly what the outcomes of his actions would be. But E.V.R. would act recklessly regardless. The problem, the team concluded, was that the outcomes projected in his mind "would not be *marked* with a negative or positive value, and thus could not be easily rejected or accepted."[48] E.V.R. *knew* the consequences, but he could only dimly *feel* their impact. This, they conjectured, had something to do with his dismal performance on the IGT.

The team explained this using Damasio's *somatic marker hypothesis* (SMH), first put forward in another article about E.V.R. a few years previously.[49] According to the SMH, *cognition by itself is incapable of making decisions*. Much as Hume argued that reason can't act without consulting feeling, Damasio suggested that rationality on its own can't make decisions in response to information. Instead, we need to have attributions of *value* placed on pieces of information in order to compare and select between them. This happens through the body. Somatic markers, Damasio suggests, would not necessarily be *consciously felt*, but "they would still act covertly to highlight, in the form of an attentional mechanism, certain components over others, and to direct, in effect, the go, stop, and turn signals necessary for much decision making and planning on even the most abstract of topics."[50] The ongoing affective dynamic created by the interaction of these markers is one way of understanding the key players in the agonism of thought. Without this churn of feelings, reason is inert. E.V.R.'s cognitive capacities were like a building on a Hollywood movie set. The facade, propped up on a beam, looked great. But the interior was a vacant lot.

These articles became the on-ramp to Damasio's best-selling 1994 volume *Descartes' Error*. Damasio used this book to interpret his findings more broadly. The book begins with a dramatic account of the experience of talking to E.V.R., who was cognitively pristine but whose day-to-day decision-making was a spiral of self-destruction. The only possible conclusion, Damasio wrote, was that "feeling was an integral component of the machinery of reason."[51] Emotions and feelings, he proposed, are "enmeshed in [reason's] networks, for worse *and* for better."[52] Emotions "are not just messy toddlers in a china shop, running around breaking and obscuring delicate cognitive glassware," Damasio's protégé Mary Helen Immordino-Yang wrote a few years later. "Instead, they are more like the shelves underlying the glassware; without them cognition has less support."[53] Without feeling, thinking never gets off the ground.

In the book's final chapter, Damasio went even further, exploring the correlation between thought and pleasure. We are "possessed by *a passion for reason*," he wrote, "a drive that originates in the brain core, permeates other levels of the nervous system, and emerges as either feelings or nonconscious biases to guide decision-making."[54] Emotion and cognition are a single stream, flowing from the same neural location or network. Damage to that network can shut down the whole system, leading to patients paralyzed not by disruption of motor circuitry but by indifference.[55] Tomkins wrote that the zeroing out of interest would be just as fatal to thought as severe brain damage.[56] Damasio points out that these can be co-occurring afflictions.

Damasio continued exploring the *passion for reason* in his 1999 book *The Feeling of What Happens*. Like Polanyi and Titchener, he pointed out that the basic operating system of animal life is a distinction between aversive and attractive stimuli—marked by pain and pleasure. We see this in a simple sea anemone, alternately opening and contracting its body to receive or rebuff material in its environment.[57] This affective nucleus, Damasio contended, is the emotional infrastructure of what, in more advanced animal organisms, we call cognition.[58] A little further up the scale of neurological complexity we find animals increasingly expressing excitement as they search their environments. The passion for reason emerges from this matrix of interest.[59]

Writing concurrently with Damasio, another affective neuroscientist, Jaak Panksepp, also explored the pleasure dimension of thinking. Panksepp insisted (like Damasio and Tomkins) that "the cognitive apparatus would collapse if our underlying emotional value systems were destroyed."[60] But Panksepp went into more detail about the neurological grounding for the passion of reason. What he called the SEEKING system is an affective engine located in the brains of mammals. It leads to "persistent feelings of interest, curiosity, sensation seeking, and, in the presence of a sufficiently complex cortex, the search for higher meaning."[61] Animals needed to evolve this emotional structure to push them to learn about threats and resources in their environments. (Think of how your domestic mammals eagerly sniff around the corners and crannies when they come to a new place.) It's affectively isomorphic with the high of cocaine or amphetamines—substances that artificially stimulate SEEKING behavior in mammals.[62]

Damasio and his collaborators also set their gambling task for neurotypical subjects.[63] In a 1997 article, for instance, they administered the IGT to both vmPFC-damaged patients and control groups, but with a twist. This time, they attached electrodes to their subjects' hands to test skin conductance response (SCR), which measures emotional arousal by gauging moisture—quantifying the sweat on our palms when we're nervous or excited. They also asked the participants to periodically describe what they thought was going on. Their findings were startling. The vmPFC-damaged subjects continued to perform badly on the task and generated no SCRs. But the neurotypical subjects developed a pattern of SCR responses *before* drawing cards from the bad decks—even after only two penalizing card draws.

The non-neurodamaged subjects eventually developed a behaviorally appropriate response. They figured out how to work the decks (much as the control group did in the earlier experiment). But the right strategy—and the SCRs—kicked in *before* they were able to articulate an awareness of what was happening.[64] The team concluded that the transition to full conceptual awareness *lagged behind* playing the game well. Even the handful of subjects in their group who never reached the full conceptual phase still developed advantageous play strategies.[65] In other words, the non-vmPFC-damaged subjects felt their way to the right strategy *before* they knew what the strategy was. Thought was an afterthought.[66]

Here the scientific debate picked up. This was because these findings—both the SCR results and the question of how far the behavioral response runs ahead of conceptualization—produced mixed replication responses throughout the 2000s. Tiago Maia and James McClelland, for instance, asked their subjects a much more detailed set of questions during in-game interviews. They found both better conceptual awareness as soon as an advantageous strategy had been locked in *and* a much quicker arrival at the conceptual stage. This contradicted the 1997 study.[67] But in a variation of the experiment from a team led by Navindra Persaud, participants were asked to place bets on whether they were choosing from a good deck or a bad deck as a different way of measuring their awareness, with a finding that smart betting substantially lagged behind smart deck selection.[68] Helen Steingroever and colleagues suggested that there should be much more attention to healthy subjects and their response to the IGT. Their findings were that healthy subjects performed much *worse* than Damasio's team had found.[69] There were reports of subjects never developing full conceptual knowledge of the game yet playing it well. Other subjects declared that they understood the game, but still played it badly.[70] Similarly, there seemed to be a consistent subgroup (often in the 20 percent range) of subjects who, although perfectly healthy, *never* learned the game well.[71]

The IGT was designed to simulate a live-fire decision-making and learning exercise to control for cognition. It sought to eliminate cognition as a variable and directly measure the noncognitive dimension of decision-making. But maybe cognition is hard to control for precisely because it *isn't separate from emotion*. The processes just aren't divisible. Instead, what gets called *emotion* and *cognition* are two-dimensional facades, abstract renderings of a three-dimensional process. At the micro-level, the elements of mind are *feelings*, rather than *thoughts*; thinking always has to be carried by feeling.[72]

Three Reviews of Neuroscientific Emotion-Cognition Research

Damasio's work helped establish the correlation of feeling and cognition within affective neuroscience in the 1990s and 2000s. But a series of review articles published in the 2000s highlight how the elimination of the reason/emotion binary emerged as a consensus within neuropsychology. These reviews show ongoing debates about the extent of localization versus generalization of function within the brain and the roles of different structures. By this point, though, all these debates take it for granted that emotion and cognition are inseparable.

Let's start with a 2006 review article from psychologist Elizabeth Phelps. She focuses on the relationship between emotion and cognition as revealed by studies of the amygdala. As Phelps points out, the amygdala is an excellent candidate for thinking about this connection not because it serves a single function—as the triune brain model had it—but because it acts as a nexus linking other brain regions.[73] Phelps identifies five areas where the amygdala highlights a link between emotion and cognition: emotional learning; emotion and memory; emotion's influence on attention/perception; emotion-processing in social stimuli; and cognitive ways of modulating emotional responses.

In terms of *emotional learning*, Phelps reviews studies on the inculcation of learned terror responses, which show that we can both *know* and *fear* at the same time.[74] At the level of *memory*, she notes that emotion enhances episodic memory during encoding, consolidation, and dictating *where attention goes*.[75] Just as Tomkins saw *interest* as necessary to guide what enters the stream of our attention from our whole perceptual field, emotion's shaping influence on *attention and perception* is well established, going back to the *cocktail party effect* first described in 1953. Animals selectively filter the field of information in their environments by focusing on an emotionally salient piece of information—like how overhearing your name spoken a few feet away at a cocktail party steals your attention.[76] The amygdala's high connectivity with sensory regions makes it a contact zone between emotion and perception.[77] Phelps concludes that the "mechanisms of emotion and cognition are intertwined from early perception to complex reasoning."[78]

In a 2007 review article, Seth Duncan and Lisa Feldman Barrett turn to the theoretical problem of the cognition/emotion split. Based on a review of neuroanatomical and neuroimaging studies, they argue that "no brain areas can be designated specifically as 'cognitive' or 'affective.'"[79] Evidence of subcortical regions *regulated* by prefrontal regions, they argue, shouldn't be misconstrued as cognitive structures *controlling* affects. Instead, they suggest, "affect is instantiated by a widely distributed, functional network that includes both subcortical regions (typically called 'affective') and anterior frontal regions (traditionally called 'cognitive')."[80] The so-called cognitive regions are necessary for affect; the affective regions are indispensable for cognition.

Their argument rests on the concept of *core affect*—the idea that the body-brain system is mediated by a continuous transmission of shifting affective signals. Core affect is our operating system, a real-time, sensitive system for assessing a body's relationship to the surrounding environment.[81] It enables the body to signal to itself how its needs and priorities are being satisfied or defeated by its environment. Core affect directs our feelings. But it's also the foundation of lots of different forms of thinking. Although we "experience core affective feelings as phenomenologically distinct from thoughts and memories," they write, "the circuitry that implements core affect serves as a core feature of cognitive processing in the human brain."[82]

Rather than a hierarchical arrangement of *cognition* over *emotion*, the studies they review suggest that *different configurations* of core affect define the whole sweep of the mind's features.[83] "Since all objects and events have somatovisceral consequences, cognitive and sensory experiences are necessarily affectively infused to some degree," they write. "There is no such thing as a 'non-affective thought.'"[84] This is why, rather than a domination of feeling by reason in learning and discovery, all cognitive operations result from agonism between different emotional channels. Core affect is the arena of agonism. "Any thought or action can be said to be more or less affectively infused," Duncan and Barrett write, "so that there is no ontological distinction between, say, affective and non-affective behaviours, or between 'hot' and 'cold' cognitions."[85] Or, put another way, there may well be *hot* and *cold* cognitions, but—as Hume had realized two centuries earlier—both are essentially emotional.

Finally, in "On the Relationship between Emotion and Cognition," a 2008 review article, Luiz Pessoa makes a parallel case, but with a more specific focus on neuroanatomy. "Parceling the brain into cognitive and affective regions is inherently problematic, and ultimately untenable," he writes, because "cognition and emotion are integrated in the brain."[86] The triune brain model stratified the brain into divergent functions. But neuroanatomical research of the past few decades, as we've seen, sharply contradicts this picture. Rather than the old model of highly localized functionality—the phrenologists' dream—Pessoa points out that in our new understanding of brain connectivity, synaptic connections jostle together much more tightly.[87] This means that brain regions don't correspond to specific functions in a *one-to-one* mapping relationship. Pessoa proposes *many-to-many* mapping: different networks within the brain exhibit multiple functional profiles, typically in collaboration with other networks.[88] The brain is actually controlled by "large-scale integration mechanisms" rather than a single stratum perched atop all the rest.[89]

Based on this remapping of the brain as primarily organized by its connections, rather than its divisions, Pessoa insists that "there are no truly separate systems for emotion and cognition because complex cognitive-emotional behavior emerges from the rich, dynamic interactions between brain networks."[90] This is exactly why *affect* and *cognition* have proven so difficult to define in the psychological literature: the affective systems are sunk so deep in the brain that they are functionally *everywhere*.[91] From the perceiving brain's initial process of determining what matters all the way down the line to the body's final behavioral output, the affective/cognitive stream is a unity.[92] The brain's operating system *is* affect. Thought is the effluvium of the core dynamic of feeling.

These reviews point to the neuroscientific consensus in the wake of the post-1990s interest in the affect-cognition relationship. They diagram how an affective account of cognition and decision-making has become dominant in so many branches of psychology. Emotions researcher Richard Davidson identifies the supposition that affect and cognition are neurobiologically distinct as the first on his list of the "seven deadly sins" of emotion science.[93] In moral psychology, the link between *moral reasoning* and *moral feeling* is now a central research paradigm.[94] As Jonathan Haidt wrote in his 2012 book *The Righteous Mind*, his early research was derailed by his failure to see over the "prevalent but useless dichotomy between cognition and emotion. After failing repeatedly to get cognition to act independently of emotion," he continues, he "began to realize that the dichotomy made no sense."[95] Haidt describes how reading Damasio led him to embrace Hume's understanding of rationality as completely dependent on feeling.

This consensus about the emotional foundation of cognition even straddles one of the big debates in contemporary psychology—the dispute around the status of Basic Emotions. Psychologists remain divided about whether the brain brings with it a set of distinct emotional states or whether the emotions we feel are constructed by cultural learning. Panksepp would be typical of the former approach, Barrett of the latter.[96] Barrett may be skeptical, for instance, of Panksepp's proposal that there is a distinct SEEKING system hardwired in the brain.[97] But all the same, Barrett proposes that affect has two dimensions—*valence* (pleasantness or unpleasantness) and *arousal*. Arousal means the "energized feeling of anticipating good news."[98] Whether we understand this as a freestanding affect system or as a more fluid mental property, the result is the same. Both posit the existence of a structure of anticipation that pleasurably pursues knowledge about the world. "Affect is in the driver's seat," Barrett writes, "and rationality is a passenger."[99] With the collapse of the triune brain paradigm, seeing cognition as *cogency*—a dynamic directed by interacting feelings rather than abstract reason—has broad currency across the brain-mind sciences.

The Mere Exposure Effect: Perspectives from Experimental Psychology

Neuroscience shines a light on the little argument of this book. Neuroscientists have largely concluded that rationality and emotionality are facets of a single three-dimensional structure. Thinking feels—without exception. A *conceptual* divide between cognition and affect may sometimes be useful, but cognition never transcends the parameters set by feeling. Damasio's *passion for reason* is the feeling of click—the pleasure we feel when information in the world falls into place.

What about the big argument? Can psychology illuminate the way knowledge makes up a landscape that we navigate by feeling, a landscape on which what *seems* true is what *feels* true—which includes not only the *passion for reason* but also other affective preferences and priorities messing together with our cognitive feelings? The rest of this chapter considers research in experimental psychology on the mere exposure effect. Studies of the MEE flesh out how experience transforms the way knowledge feels, shaping our patterns of reasoning going forward.

In 1968, Robert Zajonc set out to better understand the relationship between familiarity and preference. He was inspired by earlier, informal observations that exposure leads to liking.[100] Zajonc wanted to study this scientifically. In his first experiment, he presented his participants with a series of seven-letter words (like *iktitaf* and *afworbu*), which they were told were Turkish. He asked the subjects to pronounce a selection of these words, sometimes more than once. After this exercise, they had to guess what the words might mean. Instead of asking for an exact definition, however, the experimenter had them guess how *good or bad* the word meanings were on a seven-point scale. *Furious* would be a seven, for instance, while *lovely* would be a one. So what was *iktitaf*? Zajonc discovered that by increasing the number of times subjects were exposed to words, he could *increase their felt sense of how positive the words were*. Every single one of the twelve words was judged to have a more positive meaning as long as it was encountered more than once.[101]

Next, Zajonc rebuilt the exercise. He swapped out pronouncing nonsense words with flipping through a series of made-up Chinese characters. Then he did the same with unfamiliar faces from the yearbook of a nearby university. In each version of the experiment, he found preference for characters or portraits that had been encountered before.[102] He even redid the experiment measuring SCR (rather than relying on reported preference) and found he could directly modify SCR by increasing familiarity with an unknown word.[103] They say familiarity breeds contempt. Zajonc found the opposite. Familiarity *bonded* subjects to the things they encountered in their environment.

Zajonc called his new theory the *exposure-attitude hypothesis*, but later renamed it the *mere exposure effect*.[104] In simple terms, it suggested that our initial exposure to a new stimulus changes how we feel about it. Exposure fashions our dispositions into preferences. When we reapprehend an object through cognitive channels like recollection or recognition, the affective infrastructure is already there. This is probably not an unlimited process—we eventually reach a point of what Zajonc calls *semantic satiation*, after which exposure reduces preference.[105] But Zajonc pointed out that even the seemingly contradictory evidence of subjects (human or animal) preferring a novel stimulus to a familiar stimulus doesn't overturn his theory: "It is more likely," he proposed, "that orienting toward a novel stimulus in preference to a familiar one may indicate that it is *less liked* rather than it is *better liked*."[106]

The Zajonc-Lazarus Debate

Zajonc's research into the MEE was the prompt for one of the most famous debates in psychology of the past half century, the back-and-forth between Zajonc and Richard Lazarus about whether affect was *prior* to cognition, or simply indissociable from it. What's critical to note here is that, already by the early 1980s, affect had become so central to cognitive psychology that the issue at stake was not *whether* cognition was separate from emotion, but *how far emotion goes in determining cognition*. Zajonc's position was that emotion and cognition were separate. But he affirmed this as a way of asserting emotion's *priority* over cognition.

In his opening salvo from 1979, "Feeling and Thinking: Preferences Need No Inferences," Zajonc began by attacking the vestiges of cognitivism in psychology. Modern psychology still, he contended, too often started from the assumption that the chain of a mental process runs from a *sensation* to a *cognition* to a *feeling* based on cognitive assessment. Objects, in this view, "must be cognized before they can be evaluated."[107] Zajonc proposed the opposite: cognition is always *enveloped in evaluation*. "There are probably very few perceptions and cognitions in everyday life that do not have a significant affective component," he wrote, before continuing:

> We do not just see "a house": we see "a *handsome* house," "an *ugly* house," or "a *pretentious* house." We do not just read an article on attitude change, on cognitive dissonance, or on herbicides. We read an "exciting" article on attitude change, an "important" article on cognitive dissonance, or a "trivial" article on herbicides. And the same goes for a sunset, a lightning flash, a flower, a dimple, a hangnail, a cockroach, the taste of quinine, Saumur, the color of earth in Umbria, the sound of traffic on 42nd Street, and equally for the sound of a 1000-Hz tone and the sight of the letter Q.[108]

Just like the neuroscientists reviewed above, Zajonc was convinced that affect comes first, providing the coordinates within which our thoughts and responses unfold—the pushes and pulls of feeling that make up the agonism of our minds.[109] Even the most seemingly insignificant mental object—a letter, number, or musical tone—had a micro-hit of feeling. As Zajonc noted, this all lined up neatly with Hume's claim that reason is at the disposal of the passions.[110] The MEE—now replicated many times in subsequent studies—was a major component of Zajonc's evidence for his broader theoretical claim.

But Zajonc's closing arguments for a *rigorously* separate cognitive system ultimately rested on a semantic idiosyncrasy.[111] After having stated that "in nearly all cases ... feeling is not free of thought, nor is thought free of feelings," he identified certain extremely specific laboratory conditions—all involving strategic use of *distraction*—as evidence of the possibility of feelings divorced from thought.[112] Zajonc's definition of *cognition* was something like *conscious awareness*. That's exactly why it could be experimentally isolated by adding distractions to the laboratory setup.[113] His overarching point was that "affect is *always* present as a companion to thought, whereas the converse is not true for cognition."[114] All thinking feels; not all feeling thinks.

The narrowness of Zajonc's working definition of *cognition* (really more like *consciousness*) was a major fulcrum of the debate that followed. In his 1982 response, Lazarus began by identifying two areas where he and Zajonc differed: first, that Zajonc assumed that affect determines cognition; and second, that Zajonc saw cognition and emotion as "relatively independent subsystems" rather than, in Lazarus's view, "as fused and highly interdependent." Lazarus suggested that Zajonc's mistake was defining cognition using the outdated *computationalist* approach to information processing.[115] It was this misbegotten concept of cognition, Lazarus argued, that prompted Zajonc to draw a hard distinction between cognition and emotion. Zajonc's response a few years later was complex.[116] He acknowledged that the disagreement was rooted in definitions, but insisted that his definition of cognition could be proven experimentally. His evidence for this was neuroanatomical—an appeal to triune-brain-style research showing an autonomous limbic system.[117] But he also doubled down on a definition of cognition as a consciously discriminated stimulus.

What matters for our purposes is that the debate between Zajonc and Lazarus was actually over a narrow issue of the definition of *cognition*. Throughout the exchange, they were on the same page that, in Lazarus's words, "cognition and emotion are usually fused in nature."[118] Writing in 2007, Dutch psychologists Mark Rotteveel and Hans Phaf agree that the issue all along was a *conscious-nonconscious* distinction rather than an *affect-cognition* distinction.[119] Justin Storbeck and Gerald Clore arrive at the same conclusion.[120] "The concepts of 'cognition' and 'emotion,'" they write, "are, after all, simply abstractions for two aspects of one brain in the service of action."[121]

When we look at Lazarus and Zajonc's dispute about interpreting MEE, we see a debate where the two sides fundamentally agree about the main point of cogency theory. Affect, for all concerned, is the necessary infrastructure of cognition. Quibbling about the relationship between *cognition* and *consciousness* aside, this is a debate in which the background contours already align with the big argument of cogency theory. No one involved would disagree that every thought is enmeshed with feeling.

Recent Studies on the Mere Exposure Effect: The Feeling of Familiarity and Racial Bias

The debate about the extent to which feeling shapes cognition also sheds light on the big argument of this book. What is cogent for us is what *feels true*. But this feeling is not necessarily a reliable guide. The MEE shows that we harbor preferences based on familiarity. The landscape of what we call rationality is built, in part, by the sedimentation of these preferences. Things that feel true to us are based on this mostly arbitrary topography. Cogency is an effect of these dispositions messing together. To flesh this out, I want to look at three series of experiments studying the MEE's relationship to cognition in more detail. The first two consider the affective dimensions of recognition and cognitive processing; the third connects MEE research to the affective dimension of racialized reason. These experiments build on each other, so even though I'm going to describe the whole series, the most important experiments for our purposes come toward the end.

Series 1: Jacoby and Whitehouse; Phaf and Rotteveel

In a 1989 study, Larry Jacoby and Kevin Whitehouse set up a new experiment to better understand the MEE. Their interest was the *warm glow of familiarity* described by Titchener way back in the 1910s. They wanted to see if they could, in essence, reverse engineer the warm glow. If you *simulate the feeling* using the positive response generated by the MEE, does it trigger recognition? It was basically an effort to trick the brain into thinking a certain way by faking a feeling. The experiment began with a study list, a long sheet of words that subjects were asked to memorize. Then followed a recognition test. During the test, they had subjects indicate whether the word was *old* (from the study list) or *new* (not on the list). What subjects didn't know was that during the test, which was carried out on a computer, a word was briefly flashed on-screen—too fast to register—immediately before the target word was displayed. As with the Winkielman and Cacioppo study discussed at the outset of this chapter, this word was sometimes matched to the test word, sometimes mismatched. The researchers measured *how long it took* for subjects to decide whether a word was *old* (studied) or *new* (unseen).

Their results showed that subjects were "faster in correctly calling a test word 'old' when that test word was preceded by a matching context word (977 ms) rather than by either a nonmatching context word (1,083 ms) or no context word (1,115 ms)."[122] So the *warm glow of recognition*—simulated by the MEE—slightly sped up the subjects' capacity to recognize an old word. The hypothesis was that a matching word would create *fluency of processing* and a *feeling of familiarity*, but a mismatched word would *disrupt* processing and so prompt a *feeling of strangeness*.[123] In other words, the cognitive assessment of a word as old (studied from the list) or new (never seen before) was nudged along by a quantum of positive feeling based on having just seen a matched or mismatched word. Rather than memory operating as a standalone cognitive faculty, the affective halo surrounding the words shaped and guided it.[124]

This experiment was important, but even more suggestive for cogency are the experiments inspired by it later on. Fifteen years on, Hans Phaf and Mark Rotteveel took the same idea further. Like Jacoby and Whitehouse, they wanted to measure the effect that an affective halo would have on a cognitive operation. But they set up the experiment differently. First, they changed the affect-inducing mechanism. Instead of using MEE priming with a flickered word, they built on earlier work that showed that artificially inducing a facial expression could hot-wire an affective response. Getting a subject to smile—for instance, by holding a pen between their teeth—made them respond in a happier way to a cartoon; getting them to frown—by holding a pen between their lips—made them peevish.[125] Phaf and Rotteveel had some subjects clamp a coffee stirrer between their teeth, while others furrowed their brow. Then they went through the word-list study/word-recognition test devised by Jacoby and Whitehouse.

And instead of measuring speed, Phaf and Rotteveel measured accuracy. They wanted to see if the *cognitive* operation of assessing whether a word was old (studied) or new (unseen) was influenced by feeling. They weren't interested in whether the prime made their subjects smarter, as Jacoby and Whitehouse were; if anything, it was the opposite. They were interested in whether the prime would lead to *mistakes*—to false positives. Sure enough, that's what happened.[126] Forced-smile subjects were significantly more likely to assess a word they were shown in the test as old (studied)—which meant more false positives in which they incorrectly identified a new word as old. Like Jacoby and Whitehouse, they concluded cognitive operations were being shaped by feelings. The forced smile juiced up the warm glow of familiarity, leading to subjects making errors of recognition.

Their interpretation of this was that the *feeling of processing fluency*, the *feeling of familiarity*, and the *cognitive operation of recognition* were all part of a single interwoven—and fundamentally affective—dynamic.[127] Another experiment a few years later corroborated this. Once again, Phaf and Rotteveel sought to use affective nudges to shape performance on a word-recognition task. But this time they maxed out the affective atmospherics. Instead of tricking them into smiles and frowns, they primed their subjects by playing videos to induce mood states directly. The different groups watched a few minutes from either the horror film *The Ring* or the American sitcom *Friends*. Phaf and Rotteveel then piped the soundtrack from either *Friends* or Alfred Hitchcock's *Psycho* into the test room for good measure.

And there was another twist: this time, the word-study list was a sham. *None* of the words on the test had been presented in the study list. *Every* response that a word was old (studied) was a false positive. Sure enough, the happy group who got to watch *Friends* were more likely to mistake the words on the screen for words they had already seen than the terrorized group.[128] Feeling good made people more likely to mistake something as familiar. "The mood-inducing capability of non-affective instructions and the mood effects on non-affective material," Rotteveel and Phaf wrote, "could illustrate further that affective and 'cognitive' processes are so closely interwoven that they cannot really be distinguished."[129] This conclusion lines up nicely with a more recent study by Sandra Ladd and John Gabrieli showing that subjects reporting higher degrees of anxiety (as in, those who always had the soundtrack from *Psycho* running in their minds) were *less likely* to demonstrate a strong MEE.[130] They just weren't feeling it.

Series 2: Whittlesea; Reber et al.; Winkielman and Cacioppo; Monin

Another series of experiments on the MEE showed a similar messing together of feeling and thinking. In a 1993 article titled "Illusions of Familiarity," Bruce Whittlesea drew on the Jacoby team's finding that the warm glow of familiarity could be simulated with unrelated positive stimuli.[131] Whittlesea built five experiments to induce the feeling of familiarity and study its effect on cognition. Each of the first four experiments had subjects identifying a word, but they manipulated the predictability of the word.

For instance, in experiment 2, the subjects were shown a series of seven words on a computer screen (basically a study list), then a target word, and asked if the target word was from the list. But in between—before being shown the target word—they were shown an incomplete sentence (like *The stormy seas tossed the* _____). Sometimes, the target word was a neat fit to finish the sentence (*The stormy seas tossed the* BOAT) and sometimes not (*He saved up his money and bought a* BOAT).

The predictive sentences led to more false alarms, in which the target word was (incorrectly) identified as old (studied).[132] Whittlesea summarized the finding of his first four experiments like this: "One will feel that the meaning of an event is familiar if its meaning is easily arrived at, regardless of the source of the ease, and one will feel that the event itself is familiar if either its meaning or its formal properties are easily processed."[133] In other words, a *neat fit* with the leading sentence nudged the subjects to find the word familiar. The cognitive operation—memory recognition—was quickened by the feeling of processing fluency.[134] Whittlesea was able to doctor a simulated MEE using the felt click of a word with a sentence.

Whittlesea's fifth experiment added a simple twist. Before being asked to identify whether a word (using the same finish-the-sentence procedure) was new or previously seen, the subjects were asked to rate whether the word was *pleasant* or *neutral*. The words that slotted in with predictive sentences were found to be more pleasant than words that came at the end of nonpredictive sentences.[135] With this setup, in other words, Whittlesea produced direct experimental evidence for click. The processing fluency effect created by a predictive sentence and a matched finishing word was not only thought but felt. The click of a word in a just-right sentence radiated pleasure.

Whittlesea's fifth experiment became the basis for a follow-up study by Rolf Reber and colleagues. Once again, they worked with the MEE. They showed their research subjects a series of twenty drawings of neutral objects like a horse or airplane. But immediately before each image, a *contour* of an image was shown for twenty-five milliseconds—too rapidly to be consciously detected.[136] This flickered contour was either a match for the target picture (matching prime) or a mismatch. After seeing the target image, the subjects were asked to rate the target images based on how beautiful they were. Reber and his colleagues found that a matching prime—a spectral outline of the image the subject was about to see—reliably inclined the subjects to assess the target images as *more attractive* than those preceded by mismatching primes. The familiarity induced by a matching prime, even an undetected one, made the pictures prettier.[137]

So this was a straightforward replication of Zajonc's MEE study. Familiarity led to preference. But in a follow-up experiment, they reran the first experiment with longer presentation times on the images of the everyday objects. Once again asking the subjects to rate the images for preference, they found that longer exposure times to the images marginally improved their ratings. Reber and colleagues evaluated these results along the same lines as Whittlesea had interpreted his findings in experiment 5: "Perceptual fluency is affectively positive, rather than neutral."[138] The Winkielman and Cacioppo experiment described at the outset of this chapter—in which primes produced the ghost of a smile—built directly on Whittlesea's and Reber's team's findings.[139] What they all point to is *hedonic fluency*. The *easier something is to think*, the more pleasant it feels. It's a synonym for click—the pleasure we feel when information falls neatly into place.

Benoît Monin's research—also developing Whittlesea's findings—provided further support for hedonic fluency. Monin, too, was interested in how you could change thinking by changing feeling. His method was to provide his research subjects with a set of faces taken from university yearbooks and have them evaluate them according to several indexes, including *attractiveness, familiarity*, and *distinctiveness*. What he found was that faces that were thought to be *familiar* were also felt to be *attractive*. This replicated an earlier study that had shown a high correlation of familiarity and attractiveness.[140]

Monin then took the collection of faces from the first experiment and divided it in half. One half became the study list of a second experiment. As in the Jacoby-Whitehouse study, he showed his subjects the complete collection of faces (of which they had studied half) and had them assess whether they were *old* (studied) or *new* (previously unseen). He found a highly significant correlation between the more attractive faces and a tendency to rate them—wrongly—as having been seen before.[141]

Monin's conclusion, like all the MEE studies we've looked at, was that "affective–evaluative reactions ('Do I like X?') are used to make judgments that are on the surface unconnected to affect (e.g., 'Have I seen X before?')."[142] Thinking buds from feeling. Building on Whittlesea's finding that perceptual fluency is interpreted as familiarity, he stated that our affective reaction to a stimulus is part of the field that dictates our cognitive assessment—for instance, by asking if we've seen it before. "In short," he concluded, "the old pickup line 'Haven't we met before?' may sometimes be the good-faith result of a cognitive heuristic gone awry rather than the calculated ruse of a lounge Casanova."[143] Invoking Titchener, he called this effect the *warm glow heuristic*.[144] The cognitive operation (recognition) unfurls from the feeling (attraction).

Series 3: Race and the MEE

As an immigrant to the United States whose parents were killed by Nazis, Zajonc was acutely sensitive to the implications of the MEE for thinking about racism. He linked his initial findings to social psychology research on race, suggesting in his 1968 study that more mixing between groups could diminish racial animosity.[145] Though simplistic, this proposal has been borne out by experimental evidence in twenty-first-century studies. Social psychologist Leslie Zebrowitz and her collaborators have put forward data supporting what they call the familiar face overgeneralization (FFO) hypothesis, which proposes that "racial prejudice derives in part from negative reactions to faces that deviate from the prototype of faces that one has experienced."[146] Not only this, other research developed by Pamela Smith and her collaborators has shown that mere exposure to white faces *decreases* favorable response to Black faces among whites.[147]

On the other hand, research with young children in China and adults in the United States has shown that the MEE is *not* sufficient to decrease either implicit or explicit racial bias.[148] These experiments rely on a setup in which research subjects have to learn to individuate faces of *one* race for a computer task, but not for another race. So, for instance, the task requires subjects to press a particular number key for particular Black faces (which they've studied) but to press *o* for *any* white face. This triggers the MEE for white faces, but builds up what a research team led by Sophie Lebrecht call *individuation training* for Black faces. In a study led by Miao Qian, the MEE had no impact, whereas individuation training was able to reduce implicit (but not explicit) racial bias.[149]

What these studies share is a framework in which cognitive and affective dimensions of experience mess together. Although the studies on race don't study the hedonic dimension of bias, it comes with the territory of using Zajonc. As Smith and her collaborators write: "When White people eat, sleep, work, and shop in predominantly White areas, they may not be merely depriving themselves of diverse viewpoints and experiences. They may actually be inadvertently contributing to their own racial biases."[150]

The way we think about race and the way we feel about race are a single cat's cradle. Pulling on one string tugs the whole system.

This is not to suggest that the MEE offers anything like a comprehensive theory of race and racialization. But all this research adds to the picture of racialized reason driven by feeling. A particular piece of information—including visual information, including our everyday encounters with people and faces—when initially encountered, gains a *felt* currency merely because it was met *first*. That currency then produces a little bubble of immunity against contradictory information encountered later. New information is emotionally gauged to see if it clicks with what we already know. Click is necessary for finding truth. But it can also easily lead us astray, consolidating our preexisting preferences and biases, making them feel like neutral ground.

Conclusion: Within Reason

The approach I take here is in line with what philosopher Jan Slaby has called *critical neuroscience*. Rejecting both total determinism and total constructionism, it braids biological data from the sciences with historical and cultural studies from the humanities to create a hybrid framework sensitive to both lines of inquiry, modeling human beings as what Samantha Frost calls *biocultural creatures*.[151] Psychologists are growing more and more sophisticated in their sensitivity to history and culture, as shown by the increasing emphasis on cross-cultural research. There are similar gestures by humanities scholars who have sought to engage with the sciences in constructive ways. Cogency theory sets out to bridge humanistic and scientific perspectives, highlighting resonances across the disciplines.

Debates about the interconnectedness of thought and feeling are in the rearview mirror for neuroscientists. A consensus that feeling is necessary for thinking has become the foundation for whole swathes of current research. Studies from the 1980s on have collapsed the neat divisions between *emotional* and *cognitive* regions of the brain—categories that always were, arguably, actually the residue of unsound scholarship in the humanities from centuries past. The reason/emotion binary and the triune brain image may have conquered common sense, but they don't stand up against scientific research on the structure of the brain. These new findings indicate a pattern of interconnectedness that shreds any kind of binary mapping.

The findings of neuroscientists have confirmed that we can only ever think by drawing on a repertoire of feeling.

The same story comes across in experimental psychology. The MEE punctures the reason/emotion divide, showing that the shape of what we think and believe is defined by an infrastructure of feeling. The level ground of *what seems obvious and true* is actually created by a sedimentation of affective experiences. This means that even though we're built in such a way that we can produce good knowledge, the same emotional machinery that helps us can easily lead us astray. The MEE even contributes some suggestive fragments to a theory of racialized reason, proposing that rationality itself is shaped by power, history, and culture to produce felt hierarchies of which bodies matter. When psychologists seem to propose a split between reason and emotion (Zajonc), they do so to create a *more* expansive domain for feeling as the cradle of all thought, not to protect sovereign reason.

This doesn't mean that there can be no localization—specific networks or functions—within the brain. Nor is the best interpretation of the MEE that it simply prioritizes *the affective* or *the cognitive*. Instead, what keeps coming up in psychology is that the cognition/emotion divide is the *wrong way* to localize. As Barrett writes, affect "is not just necessary for wisdom; it's also irrevocably woven into the fabric of every decision."[152] Rather than thinking of cognition and emotion as two poles of a binary, cogency theory says they're better understood as two different aspects of the same three-dimensional structure—like the front and side views of an architect's draft of a building. In a highly abstract sense, we can render them *as if* independent of one another. But reconstructing them using only these flat projections leads to collapse.

Part II
Feeling Science and Secularism

5.
ONLY BETTER BEASTS
DARWIN, HUXLEY, AND THE SENSE OF SCIENCE

> You do me injustice when you think that I work for fame: I value it to a certain extent; but, if I know myself, I work from a sort of instinct to try to make out truth.
> —Charles Darwin to William Fox, March 24, 1859

> Perhaps that was a more cheerful time for observers and theorizers than the present.
> —George Eliot, *Middlemarch*

Introduction: The Ballad of Mr. Vestiges

By the time Darwin began his study of medicine at the University of Edinburgh in 1825, evolution had been described many times, under many names. Jean-Baptiste Lamarck had presented his tome *Philosophie Zoologique* to an annoyed Napoleon in 1810. Describing a natural order built by bottom-up forces, it nipped at the heels of the fresh emperor's top-down vision of rule by divine right.[1] Darwin's own grandfather, Erasmus Darwin, had written a scientific treatise in verse narrating the arc of life, born as a speck in the water, swirling, unfolding, and eventually producing the cascade of plants and animals seen today.[2]

And in Charles Darwin's own lifetime, the evolution question was blown wide open by the anonymously published *Vestiges of the Natural History of Creation*, which hit the streets of London in 1844. The author, dubbed Mr. Vestiges by the press, proposed a theory of gradual *transmutation* as the explanation not only of organisms, but of all fixtures of the natural world—water, soil, planets. *Vestiges* boomed, an early example of best-seller-bound pop science. It caught fire with the working and middle classes and was read by presidents and royals.[3] The surge of fascination led to three reprints in a single year, a companion volume, and twelve subsequent editions. It beat Darwin's own flagship book in sales right up to the twentieth century.[4]

But the book also provoked a counterattack. Newly royalized Napoleon's hostility to stories of life on earth that emphasized development rather than destiny was shared by the British upper crust. To the aristocratic elite, hierarchy was ordained, not accident. The new science directly challenged the linchpin of conservativism—that hierarchies have always been, must be, and will always be so. Paleontologist William Buckland, observing the continental revolutions of 1848 (and reflecting, no doubt, on the aftershocks of *Vestiges*), preached from the pulpit at Westminster Abbey, "The God of Nature has determined that moral and physical inequalities shall not only be inseparable from our humanity, but coextensive with His whole creation."[5] Radicals, socialists, and liberals entered a complicated dance with the materialist science of what we now call evolution. On the other side of the Atlantic, Black scientists like James McCune Smith devised and explored evolutionary ideas in their counteroffensive against Thomas Jefferson's racist tracts.[6] As historian Adrian Desmond writes, in the nineteenth century, "flaming politics were fuelled by emancipatory science."[7]

The Cambridge geologist Adam Sedgwick responded directly to *Vestiges*. In an 1845 letter to his Royal Society colleague Charles Lyell, Sedgwick stormed, "If the book be true, the labours of sober induction are in vain; religion is a lie; human law a mass of folly and a base injustice; morality is moonshine; our labours for the black people of Africa were works of madmen; and men and women are only better beasts!"[8] Sedgwick concluded that Mr. Vestiges was no *mister* at all. "This mistake was woman's from the first," he insisted. "She longed for the fruit of the tree of knowledge, and she must pluck it, right or wrong."[9]

When Darwin's *On the Origin of Species* was published a decade and a half later, Darwin remembered Sedgwick's vicious attacks on *Vestiges*. So he forwarded a complimentary copy of his publication to his onetime

Cambridge mentor, hoping to coax a favorable reaction with a proactive charm offensive. But Sedgwick's response was scathing: "Tis the crown & glory of organic science," he hissed at his former pupil, "that it *does* thro' *final cause*, link material to moral. ... You have ignored this link; &, if I do not mistake your meaning, you have done your best in one or two pregnant cases to break it."[10]

Sedgwick's position was complicated. He was ready to accept some measure of change in the history of life. ("We all admit development as a fact of history," he chided Darwin in the same letter.)[11] But for Sedgwick, this jostling around of species was minor, a tinkering with basically intact forms. The *scala naturae*, an eternal ranking system of life, remained fixed. There may be a law of development, he wrote shortly after receiving *Origin*, but this law is eminently hierarchical, an "order of succession ... not a law like that of gravitation."[12]

Mr. Vestiges published a best-seller, but his salvo was rejected almost across the board by English science. Darwinism, by contrast, hit the ground running. Not only did the first print run sell out immediately, but *Origin* became the center of a transatlantic English-language conversation at the nexus of science, religion, and politics. Within five years, Darwinism had taken control in England's natural science academy, catapulting evolution—previously just a histrionic theory championed by radicals and dissenters riling up the working classes—to the organizing logic of the emerging life sciences.[13]

What Darwinism offered, though, was more than just a new research paradigm. By subverting the exceptional status of the human intellect, it also reframed science itself. As we'll see below, Darwin soft-pedaled the extent to which his theory told a story about humans in the 1859 public debut of evolution by natural selection. It would be over a decade before he would discuss human evolution in print. But the harshest skeptics—like Adam Sedgwick—saw exactly where the theory was headed and started building barricades.[14] Linking humans to animals—especially under the blind gaze of accident—meant an earthquake for morality, for religion, for the political order, and for reason itself.

Darwin's innovations, then, set the stage for cogency theory. As we saw in chapter 4, there was no question, for Darwin, that reason was inextricable from emotion. It was a necessary consequence of his grounding intuition that the deep time of evolutionary kinship unites all animal life. There could be no black monolith rending the sky and bestowing reason on one creature alone by annunciation. There was only a succession of shapeshifting animal bodies—bodies marked, Darwin came to insist, first and foremost by affect. Darwinism was, in short, an ancestor of the *sensualized epistemology* of Eve Sedgwick—no relation, one imagines, to Adam—and other affect theorists surveyed in chapter 2.

Rather than a history of ideas, this chapter narrates the Darwinian aftermath as a history of secular scientific bodies—particularly the bodies of Darwin and his most ferocious advocate, the scientist and education reformer Thomas Henry Huxley. Reassessing the biographies of scientists whose lives have been subject to extensive attention and interpretation, it sheds light on science as an emotional enterprise. The sense of science as a dynamic of alternately exhilarating and constricting emotional pulses appears as a motor developing Darwinian science. And the formations of scientific secularism that spin off from these knowledge-making enterprises are tinged by these affective cores.

As we'll see in this chapter, Darwin began his scientific career as a committed devotee of William Paley, agreeing that nature's complexity was unbeatable evidence for divine intelligence. This conviction dissolved as Darwin sailed around the world on the five-year voyage of the *Beagle*. The new scientific Darwin that emerged had a deep passion for reason, but was also sensitive to the emotional links between science, faith, and society. His task, he knew, was to make his ideas *as cogent as possible* for his audience. Moreover, the years after the *Beagle* voyage made him wary about riding the exhilarating current of science without safeguards. This helped him build up a feel for scientific caution. But even Darwin's keen sense of science was swept off course when it came to race. Though he made contributions to the battle against racist science, there were clear limitations to how far he was willing to set his science against white (or, more accurately in Darwin's context, *Anglo-Saxon*) supremacy.

Huxley, too, had a deeply felt sense of science, with all the emotional exhilaration and frustration that entailed. But unlike sheepish Darwin, he was on a constant war footing against his academic, political, and philosophical enemies. His explosive debate with Samuel Wilberforce at Oxford in 1860 would have been unimaginable with Darwin in the hot seat. Darwin and Huxley both described themselves as *agnostic*, but the ways they approached nonreligion were profoundly different, revealing the distinct tectonic affects moving them under the surface. Yet even Huxley developed a more sophisticated theory of cogency as he matured, eventually becoming a capable advocate for education reform by building political alliances and filing down his sharp teeth.

Science studies has spent the past half century rediscovering science as social and material rather than the creation of solitary geniuses extracting truth from the world under the pure light of thought. So the strong emphasis on biography in this story might seem strange. But as Desmond notes of his own study of Huxley, an acute focus on context—the social, the material, the historical—ends up returning to biography as one scene of the production of science history.[15] Cogency theory follows a parallel track. It calls for attention to scientific bodies. To understand how science is made, we need to trace the bundles of emotion that shape how scientists come to think about the world. These include what Polanyi called the intellectual passions (interest, intuition, a desire to persuade …) and what William James called the tension between *eagerness* and *nervousness*—named in chapter 1 as the *sense of science*. The Darwinian aftermath—both Darwinian science and Darwinian secularism—can't be understood without mapping these emotional contours.

Darwin's Voyage: From Paley to the Passion for Reason

Sedgwick's scolding of Darwin for neglecting the mission of science to "link material to moral" echoed the English tradition of natural theology, typified by eighteenth-century theologian William Paley. Paley's line of argument—squarely aimed at David Hume and Erasmus Darwin—drew on the eighteenth century's explosion of data in anatomy, chemistry, and zoology to cement his claim that the complexity of the workings of nature was proof positive of God's designing influence.[16] Where Newton, just a century earlier, had once asked a trepanned individual if he could see out of the artificial orifice in his skull, Paley could point to up-to-date research on the intricate workings of the eye as overwhelming evidence for the action of an intelligent designer God.[17]

The anti-Lamarck, Paley became a kind of court scientist of conservative aristocratic thinking. As historian of science Bernard Lightman writes, he "reinforced support for an alliance between natural science and religious belief during a period when British intellectuals were blaming the destructive views of the radical *philosophes* for the French Revolution."[18] So admired was Paley's work that it was enshrined as a foundational text of the Cambridge University curriculum.[19] Darwin saw Paley as a master—the consummate man of science who had transformed methodical observation of nature into a powerful theory.[20] "I do not think I hardly ever admired a book more than Paley's *Natural Theology*," he wrote.[21]

Darwin, though, was not just interested in the natural world around him. He applied his keen attention to his own ways of thinking and making knowledge, leading to a series of remarkable documents in which he traced his own passion for reason. His autobiography, written late in life and first published by his son as part of a *Life and Letters* collection five years after his death, spelled out his early interest in orchestrating knowledge. "The passion for collecting," he wrote, "which leads a man to be a systematic naturalist, a virtuoso or a miser, was very strong in me."[22] Although he was an average student, the autobiography mentioned his "keen pleasure in understanding any subject or thing."[23] Taught geometry by a tutor, he wrote, "I distinctly remember the intense satisfaction which the clear geometrical proofs gave me."[24] Darwin traced the emotional roots of his scientific skill as far back as his childhood.

Though his plan was still a country parson's life, Darwin studied under the botanist J. S. Henslow while a graduate student at Cambridge. Janet Browne describes the exhilaration of Darwin's time with Henslow—especially his exploration of the action of microorganisms under lenses—as "a watershed in his emotional life generally unremarked by historians," one of the pivot points that pulled Darwin away from ordination and toward science.[25] And it was Henslow who ultimately set up Darwin's real scientific apprenticeship: his service as a gentleman naturalist on the HMS *Beagle*. Darwin and the ship's captain, Robert FitzRoy, stocked the ship's library with scholarly books, including a copy of Charles Lyell's *Principles of Geology*—a book Darwin read and reread as they sailed. Lyell became his new academic crush, recasting the geological history of the earth not as a parkland furnished by God for the good of all creatures (as Paley had it) but as a chaotic sequence of tectonic accidents.[26]

Darwin's journals record the onset of his vocation as a naturalist on the *Beagle*. The ship's first port of call was the island outpost of St. Jago. "I do not think the impression this day has made will ever leave me," Darwin wrote after examining the coral growing on the island's volcanic rock: "Never in the wildest castles in the air did I imagine so good a plan; it was beyond the bounds of the little reason that such day-dreams require."[27] FitzRoy, who would add a creationist screed to their jointly published *Journal of Researches* years later, wrote of Darwin at the time that "a child with a new toy could not have been more delighted than he was with St. Jago."[28]

Ecstasy in discovery was a leitmotif of Darwin's writings—letters and journals—throughout the *Beagle*'s five-year journey. The exquisite seaside towns of South America paled, for him, beside the vegetation of the surrounding landscape: "The delight one experiences in such times bewilders the mind," he wrote. "If the eye attempts to follow the flight of a gaudy butter-fly, it is arrested by some strange tree or fruit; if watching an insect one forgets it in the stranger flower it is crawling over; if turning to admire the splendor of the scenery, the individual character of the foreground fixes the attention. The mind is a chaos of delight, out of which a world of future & more quiet pleasure will arise."[29] The fabric of the natural world transfixed him, from the cliffs to the canopies to the dirt. "I am at present," he wrote to Henslow in 1832, "red-hot with Spiders."[30] He declared to his sister Catherine that his naturalist pursuits—observing, catching, describing—were "sources of the very highest pleasures I am capable of enjoying."[31]

It's easy, on reading passages like these, to see Darwin as basically a nature lover, enraptured by the beauty of plants and animals. This is the figure sketched by Richard Dawkins in *Unweaving the Rainbow*, the scientist as curator of a cabinet of natural wonders.[32] This isn't wrong, but it is incomplete. Darwin loved a painterly landscape and a spray of colors in a jungle. But he also loved mosses and lichens (*"heaven favour my madness,"* he wrote to his botanist friend, invoking his love of the wild experiment[33]). He spent years of his life monographing barnacles and earthworms. Even exotic travel left him unmoved—Darwin's return to England in 1836 marked the last time he left the country. Darwin wasn't just captivated by majestic mountains and gorgeous plants. The work of organizing and assembling knowledge—what he called his "beautiful facts"—was itself pleasurable.[34] The joy of click served as a driver of science, pressing him to advance toward the theory that best explained his swelling data set. The *Beagle*-borne Darwin, Browne writes, "danced from hypothesis to hypothesis and thoroughly enjoyed himself."[35]

Darwin disembarked the *Beagle* with his faith in Paley crumbling.[36] Scientific conversion rarely happens in a flash—an instant switch-out of one hypothesis for another. It's usually a long, subtle transformation, betraying the volatile emotional agonism under the surface. Darwin's intellectual arc was like this. Sharing his findings with other naturalists as he worked on his *Journal of Researches* in 1837, Darwin faced the first significant scientific pivot point of his life. How to explain the subtle variations in species of iguanas, tortoises, finches, and rheas distributed across a spray of islets? "In a Lyellian world where living beings were tied to the geological conditions," Browne writes, "or in a Paleyian world where animals and plants were perfectly adapted to their surroundings, things like this did not happen."[37] But Lyell's theory clicked with the new data in a way that Paley's did not. Unlike his predecessor evolutionists, Darwin realized that the variations of life and the accidents of landscape were related. He "added geology to sex," planting the seed of an idea: evolution by natural selection.[38] Paley's theory no longer fit. It failed the test of cogency.

The Manuscript in the Drawer: Darwin's Delay

This felt click isn't the whole story, though. Darwin throughout his life displayed the full spectrum of epistemic feelings configuring the sense of science, including what James called *keen nervousness* about getting things right. John Brodie Innes, the vicar in the village of Downe where Darwin settled, recorded his impressions shortly after the scientist's death. Innes portrayed Darwin as someone whose fascination with truth manifested not just at excitement over click but also in pressing anxiety. He described, for instance, "a Parish meeting... on some disputed point of no great importance," after which "I was surprised by a visit from Mr. Darwin at night. He came to say that, thinking over the debate, though what he had said was quite accurate, he thought I might have drawn an erroneous conclusion, and he would not sleep till he had explained it. I believe that if on any day some certain fact had come to his knowledge which contradicted his most cherished theories, he would have placed the fact on record for publication before he slept."[39] Darwin found intellectual work thrilling, but it also caused him to fret. His sense of science meant holding his own ideas in careful suspension—even subjecting them to ferocious scrutiny.

Notes on transmutation of species appear in Darwin's notebooks as early as 1837.[40] But Darwin had faced down the skeptical laughter of his colleagues when he presented his treasured ideas in the past without a full complement of evidence to back them up.[41] By the middle of 1842, he had a working outline of the theory of evolution by natural selection. He revised it steadily over the next two years, eventually penning a 230-page manuscript, never published. This document was so precious to him he affixed a letter for Emma to the pile of papers in his desk. Browne (who has read thousands of Darwin's letters) calls it "the strangest letter of his life."[42] The letter explained that the sketch was "a considerable step in science," and named some editors to send the work to if he died prematurely.

Darwin felt the driving urgency of what he called his *instinct for truth*.[43] "You will perhaps wish my Barnacles & Species theory al Diabolo together," he trilled playfully to Joseph Dalton Hooker, one of his confidants who knew some details of his secret research. "But I don't care what you say, my species theory is all gospel."[44] Yet he was also painfully sensitive to the way his science would feel to those around him. And so evolution by natural selection stayed in the drawer. It's one of the puzzles in the history of evolutionary science, what Darwin industry scholars call *Darwin's delay*: the long pause between the emergence of the first sketches of his theory of evolution by natural selection in the early 1840s and their actual publication in 1859.

There are two main lines of speculation about Darwin's hesitation. The first is that Darwin was torn between a passion for truth and another, equally important affective priority—an acute sensitivity to the sensibilities of his friends and family, especially surrounding religion. By the time he disembarked the *Beagle*, Darwin, who saw his early ship years as a "period of Orthodoxy," had turned away from Christianity.[45] His father, hoping for a good match, advised him to conceal his disbelief from any potential wife.[46] But when Darwin began courting his first cousin Emma Wedgwood, he wanted to be completely truthful with her. Darwin told Emma everything—about not just his own religious doubts, but also his increasing attraction to transmutation as an account of species development.[47] Emma saw the implications immediately and began a doomed campaign to summon him back to faith. She sent him scripture verses. He responded with theories and arguments. Even after marriage they continued to write each other letters. On the envelope of one early proselytizing missive from Emma, Darwin wrote: "When I am dead, know that many times, I have kissed & cryed over this."[48]

The death of the Darwins' daughter, Annie, in 1851, seems to have sharpened the theological split between them. Darwin described it as the "one very severe grief" of their married life. "Tears still sometimes come into my eyes," he wrote twenty-five years later, "when I think of her sweet ways."[49] But in terms of how to face the loss, Charles and Emma were divided.[50] Faith, already a sticky topic in their relationship, became even more delicate. Darwin, Browne writes, "would prefer to be dead rather than deliberately hurt Emma's feelings."[51] This pronounced sensitivity to Emma's churchy sensibilities—not to mention his conservative friends and mentors, the Sedgwicks and Henslows, for whom evolutionism was political dynamite—fuels this line of speculation about the great delay.

The second line focuses on how Darwin perceived the scientific conversation around him. When *Vestiges* began piling up in bookstalls in 1844, Darwin watched the explosive response with alarm. It confirmed his sense that his ideas were too flammable for public view. Adrian Desmond and James Moore's biography represents Darwin as physically and psychically wrecked by the horror of the social catastrophe that the exposure of his ideas would lead to for him and his family.[52] But others have argued, less dramatically, that Darwin's delay was primarily about expanding his research base and credentialing himself as a scientist.[53] On this line of reasoning, if he were to publish, he needed both a more durable reputation as a respectable scientist and a thicker dossier of evidence. These became his secret tasks throughout the 1840s and 1850s.[54]

Roderick Buchanan and James Bradley, for instance, zoom in on Darwin's work on barnacles during the 1850s. Although it was initially intended as a small project, they suggest, Darwin pivoted to a comprehensive, full-fledged monograph on *Cirripedia* as a device to elevate his scientific status.[55] Historian Alistair Sponsel's interpretation is similar, but puts more emphasis on Darwin's anxiety about his own past hastiness in pursuing *theory* rather than diligent and disciplined empirical research.[56] What Darwin called the *sin of speculation* was the stolen fruit of his youth. Criticism of his early work from peers had singed him, prompting him to push for a more cautious, methodical approach to his mature projects.[57]

Sponsel even shows that while working on barnacles in the 1850s, Darwin would furtively turn to his species book. Whereas Desmond and Moore interpreted this secret labor as evidence that Darwin found his new theory project grueling and alarming, Sponsel's assessment is the exact opposite. "Far from being the cause of his anxiety," Sponsel concludes, "Darwin found making notes on species to be an exhilarating diversion from the high-pressure work of writing his geological book."[58] Darwin was using the intellectual thrill of the species project as a way of blowing off steam while he dedicated most of his time to the grinding work of classifying barnacles. Darwin had grasped that science proceeded by alloying excitement with caution. As he wrote at the time, "Speculative men, with a curb on make the best observers."[59] The joy of speculation plus a curb of anxiety—it was a miniature manifesto for the sense of science.

The theories in the mix here all aim to pin down *the cause* of Darwin's delaying maneuver. But cogency theory suggests that what we're really talking about is not a single *cause* so much as an agonism of blended motives and contending priorities. There were many worries looming for Darwin, prompting him to shrink back from a full public offering. This wasn't for the benefit of Darwin's own confidence in his theory. His travel, his study, and his many conversations with colleagues and correspondents had already convinced him. But it reflected his sharp sensitivity to what would be cogent *for others*. This sensitivity directed the way he approached the publication of his theory when the moment finally came.

Alfred Russel Wallace, still learning the ropes of the genteel province of science in 1865, once asked Darwin and Hooker why scientists were so guarded with their beliefs. In a letter to Darwin, Hooker muttered, "Had he as many kind and good relations as I have, who would be grieved and pained to hear me say what I think ... he would not wonder so much."[60] Although spoken by Hooker, it could have come from Darwin's own pen. It perfectly reflects the agonism of this phase of his career, urgently wishing to speak truth, but acutely attuned to the skewed way his ideas would land on the emotional landscape of the science of his day.

The Charm Offensive

On June 18, 1858, Darwin received a parcel in the mail. It was from the same Alfred Russel Wallace, then working as a sort of adventurer-naturalist-trader who made a living harvesting tropical specimens and selling them to wealthy gentlemen scholars.[61] But the parcel contained pages, not skins. The essay outlined a near-carbon-copy of the theory of evolution by natural selection that was still moldering in the pile of papers in Darwin's desk. Darwin forwarded the letter to Lyell, moping, "I never saw a more striking coincidence."[62]

But within the week, Lyell, Hooker, and Darwin's other scientific friends had hatched a plan to establish Darwin's priority—the infamous scheme to read Darwin's unpublished materials into the record of a Linnean Society meeting in July 1858. Darwin was ashamed of himself, but not enough to prevent the conspiracy from going forward.[63] In the end, it was the fear of losing priority that tipped the scales, outweighing his anxiety about courting controversy.[64] To Hooker—the member of Darwin's inner circle to whom Darwin had disclosed the most and a crucial witness to Darwin's originality—he moaned: "It is miserable in me to care at all about priority."[65] But he did care—a lot. To get back on track (and retroactively justify his sleight of hand), he immediately set out to write what he imagined as an abstract for his larger study. As the framework of his ideas was trimmed with the pebbles of evidence he'd been gathering from all corners of the world for twenty-five years, the project swelled to a book-length overview. This was *Origin of Species*.

Darwin's book was stuck between contradictory ambitions: on the one hand, setting out to make a stunning intervention in the scientific conversation; on the other, a gallant effort to minimize personal and political friction now that delay was no longer an option. This is why the first published proclamation of evolution by natural selection methodically skirted both human origins and theological consequences.[66] For extra insurance, Darwin chose epigraphs (Whewell, Bacon, and, as of the third edition, Butler) signaling harmony with the tradition of English natural theology—for which the science of life had always served as a sermonic aid.[67] Although Darwin would identify himself, late in life, as "liberal or radical" in his politics, he labored furiously to separate *Origin* from the radicals and freethinkers who had hoisted *Vestiges* as their banner.[68]

"When he needed to," Browne points out, "he spoke cautiously of the Creator, aware that his book might otherwise be labelled atheistic."[69] At the same time, Darwin stated his views as truthfully as he could, emphasizing branching development rather than the progressive, teleological frameworks of descent offered by his grandfather, or Lamarck, or Mr. Vestiges. This meant that he "was careful not to allow the Creator any active role in biological proceedings."[70] *Descent with modification*, as it was known in the first edition, was a knot of contingencies, not a ladder. It was governed by accident rather than design. For all that Darwin was willing to bend his presentation to meet his audience, he still held fast to the core intellectual supports of his theory.

Darwin's quick-footed ballet shows just how aware he was that science wasn't decided by evidence and argument alone. To make his arguments cogent, he had to shape the whole current of affects surrounding the ideas. Hence the charm offensive—a generous outlay of complimentary copies and self-effacing, flattering notes, even and especially to the skeptics. If they responded negatively—as Sedgwick did—Darwin rushed to put out the fire.[71] A pattern emerged. Darwin rode out to meet his critics, massaging their alarmed sensibilities, easing the acceptance of his theory in any way he could. This included, it would seem, cutting some corners, maintaining friendly diplomatic relations for the sake of preserving an open channel of communication—and ideally expanding his circle of publicity.

When Darwin's cousin Julia Frances "Snow" Wedgwood published a two-part philosophical dialogue commenting on *Origin*, Darwin's response to her was cagy. Considered one of the most brilliant women of Victorian England (her career stifled by her family's insistence that she devote herself to caring for older relatives),[72] Wedgwood's commentary was a moral and theological defense of Darwinism published in two installments from 1860 to 1861.[73] Darwin wrote to Wedgwood in 1861, after reading the completed text, saying, "I think that you understand my book perfectly, and that I find a very rare event with my critics."[74] Except Wedgwood had done nothing of the sort. She'd covered the book with a theological gloss that brushed against the grain of Darwin's intent. Wedgwood's interpretation saw moral meaning in nature. Darwin's text offered no such comfort. But he cordially affirmed her interpretation while keeping his own cards close to the vest.

The same pattern played out with Charles Kingsley, Christian socialist, Cambridge professor, and pastor to royals. Kingsley was also a target of Darwin's 1859 charm offensive—but successfully. In response to his complimentary copy of *Origin*, Kingsley sent Darwin a miniature theological treatise outlining the compatibility of evolution by natural selection with a Christian doctrine of creation.[75] In fact, Kingsley wrote, the elegance of Darwin's appendix to Genesis made the Creator *even more* worthy of reverence. Darwin valued this reflection so much that he requested Kingsley's permission to place it in the preface of the second edition of *Origin* (published just weeks later), citing him as a "celebrated author and divine."[76]

But Kingsley, like Wedgwood, had starkly misunderstood Darwin, who had no intention of reasserting the theological necessity of a creator. Darwin needed Kingsley's imprimatur as a shield against the attacks of conservatives already revving up their war machines against this new *Vestiges*.[77] Same with Darwin's American collaborator Asa Gray. Darwin paid for the publication of Gray's 1861 pamphlet arguing for the compatibility of Darwinism with Christianity, but Darwin, as we'll see, likely didn't believe a word of it.[78] This defensive strategy involved other feints too, like adding the word *Creator* in the final pages of later editions.[79]

Darwin's own unsweetened worldview hadn't changed—not even a little. But he became the great sugarcoater, trying to entice traffic of his theory wherever possible.[80] Was it a passion for truth eclipsed by a sudden zeal for fame? Or a Trojan horse, a colossal, shadowy engine designed to sneak past emotional fortifications—a cogency mole? Either way, his science advanced only to the extent that he could forge it as the right emotional alloy. Darwin knew that without attention to the affective coordinates of cogency, his ideas would be stonewalled.

Darwin and Race Science

For all that Darwin cultivated the sense of science, however, his work was not immune to the contortions of racialized reason. Darwin's relationship with race was complex. The Darwin-Wedgwood clan—beginning with Darwin's other grandfather, the Unitarian pottery entrepreneur Josiah Wedgwood, who mass-produced antislavery medallions—were ardent abolitionists. As a student he apprenticed to John Edmonstone, a Black man in Edinburgh, who had once been enslaved in Guyana. Darwin admired the charismatic naturalist, whose stories about life in South America may have sparked his fascination with the tropics.[81] And he hated the violence and degradation of slavery he encountered on his *Beagle* voyage.[82]

During the US Civil War, he took the side of the North. With ferocity. "Some few," he wrote to Gray in 1861, "& I am one, even wish to God, though at the loss of millions of lives, that the North would proclaim a crusade against Slavery. In the long run, a million horrid deaths would be amply repaid in the cause of humanity. ... Great God how I sh^d like to see that greatest curse on Earth Slavery abolished."[83] His main contribution to race science was a strident insistence on monogenism—the common ancestry of humans—and unyielding criticism of the view advanced by racists that the races were, in fact, separate species.[84] And he and his circle relentlessly attacked the white supremacist Anthropological Society, founded by Confederate scholars to churn out racist propaganda in Britain.[85]

But this record was checkered. Kingsley wrote to Darwin in 1862 with a theory about how the myths of Europeans surrounding forest creatures like elves and fairies probably depict "semi-human race[s]" wiped out by their conquerors. "That they should have died out, by simple natural selection," he mused, "before the superior white race, you & I can easily understand."[86] Despite his antiracist commitments elsewhere, Darwin's response to this show of support for his theory was pathetic capitulation, perhaps one of the most disturbing passages he ever inked: "It is very true what you say about the higher races of men, when high enough, replacing

& clearing off the lower races," he wrote, before adding, "In 500 years how the Anglo-saxon race will have spread & exterminated whole nations; & in consequence how much the Human race, viewed as a unit, will have risen in rank."[87] Was it more deceptive politicking—an effort to flatter a powerful ally by following suit? Or does the cloak of privacy indicate Darwin actually believed this?

Although he methodically refrained from writing about humans in *Origin*, Darwin reversed course a decade later—partly in response to Wallace's recent public proclamation that the human intellect couldn't possibly be an artifact of evolution, which left Darwin sputtering with frustration.[88] Darwin's 1871 volume *The Descent of Man* was a direct counterattack. But this meant wading into the shabby race science of his time. Differences of intellect and moral character, he wrote, "between the highest men of the highest races and the lowest savages, are connected by the finest gradations."[89] And he restated the chilling irony of Victorian racism—chiding "rude men" for only practicing kindness "almost exclusively in relation to the men of the same tribe"—even as Europeans employed mass exploitation, starvation, and genocide in their empires and colonies.[90]

Historians of science tend to share a complex assessment of Darwin and race. Terence Keel writes that Darwin's research aggressively subverted racist science, even if he failed to pursue the antiracist implications of his work to their full extent.[91] Paul White adds that almost all the racist ideas transmitted by Darwin's colonial contacts were excluded when written up in *Descent*, pruned and tossed aside as he probed for synthesis.[92] But Evelleen Richards points out that Darwin's staunch repudiation of anti-Black racism was undercut by his own embrace of the cultural racism and condescension shown by the English to Indigenous populations in the Americas and Oceania.[93] Darwin never, to my knowledge, uses the word *white* in print to refer to a race, and only seldom trots out the Victorian correlate *Anglo-Saxon*. But he frequently writes about *savages*. Although he pulled back from the sinister conclusions of what would become the eugenics movement, he affirmed that the "mental characteristics" of the various races "are likewise very distinct; chiefly as it would appear in their emotional, but partly in their intellectual faculties."[94] (He said something similar about sex difference, which needs its own discussion.)[95] Darwin concluded *Descent* by noting that the views developed in the book were "highly speculative, and some no doubt will prove erroneous."[96] That doesn't change the fact that his standard of evidence was, throughout the book, calibrated to include and embrace racist assumptions about the relationship between biology and intelligence. He was, in Richards's phrase, an "emotional polygenist."[97]

Literary critic George Levine writes that *Descent* is noxious because "so much of its discussion of human behavior seems to depend on commentaries by second-rate minds on Darwin's earlier first-rate work."[98] There's some truth to this, but it misses the fact that Darwin found these commentaries cogent enough to include them. And as Richards points out, this didn't just correspond with his own unexamined prejudices; it also enhanced his position with his white readership.[99] Racialized reason—like the mindset of all scientific racists, from early brass instrument tinkerers to social media screeders—made racist conclusions appealing, even to the point of eclipsing otherwise crisp scientific intuitions, because they *felt true*. They felt so good they *had* to be true. The wrecking ball of Darwin's mind—so effective at shattering other edifices of prejudice—cracked on the hard wall of his own racialized reason.

Enter the Bulldog

Darwin's destiny was wrapped up with that of another scientist, Thomas Henry Huxley—friend, sparring partner, apostle. The Huxley-Darwin alliance was unexpected. They were of starkly different class backgrounds and, as we'll see, miles apart in temperament. Huxley, like Sedgwick, was a committed antagonist of *Vestiges*, writing a blistering criticism of the volume on the tenth anniversary of its publication. This put Darwin on a wary footing with him.[100] But Darwin also recognized Huxley's brilliance as a scientist. After they met in 1853, Darwin began cultivating Huxley as a protégé, inviting him and other young scientists to his estate at Downe, where he would probe their views for points of intersection with his own secret ideas.[101] The cheerful, churlish cynic could be a valuable ally if recruited.

As with Darwin, Huxley's passion for reason was a defining feature of his science. Having met his future wife, Nettie Heathorn, in Australia, he had only to set up a stable career and they could marry. At catastrophic emotional cost to both parties, Huxley walked away from a lucrative, ripe-for-the-taking medical career and took on a multiyear endeavor to secure financial stability as a scholar. He chose academic poverty—and uncertainty—and made Nettie wait. "Oh I am so sick, so weary of this life without love," he wrote to her, overlooking the fact that it was his unblinking desire to live a life of the mind that had created their distance.[102] Desmond calls it Huxley's *vocation*, his devotion to science leading to a wilderness of missed opportunities, rejections, and demeaning academic grunt work.[103] Only after securing a permanent position at the Royal School of Mines in 1855 was he able to invite Nettie to join him, seven years after their initial engagement.[104] He would have been one of the eager students crowding around Weber—and ignoring his advice.

Huxley's meeting of the minds with Darwin was even more remarkable because his conversion to hectic evolutionary trees marked an abrupt departure from his own understanding of nature. Where Darwin was the great theorist of the higgledy-piggledy, Huxley's preconversion taxonomy of life was a crisp orrery of circles and spheres, "groping for symmetry and order in nature."[105] It was capital-*R* Romantic, influenced by 1840s radicalism and a sense of nature as beautiful for its own sake—yet antiteleological.[106] It all collapsed under the Darwinian shock wave. As much as Huxley might have savored Mr. Vestiges's needling of the aristocratic establishment, he couldn't tolerate his sloppy science. But when Darwin's more cogent explanation of transmutation came along, Huxley was ready to jump ship. Evolution by natural selection just clicked. He later wrote that his first reaction to Darwin's hypothesis was excited recognition: "How extremely stupid not to have thought of that!"[107]

That said, Huxley held back from fully embracing the new gospel. He noted that Darwin overstated the gradualist position and missed the necessity of sudden changes of organic structure.[108] When Huxley bought the journal *Natural History Review*, previously a failing, mainly anti-Darwin science publication, he published material from lots of perspectives—including criticism of *Origin*—insisting that it stay a free field for science where all views could be explored.[109] Huxley, Desmond writes, was "endorsing the naturalism of Darwin's vision, not the fine points of his theory."[110] Darwin was a better fit—*more* cogent than the alternatives. But Huxley was probably never a full convert to Darwinism qua evolution by natural selection.

Huxley's sense of science was aligned with Darwin's. But in other aspects of temperament, he was very different. Whereas shy Darwin was a sort of intellectual pacifist, holding his tender theory in reserve and agonizing about whether he was justified in revealing it, Huxley took the other path. Huxley's son Leonard reported that his father once said of himself, "I am Darwin's bull-dog"—a relentless, indomitable attacker.[111] Desmond's interpretation is that Huxley had a lifelong sense of himself as a kind of Luther or

Muhammad—a steel-eyed reformer on a purifying drive against oppressive traditionalism, myth, and monarch-worship.[112] This gave him no shortage of opportunities to brawl. As one paper declared in his obituary, "Cutting up monkeys was his forte, and cutting up men was his foible."[113]

Huxley, too, was targeted in Darwin's charm offensive, holding a complimentary copy of *Origin* in his hands a few days before its official release. But while Darwin was paralyzed with anxiety in the days leading up to the publication date, Huxley was howling at the moon.[114] In his letter to Darwin thanking him for the gift, Huxley was already plotting war. "I trust you will not allow yourself to be in any way disgusted or annoyed," he wrote, "by the considerable abuse & misrepresentation which unless I greatly mistake is in store for you—Depend upon it you have earned the lasting gratitude of all thoughtful men—And as to the curs which will bark & yelp—you must recollect that some of your friends at any rate are endowed with an amount of combativeness which (though you have often & justly rebuked it) may stand you in good stead—I am sharpening up my claws & beak in readiness."[115] This is exactly what Huxley delivered, in back rooms, in lecture halls, and in print. Everyone had an opinion on *Origin*, Huxley observed a few months later in a review essay: "Pietists ... decry it with the mild railing which sounds so charitable; bigots denounce it with ignorant invective; old ladies of both sexes consider it a decidedly dangerous book."[116] On the other hand, "every philosophical thinker hails it as a veritable Whitworth gun in the armoury of liberalism."[117] Darwin hunkered down. Huxley sallied forth.

"Morals and religion are one wild whirl to me," Huxley wrote in an early diary. "In the region of the intellect alone can I find free and innocent play for such faculties as I possess. ... [Truth alone] allows me to get rid of the 'malady of thought.'"[118] But Huxley's sense of science was always spiced with a delight in the fight. Late in life his wife pleaded with him "to give up controversy," his constant vice.[119] Ignoring her, he continued hammering away, resuming a public debate with the Whig prime minister, William Gladstone, about scripture, though finally announcing himself "as sick of controversy as a confectioner's boy of tarts."[120] As he lay on his deathbed, hate mail from outraged believers was still rolling in at his door.[121]

Darwin was grateful for Huxley but still wary of the rhetorical excesses of his most zealous defender. A note about Huxley in Darwin's late autobiography was diplomatic: "His mind is as quick as a flash of lightning and as sharp as a razor."[122] But he still sounded a note of alarm about Huxley's bloodthirsty approach to scholarship, writing, "It was a pity that he attacked so many scientific men, although I believe that he was right in each particular case."[123] After Huxley's review came out back in 1860, Darwin wrote that for all its brilliance, it seemed more intent on landing punches than advancing science.[124] Writing to Huxley at the time, he expressed gratitude for his "clever & solid reviews," but added, "For God's sake remember that your field of labour is original research in the highest & most difficult branches of Natural History."[125]

The Episcopophage: Huxley and Religion

Even as he refused to give Darwinism his full assent, Huxley was gleefully hostile to Darwin's antagonists—now his antagonists too. He was particularly set against Darwin's religious opponents. "In this nineteenth century, as at the dawn of modern physical science," he wrote, even though the pagan views of Egypt and Rome had been abandoned, Genesis still held sway.[126] "Who shall number the patient and earnest seekers after truth, from the days of Galileo until now, whose lives have been embittered and their good name blasted by the mistaken zeal of Bibliolaters? Who shall count the host of weaker men whose sense of truth has been destroyed in the effort to harmonise impossibilities—whose life has been wasted in the attempt to force the generous new wine of Science into the old bottles of Judaism, compelled by the outcry of the same strong party?"[127] But natural philosophy had won its revenge, and now "extinguished theologians lie about the cradle of every science as the strangled snakes beside that of Hercules; and history records that whenever science and orthodoxy have been fairly opposed, the latter has been forced to retire from the lists, bleeding and crushed if not annihilated; scotched, if not slain."[128] This was an emotional register totally unavailable to Darwin. Far from being afraid of the fight with faith, Huxley was exhilarated by it.

When Huxley took over the *Natural History Review*, he bragged to Hooker that the journal's tone would be "mildly episcopophagous"—that is, bishop-eating.[129] But even when he was brawling with believers, Huxley's antireligious fire was seldom trained on theology. His real target was what he called *parsondom*—the patchwork of intellectual fiefdoms in country churches and Oxbridge professorships, from which clerics labored to convert data from the natural sciences into theological rhapsodies—the shadow government of science left behind by Paley. Desmond argues that

Huxley is best understood as an inheritor of the radical Dissent tradition of the English Midlands, critics of the aristocratic *scala naturae*.[130] (Friedrich Engels was a Huxley fan, just as Karl Marx was an admirer of Darwin.)[131]

Traumatized by his own family's sharp downswing into poverty in the Coventry slums, Huxley loathed the use of knowledge as a metaphysical buttress of the order of things—the smug, classist science of Paley and Buckland.[132] Watching the mediocre rise and thrive, his burning desire was to demolish the system of privilege and patronage thickly entangling state, aristocracy, and church. Huxley's new science regime was open to the London laborers who flocked to his lectures by the hundreds nightly. The downfall of the Anglican scientific aristocracy, he dreamed, would allow the rise of an egalitarian, nonconformist scientific congregation.[133] But *Vestiges* wasn't scientific enough to achieve this. Darwinism was.

Unlike for Darwin (see below), religion was a constant topic of discussion for Huxley. He published dozens of articles and chapters on it, engaged extended public debates with clerical and political enemies, and coined the word *agnosticism* as a new term of art. But Huxley's actual views on religion were nuanced, episcopophagous tastes notwithstanding. Like Darwin, Huxley struggled to make peace with his future wife during their courtship on the subject of his unorthodox faith. Anticipating his later philosophical agnosticism—with its built-in modesty—he insisted he was no atheist, that his lack of faith was an outgrowth of his intellectual humility.[134]

In his correspondence with Charles Kingsley shortly after both had lost children to illness, he spoke in the rawest terms about their theological disagreements. Huxley's son Noel had been cut down by a rapid fever that ran its course in two days in September 1860. His parents were so griefstricken that they memorialized his name in the christening of their child born a few months later, Leonard. When Kingsley wrote to him as a close friend encouraging him to take comfort in the doctrine of the immortality of the soul, Huxley responded with a remarkable 2,600-word letter that was equal parts theological treatise, scientific paper, and heart-wrenching confessional.

In the letter, he admitted that his philosophical rejection of eternal life had been tested by Noel's death but declared that it had come through the fire hardened: "Truth is better than much profit," he wrote. "I have searched over the grounds of my belief, and if wife and child and name and fame were all to be lost to me one after the other as the penalty, still I will not lie."[135] His emotional core was a commitment to truth itself. Science was an empirical method for him, a compass that he used to feel his way around the towering questions of God and eternity. Faithlessness had legal consequences under Victorian law, but he committed himself to it fully. "One thing people shall not call me with justice and that is—a liar," he declared with defiance, before testifying, "If ever the occasion arises when I am bound to speak, *I will not shame my boy*."[136] It's a stunning statement of the deep emotional power science held in his life. The great scientific reformer even took Luther's credo as his own: "God help me. I cannot do otherwise."[137]

Yet this same ruthlessly doubting science was also, for Huxley, an expression of an eminently *Christian* mood of humility. "Science seems to me to teach in the highest and strongest manner the great truth which is embodied in the Christian conception of entire surrender to the will of God," he wrote. "Sit down before fact as a little child, be prepared to give up every preconceived notion, follow humbly wherever and to whatever abysses nature leads, or you shall learn nothing."[138] Huxley's dynamic sense of science was, in his telling, an extension of his admiration for the core Christian moral message. He rejected religion—empty doctrines, parsonism—with one hand while drawing it toward him with the other, insisting that he could have a "deep sense of religion" without theology.[139]

In the 1870s, Huxley joined the Metaphysical Society, a club for those with interests in religion and philosophy. This, too, would have been unthinkable to Darwin (didn't care, hated clubs). Meeting twice a month with proponents of different denominations and philosophies, he developed a new style that allowed him to scale up his campaign for science, trading some of its hard edge for respectability and reach.[140] This experience catalyzed his new organizing term: *agnostic*. According to Huxley, the Metaphysical Society compelled him to assume a denomination.[141] He was a sometime supporter of George Holyoake and other early secularists, so his enemies assumed he was aligned with their street-level atheist agenda.[142] But in fact, agnosticism was a play designed for the battlefield of lecture halls and meeting rooms.

Marching under the authority of Kant and Hume (whom he crowned "prince of agnostics"),[143] Huxley defined agnosticism as a method, rather than a creed—the method devised by Socrates, and carried forward by the Reformation, by Descartes, and by modern science. The method was simply this: "In matters of the intellect follow your reason as far as it will take you without regard to any other consideration." And by the same token, "do not pretend that conclusions are certain which are not demonstrated or demonstrable."[144] There was, then, no sect of agnosticism, no "imitation ecclesiasticism."[145] Its affective structure was an unflinching drive toward truth tempered by notice of one's own epistemic limitations. Rather than settled orthodoxy, he imagined it as a permanent maelstrom of excitement and anxiety, the agonism of the sense of science.

Devising agnosticism was a politically sophisticated move. It allowed Huxley to stand back from the increasingly wide divisions within the big-tent Darwinian movement.[146] But it also gave him a new angle as his professional profile lifted from brawling gadfly to respected man of science to major public figure consulted by the highest government offices. Much like Darwin, Huxley found that edging away from materialism gave him the sheen of respectability and widened his access to the corridors of power (even if many of his contemporaries found him disingenuous).[147] As James Moore notes, after Darwin's death in 1882, Huxley even began to distance himself from the adjective *Darwinian*, ejecting it almost entirely from his vocabulary by the 1890s.[148] Although his early public proclamations on religion were keyed to a fiery, adversarial secularism, his late work focused on bigger prizes in education reform and policy.

The slashing, sneering attitude of Huxley's early public life—the intellectual warrior barking at the bishops—has, as we'll see in the coming chapters, become the template of Huxley's legacy for contemporary secularism. But really, this misses the complicated, delicate articulation of his beliefs and disbeliefs that he advanced through the vessel of agnosticism. Huxley's objection was to the way parsondom clamped down on the passion for truth, choking scientific enquiry with a thicket of moralism. He built alliances with liberal Christians in the X Club and even outside the sphere of science.[149] Darwin's biology put a weapon in his hand—a weapon that thrilled. Yet it's worth remembering that *Vestiges*—which had the same potential for radical disruption—didn't click with Huxley's sense of science. Over time, even Huxley learned to finesse his fury.

The Battle in the Cathedral of Science

The divergence in Darwin and Huxley's approaches—how they felt about both science and secularism—is neatly illustrated by one of the most famous episodes of the Darwinian aftermath: the debate between the Darwinians and their opponents at Oxford. The British Association for the Advancement of Science (BAAS) held its 1860 annual meeting in Oxford's newly constructed Museum of Natural History, a glass and stone cathedral with Gothic detailing. Huxley attended; tormenting the Oxford establishment was intellectual sport for him.[150] Darwin did not. But after three days at the conference, Huxley was tired and bored and planning to head home to spend time with Nettie.[151] As he was leaving, he met a man on the street. The man was Scottish journalist Robert Chambers.

Chambers had a secret. Fifteen years earlier, he had written *Vestiges of the Natural History of Creation*, publishing it anonymously and deftly covering his tracks using his sophisticated understanding of the publishing industry. Incognito Mr. Vestiges had been pressing the evolutionist line behind the scenes, mass-distributing his book in low-cost editions to reach as many readers as possible (and significantly diminishing his own profits in the process).[152] He'd watched the abrupt rise of Darwinism with quiet hope, seeing it as a new tide lifting the truth of his ideas. Now, in Oxford, he knew that a conference session on the work of Darwin was about to begin. And he knew it would be attended by bishop Samuel Wilberforce, who was reportedly planning to, in his own words, "smash Darwin."[153] Huxley had blasted Chambers's book.[154] But that was the past. The fight for evolutionism was now. Mr. Vestiges knew his side needed defenders. So he convinced the bulldog to go back to the museum.[155]

The BAAS was a Victorian-era TED talk—a place for members of the public to mix with men of science, with an aim to broaden popular understanding.[156] Between seven hundred and one thousand attendees were crammed into the long side room where Section D—Zoology and Botany took place.[157] The main speaker was John Draper, professor of chemistry at New York University, later author of the hugely influential *History of the Conflict between Religion and Science*. His talk was not on organic evolution at all, but on the history of ideas. Draper's later fame notwithstanding, he didn't gain much traction in Oxford as the attendees quickly moved on from his paper and began debating Darwinism. After a few anti-Darwinian comments, the chair invited Huxley to respond. He declined.[158]

Instead, Wilberforce rose. Wilberforce—the inspiration for the tight-faced Duchess character in Lewis Carroll's *Alice in Wonderland*—was a complicated figure. The son of an influential evangelical abolitionist, he'd once been a bridge-builder between different wings of the church but had lately swung toward a more severe, orthodox posture.[159] By 1860, hemmed in between the liberal Broad Church movement within Anglicanism, on one side, and the Catholicizing Tractarians, on the other, Wilberforce was on edge. The Darwinian sea change looked to him like a boon for the liberals pursuing major theological concessions between the church and science.[160] So he stepped in to slap it down.

Wilberforce gave the exhilarated crowd what they had been waiting for. After several hours of dull lecture and aimless response, the bishop's unscripted, half-hour oration was captivating. He capped it off with one of his famous rhetorical flourishes. It's not certain what was said, but the most common version of events has it that he turned to Huxley and asked him if his descent from an ape was through his grandmother or his grandfather. "A roar of approval from Wilberforce's sympathizers was heard throughout the museum," according to historian Ian Hesketh, "as if the crowd had been waiting patiently for this one glorious moment to revel in the bishop's violent poetry."[161]

What happened next is a matter of debate. The received wisdom—that Huxley defeated Wilberforce with raw scientific firepower and Darwinism prevailed—is neither a fiction nor the whole story. But the version of record—reiterated in history books, documentaries, and reenactments at Downe House—is Huxley's story.[162] In his version, Huxley made a brief rebuttal, then fired off the line that has made the debate famous. According to a letter he sent two months later, he bested the bishop by saying: "If then ... the question is put to me would I rather have a miserable ape for a grandfather or a man highly endowed by nature and possessed of great means of influence and yet who employs those faculties and that influence for the mere purpose of introducing ridicule into a grave scientific discussion—I unhesitatingly affirm my preference for the ape."[163] Huxley wrote that on the conclusion of his remarks "there was unextinguishable laughter among the people." As the "grave scientific discussion" dissolved into an uproar, Admiral FitzRoy, who had captained Darwin on the *Beagle*, rose to his feet and stomped through the room, holding a Bible aloft and roaring about revelation. It was, Huxley added, "*great fun.*"[164] Judging by the applause he received from a previously hostile crowd, Huxley seems to have swayed at least some sympathies.[165]

So how did Darwin react as reports trickled in to his study in the days that followed about the battle fought under his standard? Hesketh contends that Darwin enjoyed the news more than anyone, bringing it up repeatedly with his correspondents that week.[166] That's not wrong—Darwin certainly seemed legitimately grateful for the help of his allies and told them he found the details of the brawl exciting.[167] And he circulated a favorable article about the debate when it was published later that year.[168] But looking again at the letters, a more ambivalent picture comes out. Highlighting Darwin's praise and gratitude to his allies after the debate obscures the fact that Darwin barely mentioned it other than when he was communicating directly with the people who were there. His interest had mostly died down within a week. A letter to Hooker—who had declared himself the day's champion—a week and a half after the debate contains one passing mention of Oxford followed by seven paragraphs about plants.[169] Even the first excited letters have about as much unrelated academic chitchat as giddy play-by-play. Discussion of the debate, for Darwin, was an offshoot of the strategic discussions he was always having with his allies—about who had been won over and who was putting up a fight.

Shy Darwin, it seems, didn't want to battle, especially not in the spotlight. This is, he admitted, why he avoided the BAAS in the first place. Officially, the reason he gave for nonattendance at Oxford was that he was ill.[170] But Hesketh's study of Darwin's letters in the weeks and months leading up to the event makes it clear that he was building a paper trail of excuses for skipping the event weeks in advance.[171] "It is something unintelligible to me how anyone can argue in public like orators do," he told Hooker. "I had no idea you had this power."[172] To Huxley he wrote: "I honour your pluck. I would as soon have died as tried to answer the Bishop in such an assembly."[173] His preference, as always, was to bury himself in his science, continuing his experiments at Downe while the intellectual battles raged in distant halls and society salons. As Browne wrote, "While the *Times* roared against Huxley's support for 'Mr. Darwin's mischievous theory,' the source of the controversy appeared to have strolled into a greenhouse."[174] This was, it seems, the crucial divergence between Darwin and the bulldog. For Darwin, the tactical aspect of science was a necessary unpleasantness. For Huxley, the blood sport was at least half the fun.

This is by no means to suggest that Darwin was the real scientist and Huxley just a publicist with a poison pen. Knowledge—true or false—always marches with an army. Darwin may not have ever joined Huxley's swashbuckling X Club, who fought to take control of the British scientific apparatus and steer it in Darwinian directions.[175] But without them, his science would never have gained the reach that it did.[176] As he himself wrote to Huxley, "I am never weary of saying I sh^d. have been utterly smashed had it not been for you & three others."[177] Huxley's war battered down resistance on all sides, terraforming the landscape of cogency by knocking down junk evidence and humiliating obstinacy. And it attracted followers, whipping up excitement and mobilizing a scientific shock troop champing at the bit to take down the old guard. Darwinian science didn't succeed by the sense of science alone. Without the emotional engagement of his network, Darwin's theory might well have birthed, lived, and died quietly in a green village estate. Darwin was fascinated by the push and pull of ideas, but he was drawn to the laboratory of their growth and nurturance, not to the scenes of combat surrounding their propagation.

Creeping Disbelief: Darwinian Secularism

So we come at last to the question of so much literature on Darwin and religion: What did Darwin believe? We can't answer this without first acknowledging *how little Darwin seems to have cared*. Unlike Huxley, Darwin wrote little about religion. Throughout his nearly half century of publications—collected in a shelf-straining twenty-nine volumes—Darwin penned maybe a chapter's worth of material on the subject: a ten-page section of his autobiography (not intended for publication, as discussed below); a few dozen private letters, especially his correspondence with Asa Gray from late 1859 to 1861; some pages on the origins of religion in *Descent of Man* and a few more on religious feeling from *Expression of the Emotions in Man and Animals*; scattered paragraph-length snippets from his other major works, including *Origin*. Other than the speculation on religious origins, this is more or less a packing list of chapter 8 of Francis Darwin's *Life and Letters*.

Nonetheless, Darwin had opinions about religion—opinions that hardened as he aged. When the *Beagle* carried the twenty-two-year-old away, he was still pious, recounting in his autobiography how he was "heartily laughed at by several of the officers ... for quoting the Bible as an unanswerable authority on some point of morality."[178] By the end of the voyage, his faith had faded, with both the biblical God and the philosopher's deity seeming hopelessly far-fetched—especially when considered beside the many other faiths and traditions he had encountered abroad.[179] "Thus disbelief crept over me," he wrote half a century later. "The rate was so slow that I felt no distress, and have never since doubted even for a single second that my conclusion was correct."[180]

This set the stage for his emotional back-and-forth with Emma Wedgwood during their courtship—an intense exchange that, along with his efforts to muffle the shock for his colleagues and friends, fueled the fifteen-year delay of *Origin*. For all the strength of his convictions, the few and furtive religious debates he engaged exhibit Darwin's diplomatic acumen, on display especially when corresponding with the many strangers who wrote seeking windows onto the famous theorist's personal faith. These include a letter to a scholar from 1871, in which he indicated he was "in some degree unwilling to express myself publicly on religious subjects, as I do not feel that I have thought deeply enough to justify any publicity,"[181] and a letter to a Dutch student from 1873, which shaded in his concerns about pain while also reflecting his conviction that the extraordinary sweep of the universe *feels designed*: "The impossibility of conceiving that this grand and wondrous universe, with our conscious selves, seems to me the chief argument for the existence of God; but whether this is an argument of real value, I have never been able to decide. I am aware that if we admit a first cause, the mind still craves to know whence it came, and how it arose. Nor can I overlook the difficulty from the immense amount of suffering through the world."[182] A letter to a German student affirming that "the theory of Evolution is quite compatible with the belief in a God; but ... you must remember that different persons have different definitions of what they mean by God,"[183] and a letter to one J. Fordyce from 1879, stating, "In my most extreme fluctuations I have never been an Atheist in the sense of denying the existence of a God. I think that generally (and more and more as I grow older), but not always, that an Agnostic would be the more correct description of my state of mind."[184]

Francis, who gathered these together in *Life and Letters*, wrote of his father that "he naturally shrank from wounding the sensibilities of others in religious matters, and he was also influenced by the consciousness that a man ought not to publish on a subject to which he has not given special and continuous thought."[185] Toward the end of Darwin's life, socialist activist Edward Aveling sought his endorsement for an atheist tract, which Darwin declined on the grounds that atheism extended his views "to a greater length than seems safe."[186]

But this still doesn't answer the question. One truism in Darwin studies is that his religious disbelief fully arrived with the death of Annie in 1851. This wrenching loss, the story goes, catalyzed his refusal to allow suffering to be explained away by justifications of the actions of the sovereign God— no matter how sophisticated. Darwin himself never says as much.[187] But it's clear that the collapse of Darwin's Christianity is strongly tied to a philosophical reflection on the problem of pain in a designed universe.

His most incisive writings on this theme are in his letters to Gray, the Harvard botanist. Darwin and Gray carried on a regular correspondence after Gray received his copy of *Origin*, exchanging something like one hundred letters in two years. In between notes about orchids and speculation on the US Civil War booming in the background, the two friends circled their cardinal point of disagreement: design in nature. Many of Gray's letters to Darwin have been lost, but his views were made clear in his early reviews of *Origin*, republished (at Darwin's expense) in 1861 as *Natural Selection Not Inconsistent with Natural Theology*.[188] Gray's theological innovation was to suggest that we can detect divine action in the production of the subtle landscape of variations in organisms—variations that are then harvested by natural selection.[189] This allowed Gray to reassert that Darwinism was compatible with an intelligent designer.[190]

But this is exactly what Darwin rejected. "With respect to the theological view of the question," Darwin wrote to Gray, "this is always painful to me.—I am bewildered.—I had no intention to write atheistically. But I own that I cannot see, as plainly as others do, & as I sh^d wish to do, evidence of design & beneficence on all sides of us."[191] His argument was a version of the problem of suffering—the argument, made famous by Hume, that the existence of a good God is incompatible with the meaningless misery braided through life. Darwin pointed to the Ichneumonidae wasps, a parasitic family known for injecting their eggs into the bodies of caterpillars, which are then eaten alive by the newly hatched larvae. What "beneficent & omnipotent God would have designedly created" this ongoing stream of pure pain, Darwin asked?[192] As their conversation unfolded, Gray asked Darwin what it would take to persuade him of the fact of divine design. "If man was made of brass or iron," Darwin answered, "& no way connected with any other organism which had ever lived, I sh^d perhaps be convinced."[193]

This back-and-forth presaged the segment on religion in Darwin's autobiography, written fifteen years later as a private family record.[194] These pages contained his most trenchant statements of skepticism. The suffering of the world, he pointed out, has been justified by some "by imagining that it serves for [our] moral improvement." But calling up again the eviscerated caterpillars, he added that "the number of men in the world is as nothing compared with that of all other sentient beings, and these often suffer greatly without any moral improvement." That a benevolent God would endorse this state of affairs "revolts our understanding," and so the "very old argument from the existence of suffering against the existence of an intelligent first cause seems to me a strong one."[195]

As Levine points out, Darwin's renunciation of a divine fingerprint on the world—and his preference for a godless mechanism like natural selection—wasn't just an abstract theodicy. It allowed him to *make suffering make sense*.[196] Rather than a *justification*, natural selection offered an *explanation*, a way of fitting the pieces of evidence Darwin had in front of him into a story that clicked. As with Huxley, the commitment to divine design didn't just violate Darwin's sense of justice. It outraged his instinct for truth.[197] He turned away in disappointment from the contortions of theology that tried to reconcile senseless misery with a good God. Darwin's passion for reason didn't allow for a wallpapering over of his own grief. In the struggle between consolation and science, science won.

But as often as Darwin returned to this idea, he also reaffirmed how unsure he was of his own thoughts. "I feel most deeply that the whole subject is too profound for the human intellect," he wrote to Gray. "A dog might as well speculate on the mind of Newton."[198] In almost every letter where the subject arises, he uses the same self-effacing vocabulary, telling Gray that he is *in the mud* or *muddled*. "I am in much the same frame of mind as an old Gorilla would be in if set to learn the first book of Euclid," he wrote in 1861. "The old Gorilla would say it was of no manner of use; & I am much of the same mind."[199] Is this a bona fide statement of modesty? Or is Darwin again playing the diplomat, trying to coax his friend toward him by feigning uncertainty?

Maybe the answer is much simpler. Maybe the analogies with dogs and gorillas are not analogies at all, but coy reminders that their minds, like ours, emerged in the long history of organisms. Darwin's commitment to toppling the black monolith extended to his approach to religion and nonreligion. By virtue of being animal, our minds are also finite, of the mud, and inherently inadequate to the task of mapping the infinite—so unlike an angel or a man of brass. In this view, Darwin's agnosticism fit hand in glove with his theory of evolution. It was part of the dynamic of modesty and eagerness for truth that made up his sense of science.

There's another way of looking at Darwin's nonreligion—perhaps the one that best explains the fact that Darwin just *didn't want to talk about it*. Maybe Darwin simply found the great library of religion *uninteresting*. Metaphysical speculation was checkers. The science of life was chess. "Our faculties are more fitted to recognize the wonderful structure of a beetle than a Universe," he wrote in his N notebook from the late 1830s.[200] This was partly a statement of limitations, but also a reminder of how the mind could flourish only in its right place. Much as William James came to loathe the endless mistiness of metaphysics—detached from consequence and oblivious to evidence—Darwin found theology *boring*.[201] Why speculate on shadows in the mirror when he could plunge his hands into the earth and unearth the dazzling, intricate truths of life? Much more than for Huxley, Darwin's neglect of the uproar around religion and evolution suggests that it never had a hold on his interest in the first place. It was thin gruel compared to the heart-pounding game of clicking the evidence streaming to him from the far corners of his global laboratory into an ever-expanding, ever-conquering theory.

Conclusion: Secularism and the Darwinian Aftermath

"I can indeed hardly see how anyone ought to wish Christianity to be true," Darwin wrote in his autobiography, "for if so the plain language of the text seems to show that the men who do not believe, and this would include my Father, Brother and almost all my best friends, will be everlastingly punished. And this is a damnable doctrine."[202] But this passage didn't see print for eighty years. The version of the autobiography published in *Life and Letters* omitted it.[203] It became a family secret, only brought to light when Darwin's granddaughter, Nora Barlow, published an uncensored edition in 1958. It represented the sharpest articulation of Darwin's skepticism, his conviction that the vision of Christianity was deeply disordered. But it was only expressed privately, in a document Darwin penned solely for his family circle.

When Aveling met Darwin, the secular agitator told the scientist that "Agnostic was but Atheist writ respectable, and Atheist was only Agnostic writ aggressive."[204] Sheepish Darwin might have agreed, even if he kept his counsel. But publicly allying himself with atheism would not only have rocked his relationships with friends and family; it would also have weakened his hand in the only game that mattered to him: advancing science. Even if Darwinism became the banner of dissent—the sectarian interest of those who saw themselves as outside an established, backward-facing system, hearts swelling to the idea that it could be transformed, that old hierarchies could fade and fall—Darwin himself stayed on the sidelines.

Darwin, the hero of the contemporary atheist movement (thick brow and cool expression gazing at us from T-shirts and memes, his name a war cry on the bumper sticker battlefield), may well have been a closeted atheist. But the fact that he never announced this orientation, and even kept his relatively respectable agnosticism close to the vest, tells us a lot about what kind of atheist he was. It shades in the affective coordinates that patterned his science and his secularism.

What would it mean for secularism today to think of scientific rationality not as neutral calculation, but as made of feeling? It should—of necessity—push secularism into a state of high alert. The failure of Darwin and his followers to decisively end scientific racism left the door open for the eugenicist horrors of the twentieth century.[205] A secularist culture that defines itself as above and beyond the play of emotions leaves itself vulnerable to taint by all those prejudices that don't land on the microscope slide.[206] Even more so when we come to see that the most toxic prejudices come to our doorstep garbed as pleasure. They mess together with the excitement we feel in better understanding the world, threatening to infest our researches and eat them from the inside. "Ignoring the historical backdrop of eugenics debates," writes feminist STS theorist Banu Subramaniam, "dooms scientists to a future as co-conspirators in the production of inequality."[207] The same could be said about formations of the secular.

But cogency theory also opens avenues for understanding how science works when it works—and works well. Where Kuhn's approach to science could only render evolution by natural selection as another dizzy language game, cogency theory looks at the pivot points, the crucial moments of persuasion, the breakthroughs. Darwinism overran skepticism (both scientific and religious) toward common descent by articulating a better way of making contact with reality—of feeling out the way things are. Along these lines, a Darwinian secularism takes the emotional strands of knowledge-making as vital for science. It recognizes the centrality of feeling for good knowledge and sound belief, while also holding onto a clear-eyed catalogue of its vulnerabilities.

Levine talks about "the almost inevitable Darwinian exclamation point," the way "close inspection of nature [yields] exuberance and excitement."[208] Levine's view may land too much on the sunny side—there's a sense of Darwin's intellectual passions, but no picture of agonism. Still, his point stands. Science in the Darwinian register doesn't drain the world of feeling. The deeper scope of science *expands* the sphere of fascination, rather than narrowing it. Placing our minds in a friendly lineage beside dogs and gorillas opens avenues for self-exploration—with all the excitement that comes with those new horizons of discovery. Our old autobiographies were always obstacles to self-understanding, presenting us as angels or men of brass, censoring our connections with our animal kin. So, too, with formations of the secular drawing on science. Far from being feelingless, secularisms always arrive with their own distinct emotional signatures. The question is whether the watermark is Darwin's or Huxley's.

Neo-evolutionary theologies that make the human central or inevitable have missed the forest for the trees.[209] Darwin's story is the story of our chain of accidents. His task wasn't just to correlate our skeletons and muscles, our limbs and organs, our fingers and toes to those of other animals. He showed that the mind itself is an animal faculty, constituted from the root up by feeling. To the horror of Adam Sedgwick but the delight of Eve, thinking and feeling really are united. Mr. Vestiges won the secret war. Humans are only better beasts, and maybe not as well-off as we'd like to believe. Even knowledge production is something we do as animals, not as angels. We savor the lusciousness of science, the delight of knowledge, the passion for truth both vulnerable and thrilling.

6.
THE SECULAR CIRCUS
SCIENCE AND RACIALIZED REASON IN THE SCOPES TRIAL

Admit [Darwin's] premise and they will have to admit that
there is no fundamental difference between themselves
and the race they pretend to despise.
—*Chicago Defender*, "If Monkeys Could Speak," May 23, 1925

Content warning: This chapter features
a figure with disturbing content.

Introduction: Morons

A few days after Donald Trump won the November 2016 US presidential election, a new face started making rounds on social media. There were a few different black-and-white photographs, but they all showed the same man—the same unmistakable gray screwdriver eyes, the same dark Brylled-down hair, parted in the middle. Beside the picture was a quotation. It read:

> As democracy is perfected, the office of the President represents, more and more closely, the inner soul of the people. On some great and glorious day, the plain folks of the land will reach their heart's desire at

last, and the White House will be occupied by a downright fool and a complete narcissistic moron.

—H. L. Mencken, *Baltimore Evening Sun*, July 26, 1920

The pictures were circulated by people who would call themselves politically progressive. But the man in the meme was no progressive. The text—taken from Mencken's reporting on the run-up to the 1920 presidential election—reflected his sincere conviction that democracy was a sham. He would later use the line "president of the morons" about Franklin Roosevelt to express his total contempt for the New Deal.[1]

The word *moron* says a lot. It entered common circulation in English in 1910 through the work of eugenicist Henry Goddard as a medical diagnosis for an adult with a so-called mental age of eight to twelve years. (*Idiot* and *imbecile* landed lower on the scale.) Eugenics in the 1920s had respectable science on its side, and Mencken, though a journalist by profession, saw himself as a man of science.[2] When Mencken used the word *moron*, it rang out as more than an off-the-cuff jeer. It was a clinical diagnosis.

Mencken was a major figure in twentieth-century US secularism. Drawn to nonbelief by his favorite writer, Thomas Henry Huxley, he was the first to translate Nietzsche's *The Antichrist* into English.[3] And Mencken was a star player in the grandest spectacle of scientific secularism in the American twentieth century, the Scopes Monkey Trial of 1925. The midsummer trial of John Scopes in Dayton, Tennessee, still looms high over America's cultural landscape. This is in part thanks to the 1955 play *Inherit the Wind* and its 1960 film adaptation, where a surrogate Mencken was portrayed by a cheerfully vicious Gene Kelly. But it's also because the underlying tensions of the Scopes trial—the place of religion in public education and science in public policy—are still with us in new forms. The Intelligent Design (ID) controversies brought to a head in *Kitzmiller v. Dover* in 2005 are still fresh. Private foundations like the Discovery Institute continue to lobby for inclusion of ID instruction in schools. Evolution-denying conservatives still wind up heading congressional science committees whenever the Republicans win the House of Representatives. And the story of Scopes is still invoked by liberals to reiterate the necessity of a secular cleaving of church and state, whether the subject is abortion or contraception or gay rights.

This chapter takes up *Tennessee v. Scopes* to study scientific secularism in the wake of Darwin. As historians of science have shown, the Scopes trial that has been passed down to us is mostly fable. *Inherit the Wind* spun the story into a morality tale about the clash between free inquiry and authoritarianism. The play was intended as a creative rearrangement of historical events, a response to the political crisis of McCarthyism in the 1950s (much like Arthur Miller's *The Crucible*, which no one takes as a faithful documentary record of the Salem witch trials). The carefully crafted drama about the urgency of freedom of conscience was a savvy response to its own historical moment, but it papered over the confusing and messy alliances of the actual event.

That doesn't mean the basic contours of Scopes can't be made out in the play. There really was a law against teaching evolution and there really was a trial, though it may have been more of a media hologram than we might expect—an American echo of the Oxford museum debate, this time with a live radio feed to Chicago, a rapidly constructed airstrip connecting the town to the cities, and a hungry national print media running down the daily play-by-play for their evening editions.[4] There really was a clash around secularism and the right roles of religion and science in state institutions like public schools.

To sift truth from fiction, this chapter will retell the story of the long Scopes trial, unlinking the myth and unearthing the bizarre twists of history that led to a man claiming to have taught evolution to put himself in the way of indictment, a trial transformed into a county fair, a defense attorney cross-examining a prosecutor on a steaming courthouse lawn, a sprawling judicial melee tripped up by a technicality. This will mean reckoning with the convoluted politics of the age of jazz and fundamentalism, the venom of racism and the audacity of eugenics and their strange tensions and combinations, and how they mapped onto the lingering tensions of rural/urban, North/South, and religious/secular in the United States. Like the previous chapter, there are two bodies at the heart of this study: Mencken and his nemesis, the progressive populist William Jennings Bryan, three-time Democratic presidential candidate, three-time loser, Christian, pacifist, prohibitionist, ally of suffragists, who dedicated the final years of his life to ending the teaching of evolution in schools.

Cogency theory sees the Scopes trial as a contest of emotions. This isn't new in itself—many textbook accounts of Scopes emphasize the high tide of feeling in the trial.[5] But cogency theory goes deeper in diagramming the case as a game of cat's cradle between scientific secularism, emotion, and racialized reason. What's most striking about the Scopes trial is how little it reflects the sense of science. Unlike in the controversies surrounding

Darwin, the heartbeat of the passion for reason throughout the trial is faint. *Tennessee v. Scopes* serves, instead, as a case study of how racialized reason—the carapace of racist ideas that forms around core racist affects—infects secular rationality.

Mencken, the most zealous partisan on the secularist side, was not just a racist. He was also an elitist—in the fullest sense of the word—moving way beyond the Black/white race binary to a virulent biological determinism. The cogency of eugenics was, for him, pinned to the way this so-called science evoked feeling. It felt so good to Mencken that it had to be true. The secular vision Mencken drew from this science reflected these racialized affects. On the other side, some contemporary historians have seen fit to reassess the creationist faction as having unexpectedly noble aims, landing on moral high ground by challenging the pro-eugenics sympathies of 1910s and 1920s science. But the cogency theory approach pushes back on this revisionist view. It sees the antievolutionist side—including William Jennings Bryan himself—as mirroring the racialized cognition of Mencken, elevating a Christian (and implicitly white) nationalist identity. The chapter concludes by considering how the Scopes trial reflects a failure of both liberal and secularist visions of the relationship between science and society.

The Long Scopes Trial

Darwin's deft downplaying of his own nonreligious inclinations paved the way for many nineteenth-century Christians to both accept and embrace Darwinian biology. Liberal Christians both inside and outside the religious establishment not only accommodated Darwinism but made it central to their theological sensibilities. Like Charles Kingsley and Snow Wedgwood, they believed Darwinism told a story of God's majesty and human redemption.[6] Theologians like Frederick Temple and Aubrey Moore in the UK and preachers like Henry Ward Beecher in the United States followed this track.

But plenty of other anti-Darwinian Christian factions retained their skepticism of the new science. By the early twentieth century, the Darwinian debates had fused with one of the defining controversies of American Protestantism: on one side, liberal modernists who favored theological accommodation with science; on the other, fundamentalists who doubled down on the unfractured integrity of the Bible. Liberal accommodation of science was seen as opaque and unsatisfying by lay believers more impressed by the apocalyptic thunder of anti-Darwinian fundamentalist preachers and politicians.[7] The word *fundamentalism* derives from a series of booklets published under the title *The Fundamentals: A Testimony to the Truth* in the 1910s. The ninety essays making up *The Fundamentals* were a color negative of the work of Kingsley and Beecher, setting out an agenda of resistance to science, liberal theology, and biblical criticism.[8] The collection included the lapsed evolutionist George Frederick Wright's essay "The Passing of Evolution," which catalogued limitations of Darwin's theory.[9] It claimed the mantle of real science for revelation, prefiguring the fundamentalist campaign.[10]

Education was one of the primary battlefields in this contest between modernists and conservatives. Public education exploded in the United States—especially in the rural South—in the decades following the turn of the century.[11] In Tennessee alone, the population of high school students had increased from ten thousand in 1910 to over fifty thousand in 1925, almost solely to the benefit of white children.[12] This expanded government involvement in child-rearing displaced the patriarchal family as the conduit of culture and values in the South.[13] Although some conservatives in the South embraced the expansion of public education as a vehicle for Bible instruction, they were put on the defensive when their kids started bringing evolution talk home to the dinner table.[14] And they worried it risked leading the United States down the track of atheism and militarism, much as evangelicals blamed the German education system for the disaster of World War I.[15] In Tennessee, the Methodists' loss of control of Vanderbilt University to secular administrators in the 1900s added even more urgency to the cause.[16]

This is the tableau of the Scopes trial: religion, politics, science, and history interlocked in a single set piece. Key to understanding the trial itself, however, is getting distance from its best-known retelling: *Inherit the Wind*. Jerome Lawrence and Robert Lee's dramatization of the trial was never intended to be a faithful historical replica, nor even a commentary on fundamentalism, evolution, or the science-religion dynamic. Although antievolution statutes were still on the books in 1955 and fundamentalism remained an active regional force, Lawrence and Lee's real concern was McCarthyism and the corrosion of freedom of speech during the late 1940s Red Scare. But the eventual inclusion of the play in high school curricula guaranteed it would warp the historical record. The fictionalized account of Bert Cates, Matt Brady, Henry Drummond, and E. K. Hornbeck was a fable; like all fables, it blanched out the stubborn complexity of Scopes, Bryan, Darrow, and Mencken.

In this context of politicized science, William Jennings Bryan—his political career over but his fund of admiration among white Protestants still running high—and the fundamentalists resumed the alliance they had formed over prohibition, lobbying states around the country to pass legislation banning the teaching of evolution in schools. The issue became a leitmotif in the 1924 presidential elections. Bryan was not on the ticket (though his brother Charles was up for the vice presidency), but Democrats, after declining to condemn escalating violence by the Ku Klux Klan at their party's convention that year, still declared fealty to "Bryan and the Bible."[17] Oklahoma and Florida passed laws preventing evolution instruction in 1923. In early 1925, Tennessee legislators followed suit with the Butler Act, prohibiting any curriculum that contradicted the Bible.

So far, so good for *Inherit the Wind*. But here we part ways with Lawrence and Lee. What launched the Scopes trial was not an upstanding schoolteacher insisting on his right to free speech—Cates heroically rolling down the diagram of a gorilla in his classroom, then frog-marched to jail by a posse. It was a press release printed in a Tennessee newspaper. The recently formed American Civil Liberties Union wanted to establish the unconstitutionality of the Butler Act.[18] But it needed a test case to rise through the system and force the Supreme Court to rule. So the ACLU offered to pay the legal expenses of any teacher willing to testify that they had taught evolution in contravention of the statutes.[19] John Scopes, a football coach and sometime science teacher at the high school in Dayton, Tennessee, didn't see the ACLU's call. But some local town boosters did. Most of them didn't care much about evolution, but they saw a chance to bring business to Dayton.[20] Only after they'd agreed on a plan did they call up Scopes. He wasn't certain, but he seemed to recall reciting from a chapter on evolution in a review session, and so agreed to put himself forward for the test case.[21]

The ACLU's priority was to sprint through the lower circuits to the Supreme Court. But, as historian Edward Larson writes, the people of Dayton "had other ideas."[22] As early as the pretrial indictment, Judge John Raulston stated: "I have set a date when all universities and schools will be through their terms of school in order that scientists, theologians, and other school men will be able to act as expert witnesses.... My suggestion is that a roof be built over a large vacant lot and seats be built in tiers. At the very least, the place should seat twenty thousand people."[23] The Daytonians—in many ways politically and theologically isolated from the rest of their state—believed they were launching a national debate, not prosecuting a heretic.[24] The scheme resembled the popular Chautauqua lectures—a franchise of festivals built around edifying talks by cultural and scientific notables. Bryan himself was a major fixture on the circuit. If the public-facing scholarly fête of the British Association for the Advancement of Science was a Victorian TED talk, Chautauqua was the Roaring Twenties edition. The Dayton city fathers' vision for the trial was in this mold.

But this was all a preamble. When Bryan himself volunteered to join the prosecution, national interest in the event exploded. Bryan's entry, in turn, caught the attention of Clarence Darrow, one of the most famous criminal lawyers in the country, with friendly links to the ACLU (and Bryan himself) through his work defending labor leaders. Civic associations and businesses began preparing for what was, in effect, a trial engulfed by a state fair. The actual attendance was only in the low thousands—many of them journalists. But the ambience was circus-like, all the same.[25] Larson writes that "Main Street merchants decorated their shops with pictures of apes and monkeys. One billboard featured a long-tailed primate holding a bottle of patent medicine; another pictured a chimpanzee drinking a soda. The constable's motorcycle carried a sign reading 'Monkeyville Police,' while a delivery van bore the words 'Monkeyville Express.'"[26] The plan backfired, and almost all the coverage in the press criticized Dayton for greedily embracing the spectacle.

With the circus came a lion. Mencken went down to Dayton to cover the trial in person for the *Baltimore Sun*. The *Sun* was Mencken's hometown paper, but by this point it was just an outpost of his one-man media empire. It's difficult to overstate how prominent Mencken was on the American cultural scene in his day, a famous figure everyone wanted to talk about, not unlike a Huxley or a Hitchens. In the postwar years, writes Mencken biographer Marion Rodgers, the question *What do you think of Mencken?* was easy kindling for refined conversation.[27] By the mid-1920s Mencken, only in his early forties, already had two major books written *about* him, in addition to his scores of single-authored volumes and thousands of articles and essays.[28] He was world-famous, influential, and, as we'll see below, extremely good at what he did: namely, hatchet jobs.

The trial itself began on July 15. The defense had begun with a motion to quash the charge on the grounds that the Butler Act was unconstitutional. This led to the first of several astonishing speeches made during the trial: Clarence Darrow's clarion call for free inquiry, which lasted for two hours and left even the mostly hostile courtroom audience exhilarated and astonished. "You have but a dim notion of it who have only read it," Mencken wrote. "It rose like a wind and ended like a flourish of bugles."[29] The speech was widely praised, and its text was printed in newspapers around the country the following day. The prosecution's only counter at this stage was to retrace, blandly, the terms of the statute. Judge Raulston sided with sobriety, affirming that Scopes's rights as a contract employee of the state were not subject to constitutional oversight.[30]

On the surface, the prosecution was narrowly focused on establishing Scopes's guilt under Butler. But there was dissent in their ranks. Although they wanted to win the trial on statutory grounds, Bryan was yearning for a bold, epic confrontation on behalf of the integrity of revealed religion. Still, the team opened with a no-frills approach. They called four witnesses: the superintendent of the school, two of Scopes's students, and the proprietor of the local drugstore. Each testified that Scopes recited prohibited teachings in the classroom and so violated the Butler Act. Then the prosecution rested.

The defense side was also divided. The ACLU attorneys were still intent on getting to the Supreme Court (which means they wanted to lose). But Darrow, like Bryan, sensing something in the air, wanted to plant a flag. He successfully pushed for a strategy that was more ambitious, if still basically legalistic. The defense set out to show that the Butler Act's presumptive target—the teaching of evolution—was missed by the printed letter of the law, which only outlawed *contradicting Genesis*. Their intent, through the calling of a dozen expert witnesses—eight scientists and four clergymen—was to prove that Darwinism and the Bible were, in fact, compatible. And therefore Scopes had not violated the act by teaching evolution. Darrow didn't believe any of this, but shielding Scopes behind an academic version of theistic evolution (humiliating his enemies while still expecting to lose) was his best available compromise with the ACLU.[31]

Their first move was to call a zoology professor to the stand. The prosecution objected, contending that the evidence the scientist offered was irrelevant to the charge. Judge Raulston's response was to send the jurors away while the two sides wrangled over admissibility. The jury would be out for the rest of the week. (When they returned to deliberate on the final day, they would have spent less than half a day in session.) The defense and prosecution made arguments for and against inclusion. Bryan delivered a stirring speech, bringing the crowd to its feet. This was followed by what, by all accounts, was one of the most extraordinary orations of the trial, from

ACLU attorney Dudley Field Malone, in defense of intellectual freedom. This speech, too, ran against the disposition of the crowd. But Malone brought the house down. During the storm of applause that followed, a policeman rapped a table with his baton so hard that he cracked it down the middle. Then everyone heard a rousing counterargument by the local prosecutor—also met with sustained applause.[32]

Judge Raulston adjourned the trial for the evening to consider the merits of the prosecution's objection. Overnight, he was lobbied by Tennessee legislators, stung by mocking coverage of the state in the press, to end the trial as quickly as possible. When he returned Friday morning, he ruled the testimony of the expert witnesses in the defense's docket inadmissible. Darrow objected and persuaded the court to accept written testimonials from them all. He then requested another adjournment to gather their statements.[33]

Over the weekend, Darrow came up with a canny plan. If the defense's expert witnesses on religion were denied access to the trial, he decided, they would use the expert witness already in the room. So on the second-to-last day of the trial, after Judge Raulston had relocated the proceedings to the lawn to escape the stifling heat, Darrow called Bryan himself to the stand. Bryan accepted with gusto, on condition that he would be allowed to cross-examine Darrow in turn. It flattered the ambitions of both men to duel for the honor of their respective worldviews. And it finally slaked the thirst of the audience—which swelled from five hundred to three thousand as word spread—for a glorious, sweaty spectacle.[34] The atmosphere on the hot grass would have been not unlike the feeling in the Church of St. Mary the Virgin, transformed into wrestling grounds during the disputations, or in the long hall of the Oxford Museum of Natural History as Wilberforce and the Darwinians duked it out before a crowd of almost a thousand.[35] It was an intellectual brawl, science as spectator sport.

Darrow's cross-examination reads today like a laundry list of atheist objections to the Bible, pouncing on extravagant stories and contradictions in the text and putting them under the vise of modern science. But there was a strict method, which revealed itself in Bryan's answer to a question about the age of the earth. Bryan claimed that the *days* of creation in Genesis need not have been actual twenty-four-hour periods, but may well have been whole epochs. (This is the *day-age theory*, developed by nineteenth-century Christian apologists, disdained by fundamentalists but endorsed by Bryan.)[36] This established Darrow's point: interpretation of the Bible was unavoidable.³⁷ The *Commercial Appeal* (Memphis) reported: "It was not a contest. Consequently there was no victory. Darrow succeeded in showing that Bryan knows little about the science of the world. Bryan succeeded in bearing witness bravely to the faith which he believes transcends all the learning of men."³⁸

Darrow's assault was followed by another sudden change of plans: Judge Raulston, still under pressure from state politicians, abruptly brought the trial to an end, junking the agreement made between Bryan and Darrow to swap places. Siding with the rest of the prosecution team (who now viewed Bryan as a rogue operative) and affirming that the debate was irrelevant, he brought the jury back in. Having heard only half a day of testimony, the jury needed just nine minutes to reach a verdict, mostly spent getting in and out of the courtroom.³⁹ They found Scopes guilty, and Judge Raulston set a fine of $100 from the bench.

And this minute detail became the defining feature of the *legal* legacy of the trial. At Tennessee's appeals court two years later, the justices accepted all the prosecution's arguments about the constitutionality of the Butler Act, refusing the ACLU's request to overturn it. So far so good for the ACLU. But under Tennessee law, a fine of more than $25 must be set by the jury, not the judge. Eager to banish the Scopes case from the papers as rapidly as possible, the justices found Scopes's penalty unlawful and voided his conviction, dispelling the ACLU's plan to bring the law before the Supreme Court. No other candidates for test cases stepped forward, and the mood of the ACLU's donor brigade, unhappy with Darrow's performance, made the ACLU reluctant to press the issue.⁴⁰ Contra *Inherit the Wind*, there was no neat narrative button—the forces of unreason collapsing with a shudder in the face of truth—though Bryan did die five days after the trial concluded, aged sixty-five.

The Butler Act remained on the books for forty years—shaping textbooks and curricula but yielding no prosecutions—before repeal in 1967.⁴¹ In the 1950s, concerns about advances in Soviet science led to a push for a more rigorous national high school curriculum, including in biology.⁴² This opened a legal battle over the Arkansas version of the Butler Act in the 1968 *Epperson v. Arkansas* trial. Susan Epperson, a high school biology teacher, put herself forward as a new test case on the ACLU's behalf, leading to the 9–0 nullification of the law by the US Supreme Court. In response, religious conservatives began passing *equal-time* laws, which mandated teaching biblical creationism alongside evolution in classrooms. In 1981, the first of these laws was struck down by an Arkansas district court in *McLean v. Arkansas*. Six years later, the Supreme Court weighed in on a Louisiana equal-time law in *Edwards v. Aguillard*, ruling that creationism was a religious viewpoint that could not be lawfully taught in US schools. So ended the long Scopes trial.

Return of the Bulldog, or *Mencken v. Boneheads*

At the time of *Scopes*, the United States was sharply divided by tensions of class, race, region, and religion. (The more things change …) Rural white constituencies—especially in the South—were increasingly frustrated by the predatory capitalism of the big cities of the Northeast. These economic powerhouses had sunk their talons in deep during Reconstruction and the economic collapse of the 1890s. Southern Blacks, meanwhile, were under siege, the victims of racial terrorism and severe economic exploitation. In W. E. B. Du Bois's words, whites rejected Reconstruction not just because of its economic terms but because they "wanted the Negro beneath the feet of the white worker."[43] Powerful white coalitions in the South, disgraced by the Civil War, Reconstruction, and economic disadvantage, defined themselves in opposition to what they perceived as a pro-bank, pro-alcohol, and pro-Black Yankee cultural takeover (see figure 6.1). "Still suffering from the ravages of the Civil War and the humiliation of Reconstruction," Larson writes, white "Southerners were conscious of their national image and sensitive to any perceived slight."[44]

Religion was part of this picture, too. The geographical distribution of fundamentalism was broad-based, with epicenters in far-flung California, Minnesota, and Pennsylvania. Its intellectual hub was Princeton Theological Seminary, while Vanderbilt University in Tennessee was a modernist stronghold.[45] But as Jeffrey Moran writes, although fundamentalism first took root in the North, it "adapted well to the southern climate," finding points of contact with existing regional grievances.[46] Every single state-level antievolution bill passed in the 1920s was in the former Confederacy or Oklahoma.[47]

This was the political and cultural backdrop of the Scopes trial. The Darwinian controversies examined in the last chapter showcased the sense of science, a test tube of how science and secularism come to be defined by an agonism of intellectual feelings. But in the summer of 1925, a very different facet of scientific secularism was on display. The rest of this chapter focuses on Mencken and Bryan. Rather than amplifying their differences, however,

Figure 6.1 J. P. Alley, *Commercial Appeal*, June 14, 1925, showing Scopes calling for Darrow's aid.

it highlights their symmetry. Although they were on opposite sides of the debate, both trafficked in versions of science defined by racialized reason. They illustrate how the emotional parameters of racialization shape the coordinates of knowledge-making, setting the parameters of *what feels true*.

Rodgers (Mencken's biographer) describes how Huxley became both the template for Mencken's "violent agnosticism" and the inspiration for his slashing literary style.[48] On the centenary of Huxley's birth, Mencken wrote: "All of us owe a vast debt to Huxley. … All his life long he flung himself upon authority—when it was stupid, ignorant, and tyrannical. He attacked it with every weapon in his rich arsenal—wit, scorn, and above all, superior knowledge. To it he opposed a single thing: the truth as it could be discovered and established—the plain truth that sets men free."[49] He even identified Huxley as the archetypal nineteenth-century genius—signaling his preference for the snarling disciple of Darwin rather than the architect of evolution by natural selection himself.[50]

But although he followed the way of the bulldog, Mencken was no scientist. He was an amateur who hitched his wagon to the science that best flattered his own self-regard: eugenics. Unlike Huxley, who underwent at least one full-blown scientific conversion in his life, Mencken's science was never more than an incubator of his own narcissism. (Mencken did quietly tone down his racist flourishes over the course of his life, though, excising over-the-top passages as his books went into reprint.)[51] Huxley's love of the fight was always calibrated to match up with his own bracing sense of science, scrutinized, weighed up, and tested. Huxley felt his truth had been bought and paid for with long toil and so allowed himself to indulge in its too-eager defense. Mencken didn't have this self-suspicion.

Mencken's politics are almost totally inscrutable from a twenty-first-century perch. To us he looks like a crisscross of contradictions: an urban libertarian and an antidemocrat, a eugenicist who blasted Jim Crow and the KKK, a snob fascinated by Nietzsche who wrote book-length rhapsodies to popular culture and vernacular speech. But elitism was a constant in his political life. He kept a well-stocked cupboard of insults—*peasant, boob, halfwit, moron*. The slogan of the first arts and culture magazine he edited, the *Smart Set*—printed right on the cover of the October 1914 issue—was: "One civilized reader is worth a thousand boneheads" (see figure 6.2).

Mencken offers a case study of the emotional architecture of elitism. He saw himself as a culture hero, a crusader for the virtues of civilization, mounting a daunting but debonair last stand against the horde. It's unmistakably racialized, especially when fused with eugenics. As we saw in chapter 2, racialized reason fronts a facade of scientific impartiality, but still gleefully plunges into the hedonicity of hate. Mencken was a master of this jubilant contempt, which meant he was always gathering boneheads to fill up the lower ranks. He had three supply lines: religion, especially evangelical and fundamentalist Christians (Mencken was the inventor of the term *Bible Belt*), race (usually in terms of an aristocratic myth of bloodlines), and region (rural people, whom Mencken called *yokels*), especially those from the South.

All three kinds of disdain are on display in Mencken's essay "The Sahara of the Bozart," published in 1917. "Bozart" was a mocking malapropism of the French *les beaux arts*. The "Sahara of the Bozart" was the South, a

Figure 6.2 James Montgomery Flagg, *Smart Set*, October 1914.

cultural garbage dump. "Down there," Mencken wrote, "a poet is now almost as rare as an oboe-player, a dry-point etcher or a metaphysician."[52] "It is," he continued, "amazing to contemplate so vast a vacuity.... Nearly the whole of Europe could be lost in that stupendous region of worn-out farms, shoddy cities and paralyzed cerebrums."[53] It wasn't always so. The planter class, the indolent slave masters Du Bois diagnosed as "arrogant, strutting, quarrelsome kinglets," Mencken saw as the last great American glitterati, a once-glorious society of learning and refinement, buried by the Civil War.[54] "The old aristocracy went down the red gullet of war," he wrote. "The poor white trash are now in the saddle."[55]

Eugenic pseudoscience was his weapon of choice. The source of Southern decay, he hypothesized, was its corrupted gene pool, dangerously skewed when the upper castes were killed off. Mencken noted that "the older stocks of the South, and particularly the emancipated and dominant poor white trash, have never been investigated scientifically."[56] So he volunteered his talents. His finding was that whereas the aristocratic orders of the cultured Old South were primarily Anglo-Saxon, the impoverished classes were mostly "Celtic." "It is highly probable," he mused, "that some of the worst blood of western Europe flows in the veins of the Southern poor whites, now poor no longer."[57] The decapitation of Southern society, he concluded, had wiped out the gene pool's upper crust, allowing the genetic losers to rise to the top.

The only hope of a future Southern rebirth, Mencken wrote, lay with its Blacks. This was because, in the antebellum golden age, noble-blooded whites would not intermarry with poor whites but *would* "take mistresses" (his vile euphemism for rape) from among enslaved Black women, producing descendants who carried their glorious blood. The poor whites now in charge were the inheritors of an undiluted line of mediocrity. But Southern Blacks carried the seed of heroism. "It is not by accident that the Negroes of the South are making faster progress, culturally, than the masses of the whites," Mencken wrote. "No Southern composer has ever written music so good as that of half a dozen white-Black composers who might be named."[58]

This prompted Mencken's strident denunciation of the Jim Crow regime, which suffocated the only real noble culture left in the South and boosted the boneheads.[59] This was the blueprint for Mencken's ruthlessly efficient degradation machine. Southern white supremacists had no quarrel with race science. They'd been eager consumers of cranial measurements, polygenism, and theories of Blackness as a "defective decarbonization process" for over a century.[60] But this was exactly what made Mencken's work so cutting. He had mastered an acrobatic double insult, lacerating racist whites with their own twisted race science *and* elevating Blacks above them.

"Homo Neandertalensis": Mencken in Tennessee

Needless to say, then, the white citizens of Tennessee were on edge when Mencken arrived to cover *Tennessee v. Scopes* a few years later.[61] Given Dayton's idiosyncratic demographics (Rhea County was the only Tennessee district *not* carried by Bryan in his presidential campaigns), Mencken was initially welcomed by some townspeople who admired his glamour and aura of culture.[62] He reciprocated by calling their home "a country town full of charm and even beauty"—very different from the "squalid Southern village, with darkies snoozing on the horse-blocks, pigs rooting under the houses and the inhabitants full of hookworm and malaria" he had expected.[63]

But his first trial dispatch liquefied this grant of goodwill. The article, "The Tennessee Circus," began with a broadside against Christianity itself. "The whole history of the church," he observed, "as everyone knows, is a history of schemes to put down heresy by force."[64] And yet, he continued, the tactic was increasingly ineffective. Southern Christian authorities—the "Ku Klux Klergy," he called them—were intellectually "still medieval. They believed that the devices which worked in the year 1300 will still work in 1925."[65] Far from horrifying Mencken, however, this thrilled him. "As a life-long opponent of their pretensions," he beamed, "I can only report that their fidelity to this belief fills me with agreeable sentiments. I rejoice that they have forced the fighting, and plan to do it in the open."[66] There's the shade of Huxley on Mencken's shoulder, sharpening his claws and beak.

In the second article of the series, "Homo Neandertalensis," he phrased the battle even more starkly in terms of a zero-sum contest between religion and civilization. Giddily, he told the story in racialized terms. "The so-called religious organizations which now lead the war against the teaching of evolution," he proposed, "are nothing more, at bottom, than conspiracies of the inferior man against his betters."[67] The motivation was simple laziness. Evolution is a hard thing to understand. But the story of Genesis "is so simple that even a yokel can grasp it. ... So he accepts it with loud hosannas, and has one more excuse for hating his betters."[68] It was Mencken's own jury-rigged theory of cogency: fundamentalism was a simplex system, a preference for easy ideas that click. But Mencken had no intention of turning this laser of scrutiny on himself.

Through a series of almost a dozen more pieces, Mencken continued to hammer his message home. He lumped together the rural, the religious, and the Southern: they became the peasants, the boobs, the morons, the boneheads. In another column, he described the trial itself as having taken on "something of the air of a religious orgy."[69] This was due not only to the celebratory noises of the attendees but also to the circus atmosphere around town, especially the noisy preachers. "One and all they are Fundamentalists," Mencken wrote, "and their yells and bawlings fill the air with orthodoxy."[70]

In advance of his July 13 column, Mencken seems to have gone out into the hills and found a nighttime tent revival. He portrayed it as a sort of midnight horror show, happily flirting with the slanderous slippage between Christian and pagan rites. "What they crave," he wrote,

> is a continuous experience of the divine power, an endless series of evidence that the true believer is a marked man, ever under the eye of God. It is not enough to go to a revival once a year or twice a year; there must be a revival every night. And it is not enough to accept the truth as a mere statement of indisputable and awful fact: it must be embraced ecstatically and orgiastically, to the accompaniment of loud shouts, dreadful heavings and gurglings, and dancing with arms and legs.[71]

Historian Sean McCloud has noted that eugenicists of this period correlated inferior blood not just with race but also with primitive religious practices. These were typically Roman Catholic, fundamentalist, sectarian, ecstatic, minority, and new religions.[72] So Mencken's assessment of Southern religion as *barbarism* looped back into his use of race science. "Fundamentalism borrows the magic of Christian Science," he wrote, "and idiot kisses idiot."[73] Here again *idiot*—like *moron*—is a technical term.

And rising above them all was Bryan, an imperious clown, "the peasants' Pope."[74] Bryan brought out Mencken's most dogged tendencies. He relished painting the politician as a bitter, broken monarch who had retreated to his rump state to dwell with animalistic mountainside acolytes. "He hates the learning that he cannot grasp," Mencken wrote. "He hates those who sneer at him. He hates, in general, all who stand apart from his own pathetic commonness. And the yokels hate with him, some of them almost as bitterly as he does himself. They are willing and eager to follow him—and he has already given them a taste of blood."[75] That was during the trial. In his obituary after Bryan's death a few weeks later, when most newspapers were cranking out hagiography, Mencken sneered: "He was born with a roaring voice, and it had the trick of inflaming half-wits. His whole career was devoted to raising these half-wits against their betters, that he himself might shine."[76]

The only science Mencken brought to the table was his crude cartoon of the already shaky field of eugenics. He was drawn, like a moth to a flame, to knowledge that installed him on the upper deck. What was cogent for Mencken? It was the science that clicked with his sense of superiority. Unlike Huxley, who opened up a private war against Southern white supremacists—the same wasted aristocrats Mencken garlanded with praise—and took them to task for their junk biology, Mencken snuggled up to race science.[77] Science, for him, surged with what Sharon Patricia Holland calls the erotic part of racism, lustily messing together with the affects of knowledge-making.[78] This is not just racism understood as Black/white, of course, but all the different ways of arranging USes and THEMs. Mencken choked science under a thicket of insults—powerful, world-moving insults that have shaped political formations for generations.

The targets of Mencken's smears counterattacked with insults of their own. Daytonians called him "the stinker." Austin Peay, the governor who signed the Butler Act, dubbed him an "intellectual skunk."[79] Mencken's columns were being reprinted in the *Chattanooga Times* but were so reviled that the editors began redacting them and even, it seems, publishing them with deliberate misprints to humiliate him.[80] A Southern pastor was quoted in a local paper stating, "Mencken is just a dirty buzzard and the folks that follow him are no more than damn scoundrels." He added, "I'm here to tell you that the biggest set of fools that walk on earth today walk on Broadway. Why, there are more ignorant, pot-headed fools to the square inch in New York than in any part of America."[81] Another Southerner wrote to Peay that "the Great Commoner [Bryan] fell at this post maintaining that Tenn. had sense enough to run her own affairs without Yankees from the North to meddle in them."[82] The trial had descended from battle of ideas to food fight, with all sides giddily flinging scorn.

Mencken received written threats that he would be tarred and feathered if he stayed in town, forcing him to exit Dayton early (and miss the Bryan-Darrow showdown). It was the sorry conclusion of his effort to take up the side of science, a snarky, self-indulgent parody of Darwin's wildly successful charm offensive. The Butler Act, as Larson writes, became "a symbol of pride and regional identity for some [white] Southerners."[83] Mencken did nothing to improve this state of affairs. He almost certainly made it worse. But he never had any intention of doing otherwise. His passion for persuasion—for Polanyi a vital part of the emotional alloy of science—was nil. Science was a weapon for Mencken, cogent only to the extent that it aligned with racialized reason. Is it any surprise this led to a widening cogency schism—that what felt true for Mencken and for his targets came to be miles apart? In Mencken's hand, evolutionary science became a lash of degradation to use on rural, white, Christian Southerners. How could it possibly be cogent for them?

William Jennings Bryan, the Great Commoner

It was this same slow-boiling regional resentment that lifted again the career of William Jennings Bryan. As we've seen, the kaleidoscope of political factions of the 1920s was dizzyingly complex, all the more so since our twenty-first-century ideological schematics don't fit the times. Race, class, region, and religion were all part of this maze. Writing about Bryan's first presidential campaign in the late 1890s, for instance, historian Michael Kazin notes that Southern Democrats "accused their political enemies of shedding tears for unworthy Blacks but sneering at the language and manners of the productive white majority."[84] But many of these populist Democrats were also *anti-imperialist*—on racist grounds. One of Bryan's allies, a senator from South Carolina, objected to the seizure of the Philippines during the Spanish-American War on the grounds that it would "inject poisoned blood" into the American body politic.[85] Religiously, too, Bryan's position was complicated. Although Bryan was their champion in Dayton, he was only passingly attached to the fundamentalist movement. He seldom used the word to identify himself and never publicly engaged with the pamphlets themselves.[86]

Bryan's populism was built on his terms, not ours. But like all populists, he was a master of manipulating dignity, resuscitating the shame of his audience in order to vanquish it.[87] He knew how to turn almost any political situation into a soap opera. Kazin writes that "down South, Bryanism was a popular persuasion. Most whites resented and envied the power and wealth of the urban industrial establishment, and Bryan played to such sentiments whenever he visited the region."[88] When he walked into the 1896 Democratic National Convention, an unknown thirty-six-year-old Nebraska lawyer, taking the stage to denounce the Cleveland administration's policy on bimetallism, he reforged an esoteric controversy about currency into one of his most famous speeches. At the climax of the orientation he declared that farmers and workers would not be crucified "on this cross of gold." He even splayed his arms for effect. The storm of applause lasted longer than the speech itself.[89] Bryan walked away from the convention as the party's presidential candidate. Though he lost all his elections, he still became a beloved heartland icon, his picture on the wall of every home in some towns. Bryan had a gift, strumming the political tensions of his time like a maestro.

The conventional wisdom has rendered Bryan as a figure of scorn, an insincere panderer and a huckster—an impression consolidated by *Inherit the Wind*. But Bryan's proxy in *Inherit*, Matt Brady, was really a replica of Joseph McCarthy. As Kazin notes, in more recent academic accounts, "the recognition that most evolutionists in the 1920s were dedicated to 'improving' the human race through eugenics has made Bryan seem more sympathetic."[90] Larson, for instance, stresses that the *survival of the fittest* concept was invoked as justification for the shock-and-awe capitalism of Rockefeller and Carnegie so loathed by Bryan.[91] And Ronald Numbers emphasizes that Bryan was well versed in studies linking evolutionary ideas to militarism, especially among the German officer corps during World War I.[92] These associations with evolutionary theory, according to the revisionist view, prompted Bryan's counterattack.

How did the progressive Bryan of the late nineteenth and early twentieth centuries become the reactionary Bryan of the 1910s and 1920s? Or did he? The solution offered by historians of science and religion has been, increasingly, to suggest that the two Bryans are one and the same. Stephen Jay Gould's chapter on the Scopes trial in his best-selling *Rocks of Ages*, for instance, starts off with a long denunciation of the teaching of creationism in schools—with details filled in by Gould's own experience serving as an expert witness in the 1981 *McLean v. Arkansas* trial. While taking care not to allow creationists to stand as representatives for all religion, he pulls no punches in labeling them as "well-funded and committed zealots."[93]

But then Gould rapidly switches gears. The second half of the chapter sees him stoutly *defending* Bryan. He draws up Bryan's pacifism, his populism, and his critique of eugenics as forerunners of his suspicion of Darwinism.[94] Gould highlights the nasty eugenicist content of the 1914 edition of *Civic Biology*—the textbook Scopes claimed to have read from—as an instance of science illegitimately intruding into the sphere of values, mirroring the transgression of creationists who make religion about matters of fact. "Bryan," he concludes diplomatically, "advocated the wrong solution, but he had correctly identified a serious problem."[95]

This new interpretation casts Bryan sympathetically, seeing his late campaigns for Prohibition and against evolution as outcroppings of his deep-rooted, principled populism—a populism that also led him to champion women's rights, radical pacifism, labor unions, and a universal income tax— the policy positions that earned him the nickname the Great Commoner and Mencken's scorn.[96] It casts the spotlight on Bryan's friendship with Leo Tolstoy, the unbending pacifist champion of the poor, who admired Bryan so much he had a framed picture of him on the wall of his study.[97]

And it reaffirms that Bryan set the Democratic Party on track to becoming the party of Franklin Delano Roosevelt and civil rights rather than the libertarian-lite, antistatist party of Thomas Jefferson.[98]

But this misses the importance of how science *felt* for Bryan. And that in turn overlooks the way his involvement with the trial was defined by racialized reason—a grotesque brew of white nationalism and Christian supremacism that set the coordinates for how he engaged with science. Kazin documents how Bryan's political priorities changed over the course of the 1910s. Although he cultivated friendships with Black religious leaders, denounced lynching, and was endorsed by Du Bois in 1908, Bryan's race politics became more poisonous over time.[99] He presented himself as an impatient crusader for justice but was actually picking his battles shrewdly, cultivating northern Blacks and Southern white supremacists alike as allies.[100] After moving to Florida from Nebraska in 1915, he was pulled even more deeply into the racialized orbit of Southern Democratic politics. Down South, Bryan became "more convinced that the region's white majority, to protect the civic order, had to hold a whip hand over the minority race."[101]

He increasingly sided with the traditional white power apparatus—by forcing anti–Ku Klux Klan language out of the 1924 Democratic platform and opposing a federal antilynching law, for instance.[102] Klan researcher Kelly Baker reports that the knights—who saw evolution science as a Catholic-Jewish-Bolshevik conspiracy—repaid the quiet favor he showed them by declaring him an honorary member after his death and burning a cross in his memory.[103] By the 1920s, his support of Jim Crow had made him so toxic to Blacks in the South that Black journalists who might have been sympathetic to some of his views refused to support him.[104] As for the clergy, Moran has argued that although most Black Protestants were theologically conservative and skeptical of evolutionary biology, they shied away from the militant culture war vendettas of Bryan and his white fundamentalist allies.[105]

Sociologist of education Shantá Robinson, in a detailed study of the African American press, has found both deep fascination and a wide range of perspectives among Black observers of the trial.[106] Common to many, however, was hostility to Bryan as a representative of white power and enthusiasm for Darrow and Scopes as figureheads of progress—much as nineteenth-century reformers and dissenters in the UK took up Darwinism as a weapon against their own oppressive systems of rights and privileges.[107]

And some Black writers, echoing the nineteenth-century debates around monogenism and polygenism, accused white racists of rejecting Darwinism to avoid the implication of kinship with those they saw as their inferiors.[108] "The folk who leave white Tennessee in blank and ridiculous ignorance of what science has taught the world," wrote Du Bois, "are the same ones who would leave black Tennessee and black America with just as little education as is consistent with fairly efficient labor and reasonable contentment ... who permit lynching and make bastardy legal in order to render their race 'pure.'"[109]

And there's no question that during this same period, Bryan saw himself more and more in the mantle of a crusader, picking up the flag of Christianity and condemning its enemies. Although Bryan had always centered Christianity in his politics, a rising emphasis on Christian nationalism—not social gospel but Christianity for Christianity's sake—marked his career from the 1910s on.[110] Bryan's new defenders note his preoccupation with two books: Vernon Kellogg's *Headquarters Nights* and Benjamin Kidd's *The Science of Power*, both of which made links among Darwinism, atheism, and German militarism. But Larson argues that Bryan was even more horrified by another book, James Leuba's *The Belief in God and Immortality*, which showed that Christian commitment was negatively correlated with education.[111]

Leuba found that university professors, in particular, exhibited shockingly low levels of faith. Like a one-man campus watchdog group, Bryan's public presentations constantly rehearsed insults to the faith from professors. "At the University of Wisconsin," he reported in one speech, "a teacher told his class that the Bible was a collection of myths. A father (a Congressman) tells me that a daughter on her return from Wellesley told him that nobody believed in the Bible stories now. Another father (a Congressman) tells me of a son whose faith was undermined by [Darwinism] in Divinity School."[112] This was not about a progressive politics, or at least not in the main. It was a way of reasserting the dignity of Christian nationalism in the face of insults to the faith. Larson's analysis is that *this* was Bryan's "ultimate justification" for going to Dayton.[113]

Bryan's 1922 *New York Times* op-ed "God and Evolution" provides more evidence of this Christian supremacist outlook. This was a high-profile venue, granting Bryan immediate access to a vast audience—and exactly the people he needed to persuade. But his primary objections to evolution had nothing to do with peace or morality. His three concerns about Darwinism were that it was a guess (the standard misunderstanding of scientific hypothesis still used by creationists today); that it wasn't supported by the Bible; and that there was no hard evidence for it (like transitional species).[114] A little later in the essay, Bryan asserted in passing that Darwinism was "harmful," but all this meant for him was that "it entirely changes one's view of life and undermines faith in the Bible."[115] He was defending Christianity for Christianity's sake.

The highwater mark of passion in the piece came when Bryan discussed Darwin himself. "Darwinism made an agnostic out of Darwin," he exclaimed. "When he was a young man he believed in the Bible; just before his death he declared that he did not believe that there had ever been any revelation; that banished the Bible as the inspired Word of God, and, with it, the Christ of whom the Bible tells."[116] Darwin's departure from Christianity stood on its own, for Bryan, as an indictment of evolution. Then Bryan brought up, once more, Leuba's findings and the Wisconsin insult with horror. Only at the very end of the essay's four thousand or so words did Bryan mention the importance of Christianity for "morality and civilization."[117] But this was an afterthought. The essay's center of gravity was not an affirmation of Christian values or progressive politics. It was a barking reassertion of Christian supremacy.

We see the same pattern in Bryan's *Seven Questions in Dispute* from 1924, his final book. The last chapter, on "The Origin of Man," listed objections to evolutionary science, challenging the evolutionary account of the emergence of the eye and objecting that by the evolutionists' logic, we must be more physically perfect specimens than the ancient Greek athletes, which Bryan insisted couldn't be true.[118] The book was a gallery of caricatures, with little meaningful effort to engage the state of the scientific conversation. Notably absent, too, was any discussion of values. The heart of Bryan's condemnation didn't mention morality: once again, the most sinister consequence of Darwin's acceptance of evolution was simply that it caused him to abandon Christianity.[119] Kidd got a mention—Darwinism as the philosophy of might makes right—but Bryan quickly jumped back to Leuba and the erosion of the community of faith.[120] The final section—"Evolution: The Menace of Civilization"—summed it all up: "Darwin's God was nowhere—he could not find him; Darwin's Bible was nothing—it had lost its inspiration; Darwin's Christ was nobody—he had an ape for an ancestor on both his father's and his mother's side. Such a Christ is impotent to save."[121] Bryan's real defense of Christianity wasn't its moral message. It was Protestant *solus Christus* soteriology held up as the tentpole of Christian supremacism.

During the famous cross-examination at the trial, it's hard to ignore Bryan's defensiveness as he answers Darrow.

> DARROW *Now, you say, the big fish swallowed Jonah, and he there remained how long—three days—and then he spewed him upon the land. You believe that the big fish was made to swallow Jonah?*
>
> BRYAN *I am not prepared to say that; the Bible merely says it was done. ...*
>
> DARROW *But do you believe he made them—that he made such a fish and that it was big enough to swallow Jonah?*
>
> BRYAN *Yes, sir. Let me add: One miracle is just as easy to believe as another. ...*
>
> DARROW *Perfectly easy to believe that [the whale] swallowed [Jonah]?*
>
> BRYAN *If the Bible said so; the Bible doesn't make as extreme statements as evolutionists do.*[122]

And then:

> DARROW *Have you an opinion as to whether—whoever wrote the book, I believe it is, Joshua, the Book of Joshua, thought the sun went around the earth or not?*
>
> BRYAN *I believe that he was inspired.*
>
> DARROW *Can you answer my question?*
>
> BRYAN *When you let me finish the statement.*
>
> DARROW *It is a simple question but finish it.*
>
> BRYAN *You cannot measure the length of my answer by the length of your question.*
>
> DARROW *No, except that the answer be longer.*
> *[Laughter in the courtyard.]*
>
> BRYAN *I believe that the Bible is inspired, an inspired author. Whether one who wrote as he was directed to write understood the things he was writing about, I don't know.*[123]

This wasn't moral inspiration; it was a touchy proclamation of faith, shoring up an identity rather than proclaiming a vision of a more just society. (In fairness, Darrow's prickliness is on full display here, too.) Even though Bryan waved a copy of *Civic Biology* around in the trial as he denounced its contents, he made no mention of its support of eugenics.[124]

There was one exception to this pattern. As soon as the trial ended, Bryan released the questions he'd intended to put to Darrow.[125] Here Bryan offered four specific criticisms of Darwinism. It not only contradicted literal Genesis but also destroyed faith and love, posed a distraction from spiritually and socially uplifting work, and weakened our resolve to improve society.[126] But the fact that this showed up only days before Bryan's passing suggests just how *late* it arrived in his thinking. The intense attention of the trial, it seems, helped Bryan hone his line of criticism as he realized—finally—that moral denunciations of evolution might be more cogent for his intended audience. His rhetorical strategy evolved in response to a changing environment.

This is consistent with other evidence that Bryan, the fundamentalists, and the Southern political machine were worried about Christian identity way more than the moral cesspool of eugenics. Larson's research shows that although states in the Deep South were slower than their northern counterparts to adopt eugenicist policies, this was mainly owing to secondary factors like the lack of an academic and medical establishment or a concern over costs.[127] After the 8–1 *Bell v. Buck* ruling in 1927 (a case that began in Virginia), the legislative floodgates opened in the South. "Within days of the Supreme Court decision," Larson writes, "comprehensive sterilization proposals surfaced in the Alabama and Florida legislatures," with Georgia following suit shortly after.[128] These eugenicist policies then held on long after the rest of the country had dismantled its eugenicist machinery. Just three Southern states made up three quarters of annual sterilizations in the country by the 1950s.[129] The South became a eugenicist redoubt. And its antievolution laws were still on the books.

The same point is made by intellectual historian Adam Shapiro, who has looked at the correspondence between George Hunter, author of *Civic Biology*, and his publisher, the American Book Company. Concerned about sales in the South, the American Book Company pressured Hunter to revise his textbook in the aftermath of *Scopes*.[130] Hunter gave in, producing a new manuscript that avoided the word *evolution* entirely but *kept the eugenics material*. The revised volume, *New Civic Biology*, was widely adopted.[131] This is why Shapiro dismisses Gould and Larson's claim that Bryan was primarily motivated by a concern over eugenics.[132] The bottom line is this: if Bryan and the fundamentalists had been worried about eugenics, they would have gone to war against eugenics. They went to war against Darwin. And eugenics waltzed through the open gates.

Figure 6.3 E. J. Pace, *Moody Monthly*, March 1922.

When we consider how brazenly empty of real values talk Bryan's proclamations were, his Christianity looks like little more than a racialized identity game—a badge of affiliation that, as Anthea Butler has shown, was deeply implicated in American white supremacy, even where it kept explicit race talk in the closet.[133] Bryan didn't think he was abandoning science. Like Wright, he insisted he had *real* science on his side (figure 6.3). But the science that was cogent for him was itself a specimen of racialized reason—just as the same white Southern politicians who penned the antievolution laws were happy to embrace eugenics. Creationism made the Bible an identity machine, dividing the world into believers and infidels. This felt frame of separation dictated how fundamentalists aligned themselves with some science and rejected the rest. Their so-called science felt so good it had to be true.

Conclusion: Descendants of Ours

Unlike the earlier Darwinian aftermath, Mencken and Bryan's contributions to the Scopes trial don't show off scientific secularism as a dynamic between belief, disbelief, and the sense of science. They're hardly about science at all. Instead, they look like a wrestling match between rival regimes of racialized reason, a playground for turbulent identity games. The passion for reason recedes way into the background. Looking at Mencken and Bryan, we can trace the tangled skeins of race, region, religion, and identity directing cogency, dictating what Christians and atheists alike felt to be true or untrue. So-called science became a proxy war puppeteered by affective templates clashing beneath the surface.

Mencken presented himself as science's crusader, the heir to Huxley. But Huxley, for all his sharp edges, was committed (usually) to the sense of science. Mencken's scientific passion, on the other hand, was dominated—completely—by racialized reason. The science that clicked for him was whatever confirmed his sense that he stood on society's upper shelf and afforded him the best vantage point for looking down on everyone else. And his secularism was the kind that parades under science's flag while quietly choking the passion for reason beneath a thick canopy of racism and elitism. Mencken's real interest was not science, but boneheads.

Bryan was deeply invested in preserving the integrity of literal Genesis. But against what his modern admirers might claim, Bryan by the 1920s was not particularly interested in advancing Christian visions of radical love or justice. Nor does there seem to be any real concern with surfacing truth. Instead, Christianity was an identity defended for its own sake, a last-ditch charge to revive a sense of superiority after a loss of influence and cultural clout. It was propelled by racialized reason, often with conspiracist elements. One fundamentalist pastor echoed the KKK in calling evolutionary biology the work of an "international Jewish-Bolshevik-Darwinist conspiracy."[134] Bryan kept his own racial views close to the vest, but he, too, clearly found science most cogent when it matched his own sense of who was in and who was out.

There aren't many figures in the long Scopes trial who come across as especially admirable. But if there's any light in the dark, it's with the teachers. Gould writes about sitting in the docket during *McLean v. Arkansas*, listening to the testimony of educators horrified by the order to serve creationist dogma to their students under Act 590, Arkansas's equal-time provision from 1981. When a high school biology teacher took the stand, he was asked what he would do if forced to comply with the law. "I've given it a great deal of thought," he responded. "I'm very much inclined not to comply with Act 590. I do not want to appear to be a revolutionary or a martyr or anything of this nature, but as a science educator I think I know what science is. I think I know what professionalism and ethics are. I think I realize my obligations to my students."[135] The other teachers echoed this conviction. To teach their students something they knew to be a falsehood would be a betrayal.

This deeply felt ethic doesn't make sense unless we can name the *passion for reason*, not just as an empty cognitive formalism but as an urgent emotional need to connect with the truth. Why *not* lie to your students? What does it cost you to lie, if that's your job? The same liberal common sense that defends equal-time provisions scratches its head. *You get paid either way, right?* But it does cost something. It costs a lot. To deceive students—to knowingly teach error—inverts the joy of the sense of science. It poisons the passion for reason.

The liberal focus on freedom of inquiry—although it proved an effective solvent against antievolution laws—actually set the table for the subsequent controversies in the long Scopes trial and the intelligent design campaigns of today. Creationism adapted by commandeering the language of free inquiry through the equal-time laws that cropped up in the wake of the fall of evolution bans in the 1960s. The modern ID movement—a network of deep-pocketed private foundations artificially elevating their tiny stable of handpicked renegade scientists—has used the same playbook.[136] They demand that high school biology classes *teach the controversy*, give ID *equal time*, then let the kids *decide for themselves*. They've managed to hack liberal common sense, jury-rigging a platform for all those ideas biology left in the trash heap.

What could be wrong with letting students decide for themselves? It's simple: presenting myth as on par with the accumulated mass of data gathered and organized by the modern life sciences is confusing, not empowering. At best, it lards up the classroom with empty calories, denying students a rich opportunity to *learn*. Simply enabling *free inquiry* isn't enough. Knowledge needs room to grow. Crowding its patch with nonsense denies it daylight. As Naomi Oreskes and Erik Conway note, giving airtime to bad ideas doesn't purge them.[137] It creates a miasma of confusion in which exciting falsehoods gain traction at the expense of complex, unsatisfying,

Figure 6.4 Leslie Rogers, *Chicago Defender*, June 13, 1925.

stress-tested scientific facts. This is how *free inquiry* gets used to suffocate science in the ID debate.[138]

So cogency theory offers a new perspective on public discourse about science. The liberal assumption that everyone will eventually *see reason* when the truth presents itself is flawed. It's precisely because the sense of science is so delicate that it's easily paved over by the freeway of thrilling fictions—creationism, eugenics, ID, and all the rest. When the philosopher Jacques Derrida warns us that "nothing risks becoming more poisonous than an autobiography," he's concerned with exactly the way self-flattering fantasies of human specialness always have a field advantage in the battle for

Figure 6.5 Leslie Rogers, *Chicago Defender*, July 18, 1925.

truth.[139] They feel so good—especially to those who have already bet their dignity on the identity package that goes along with them—that they *have to be true*.

But the scientific debates, as important as they are, can't be the whole story when we reconsider *Scopes*. The closing statement of this chapter is offered by two cartoons inked by artist Leslie Rogers for the Black-owned *Chicago Defender* newspaper around the time of the trial. In the first, a pair of monkeys high up in a tree look down on a lynching (see figure 6.4). "Joe," one asks, "do you believe fiends like those are descendants of ours?" "NO!" replies Joe. Down below, the lynching is portrayed as more party than crime scene, white spectators rushing to revel in murder. In the second, a country doctor (*Public Interest*) performs a checkup on a boy (*The Evolution Question*). Behind them, Uncle Sam points at a squalling baby in a cradle (*The South*). The baby's cries are a litany of social evils—*Lynching, Race Hatred, Jim-Crowism, Peonage* (see figure 6.5).

These images reiterate the views of Black American commentators watching the trial and using it as a lens to consider the interlocking political crises of their time. But the theological content of the trial—the clash of secular and religious—recedes into the background. Rogers uses *Scopes* to amplify attention on a very different set of injustices—racial terrorism, poverty, and segregation. What, to the Black American, was the Scopes trial? The theological point/counterpoint, in Rogers's view, was much less urgent than the way it pointed to the life-or-death issues lurking outside the courtroom.

Side by side with Rogers's cartoons, the Scopes trial looks like much more of a parochial concern than contemporary secularists—especially white secularists—might imagine. It looks like a secular circus. A sideshow. It was a lost opportunity for secularists to articulate a moral vision. Rogers's cartoons pose a challenge to secularists who see themselves as offering a decisive transformation of society. Secularism may offer itself as an abrupt break with past prejudices and superstitions caused by the sudden illumination of scientific reason. But modern formations of the secular as a gladiatorial spectacle—served up with a sneer, wielding science as a blunt instrument—are nothing more than a blithe extension of what came before.

7.
THE FOUR HORSEMEN
NEW ATHEISM AS SECULAR CONSPIRACY THEORY

> When you get me a good man, made out of arguments,
> I will get you a good dinner with reading you the
> cookery-book. —George Eliot, *Middlemarch*

Introduction: Sane and Decent People

On a February morning in 2015, police were called to a rented apartment in Chapel Hill, North Carolina, where they found three local university students slain by gunshots. A few hours later, forty-six-year-old Craig Stephen Hicks, a neighbor of the victims, turned himself in. Having at first fled in his car, Hicks now confessed, claiming that the three murders were prompted by a dispute over a shared parking space at their apartment complex.

Almost immediately, Hicks's story about his motive for the killings was put in doubt. This is because the three students—Razan Mohammad Abu-Salha, nineteen; her sister, Yusor Mohammad Abu-Salha, twenty-one; and Yusor's new husband, Deah Shaddy Barakat, twenty-three—were Muslim. Both Razan and Yusor wore hijab. Although Hicks's parking disputes with the students were well known around the complex, no car was parked in the shared parking space at the time of the shootings. He was also known to have had similar disagreements with other neighbors. But it was the three young Muslims who were singled out.

Moreover, Hicks was an atheist. Reporters found a string of social media posts asserting his aggressively secular views. The cover photo of his Facebook page was a banner reading "I don't deny you your right to believe whatever you'd like; but I have the right to point out it's ignorant and dangerous for as long as your baseless superstitions keep killing people."[1] Members of the Abu-Salha and Barakat families speculated that the killing was motivated by racial hatred.[2] Yusor's father said in an interview that his daughter had told him about Hicks the previous week, saying, "I think he hates us for who we are and how we look."[3]

But Hicks's version of his story was corroborated, sort of, by other facts. For one thing, he didn't seem to show, in his public Facebook proclamations, any special antipathy toward Islam. He was even critical of conservative American Christians who had resisted the construction of the Park51 Community Center, the so-called Ground Zero Mosque, in Manhattan near the site of the World Trade Center attacks in 2010.[4] He described himself as an *atheist for equality* and a *gun-toting liberal*.[5] A neighbor said Hicks had "equal-opportunity anger" toward residents. He seems to have taken the same approach to religion.[6]

Karen Hicks, the confessed killer's estranged wife, held a news conference defending her husband, stating, "[This] is one thing that I do know about him. He often champions on his Facebook page for the rights of many individuals. For same-sex marriages, abortion, race. *He just believed ... that everyone is equal*. It doesn't matter what you look like or who you are or what you believe."[7] Her husband, she insisted, was no Christian supremacist—unlike, say, the gun-toting conservative Christians who menaced Muslims during prayer time outside an Arizona mosque a few weeks later.[8]

Yet the questions remained. How did a parking dispute turn into homicide? And why, if, as other neighbors claimed, Hicks was a known menace who had made threatening remarks toward many of them, was it three Muslim kids who were shot to death? As Omid Safi, a professor of Islamic studies at nearby Duke University, wrote, when "was the last time a parking dispute in North Carolina ended in execution-style murder? Something else had to have been at work."[9]

Richard Dawkins—often cited in Hicks's posts—wrote in *The God Delusion* about the suicide bombings on the London subway system in 2005 carried out by four young Muslim men, claiming that only "religious faith is a strong enough force to motivate such utter madness in otherwise sane and decent people."[10] How, then, do we wrap our heads around the *gun-toting liberal*, the secular terrorist who perpetrates not just antireligious violence, but *racialized* antireligious violence? How does equal opportunity antitheism turn into special hatred toward Muslims? How does secular reason—the thoughts and beliefs of sane and decent people—get swept up in unspeakable violence?

From the perspective of cogency theory, secularism—in this case, the New Atheism, still today the most prominent version of what Charles Taylor calls *secularism 2*—is more than just a set of concepts and ideas animated by pure reason. Maybe it's true that Hicks really *believed* in equality. Maybe he had the right words and the right ideas. But the cognitive layer of words, beliefs, and ideas is not the whole story of secularism. Secularism feels, and New Atheism as a case study of scientific secularism illustrates this perfectly. While presenting itself as cut from the glacier of neutral rationality, its affective coordinates shape how its partisans act and interact. This includes patterns of racialized reason and an aggressively simplistic approach to religion. They're the ingredients of a sort of secular conspiracy theory.

The New Atheists—a cluster of secularist thinkers who came to prominence in the early 2000s—invoke Darwin to advance their views. Dawkins and Daniel Dennett, for instance, built careers around best-selling affirmations of a narrow interpretation of Darwinian evolutionary biology. As their interest turned to atheism, science became central to the arguments they made against religious belief. But the contrast between the New Atheists and Darwin himself couldn't be more stark. Sheepish Darwin carefully concealed his religious views—and their complex relationships with his science—in order to avoid offense (and create a public platform for his theory to flourish). The New Atheists retooled Darwinian biology into a war machine designed to batter down faith.

Like Darwin, New Atheist writers mobilize the passion for reason. Although it presents itself as having risen beyond mere feeling, New Atheism revels in the emotional electricity of knowledge-making. It's no accident that Dawkins and Dennett were principal litigants in the conflict around *sociobiology*, contending against an alliance of progressive scientists like Stephen Jay Gould, Richard Lewontin, and Steven Rose. This chapter argues that New Atheism makes religion a simplex system—flattening it to a set of easy and obvious relationships, making it easier and more enjoyable to study (and blame)—just as adaptationist sociobiology does with biology.

Both are so fascinated by the click effect of intelligibility that they wind up obscuring the messiness and strangeness of actual scientific truth.

Simplexity, as we saw in chapter 1, is a key ingredient of conspiracy theory. And just like conspiracy theory, it's clear in reading New Atheist writings that something extremely serious is going on—just beneath the surface—with race.[11] Racialized groups are all over the place in New Atheist writings. This operates on two stacked levels. On the one hand, there's a lumping together of religious people into a uniform mass. Time and again, New Atheists equate rank-and-file believers with extremists. This is amplified by an insistence on seeing religions as simplex systems—nothing but packets of ideas, handbooks that dictate actions like marching orders. It's the linguistic fallacy applied to religion, what Manuel Vásquez calls *textualism*. That's the first level.

On the other hand, special pressure is placed on Islam, which becomes first among equals in the New Atheist rogues' gallery of religion. Islam is constantly singled out for contempt, reflecting what we might call, following Mel Chen, a sort of felt *secular animacy hierarchy*.[12] Just as we noticed an uncanny similarity between Mencken and Bryan in the last chapter, New Atheism and Christian supremacism, from this stance, look a lot alike: for both, Islam coalesces into a de facto racial other, a supervillain whose plans are always looming over us. What feels like an unbiased and objective criticism of Islam, to New Atheists, is an affectively encrypted racial hierarchy. Identifying the streak of Islamophobia rippling through so much New Atheist work helps us understand the nightmare at Chapel Hill. These two motivated mistakes—the errors that keep coming back—light up how cogency works. They're formations of desire organizing knowledge beneath the skin. They're hard to let go of because it's pleasurable to keep them close. They feel so good they have to be true.

Two important caveats need to be placed here. First, this chapter is not about blaming New Atheism for the Chapel Hill killings. The picture of human thoughts, feelings, and actions sketched by cogency theory is too complex for that. But it does ask what role the New Atheism as a secular conspiracy theory plays in building the background coordinates for this and other acts of secular violence. Nor is this an argument that atheism is inherently toxic or wicked. That's just as much a caricature as the funhouse mirror depiction of religion offered by New Atheism. It's exactly the naive assumption that propositional beliefs directly convey bodies to a predictable set of actions that's on trial here. This chapter closes, then, by looking at another set of secular writings that has cropped up in the past decade. These other atheisms, especially from Black, queer, and feminist perspectives, map out a radically different vision of how the secular can feel. They embrace the passion for reason, while sharply scrutinizing secular reason for the affective traces of racialized cognition.

From Sociobiology to New Atheism

The New Atheism was so prominent by the late 2000s that it's easy to forget the state of decline atheism was in across the Anglophone world at the turn of the millennium. A few days after the inauguration of President George W. Bush in January 2001, science writer Natalie Angier commented that "in an age when flamboyantly gay characters are sitcom staples, a Jew was but a few flutters of a butterfly wing away from being in line for the presidency and women account for a record-smiting 13 percent of the Senate, nothing seems as despised, illicit and un-American as atheism."[13] Theologian Alister McGrath linked this to the collapse of world communism a decade earlier, calling it the *twilight of atheism*.[14]

So it would have surprised most observers that anything like New Atheism was stirring in the cracks in the early 2000s. The story told now is that the election of Bush and the 9/11 attacks ten months later triggered a new push for organized secularism.[15] In 2003, Daniel Dennett used a *New York Times* op-ed to call for a new movement of *Brights*, those individuals who "don't believe in ghosts or elves or the Easter Bunny—or God."[16] The next year, Sam Harris published his surprise best-seller *The End of Faith*. He later said he started writing the day after 9/11.[17] This was followed by Harris's *Letter to a Christian Nation*, Dennett's *Breaking the Spell*, and Dawkins's *The God Delusion* in 2006, and Christopher Hitchens's *God Is Not Great* in 2007.[18] They burned up the best-seller lists and formed the nucleus of what came to be called New Atheism.[19]

Journalist Gary Wolf (who coined the term *New Atheism* in 2006) suggests that *The God Delusion* was a departure from Dawkins's previous work—public-facing scholarship on evolutionary biology.[20] This is not exactly wrong, but it overlooks the fact that Dawkins was already fixating on religion as far back as his first book, the 1976 pop-sci best-seller *The Selfish Gene*. It was in *Selfish Gene* that Dawkins wrote that humans and other organisms "are survival machines, programmed to preserve the selfish molecules known as genes."[21] Everything we do, Dawkins proposed, can be slotted into the cost-benefit calculus of improving fitness for genes. And this had serious implications for religion.

The Selfish Gene was sociobiology, understood in E. O. Wilson's terms as the study of the biological basis of behavior.[22] But it was also a particular spin on sociobiology—a *strong adaptationist* interpretation—in which every feature or behavior of living organisms could be justified by the advantage it offers in a zero-sum game of reproduction and survival. The focus wasn't on the organism itself, though. Dawkins's book looked at genes, which he argued were fixed on a fanatical mission to mass-produce and preserve copies of themselves. Cannibal animals were his favorite examples. Black-headed gulls who consume the offspring of their conspecifics and female praying mantises who both gain reproductive material from their hapless mates *and* "obtain a good meal" epitomized the theory that genes are selfish.[23] Even altruism, from the gene's perspective, was math. Protecting conspecifics (or, even better, kin) meant more replicas. Dawkins's source for this idea, biologist W. D. Hamilton, wrote in a 1964 essay that "no one is prepared to sacrifice his life for any single person, [but] everyone will sacrifice it when he can thereby save more than two brothers, or four half-brothers, or eight first cousins."[24] In Dawkins's adaptationist sociobiology, every action was a fitness calculation benefiting the gene's relentless quest to replicate itself.

Other biologists challenged this adaptationist approach. Stephen Jay Gould and Richard Lewontin, for instance, mocked Dawkins and other adaptationists in their 1978 paper "The Spandrels of San Marco and the Panglossian Paradigm: A Critique of the Adaptationist Programme." They argued against the idea that every feature of an organism can be assessed as *useful*. While the adaptationist approach sometimes comes up with the right answer, they wrote, *strong adaptationism* closes off the possibility that a feature of an organism may not exist for an adaptive purpose.[25] (There's an intriguing parallel here with the wariness of postcritique scholars toward paranoid reading—the assumption that suspicion will always yield the right answer—as we saw in chapter 3.)[26]

"Odd arrangements and funny solutions" rather than streamlined, hyperefficient survival machines "are the proof of evolution," Gould wrote a few years later, because they exhibit the paths "that a sensible God would never tread but that a natural process, constrained by history, follows perforce."[27] Feminist philosophers of science have also been skeptics of strong adaptationism. Evelyn Fox Keller noted that adaptationism reduces organisms to atomized individual genes, rather than grasping the multilevel dynamics between genes, organisms, environments, and groups.[28] She argued that the actions and features of organisms result from a hypercomplex field of variables and forces, not textbook arithmetic.[29]

What's most startling, though, is that Dawkins's own commitment to adaptationism hit a wall when he came to religion. The strangest part of *The Selfish Gene* was the way it ended up creating a carve-out for all kinds of behaviors that Dawkins saw as *not* adaptive by flinging them into the domain of *memes* rather than *genes*. A *meme*, as Dawkins defined it, is a copiable unit of information.[30] Memes are the Lego bricks of human culture, chunks of thought that circulate through conversation, writing, and other media. They are, however, totally detached from biology. They operate analogously, Dawkins wrote, because they compete for influence and outstrip and eliminate their rivals. But the mechanisms are mental, not biological. Memes are the new replicators, producing behaviors that don't line up with biological natural selection.

What's remarkable is that Dawkins seems to have created the concept of the meme *specifically to undermine religion*. There were already adaptationist explanations for the existence of religion in circulation in the 1970s, most of which focused on the role of religion in producing effective cooperative units (what we now call group selection).[31] But Dawkins rejected these out of hand.[32] He refused to even consider the possibility that religion might be biologically adaptive, so he had to explain it as memetically adaptive. He took almost every one of his examples of meme power from religion: the *god meme*, which explained away injustice; the "threat of hell-fire," a powerful enforcement mechanism; blind faith, the ultimate smokescreen to defeat questions and challenges to authority; and monastic celibacy.[33] Each of these was biologically *maladaptive*. But they survived and reproduced on the field of memes. As Chris Hedges points out, Dawkins's abrupt emphasis on humans as *dis*continuous with the natural world was actually deeply *unfaithful* to Darwin.[34] In other words, Dawkins was so determined to attack religion—already in the 1970s—that he developed an *entirely new branch of evolutionary theory* to explain it.

Although tucked away in the eleventh chapter of *The Selfish Gene*, Dawkins's hostility toward religion didn't go unnoticed. At the beginning of *Unweaving the Rainbow*, published twenty years later, Dawkins describes some of the correspondence he received from readers of his first book. One man "confessed that he could not sleep for three nights after reading it, so troubled was he by what he saw as its cold, bleak message."[35] And in the preface to the thirtieth anniversary edition of *The Selfish Gene*, Dawkins quotes extensively from an Australian reader who "largely blame[s] *The Selfish Gene* for a series of bouts of depression [they] suffered from for more than a decade."[36] Dawkins is unbothered. Religion was already a punching bag for him as far back as the 1970s.

New Atheism, Scientism, and the Linguistic Fallacy

The Selfish Gene, then, was the prototype of the New Atheist books of the 2000s. It had the sassy, scathing tone toward religion, and it couched its contempt in science.[37] Its account of religion as a *meme*—a molecule of information with its own malignant agenda—set the table for the New Atheist criticisms of faith. Dennett (whom Gould icily writes off as "Dawkins's lapdog")[38] says *The Selfish Gene* inspired his own shift into thinking about biology.[39] He brings Dawkins's adaptationist slant onboard at every level of his project. It's at the root of his theory of consciousness and his interpretation of Darwinism.[40] And it's embedded in his atheism. *Breaking the Spell* uses contemporary cognitive science research to hotwire an entire theory of religion inside the framework of meme analysis, reprinting Dennett's own earlier essay on memes as an appendix for good measure.[41] Shoddy religious beliefs, Dennett writes, are outlaw memes.[42]

Taking this approach, though, means taking it as a given that religions are about belief and nothing but belief. Both *Breaking the Spell* and Dawkins's *The God Delusion* start out by surveying alternative definitions of religion—like William James's emphasis on experience and Einstein's *cosmic religious feeling*—then immediately conclude that these are *spirituality*, rather than *religion*, properly speaking.[43] Religion—real religion—has to be about belief. God, for Dawkins and Dennett, is just a hypothesis. What's more, these beliefs are central to understanding the motivation of religious people. Harris's *The End of Faith* contains an entire chapter titled "The Nature of Belief," where he argues that "a belief is a lever that, once pulled, moves almost everything else in a person's life."[44] Analyzing *what beliefs make people do* is the core procedure of New Atheism. Writing about the 9/11 attacks, Harris asks, "Why did nineteen well-educated middle-class men trade their lives in this world for the privilege of killing thousands of our neighbors?" And answers: "Because they believed they would go straight to paradise for doing so. It is rare," he adds, "to find the behavior of humans so fully and satisfactorily explained."[45] Dawkins concurs, insisting, "*These people actually believe what they say they believe.*"⁴⁶ To know a religion is to know its belief system, the operating system for how its followers think and act.

This may chime with the conventional wisdom in the West, but it's one of the main areas where scholars of religion have criticized the New Atheist approach. As we saw in chapter 3, scholars of religion see the effort to reduce religion to belief as an echo of the Protestant fixation on scripture. The anthropologist of religion Manuel Vásquez, building on Talal Asad's call to push past the exclusive focus on religion as symbol system, directly criticizes Dawkins & Co. for producing a flat, one-dimensional picture of religion as meme complex.⁴⁷ Vásquez calls this approach the "suffocating textualism that approaches religions as essentially systems of symbols, beliefs, narratives, and cosmologies, ignoring other important material dimensions of religious life."⁴⁸ Religion's critics (and, let's face it, no small number of its advocates) fall for the linguistic fallacy—the error that belief is all that matters for understanding motivation.

From the perspective of cogency theory, compressing religion to a booklet of beliefs is a way of making it into a simplex system, and so changing how knowledge about it feels. As we saw in chapter 1, simplexity makes an intellectual field more interesting by maxing out opportunities for click. Through the filter of textualism, human motivation is literally spelled out for us. Whether it's a catechism, a prayer, or a sacred book, a contraption of sentences provides all the puzzle pieces of the secrets of subjectivity. The messy, complex questions of history, power, and feeling are ignored. It's the wrong way to understand religion, yes, but *it's a joyful error*. It transforms religion into a toy with a prefabricated solution. If everyone *really believes* the books they read, then the chords of understanding are clear as day. We can track a straight line from book to belief to action. Everything clicks together with satisfying ease. Religion compressed to belief is seductive as an explanation *because it's simple*.

This lines up with what philosopher Massimo Pigliucci identifies as the overriding *scientism* of the New Atheists—their conviction that everything in the world fits under a microscope.⁴⁹ Like conspiracy theory, scientism creates a simplex system. By assuming that everything can be known through measurement—and known easily—it turns up click everywhere. Harris, for instance, argues in his book *The Moral Landscape: How Science Can Determine Human Values* that advances in brain science are on the brink of cracking the code of pain and pleasure. This will lead, he contends, to a *science* of good and bad outcomes that will eliminate the need for ethics by reducing morality to arithmetic.⁵⁰ Of course, advances in science have produced means of prediction and control that allow for indispensable life-saving and life-enhancing interventions. And the voice of science in combating anthropogenic climate chaos has never been more urgent. It's not that science doesn't have an extraordinary track record to point to. But scient*ism*, like conspiracy theory, is drained of humility, painting a one-dimensional picture of science that ignores its limitations, gaps, and fissures.

Dennett's book *Breaking the Spell* does the same thing. He proposes that religious phenomena, too, need to be subjected to scientific analysis.⁵¹ Religion, he writes, is a sort of economy. *Cui bono?* is the refrain of the book—*who benefits?* Religion can be measured using the same cost-benefit analysis Dawkins tells us to apply to biology and Harris wants us to apply to morality. "What pays for religion?"⁵² Watching a ritual, Dennett asks: "Who or what is the beneficiary of all this extravagant outlay?"⁵³ Religion is flattened to a kind of balance sheet of credits and debits. We do *x* only if we will gain *y*. The answers are organized into tidy columns, simple, straightforward, computable.

It's one thing to say that scientism is a methodological mistake. But cogency theory lands a different point. Scientism, from the perspective of cogency theory, makes knowledge *feel* a certain way. Everything is *deeply intelligible*, a perfect symphony of clicks. This goes hand in hand with the hatred of so-called postmodernism, which, led astray by "the demon of relativism ... pour[s] scorn on the search for truth."⁵⁴ What the New Atheists and other pop authors (including plenty of theists eager to join their crusade for certainty) call postmodernism is any challenge to the possibility of absolute truth.⁵⁵ Postmodernism is the click-killer. It flips the tables on a prepackaged world eager to arrange itself into a neat grid for our pleasure. Exquisite geometry becomes a splat. Ambiguity, for scientism intoxicated by click, is repellent.

And, of course, adaptationism is itself a form of scientism. Dawkins writes that "we animals are the most complicated and perfectly designed pieces of machinery in the known universe."⁵⁶ Every part of every organism yields a neat adaptive storyline when put under the microscope. E. O. Wilson's 1978 explanation for same-sex desire, for instance, was that even though they can't have children of their own, "homosexual specialists" help their close kin with "domestic occupations at the dwelling sites," which allows their group to more effectively pass on the genetic predisposition to queerness.⁵⁷ Gould calls these *just-so stories*—like the famous fables in which every animal has a cute origin story for how it earned its distinctive feature. As critics have noted, breathless monologuing about *why things evolved* is the stock-in-trade of adaptationism, but the answers produced can never be tested.[58] Adaptationism mass-produces clicky origin stories without ever subjecting them to the tempering pressure of a skeptical glance.

What needs to be emphasized, too, is that this all flies in the face of Darwin's own method. He saw life as a staggeringly complex maze, produced not only by natural selection but also by other angles of selection pressure. As George Levine writes, Dawkins and Dennett offer "a vision ... of universal order, where Darwin's laws are no longer 'higgledy piggledy' but the expression of an ultimately unified and coherent world."[59] Gould, in a review of *Darwin's Dangerous Idea*, says that Dennett "*only gets excited when he can observe adaptive design ... but such an attitude surely represents a blinkered view of nature's potential interest.*"[60] Scientism, the Panglossian paradigm, and the fight against postmodern relativism are fueled by the same "rage for order."[61] Weber says that our disenchanted worldview renders everything subject to a scrutable explanation. But as we saw in chapter 3, this isn't a grim trap we've stumbled into. It's a skillful seduction of our intellectual desires. Scientism, conspiracism, and simplicity all set out to make everything easily explainable—humming with interest.

Bulldogs on Parade

New Atheism resembles conspiracy theory not because it's focused on secret events, then, but because of the way it feels its way through knowledge. And like conspiracism, it tends to walk arm in arm with racialized reason. There are two levels of this. On one level, New Atheism consistently presents all religion (including so-called moderate religion) as interchangeable with extremism. Dawkins puts this succinctly, mocking the term *religious extremism*, "as though that were some kind of terrible perversion of real, decent religion."[62] The second level is smaller in scope but probably wider in impact. It's the strand of New Atheist writing that insists that Islam is a *special problem*. Both mistakes are forms of racialized reason, taking the part as representative of the whole. But the latter is run through the filter of white supremacy, producing a stratification into *silly white religion* and *evil brown religion*.

The first mistake, the conflation of all religious people with extremists, shows up in a Lennonist screed in *The God Delusion*, in which Dawkins invites us to imagine a world without religion, with "no suicide bombers, no 9/11, no 7/7, no Crusades, no witch-hunts, no Gunpowder Plot, no Indian partition, no Israeli/Palestinian wars, no Serb/Croat/Muslim massacres, no persecution of Jews as 'Christ-killers,' no Northern Ireland 'troubles,' no 'honour killings,' no shiny-suited bouffant-haired televangelists fleecing gullible people of their money ('God wants you to give till it hurts')."[63] For Dawkins, this is not limited to fundamentalism. "To the vast majority of believers around the world," he insists, "religion all too closely resembles what you hear from the likes of Robertson, Falwell, or Haggard, Osama bin Laden or the Ayatollah Khomeini."[64] There's a willful conflation here of the spectacular few with the invisible many.[65] Dawkins can't help himself. The temptation to dismiss *all* religious people as zealots hazardous to democracy is too incandescent for him to resist.

Christopher Hitchens has a similar habit of thinking. It's there in the overheated intertitles of his book: *religion poisons everything*; *religion kills*; *is religion child abuse?* "As I write these words," he warns us, "and as you read them, people of faith are in their different ways planning your and my destruction, and the destruction of all the hard-won human attainments."[66] "I certainly do believe that totalitarianism is innate in all religion," he affirms in the documentary interview *The Four Horsemen*, a meeting of minds with Dawkins, Dennett, Harris, and Hitchens filmed in Dawkins's North Oxford home. Religion "has to want an absolute, unchallengeable, eternal authority. It must be so. A Creator [for whom] our comments on His will are unimportant. His will is absolute. ... That is the origin of totalitarianism."[67] It's the textualist assumption that ideas and behavior are in an inflexibly tight causal relationship, and Hitchens sees it at the heart of all religious systems of thought. This idea, he contends, is the trigger of all forms of despotism.

The documentary film *Religulous*, starring comedian Bill Maher, is part of the same New Atheist constellation. The religious people Maher interviews for the documentary look silly, sometimes even disingenuous. It's lighthearted, gently mocking, conversational. But the final sequence abruptly changes tone. Returning to the archaeological site of Megiddo in Israel, the prophesied site of the battle of Armageddon in Revelation, Maher suddenly launches into end-of-days talk. Maher insists that the religious "irrationalists" can no longer be trusted to make decisions with world-spanning consequences. "The plain fact is," he advises us, "religion must die for mankind to live."[68] It's Dawkins's quip that only religious faith could motivate fanatical violence all over again. Even moderate religionists are "mafia wives"—passive enablers of a wicked regime.[69] "That's it," he concludes. "Grow up or die."[70] In the background, we're blitzed by grainy footage of wars, explosions, armed irregular soldiers, protests. An apocalyptic soundtrack of choppy choral vocals and kettledrums is the finishing touch.

Richard Cimino and Christian Smith contend that what's unique about the New Atheism is its argument that "even moderate religiosity is deeply implicated in the moral catastrophes perpetuated on the world in the name of religion."[71] But as other critics have pointed out, this mistake is, simply put, totally *unscientific*: it ruthlessly skews the data, cherry-picking examples of religious people behaving badly, glossing over instances where nonbelievers do the same.[72] It's a secularist analogue to race science, laundering white supremacy and calling it objective truth.

Reza Aslan calls Dawkins "Darwin's Rottweiler."[73] And Dawkins isn't alone in loving a fight. *All* the New Atheists seem to have the same Huxleyite battle lust. But Huxley, for all his growling, gradually became convinced of the need to work alongside religious people to achieve his goals in, for instance, education reform. He was more of a gate-crasher than Darwin, but he had at least some of the same self-skeptical tendencies in his science. He followed James's advice to express a sincere nervousness about getting the truth wrong, taking a hard pass on *Vestiges*. It's hard to say the same about the New Atheists, who never met an antireligious polemic they didn't like. The cogency of the great conflation between violent extremists and run-of-the-mill believers is built by approaching the evidence with extreme selectivity. Some data points don't fit the picture, so they dim into the background. The counterexamples don't click. It's the same pattern of self-serving, exciting interpretation that underlies conspiracy theory, now scaled up to a full-fledged formation of the secular. It feels so good it has to be true.

Secular Animacy Hierarchies

The motivated mistake that religion can be defined by its extremes is a form of racialized reason. It eagerly overlooks the evidence because it wants to believe the worst. But this gleeful fascination with otherness takes on an even more clearly racial cast when New Atheists talk about Islam. The second big mistake of New Atheism is that Islam is the worst among equals. Race, a felt sense of foreignness, is directing the cogency of their ideas. Sara Ahmed writes that affect "can stick words like 'terrorist' and 'Islam' together *even when arguments are made that seem to unmake those links.*"⁷⁴ Rationality messes together with the racialized affects of Islamophobia, and Islamophobia comes to *feel reasonable*. It's a *secular animacy hierarchy*, to use Mel Chen's term discussed in chapter 2—a structure of racialized reason that emerges when some groups are felt to be more valuable or worthy of life and respect than others. It still works when no one is saying it out loud—and even when no one is quietly thinking it to themselves. Racialized reason is the skin that forms around raw racist feelings. Just as a racist society tends to produce racist science, an Islamophobic society tends to produce Islamophobic formations of the secular. It just feels right.

Hitchens's work is Exhibit A here. *God Is Not Great* is even-handed when it comes to Islam. Hitchens, as a war correspondent who covered the 1990s Balkan conflicts in which Christian forces massacred Bosnian Muslims by the thousands, has no illusions about Christianity turning the other cheek. In Belgrade, he tells us, the media would specify that victims were Muslim while ignoring the sectarian affiliations of Christians, "even as their murderers went to all the trouble of distinguishing themselves by wearing large Orthodox crosses over their bandoliers, or by taping portraits of the Virgin Mary to their rifle butts."⁷⁵ He even pens a motto of religious respect in the first chapter. "I leave it to the faithful to burn each other's churches and mosques and synagogues," he writes. "When I go to the mosque, I take off my shoes. When I go to the synagogue, I cover my head."⁷⁶

But that's his book. Hitchens's speeches, interviews, and articles are very different, offering a stunningly vicious racialized slant. Hitchens describes his emotional response to 9/11, for instance, in an article published a few weeks after the attacks. "To my own surprise and pleasure," he confesses, it "turned out to be exhilaration. Here was the most frightful enemy—theocratic barbarism—in plain view."⁷⁷ The hedonicity of racism is firing on all cylinders, creating a sprawling, faceless enemy. It's an uncanny echo of H. L. Mencken's *I rejoice that they have forced the fighting*.⁷⁸ Hitchens is actually disdainful of Mencken, whom he dismisses in a review essay as "an insecure small-town petit bourgeois ... , an antihumanist as much as an atheist."⁷⁹ But it's hard not to suspect that this was a narcissism of minor differences. The same compassionless cleverness is in their DNA. Hitchens, Mencken, and the early Huxley all branch off from the same canine lineage—snarling, grinning, brawlers, never content without an enemy.

Take this September 2002 interview, in which Hitchens is prompted to assess the war in Afghanistan. "I don't think the war in Afghanistan was ruthlessly enough waged," he replies. The confused interviewer asks if Hitchens endorsed the US-led coalition's use of cluster bombs. Here's Hitchens's response: "If you're actually certain that you're hitting only a concentration of enemy troops ... then it's pretty good because those steel pellets will go straight through somebody and out the other side and through somebody else. And if they're bearing a Koran over their heart, it'll go straight through that, too. So they won't be able to say, 'Ah, I was bearing a Koran over my heart and guess what, the missile stopped halfway through.' No way, 'cause it'll go straight through that as well. They'll be dead, in other words."[80] Hitchens's thinking has mutated into something unbelievably dark. It's exactly what Chen means by an animacy hierarchy. In print, Hitchens *says* all the right things—about respecting Islam and rejecting anti-Muslim bias. Like Hicks, he may even have the right *beliefs*. But his speech is marked by pockets of horror, a distinct *way of feeling* about some bodies as so base that their death and humiliation is desirable. It's hard to imagine Hitchens so quick to celebrate steel pellets puncturing the bodies of Christians or Jews.

Dawkins is less introspective than Hitchens, less apt at tracking and surfacing his own emotional processes. But the same racialized obsession is on display throughout his public statements, especially when he's letting loose on Twitter. "Haven't read Koran so couldn't quote chapter & verse like I can for Bible," he tweeted in 2013, "but often say Islam greatest force for evil today."[81] In 2014 it was "Suggest always put Islamic 'scholar' in quotes, to avoid insulting true scholars."[82] Some similar tweets have now been wiped, including Dawkins's now-vanished signal boost of a conspiracy theory website claiming to expose the "secret Islamist infiltration of the Obama administration."[83] Dawkins has revamped his tone (and maybe changed his mind) in the intervening years, but there's still a consistent pattern of racialized response. In 2015, even while condemning the murders of the young Muslim students in North Carolina, Dawkins couldn't resist getting a dig in at Islam. "Alas, criminal individual killers exist," he tweeted. "But there's only 1 ideology now that preaches the legal killing of dissenters. And it isn't atheism."[84]

Then there was the *cultural upbringing* dustup. "Listening to the lovely bells of Winchester, one of our great mediaeval cathedrals," he tweeted with a summery selfie in 2018. "So much nicer than the aggressive-sounding 'Allahu Akhbar.' Or is that just my cultural upbringing?"[85] Facing down an internet backlash ("Feeling lovely tweed, one of our great materials," one of my whip-smart doctoral students shot back, "So much nicer than aggressive-feeling cotton. Or is that just my cultural upbringing?"),[86] he quickly reversed course. "The call to prayer can be hauntingly beautiful, especially if the muezzin has a musical voice," he clarified, but "'Allahu Akhbar' is anything but beautiful when it is heard just before a suicide bomb goes off."[87]

It all goes to show that even though secular reason *feels like neutral*, it's inflected by racialized affects. They make an invisible hierarchy cogent. Dennett, to his credit, seems to get this. He writes that during his childhood in Lebanon, the "rhythm of the muezzins calling the faithful to prayer from the nearby minaret was my everyday experience, along with my teddy bear and toy trucks, and the beautifully haunting call never fails to send chills through me when I hear it today."[88] We might feel wary toward a different culture—and imagine that hostility to be based on its objective features and qualities—simply because it's unfamiliar. But Dawkins never catches on that what divides *scary* from *lovely* may be about how we have learned to feel about racial difference—and that this in turn might shape what feels like objective reason.

It's typical of how Dawkins talks, too. "If you look at the actual impact that different religions have on the world," he told an audience at a public festival of science in 2017, "it's quite apparent that at present the most evil religion in the world has to be Islam."[89] For what it's worth, he then denounced Donald Trump for demonizing individual Muslims. This was in keeping with his recent tendency to call himself a *Muslimophile*, claiming that Islam (represented by ISIS or the Iranian IRGC regime) abuses Muslims.[90] In the *Four Horsemen* symposium, Dawkins makes the point that "the present savage Islam" is "really rather recent."[91] But this is buried under the mountain of Dawkins's attacks on Islam. It's consistently singled out as a unique threat.

Then there's Harris. Islam is the only religion with a chapter all to itself—"The Problem with Islam"—in *The End of Faith*. "There are good beliefs and there are bad ones," he writes in the opening paragraph, "and it should now be obvious to everyone that Muslims have more than their fair share of the latter."[92] "We are at war with Islam," he doubles down a few pages on, insisting that it "is not merely that we are at war with an otherwise peaceful religion that has been 'hijacked' by extremists. We are at war with precisely the vision of life that is prescribed to all Muslims in the Koran."[93] In *The Four Horsemen*, Harris lines up behind the controversial "clash of civilizations" thesis, declaring that Islam has "bloody borders." Only under the historical Islamic caliphates, he writes, is Islam "totalitarian and happy with itself ... and you don't see the inherent conflict and the inherent liability of its creed."[94] The only time Islam isn't "waging jihad," he tells us, is when "they've already successfully waged jihad."[95] Islam is the special problem of special problems—and not a bizarre perversion of Islam, as even Dawkins would have it. For Harris, this is real Islam—the only real Islam.

Intellectual historian Mohammad Hassan Khalil has studied Harris's approach to Islam in detail. His assessment is that Harris makes two glaring errors. The first is the mistake we looked at earlier: Harris consistently holds up outliers like Osama bin Laden and the Taliban as the type case of the world's 1.8 billion Muslims. But Khalil also finds a second, unique problem with Harris's work. Harris accuses the vast majority of Muslims—those who do not share *his* violent interpretations of their tradition—of *incorrectly interpreting their own faith*. If they'd only read their own scriptures, Harris is convinced, they would be much worse. Both of these mistakes are by-products of Harris's own suffocating textualism. Harris is the worst offender among the New Atheists in thinking that subjectivity is in a one-to-one correspondence with religious beliefs—and that these beliefs are encoded in a set of books that can be taken as a literal blueprint for how religious subjects will behave. That this claim is empirically unsound—*Shock, horror! Religious people have complicated, inconsistent ways of interpreting beliefs!*—is lost on him.

It gets worse. Even if we take the texts as seriously as Harris wants us to, Khalil shows, he *still* interprets the Qur'an in a way that methodically errs on the side of the most damning possible conclusions—no matter how improbable. Khalil spends the first two-thirds of his book patiently surveying Islamic understandings of war, first in the texts, then in the writings of contemporary militants like bin Laden. His conclusion is that "the most distinctive features of radicals such as bin Laden are not their alleged literal readings of the foundational texts of Islam—in some cases, they go to great lengths to circumvent such readings—but rather their aberrant, expansive conceptions of justifiable combat and retaliation."[96] Far from being fundamentalists, Khalil shows, these militants have actually developed winding, convoluted interpretations of their tradition that lead them an amazing distance from their own texts and sources.

The New Atheists are willfully oblivious to this. Khalil zooms in on Harris and fellow New Atheist Ayaan Hirsi Ali, the Somali British ex-Muslim who has made common cause with neocon military adventurism in the Middle East. Khalil shows that their cherry-picking of sources (and their general lack of understanding of how Islamic textual interpretation works) has led them to an assessment of scripture that is much closer to the eccentric views of bin Laden than the Islamic mainstream.[97] For example, over the course of *The End of Faith*, Harris cites sixty Qur'anic passages condemning *unbelievers* as evidence that Islam is irreversibly hostile to other religions.[98] But he misses that many of these refer to specific groups during the military campaigns of the early Muslim community, and that contemporary Muslim theologians interpret them liberally.[99]

Atheist philosopher of science Meera Nanda has an even sharper take on Harris. She notes that Harris, who traveled for years in South Asia studying Buddhism and Advaita Vedanta, uses *The End of Faith* to quietly advance his own metaphysical ideas—even supernatural ones.[100] "While he is quick to pour scorn on such childish ideas as the virgin birth, heaven and hell," Nanda writes, "the great rationalist has only winks and nods to offer when it comes to such 'higher' truths as near-death experiences, ESP and the existence of disembodied souls, all of which he finds plausible."[101] Nanda's diagnosis is that Harris has absorbed the spiritual orientation of contemporary right-wing Hindu nationalism, including its vendettas against Christianity and Islam. This comes along with a sort of mystical theology—drawing on Hindu intellectual coordinates—what Harris calls "The Wisdom of the East."[102] Harris presents himself as an objective observer, coolly probing the belief systems of the world's religions and finding them filled with horrors. But he's created a secret harbor for a dictionary of religious ideas that are immune to scrutiny.

The opening image of *The End of Faith* is a suicide bomber getting ready to destroy a bus. Harris sets it up as a thought experiment, stating that although we know nothing about him, it's "bet-your-life-on-it-easy... to guess the young man's religion."[103] But as Khalil points out, this is an extremely historically narrow view. As recently as the 1970s, an American probably would have assumed the bomber was a communist partisan—a revolutionary taking on a daring suicide mission for a *secular* cause.[104] So why make *this* historical moment the prism for understanding all of Islam? What motivates Harris's reckless conclusions, his hasty insistence that Islam is "a fringe without a center"?[105] Not to mention his strange carve-out for the "wisdom of the East"?

From the perspective of cogency theory, this is exactly how racialized reason infests secular rationality. The cartoon version of Islam is too much fun to let go of. New details that complicate the pretty picture get swept aside. What Chen calls *animacy* is a web of intuitions—about which things are valuable and which are debased—laced into our everyday speech, both reflecting and reiterating a field of power.[106] The things we find cogent—what *feels true* to us—about particular bodies or groups will be configured by these coordinates. It's racialized reason, a structuring net that stratifies the bodies that matter before we even speak. Violence committed in the name of this simulated objectivity is felt to be just.[107] *Racism* (patterned after biological types) is only one salient form of *racialization*—the bigger matrix of in-group/out-group identification.

Of course, neither of these layered mistakes feels like a mistake to the New Atheists. They're both held as gospel truth, even as the evidence against them piles up. It's exactly what cogency theory—as an account not only of ordinary knowledge-making, but of formations of the secular—sets out to explain. These errors gain traction because they produce good feelings, which mess together with our sense of what clicks. This makes staggering simplifications *feel like* the outputs of objective reason. The myths that all religious people are fundamentally the same, or that Islam has a basically evil disposition, feel so good they *have* to be true.[108] The affective elements of conspiracy theory are all there. The New Atheist passion for reason withers—almost instantaneously—when presented with an opportunity to feel good about US against THEM.

Atheism in the Aftermath

Many of the criticisms of New Atheism focus on its strident tone or its narrow view of religious belief.[109] This is part of what I'm talking about here, but not the whole story. We could fix those things and there would still be deadly intellectual problems at the heart of the New Atheist project. The fact that these deeper flaws are so hard to uproot reveals what cogency theory sets out to show: secular reason is composed in a mesh of passions. That's not a bad thing in itself. But it becomes dangerous when we buy into the corrupt, commonsense claim that reason and emotion are fundamentally separate, leaving *what feels neutral* unchallenged.

Some might say that the secular always falls into this trap. But this, too, succumbs to textualism. It shares the same assumption that our propositional beliefs always fix our actions. If we want to take Asad's *formations of the secular* hypothesis seriously, we need a textured account of the different ways the coordinates of nonbelief play out in different historical moments for different communities and different bodies. Scholars of religion would reject as painfully naive any claim that *the Christianity* or *the Buddhism* leads to a single way of living and being—let alone that it was just *good* or *bad*. The secular needs to be seen in the same light, not only as plural but as an active, ongoing plural, constantly reconstructing its own horizons. The backlash provoked by New Atheism *within atheism itself* shows that there are other ways of making the secular. This countercurrent has been called the *New New Atheism* or *soft atheism*, a loosely identified group of writers including Alain de Botton, Greg Epstein, John Gray, A. C. Grayling, Martin Hägglund, Philip Kitcher, Corinna Nicolaou, and Kaya Oakes, who have advocated for a rethinking of the aims and tactics of contemporary atheism.[110]

There's lots to say about how these new approaches recast the affective alloys of the secular. But I want to focus on a cluster of writers who have explicitly raised race and racialization as central: Anthony Pinn, the architect of *African American humanism*; Black feminist Sikivu Hutchinson; and white interfaith activist Chris Stedman. What's distinctive about these thinkers is that they *refuse to take secular reason's claim to neutrality as a given*. Their goal has been to steer atheism away from conspiracism and build it instead around something like the sense of science—a dynamic of humility and excitement.

African American humanism is going through a golden age, as recent historical studies linking the Black intellectual tradition and secularity have shown.[111] It's an interesting feature of the aftermath of New Atheism precisely because it thinks about race and difference in ways that Dawkins & Co. are totally oblivious to. Pinn, a philosopher of religion at Rice University, is one of its founders, a frequent speaker at atheist and humanist events and the winner of awards from national humanist organizations. His philosophical outlook presents a studied contrast with the New Atheist approach, a vividly different way of composing secularism by drawing on a different cocktail of felt ingredients.

For one thing, he defines his thought not in opposition to *religion* but, rather, in opposition to *theism*. Much as Huxley insisted he was both religious and totally without theology, *religion*, for Pinn, "assumes no gods and requires no concern with superhuman worlds of wonder."[112] Instead, it's a reservoir of reflections on how to live meaningfully. Unlike Huxley, though, Pinn extends this recuperation to theology itself. His contention is that theology can be taken seriously as "a method for critically engaging, articulating, and discussing the deep existential and ontological issues endemic to human life."[113] It's a cautious, even-handed approach—the reparative counterpart to the paranoid perspective of New Atheism—that immediately sets Pinn's version of atheism on a different affective foundation. Rather than a posture of total war, his starting point is that the resources of religion can be subtracted from their theistic frames and worked into humanism.

But Pinn still maintains a passion for reason as part of the atheist project, stressing that only fragments of the theological project can be saved. "I think there are ways in which the conceptualization and practice of humanism ... might benefit from theological analysis," Pinn tells us, before resolutely emphasizing that "much of theological grammar and vocabulary has run its course and offers nothing of value."[114] In some moments—as when Pinn writes of the "willingness to be guided by an imaginary force" and the "otherwise counterproductive thinking and behavior stemming from this allegiance"—there's even a bit of a bite, a sense that the edge is being savored—if not quite at bulldog-level jaw pressure.[115]

Moreover, Pinn's African American humanism is organized around a much more nuanced approach to race than one finds in the New Atheism. First and foremost, he rejects *color blindness*, the fantasy of secular neutrality when it comes to race. Pinn confesses to finding it annoying when white atheists ask him to explain why so many Black Americans are Christian.[116] Without a grasp of how Christianity and Islam have provided "a sense of identity and agency that contradicted dehumanization produced through racial injustice," he writes, white atheists are operating out of ignorance at best, complicity in oppression at worst.[117] Angrily reasserting the sovereignty of so-called objective reason is not enough. Rather than asking why Black folks are invested in Christianity, Pinn suggests white atheists should be working around the clock to figure out why humanism has failed to entice a diverse constituency.[118]

Sikivu Hutchinson, who sees herself as working out a Black feminist atheism, develops a similar line of thought. Her work, though, explicitly connects Black atheism to traditions of Marxist-socialist critique, which she sees as the inspiration for earlier Black freethinkers like Hubert Harrison.[119] Her vision of *radical humanism* advances "a vision of secular social justice that challenges Eurocentric traditions of race, gender, and class-neutral secularism."[120] It directly confronts the way secular reason is determined by something more than just a surface-level grid of beliefs and disbeliefs.

Although she writes favorably about Dawkins's Foundation for Reason and Science and its efforts to promote the work of feminist atheists,

Hutchinson doesn't hesitate to dress it down for appointing an all-white board of directors when it merged with the Center for Inquiry in 2016. For her, this was yet another lost opportunity for the atheist movement to refocus attention on atheism beyond the pale of whiteness.[121] Radical humanism, in her eyes, demands sustained, street-level engagement with social justice. "In the absence of an explicitly anti-racist, anti-sexist, anti-heterosexist and anti-imperialist critical consciousness," Hutchinson predicts, "there will continue to be a major divide between white atheist discourse and the lived experiences of humanists of color."[122] This commitment to a broad-based social justice mission for atheism comes across in her own antiracist work—fighting discrimination in schools, gentrification, subprime mortgage scams, and bias in hiring and tenure decisions at universities—all areas where racialized reason masks its emotional infrastructure as color-blind policy.

And she targets the "Islamophobic atheist rock star" style of Dawkins and Harris.[123] She rejects the triumphalism of New Atheists like Ayaan Hirsi Ali who trade on a binary between the civilized West and the barbaric Islamic world, relying on a deceptive "portray[al of] feminism as a battle that the West has already won" and "absolv[ing] bourgeois democracies like the United States" of their own defective human rights records—not to mention their imperialist wars on the global stage.[124] It's a project that converges with Jasbir Puar's criticism of *homonationalism* and Sara Ferris's derived concept of *femonationalism*—a superficial commitment to gay and women's rights used to justify imperialist violence.[125] These critical approaches call out the pretense to objectivity in Western rationality, which obscures its racial determination.

But—like Pinn—Hutchinson is ruthless in prosecuting Christianity's complicity with oppression. She uses a Marxist framing of religion as a toxic by-product of economic inequality, pulling no punches on white televangelists and Black prosperity gospel churches—"the community's biggest parasites."[126] She further insists that even progressive versions of Christianity will always fail because they rely on "on cherry picking scripture to articulate a social justice agenda fundamentally incompatible with the patriarchal, imperialist, sexist, homophobic, inhumane thrust of the Bible."[127] The Bible, she writes, is and only ever will be a blueprint for capitalism and fascism.[128] It's a pared-down version of the overwhelming textualism of the white New Atheists explored above—and in many ways Hutchinson's style of secularism *feels* more like New Atheism than Pinn's does. The signal difference is that for her the mission of antiracism is embedded in the foreground. She has no confidence that an unexamined secular reason will be able to maintain its neutrality when it's determined by the coordinates of a racist society.

The center of gravity for Pinn is elsewhere. He brings social justice onstage, but his focus is on coming up with a "system of life meaning"—a nontheistic religion.[129] This means pulling up resources from religious art, architecture, material culture, music, science, even the Bible itself. Unlike Hutchinson, he sees both the Hebrew Bible and the New Testament as holding "metaphorical or symbolic value through their teaching of both positive and negative life lessons," so long as they've been subtracted from the metaphysical framing that comes along with theism.[130] Where Hutchinson's frame of reference is textualist, Pinn has a more flexible sense of the relationship between books and bodies.

Science and Secular Introspection

Pinn also sees science as a resource for building African American humanism. The best way to understand our bodies, in his view, is to move on from *imago Dei* theology. (He argues that the "theoretical basis for racial inferiority came originally out of theology, not science.")[131] This means learning about our evolutionary makeup and its dynamic relationship with culture.[132] But he steers away from a positivist version of science that insists on its own infallibility. He cites Gould as an example of a scientist who highlighted science's susceptibility to contamination by racism and sexism, while still advancing public science as a resource for human self-understanding.[133] Science, in his view, gives us a window into "the nature and meaning of the human animal."[134] It's a form of scientific secularism, though the emphasis is not so much on how science *feels* but the way it gives us tools for mapping our emotional interiors. That includes knocking down the black monolith myth.

Science for the other thinkers in this group is less enticing. Coming from a perspective shaped by his experiences as white, queer, and ex-evangelical, Chris Stedman is similar to Hutchinson in wanting to radically center social justice as the real work of secularism. Stedman's 2012 memoir, *Faitheist*, begins with a reception after an atheist lecture, held in an upscale apartment in downtown Chicago. It's here that he learns that *faitheist* is a term of abuse lobbed by atheists against their own kind—specifically, those found to be insufficiently outraged by religion.[135] Stedman sees this as a destructive habit of the movement. "Disengaged or antagonistic atheism," he writes, "weakens our community's claim that an ethical life is possible without a belief in God."[136]

Stedman's contention is that *movement atheists*—the consumers of angry books, angry lectures, angry social media—are actually a minority among the broader atheist world. He talks about how some of his atheist friends blanch at the word *atheist* because of its association with the recreational outrage of the New Atheism. "The atheist movement is doing something very wrong," he writes, "when a sizable number of the atheists I meet in my day-to-day life want nothing whatsoever to do with it."[137] This is also why Stedman is determined to root out atheism's Islamophobic streak. "Whatever the killer's motive," he wrote in response to the Chapel Hill murders in 2015, "we atheists need to address anti-Muslim prejudice in our community."[138] Stedman, Pinn, and Hutchinson share a strong sense that atheism has been organized by a vision of secular reason that passes itself off as neutral but is actually defined by the parochial experience of a particular privileged group.

For the same reason, Stedman is wary of versions of secularism that fixate on salvation by science. Atheism, he argues, is seen as a playground for elites preoccupied with science.[139] This closes doors into the atheist community from those who feel displaced by its race and class priorities. Hutchinson's take is similar. While condemning what she calls the state of *educational apartheid* in the United States (another missed opportunity, she notes, for the atheist movement to rally around a meaningful unifying cause), she also disdains the "arrogance of New Atheist discourse that reductively focuses on raising 'science' ... to the status of shining antidote to social injustice"—a discourse that "is especially insidious for communities of color"—particularly without a reckoning with the history of scientific racism.[140] For both thinkers, science holds no *interest*. It just isn't part of the way they want secularism to feel.

But Stedman is adamant that feeling is part of the new secular culture he wants to build. Reflecting on his work with Eboo Patel's Interfaith Youth Core—a service group that brings together volunteers of different religious backgrounds, including atheists—Stedman explores how their events induced "an entirely different feeling" compared to the movement atheist events he attended—a feeling of nurturing warmth rather than hot-blooded rage.[141] While taking a master's degree in theology, he describes "sitting in class the day after my botched attempt at seeking secular community, [realizing] that

I felt more at home with my religious colleagues than with the atheists from the day before."[142] That feeling of home, for Stedman, isn't about shared beliefs. Instead, the feeling of home is made by the affective resonance running beneath the surface. Rather than agreement at the level of creeds, community is created by what José Esteban Muñoz calls *shared vibes*.[143]

Stedman, then, proposes a different formation of the secular using a different ensemble of emotional elements. It comes along with a recognition that being secular may well *feel like* religion.[144] The New Atheists rub elbows with fundamentalism not by virtue of their epistemological commitments, but by the way both are patterned like conspiracy theory. On the opposite pole, Stedman wants secular feelings that put atheists at the same table as religious believers who see their faith as oriented primarily to the work of social justice. The polarity isn't between *religion* and *secularism*. It's about uniting *affectively similar* forms of religion *and* secularism, while a different affective alliance—which also includes both believers and nonbelievers—parades on the other side of the field. New Atheists and Christian fundamentalists (or Mencken and Bryan) may be flying different colors, but from this perspective, they're on the same team. Shared vibes.

This leads into some of Stedman's most thoughtful reflections on secular feelings—and their political consequences. Although he's at the intersection of two stigmatized identities (gay and atheist), Stedman says he receives *more hate mail from his fellow atheists* than from religious people.[145] The dynamic of racialization within atheism is so intense that it even has its own internal purges. Thinking back on his rapid evolution from angry progressive queer evangelical to angry atheist while attending college, Stedman writes that "directing anger at others can feel good, but I've found that a hangover follows."[146] Anger, he suggests, has a complex psychological half-life. Like a sugar high, it starts out sparkling and exciting, but leaves a malaise in its wake, followed by cravings. His view is that this kind of atheism is turning off people who would otherwise join the movement—the people who tell him, "Well, I don't believe in God, but I'm not an atheist."[147]

There's a similar sort of emotional self-inventorying in Pinn's work. Unlike the New Atheists, Pinn is acutely concerned about the power of the felt WE to produce hard borders, which in turn leads to violence. Thinking through both the history of anti-Black racism and the way African American humanists are often asked, "But you believe in God, don't you?" as a sort of identity confirmation marker, Pinn lays out a sophisticated philosophy of community for humanists.[148] At its center is a conviction that communities are made with our bodies—the hinge between the emotional and the political—and that talk about the community, to avoid producing racialized others, needs to emphasize inclusion as an ongoing mission. Community, he writes, "pulls at embodied life, enveloping it—including it but extending beyond it, leaving behind awareness and a feeling of '*and* …'"[149] Rather than a fortress of the faithless, Pinn's starting point for secularism is the urgent need to jam the signal of identity-making at its source.

But with all of this said, Stedman, like Hutchinson and Pinn, keeps open a facet of his atheist profile for a policy of truth. One of the most poignant moments of Stedman's memoir takes place after a fatal bridge collapse happens near his place of work. Stedman is an evangelical college student. His faith is flickering. During a vigil at the disaster site with his Christian friends, he writes, "I couldn't abide the prayers I overheard." They seemed "futile at best, and inappropriate and disrespectful at worst."[150] Listening to a friend pray, he finds himself mumbling, "This is bullshit."[151]

But why? Why the flash of rage in the circle of grief? Why not just ease into a comforting habit, even if it had the ring of untruth? For some, that would have been right. But for Stedman, in that moment, the truth mattered too. To overlay searing pain with an ice-cold lie was too much. He finds himself debating one of his professors, a Christian, on exactly this point. "When I talk about God, I mean love and justice and reconciliation, not a man in the sky," the professor tells him, before asking, "You talk about love and justice and reconciliation—why can't you just call that God?" Stedman's reply is part of his realization that his faith had left him: "Why *must* you call that God?" he responds. "Why not just call it what it is: love and justice and reconciliation?"[152] These scenes of contention are rare in his writing, but they illustrate how his atheism is still plugged in to a felt commitment to truth-making.

In a meditation that offers a distinct afterimage of Darwin, Stedman reflects on how his Christian friends tried to persuade him that faith had a sort of lunar cycle and that if only he waited, it would wax again in his heart. But his own finding was that "years later I am surer than ever that I don't believe in God, and struggle to recall why I did in the first place." Moreover, he adds, "the question no longer intrigues me—I'm much too interested in the complexities of being human to spend much time thinking about anything beyond that."[153] Like Darwin, metaphysical speculation simply fell away as an object of interest. There were other passions to pursue. For Darwin these were looped in with the wild experiment of natural science.

For Stedman they came along with the wild experiment of building a new form of secular community.

In *Is Critique Secular?*, Talal Asad issues a challenge to secularism. "What would happen," he asks, "if religious language were to be taken more seriously in secular Europe and the preventable deaths in the global South of millions from hunger and war was to be denounced as 'blasphemy,' as the flouting of ethical limits for the sake of what is claimed to be freedom?"[154] This is exactly what these atheists in the aftermath are up to. They've set out to build formations of the secular that make violence, racism, neglect, and exploitation into blasphemy—anathemas loathed no less than heresy. To do this, they take as their starting point an anatomy of secular reason not as a self-evident, towering monument of truth but as a construct made up by its own circulations of feeling. Studying and rewiring these feelings, they create a sense of the secular that balances the pursuit of truth with a nervousness about the emotional stowaways that might contribute to racialized reason.

Conclusion: Laboratories of the Secular

The New Atheists call themselves the Four Horsemen. The name captures all the emotional force packed into the pages of their books: an apocalyptic fantasy, horsing around with religious texts, cavalier to the ways those pages are read, felt, and lived by real religious people. And it points beyond this, too, to the undeniable fact, after Darwin, of the animality of our bodies, our proximity to animals, even when we seem to be doing eminently nonanimal things like reading, speaking, thinking, believing, or disbelieving. The thinking/feeling binary falls apart. Rather than floating over the world of ideas, selectively illuminating truth with lucent beams of thought, we are lushly connected to it. Belief and nonbelief draw on reason, yes, but reason itself emerges from dynamics of feeling. What does secularism feel like? It's a menagerie of passions and pleasures, configured differently for different bodies in different times and places. Secularism is a thing we do as animals, not as angels.

The New Atheists are oblivious to the feelings that carry our thoughts. Although they put Darwin on their standard, they sharply cut against his science, reasserting the black monolith myth's divide between human and animal, between memes and bodies, between thinking and feeling. This leaves them with limited capacity to scrutinize how what they call neutral reason is constructed from a layered collage of feelings. As Amy Hollywood writes, "Despite the desire that rational discourse be undertaken in a spirit of calm and order, modern Western rationality bears within it the marks of a purificatory fever."[155] The result is a version of the secular in which the only thing that matters is winning theological arguments. New Atheism couldn't be further from Darwin's quiet secular garden.

But other secular experiments that have surged in the wake of New Atheism more clearly reflect something like the sense of science, carefully tending the agonism between discovery and humility. They start with a clear-eyed awareness that secularism's claim to neutrality is an invitation to arrogance. Nonbelievers like Pinn, Hutchinson, and Stedman, reflecting deeply on the intransigent dynamics linking reason, racialization, and feeling, offer versions of atheism that turn down the volume on the paranoid style. Rather than assuming that reason is drained of feeling, they scrutinize it carefully, studying its composition, both celebrating its successes and seeking to correct its many missteps. For some, the secular is not even the opposite of religion. Their atheism lives in many phases of dynamic encounter, intimacy, and exchange with faith.

Yet they're still *more* invested in truth than the New Atheism is. At its heart, conspiracy theory is a cluster of motivated mistakes. New Atheism is the same. It's not just the problem of being mean to religious believers. It's crisscrossed by a series of intransigent conceptual errors that are held in place because they feel too good to let go. These errors flourish by parasitizing our pleasure in click and messing it together with racialized affects. Like the *scientia sexualis* that turns out to be an *ars erotica*, the conspiracy theory approach to science and secularism is really a shrewdly disguised apparatus of pleasure. These other atheists refuse these temptations, more faithfully exercising the passion for reason by subjecting our own sense of pleasure in knowledge to scrutiny, playing feelings off against each other to produce a disciplined policy of truth. This lets them cut through the delirious belief that religious moderation is a short slide away from religious extremism, or the racist claim that Islam is essentially more dangerous than other religions. They call us to challenge what gets called rationality when it tries to smuggle racialized reason in under a sheet.

After Deah Shaddy Barakat, Razan Mohammad Abu-Salha, and Yusor Mohammad Abu-Salha were killed, their community memorialized them with, among other things, a Facebook page called "Our Three Winners." The page celebrated Deah's charity work—providing dental services to Syrian refugees in Turkey, for instance, as well as dental supplies to the homeless in and around Chapel Hill—and Razan's work with charities like Global Deaf Muslim. If the situation had been reversed, and it was Craig Stephen Hicks whose life had been cut short, the memorials would have looked very different. Forty-six years old, one failed marriage behind him, another on the rocks, an estranged twenty-year-old daughter who refused to speak to him: What did he see when he looked at them? He saw what so many flailing white American men see when they look at flourishing people of color: he saw a world out of joint, in which the correct hierarchy of dignity had been turned upside-down. He left Christianity behind, but his atheism remained in full communion with white supremacy. He became a gun-toting liberal, descending into a fantasy zone of self-righteousness under the banner of rational disinterest. Then he armed himself to the teeth to defend that mirage.

We don't know why the winter day when he knocked on his neighbors' door turned into a day of horror, but I have argued that we know why he chose those people, rather than any of the other neighbors he'd menaced. Because even though, in Karen Hicks's words, he "just believed everyone was equal," secularisms are always constituted not simply by a set of intellectual commitments but also by a convergence of affects, shaping animacy hierarchies that determine the depth dimension of our values. Wordlessly, they dictate who rises and who falls. As Pinn points out, atheists and humanists "can knowingly and unknowingly support racial injustice through the assumption humanism puts them beyond the realm of such illogical thinking and behaving."[156] Without self-scrutiny, racism bleeds into secularism just as it bleeds into religion or science.

This is not to posit a straight line from Hitchens to Hicks. That would only replicate the linguistic fallacy theory of motivation that this book has tried to unsettle. As Omid Safi writes, "There doesn't have to be a concerned and targeted campaign against Muslims; 15 years of post-9/11 vitriol against Islam and Muslims has poisoned the public discourse. The constant dehumanization of Muslims and the automatic, immediate association of the Islamic faith with terrorism and violence combined with the American addiction to guns ... creates a charged political context which can erupt at any moment."[157] This is what cogency theory aims for: to show how something that masquerades as neutral—secular rationality—absorbs the dispositions that enfold it. Rationality is always susceptible to being messed together with the emotional priorities of where it came from, precisely by shaping *what feels true*. Secularity absorbs a repertoire of feelings that continues to operate and shape subjectivity under the surface of new regimes of belief. These are the sources of the secular fanaticism that New Atheism insists is impossible. The Big Break of secularization isn't the top-to-bottom transfiguration atheists like to think it is. Believer or nonbeliever, we all lose when we allow secularism to become just another slush fund for white male rage. If there's a way forward for atheism, it starts with the defeat of that longing for a horde of racial others (not to mention the morons and boneheads) to step over while loudly insisting on its own innocence.

Thinking feels. And because thinking is made by feeling, it messes together with all the other affects swirling around it. There are and must be many secularisms, many atheisms, an array of nonreligious improvisations tempered by passionate self-suspicion. These secularisms need their laboratories, but more than test tubes, air pumps, thermometers, prisms, and EMGs, these are laboratories that explore and retune our bodies, recalibrating our emotions into finely tensed agonisms, guiding us to meet the world more vividly, more sensitively, more honestly, more compassionately. At the core of this is a resolute vigilance to keep in check the all-too-human disposition to find pleasure in writing people off. It's the secular as oriented to what Achille Mbembe calls the *project of nonracialism*, demanding new forms of feeling and thinking together.[158]

EPILOGUE
FROM CREATIONISM TO CLIMATE DENIALISM

In 2013, the Pew Research Center published the results of a survey on evolution and political affiliation in the United States. They also compared these 2013 responses to the findings of a similar survey from 2009. The comparison told a surprising story. Among self-described Democrats and independents, the number of believers in evolution held steady across those four years, showing almost no change in those who accepted the evolutionary story. Among Republicans, however, the number of respondents who affirmed evolution *dropped by eleven points*, from 54 to 43 percent.[1]

It's another nail in the coffin of the classic secularization narrative, the claim that religion is on a downward slide, never to regain ground. But why? Why does confidence in scientific accounts of the history of life plummet among American conservatives in the first term of the presidency of Barack Obama? Cogency theory's answer is that it has everything to do with the way science feels. It's not about new information, new research, new books, new ideas. It's about a new tilt on the landscape of belief, a change in the coordinates of *what feels true*. Conservatives think they're under assault by a secular agenda and ramp up their opposition to secular ideas. Racism is probably in the mix too—white supremacy's escalating immune response to America's first Black president. As science comes to feel more and more like enemy territory, it becomes less and less cogent.

No part of science happens in a vacuum. It's engineered by living bodies, saturated by culture, power, and history, and enfolded within feeling. Naomi Oreskes writes in *Why Trust Science?* that the reliability of science is based on both "its sustained engagement with the world" and "its social character."[2] Cogency theory adds a third dimension to this picture. It suggests that science works when it stages an agonism of different *cognitive emotions*, tracking the excitement of click while holding on to nervousness about getting things wrong. Science doesn't need the thinking/feeling binary to make good knowledge. The same emotional machinery that sends us down the wrong track can also, with just a bit of fine-tuning, build durable science. But this means that science—and formations of the secular tinged by science—*always* have an emotional dimension, even when it's submerged beneath the threshold of awareness. From the micro to the macro, knowledge-making is always guided by a subtle web of emotional priorities, intimate threads that lace cognition into a dense weave of information and inspiration.

Theories of Denial

Science denialism today is driving one of the most stunning unfolding disasters of our time: anthropogenic climate change. Some theories of climate denialism coming out of STS have lapsed into a sort of *denialism denial*. They insist that no one could actually look at the evidence for the climate crisis and *fail to believe*. Bruno Latour's recent work, for instance, claims that the denialist elite—smarmy politicians, professional gasket-blowers in the right-wing mediasphere, smirking CEOs—aren't actually denialists at all. In fact, they "have taken the threat seriously" and have simply decided to *feign* denial for as long as possible, deliberately concealing their fidelity to science while they build their own escape hatches.[3] So they stock their island fortresses or invest in schemes to run off to the moon. In turn, rank-and-file denialists are absolved by Latour of *their* rejection of climate science. They see elites failing to commit to change and so reject the warning signals sent by science altogether.[4]

For someone who has so shrewdly diagnosed the erosive effects of conspiracy theory, Latour's confidence that no one could sincerely *fail to believe* the science of climate crisis seems strange. But this is exactly the kind of mistake we're led to in the absence of a robust account of how feeling terraforms the landscape of plausibility. Without a theory of cogency, we have to conclude that climate denialism is either sheer obliviousness or a bizarre decoy. The truth is more complicated. From the perspective of cogency theory, two bodies can look at the same evidence and arrive at radically different conclusions because *the way they feel* about that information is split. When we see reason as *organized* by affect rather than as its binary opposite, we can pose a new set of questions about why someone believes or disbelieves. Instead of trying to explain away denialism, as Latour does, cogency theory takes the bull by the horns. It directly confronts the question of why the same science is cogent for some but not others.

Cogency is the raw material of conviction. It's the agonism of compulsions in our bodies, the traces of the rambunctious passion for reason messing together with the sticky affects that surround it to make weird conglomerates of belief. It affirms that thinking and feeling are not just *intertwined*. Rather than a stiff-backed *pas de deux*, they're a single, sprawling, synchronized ballet of faculties. That means cogency is about how tense knots of power, desire, knowledge, and history pull on our bodies, and how they're worked by people, places, and things around us, by relationships and antipathies, by hopes and frustrations, by memory and pain, exhilaration and shame, bliss and rage. It's about how the emotional structure of obviousness is composed in real time, and how hotwiring that emotional infrastructure can rotate the landscape of plausibility. It's about how we make up our minds by feeling our way forward, and how new injections of feeling—including the feelings carried by information, fact or fiction—remake belief.

Cogency theory, then, is about the enigma of persuasion. It offers new maps for how to get people into the persuasion zone and new techniques for what to say when they get there. In diagnosing the logjam of science skepticism and trying to find a way through, it highlights three features of the crossroads of feeling and conviction.

1. The Emotional Makeup of Science Skepticism

Jesus Camp, from 2006, is a documentary about evangelical kids attending a Christian summer leadership camp.[5] Early in the movie we meet a homeschooled boy named Levi as he watches a creationist video at his parents' house in rural Missouri. His mother calls him into the kitchen, where they sit down for a lesson, a portrait of President George W. Bush tacked to the wall behind them. She quizzes Levi on evolution, Galileo, and climate change. "One popular thing to do in American politics," she reads from their textbook, "is to note that the summers in the United States over the past few years, have been very warm. As a result, global warming must be real. What's wrong with this reasoning?" "It's only gone up 0.6 degrees," Levi replies, eagerly. "Ah," she says, "yeah, it isn't really a big problem, is it?" "No," Levi says reflectively, before adding, "I don't *think* that it's gonna hurt us."[6]

What happens next reveals the emotional linchpin of the scene. Levi's mom is making a point about bias in education. "What if you had to go to a school where the teacher said 'Creationism is *stupid*, and you're *stupid* if you believe it'?" she asks. "Or what if you had to go to a school where your teacher said 'Evolution is *stupid*, and you're *stupid* if you believe in it'?"[7] The play of pitch in her voice exposes the affective currents shaping her words, the dense infrastructure of cogency. It's all in the way she says *stupid*. Each and every time, like she's spitting, *You're stupid*. You can hear the venom, the pain, a history of having been lashed by that word, shamed by it, passed down through generations. When Mencken wrote "Homo Neandertalensis" or printed "One intelligent reader is worth a thousand boneheads" on the cover of the *Smart Set*, he meant her. Science has been used as a weapon against her. Is it any wonder she's kicking back?

This isn't to say that *religious beliefs* are sacrosanct or immune to challenge. But it is to say that the *emotional* format of science-religion interaction needs to be studied and approached with a feel for tracing the affective backdrop of the conversation. To understand why someone might be hostile to science, we need to locate them in a history of feeling. We need to know why their trust in science might be contaminated. Then we need to extend bridges and rebuild that trust. This means rearranging the landscape of cogency.

So the first finding of cogency theory is this: we can't assume that *more knowledge* alone is powerful enough to overcome opposition to science skepticism, just as we saw that *teaching the controversy* around creationism or Intelligent Design doesn't necessarily produce better classrooms. In fact, our starting point should be that new information about things that matter is *almost always going to face resistance*. Unlike the phony Chinese characters Zajonc slipped to his test subjects in 1968, we seldom have the benefit of default indifference. The people you're trying to persuade see you coming a mile away, and how they feel about *you* is already shaping how they feel about *what you say*.

We need maps of where resistance comes from. Is it a question of money or livelihood? Is it about identity—race, class, religion, political stripe—the coordinates of who's in and who's out, who gets listened to and who gets shouted down? Is it because science isn't trusted by those who have come to see it as a soldier of fortune for secularism, class condescension, or racism? Without a diagram of how knowledge feels—all the softnesses and hardnesses a body has toward new science—we're lost. Nothing is off the table in this process. Shame may be just as valuable a tool for transformation as patience, for instance. But compassion is always part of the equation. Persuasion means learning our landscapes of feeling, exploring them, and then artfully rearranging them, all with an eye to letting ourselves more graciously acquiesce to truth.

2. The Emotional Structure of Obstinacy

In his 1899 book *The Interpretation of Dreams*, Freud described what has come to be called *kettle logic*.[8] It goes like this. Your neighbor borrows your kettle and returns it to you with a hole in it. You protest. But your neighbor is all denials. He insists, "first, that he had given it back undamaged; secondly, that the kettle had a hole in it when he borrowed it; and thirdly, that he had never borrowed a kettle from [you] at all."[9] It's a study in the emotional logic of obstinacy. He *wants it not to be true*, so he gets busy fortifying his position with reasons. Thinking buds from feeling. His passion for truth has been eclipsed—completely—by his *refusal to be wrong*, his deep desire to feel okay about himself.

As Oreskes points out, climate denialism follows the same self-seducing logic: first they tell us climate chaos isn't happening. And if it is happening, it's not caused by humans, so there's nothing we can do about it. And if it is human caused, maybe it's a good thing?[10] Climate denialists often come armed with their own little arsenal of pseudo-facts. They have their own pseudoscience and their own pseudo-theory, often mobilized, as Oreskes and Erik Conway have documented, by pseudo-experts.[11] It's structured like a conspiracy theory—a chintzy knockoff of real insight that trumps existing knowledge and lets you feel smarter than everyone else. It gets an extra jolt from the thrill of dealing in stigmatized knowledge.[12] This is part of what makes denialism cogent.

But climate denialism has another powerful weapon at its disposal. It draws on the immune system of *feeling okay about things*. Contentment has a built-in defense mechanism. The force of climate denialism is amplified by the fact that *we really don't want to know*. It's not just that there's a catastrophe on the horizon. What-we-believe has an immune system, and that immune system feels like happiness. The climate crisis is an outgrowth of the fact that we're anything but creatures of pure reason. Confronting unwelcome truths is unpleasant precisely because they disrupt our emotional equilibrium. Our failure to listen to climate science is partly a by-product of our own thirst to be content. Could simple things—fuel, meat, plastic—be sowing the seeds of disaster? It feels so awful it can't possibly be true.

But contra what the New Atheists tell us, *religion* is not the problem. Some forms of religion are marching in lockstep with denialist agendas, but so, too, are some formations of the secular. Marx knew that capitalism is formidable exactly because it creates a hologram of *this is fine* around those who have been carried by the winds of fortune into its upper stories.[13] This hologram has an emotional immune system. It refuses to accept that we might be in serious trouble. For the chosen ones of global capitalism, the climate crisis has, in a sense, hacked us, exploiting our inability to muster the self-awareness we need to confront it, artfully finessing our emotional limitations. There are lots of factors—social, historic, economic—leading to climate denialism. But much like with conspiracy theory, finding persuasion zones requires a clear account of the emotional anatomy of how denialism works. What makes it cogent? What prevents people from responding to it and then voting, mobilizing, and acting in meaningful ways? And how can we turn the tables? The bulwark of denialism is not a person, or a group, or even an ideology. It's a structure of feeling—the feeling of *this is fine*. The harder the truth, the more difficult it is to bring it into view.

3. The Emotional Force of Truth

But this shouldn't leave us without hope. For all the pessimism about obstinacy and its thick emotional roots, cogency theory also directs us to be clear-eyed about the force of truth. Facts are powerful. Their power comes from our makeup as bodies that *want to feel the click of things coming together*—things we know even though we haven't quite admitted it to ourselves—even if we *also* want to avert our eyes. Denialism has developed an extremely effective weapon against science: obstinacy, the bullish self-confidence of the kettle-wrecker, so determined to not be found in the wrong that they believe their own falsehoods. But the art of changing minds about climate science can harness this felt force of facts.

Obstinacy is demoralizing. It's often said these days that persuasion is dead, that no one changes their minds anymore. But we know that's not true, even if the conditions under which people change their minds have transformed. Cogency theory proposes that obstinacy is also limited. From the perspective of thinking as cogitation, if you don't see the truth of something the first time it's served up, you never will. You're just *unreasonable*. But cogency theory says that persuasion is about agonism. It's a struggle. Obstinacy is just a force, like any other force. And like any force, it can be overwhelmed. Truth is a current that can sand down obstinacy, like tides weathering away stone. Facts may not be all-powerful, but they are far from powerless. Part of the response to denialism has to be to carefully restage the science, to show how the facts of climate chaos are being researched, and to aggressively confront lies and distortions. When denialism mobilizes its immune response, the task is to keep pushing rather than give up.

Academics, for our part, can reaffirm a commitment to truth as central to scholarship. In many places, this is already happening, with a thoughtful postpositivist approach underwriting interesting research in every department. But disavowing the search for truth altogether is just as dangerous as embracing the naive view of reason as untainted by feeling. Latour laments that "entire Ph.D. programs are still running to make sure that good American kids are learning the hard way that facts are made up, that there is no such thing as natural, unmediated, unbiased access to truth, that we are always prisoners of language, that we always speak from a particular standpoint, and so on, while dangerous extremists are using the very same argument of social construction to destroy hard-won evidence that could save our lives."[14] We can't just teach our students the impossibility of certainty over and over again. The urgent task in front of us is learning how to move with confidence through a world where certainty is impossible, but resolute action is vital.

Most scientists have moved on from positivism and are bustling away in their laboratories, making discoveries and crafting tools to try to heal this planet. And they're making mistakes—in part because they often borrow concepts, like the reason/emotion binary itself, that are the residue of thousands of years of humanistic conversations. Humanities scholars can help correct those errors. Science and the humanities don't have to be at odds. Breathing the fallout of science wars fought generations ago is exhausting and counterproductive. There has to be a better way to map the relationships between the islands of study we all love than as a sprawling battlefield.

The gamble of cogency theory is that taking the role of feeling in thinking seriously will allow us to chart new bridges and build new conversations.

Saeculum means "century." The twenty-first century is our century. It's what we have left to halt the catastrophic machinery our species has built to rake the planet. This catastrophe—broad-based ecosystem collapse, resource scarcity, mass migration, war—isn't going to be like the swift-but-gentle snuffing out of a candle. It won't produce redemptive misery—the romantic myth of apocalypse trafficked by chic fatalists across the religio-secular spectrum. It will be a long, exhausting endgame. It will mean mayhem, violence, and starvation for every human alive and for our animal kin. No one wants the pain that climate chaos has already started to distribute around the world—starting with those who are least responsible for it—let alone the even more frightening landscape we are leaving to our descendants. Einstein believed religion and science spring from the same emotional root. If the secular, as the project of the century, is to mean anything, it needs to look for these affective connections—emotional, intellectual, and moral—and make common cause.

Acknowledgments

I'm grateful to friends, colleagues, and students who have helped me think through every facet of this book over the past decade. My extraordinary colleagues at the University of Pennsylvania and Oxford—especially but not solely in Religious Studies at Penn and Theology and Religion at Oxford—have offered so much inspiration and so much kindness I don't know how to even begin to thank them. I can also only attempt to express my immense gratitude to all the students in my classes, seminars, and tutorials who have challenged and provoked the ideas explored here. This extends, especially, to three undergraduate assistants (Luis Ortiz Juarez, Jack Kiyonaga, and David Roza) and three graduate assistants (Max Dugan, Justine Ellis, and Scheherazade Khan) who helped with different aspects of research and manuscript preparation. David Azzolina at Penn Libraries generously helped me chase down some of the book's images. Many thanks, too, to Mark and Michele Aldrich for permission to draw on their online archive of images related to the Scopes Trial.

I've had the privilege of working out the details of this project through conversations at dozens of talks, conferences, and workshops. These include events at Albright College, Australian Catholic University, Australian National University, Boston University, Bucknell University, Dartmouth College, Eastern University, Emory University, Freie Universität in Berlin,

Georgetown University, Lehigh University, Leipzig Universität, Le Moyne College, Macquarie University, New York University, Queen's University, Ryerson University, Yale–National University of Singapore, and the Universities of Cambridge, Dayton, Florida, Manchester, North Carolina–Charlotte, Oxford, and Nottingham. This work has also been presented at meetings of the American Academy of Religion; the British Association for the Study of Religion; the International Society for the Study of Religion, Nature, and Culture; the Nonreligion and Secularity Research Network; the Society for the Scientific Study of Religion; and the Society for the Study of Affect. I'm grateful to audiences, hosts, and discussants at all of these events, and especially grateful to the Departments of Religious Studies at Haverford and Swarthmore College, Yasemin Ural and the Affective Societies Collaborative Research Centre at the Freie Universität in Berlin, Kylie Crabbe and the Institute for Religion and Critical Inquiry (IRCI) at Australian Catholic University, John Corrigan at Florida State University, Claire Monagle of Macquarie University, and Shaun Henson at Oxford for hosting residencies, fellowships, and workshops that served as crucial inflection points in the book's development.

This research was funded in part by the grant *Affect and Knowledge Production in Theology and Religious Studies*, from the Templeton World Charity Foundation (TWCF), which I received with Simeon Zahl. I'm grateful to TWCF for its generous support. Simeon's friendship and fellowship has been one of many joys that have come along with this project. The grant allowed us to consult with two psychologists, Wendy Berry Mendes of UC–San Francisco and Michael Spezio of Scripps College. These outstanding colleagues provided us with reading lists, from which much of the research in chapter 4 is drawn, and also offered generous and extensive comments on a draft version of that chapter. Although they both approved of the main thrust of chapter 4, there were differences in their viewpoints (and mine) around the edges. When this happened, I triangulated the dissenting views with my own analysis as best I could. I take full responsibility for the contents of this chapter and any and all errors throughout the book. Additional research and writing support was provided by the Office of the Dean of the School of Arts and Sciences at Penn.

I also owe thanks to Allison Covey, Monique Scheer, Bill Wood, and Simeon Zahl for comments on individual chapters, as well as to the Religion and Theology research fellows at the IRCI, including Alda Balthrop-Lewis, Michael Champion, Nevin Climenhaga, Kylie Crabbe, Matthew

Crawford, David Newheiser, and Jonathan Zecher, who worked closely with me on chapter 5. Special gratitude goes to three readers at Duke University Press who provided invaluable feedback on earlier drafts of the manuscript. I am, as ever, extremely grateful to Miriam Angress, my editor at Duke, for her support.

My grad students at Oxford and Penn have been some of my most valued conversation partners as I've worked out these ideas. You've helped make this book in so many ways, appearing over my shoulder to ask just the right question while I was slogging through a paragraph. Thank you. And I want to thank my parents, Anny and Val, and my brother, Gavin, for endless love and support.

This project owes a lot to Oxford itself, not only my wonderful colleagues, students, and friends but more generally its culture of thinking done in fellowship—with other bodies—in the spaces and community that infuse intellectual life. This is scholarship not just as reading and writing but as eating and drinking together, chatting, walking, sipping tea, praying, singing. I found Oxford daunting at first, but soon came to understand that it was designed to be not frozen and forbidding but joyful and generative. This was, after all, where a bookish don and his friends gathered in a pub, fireside, and invented orcs.

And it was where I proposed to you, Allison, and where we made a home near the river island after we were married, and I dedicate this book to you, with all my gratitude and love.

Notes

Earlier versions of portions of the introduction and chapters 1, 5, and 7 appeared in "Beautiful Facts: Science, Secularism, and Affect," in *Feeling Religion*, ed. John Corrigan (Durham, NC: Duke University Press, 2018), 69–92; "The Secular Experiment: Science, Feeling, and Atheist Apocalypticism," in *Affect and Emotion in Multi-Religious Secular Societies*, ed. Christian von Scheve, Anna Lea Berg, Meike Haken, and Nur Yasemin Ural (London: Routledge, 2019), 211–27; and "The Wild Experiment: Emotion, Reason, and the Limits of Science," In *Are There Limits to Science?*, ed. Gillian Straine (Cambridge: Cambridge Scholars Publishing, 2017), 61–79.

Introduction

1. Darwin Correspondence Project, letter no. 4061, http://www.darwinproject.ac.uk/letter/DCP-LETT-4061.xml.
2. Browne, *Power of Place*, 169.
3. Browne, *Voyaging*, 185–86.
4. Keller, *Feeling*, 198.
5. Quoted in Ranganathan, *Ramanujan*, 88.
6. Quoted in Jammer, *Einstein and Religion*, 56. See also Einstein, "Religion and Science."
7. Polanyi, *Personal Knowledge*, 201.
8. In Ayer, *Hume*, 2. René Rosfort and Giovanni Stanghellini point out that this comes out strongly in the play of Hume's style, allowing "his passions, sentiments, and taste to animate the text" ("Mood for Thought," 411). See chapter 1.

9 Berlant, *Female Complaint*, 4.
10 See, for instance, Fleck, *Genesis*; Harding, *Science Question*; Latour and Woolgar, *Laboratory Life*; Longino, *Science as Social Knowledge*; Oreskes, *Why Trust Science?*; and Shapin and Lawrence, "Introduction." One exception would be Isabelle Stengers, whose *Cosmopolitics I* does gesture at science as a passionate search for truth (Stengers, *Cosmopolitics*, 6). See also Shah, *Who Is the Scientist-Subject?*; P. White, "Introduction"; and associated special issue of *Isis* for an overview of how emotion has been explored in the history of science.
11 Latour, *On the Modern Cult*, 104.
12 See, e.g., Deleuze, *Bergsonism*; Manning, *Always More Than One*; Massumi, *Parables*; and Shaviro, *Discognition*. For a critique of this approach to affect, see Leys, *Ascent of Affect*. For a response to Leys, see Schaefer, *Evolution of Affect Theory*.
13 See Sorabji, *Emotion*, for an overview, as well as Nussbaum, *Political Emotions* and *Upheavals of Thought*.
14 See Dixon, *Passions*; and essays in Coakley, *Faith, Rationality, and the Passions*. Christian thinkers working on Pascal—author of the phrase "We know truth, not only by reason, but also by the heart"—have reached similar conclusions (see Pascal, *Thoughts*, 99; Ryrie, *Unbelievers*; Wood, *Blaise Pascal*). Ryrie's work is especially interesting in conversation with cogency theory, though he tends to see feelings as producing thoughts that are unmovable by new ideas and reasons (11). In some ways this ends up reinscribing the feeling/thinking binary, while cogency theory seeks to replace it with an intricate cat's cradle model in which pulling on feeling changes thinking and vice versa. For consideration of how Christian thought can be strung together with an affective account of belief, see Ward, *Unbelievable*; and Zahl, "On the Affective Salience" and *Holy Spirit and Christian Experience*.
15 See Colombetti, *Feeling Body*; Maiese, *Embodied Selves*; Protevi, "Adding Deleuze"; Svendsen, "Moods"; and Thagard, *Hot Thought*. See also Spinoza, *Ethics*, esp. part 3; Dumler-Winckler, *Modern Virtue*, on the work of Mary Wollstonecraft; Whitehead, *Process and Reality* and *Science*; and thinkers influenced by Whitehead like Manning and Shaviro.
16 See Riskin, *Science*; and M. Sullivan, *Secular Assemblages*.
17 See Levinson, "What Is New Formalism?"
18 See Heidegger, *Being and Time*; Rabinow, *Essays on the Anthropology of Reason*; Rubenstein, *Strange Wonder*; Maiese, *Embodied Selves*; and Kochan, *Science as Social Existence*. See Ahmed, *Queer Phenomenology* and *Promise of Happiness* for discussion of links between phenomenology and affect theory.
19 See Crawley, *Lonely Letters*; Harney and Moten, *Undercommons*; hooks, "Theory as Liberatory Practice"; Prescod-Weinstein, *Disordered Cosmos*; Quashie, *Black Aliveness*; McKittrick, *Dear Science*; Ferreira da Silva, *Global Idea*; and Wynter, "Disenchanting Discourse" and "Unsettling the Coloniality of Being/Power/Truth/Freedom." Wynter's larger body of work is particularly interesting here; McKittrick, commenting on Wynter commenting on Fanon, sums up their epistemology as "*knowing is feeling is knowing*" (*Dear Science*, 60, emphasis in original).

20 See Haidt, *Righteous Mind*. See also those influenced by the work of Jaak Panksepp, e.g., Asma and Gabriel, *Emotional Mind*.
21 See Blackman, *Haunted Data*; Hamner, "Affect Theory"; and Manning and Massumi, *Thought in the Act*.
22 For Indigenous North American perspectives on disrupting the feeling/reason binary, see, e.g., Deloria, *Metaphysics of Modern Existence*; Harjo, *Spiral to the Stars*; Kimmerer, *Braiding Sweetgrass*; and Wilson, *Research Is Ceremony*. For Islamic perspectives, see Asad, *Secular Translations*, esp. chap. 2. For approaches from Indian philosophy, see Dharwadker, "Emotion in Motion"; and Prakash, *Another Reason*, chap. 2. Some other promising sources have also been neglected: conversations on intellectual emotions taking place in analytic philosophy of science (see Kochan, *Science as Social Existence*, appendix, for an overview); reflections on scientific feeling in scientists' autobiographies (see Thagard, *Hot Thought*, for an excellent survey); and debates about the role of beauty in scientific reasoning (especially physics).
23 Deleuze, *Spinoza*.
24 I don't, for instance, use *affect* to mean *becoming*, as in the works of affect theorists influenced by Gilles Deleuze (see n16 above), or *susceptibility*, used in the work of scholars influenced primarily by Spinoza and Whitehead. See, e.g., Bennett, *Vibrant Matter*; and Shaviro, *Discognition*. See Dixon, *Passions*, 247, for a helpful note of caution about pinning too much hope on precise definitions of key terms like *passion* and *emotion*.
25 Bloor, *Knowledge and Social Imagery*, 7.
26 Foucault, *Order of Things*, xxiv.
27 Fanon, *Black Skin, White Masks*, 28–29.
28 Jordan-Young and Karzakis, *Testosterone*, 60.
29 Perry, *More Beautiful*, 42, emphasis added.
30 Chen, *Animacies*. See chapter 2, below.
31 Eliot, *Middlemarch*, 156, emphasis added.
32 Sedgwick, *Touching Feeling*, 167, emphasis in original.
33 Other terms proposed to consider this relationship include *cogmotive* and *cogaffective* in psychology or affect theorist M. Gail Hamner's notion of the *affecognitive* (Plamper, *History of Emotions*, 246; Hamner, "Affect Theory"). These are helpful terms, but my focus is on hearing existing words differently rather than creating a new technical vocabulary.
34 Shapin and Lawrence, "Introduction."
35 Daston and Galison, *Objectivity*, 52.
36 Latour, "Why Has Critique . . . ?," 231.
37 Kuhn, *Structure*, 6.
38 Kuhn, *Structure*, 4.
39 Kuhn, *Structure*, 112.
40 There are ambiguities in Kuhn's position. Even in his famous postscript—added to the 1970 second edition of *Structure*—Kuhn is difficult to pin down. "I am a convinced believer in scientific progress," Kuhn tells us, but then he scolds us for

thinking this means that "successive theories grow ever closer to, or approximate more and more closely to, the truth" (Kuhn, *Structure*, 206). Maben Poirier reads the postscript differently, seeing it as Kuhn's total capitulation to the empiricists and an invalidation of the argument of the first edition. This seems extreme to me, but it does speak to the stunning ambiguity in Kuhn's own attempts to explain himself (Poirier, "Comment," 266n5).

41   Latour, *Pandora's Hope*, 1, emphasis added.
42   See Alaimo and Hekman, *Material Feminisms*; Barad, *Meeting the Universe Halfway*; Coole and Frost, *New Materialisms*; and Elizabeth A. Wilson, *Gut Feminism*. See also Haraway, *Simians, Cyborgs, and Women*, the philosophical antecedent of contemporary feminist new materialisms, which moves on from Kuhn's mind-only epistemology by thematizing the thinking body as a "material-semiotic generative node" (200). Cogency theory extends this insight by adding feeling to the equation, framing knowledge production as a *material-semiotic-affective* process.
43   Alaimo and Hekman, "Introduction," 4.
44   Oreskes and Conway, *Merchants*; Oreskes, *Why Trust Science?*
45   Latour, "Why Has Critique … ?" See chapter 3 below for discussion.
46   Jaggar, "Love and Knowledge," 155. See also Code, "Taking Subjectivity into Account."
47   See Poirier, "Comment"; Moleski, "Polanyi vs. Kuhn"; Jacobs, "Polanyi and Kuhn"; and Timmins, "Kuhn's *Structure*."
48   In Moleski, "Polanyi vs. Kuhn," 14.
49   Moleski, "Polanyi vs. Kuhn," 17.
50   Jacobs, "Polanyi and Kuhn," 26; Timmins, "Kuhn's *Structure*," 310.
51   Moleski, "Polanyi vs. Kuhn," 17; see also Kuhn, *Structure*, 44.
52   Poirier, "Comment," 264.
53   Polanyi, *Personal Knowledge*, 151.
54   Poirier, "Comment," 267.
55   Poirier, "Comment," 274.
56   Even Kuhn's friendly nods to Polanyi read him as rhyming with the language-obsessed philosophy of Ludwig Wittgenstein. For instance, *tacit knowledge* for Kuhn is nothing more than the pieces of the *language game* of science that remain unsaid (Kuhn, *Structure*, 45–46).
57   Poirier, "Comment," 272; Moleski, "Polanyi vs. Kuhn," 21.
58   Polanyi, *Personal Knowledge*, 140, emphasis added.
59   Polanyi, *Personal Knowledge*, 141.
60   Polanyi, *Personal Knowledge*, 206.
61   Polanyi, *Personal Knowledge*, 143.
62   Polanyi, *Personal Knowledge*, 159.
63   Polanyi, *Personal Knowledge*, 141.
64   Polanyi, *Personal Knowledge*, 142; see also Feyerabend, *Against Method*, 17.
65   Polanyi, *Personal Knowledge*, 200.
66   In Moleski, "Polanyi vs. Kuhn," 14.

67 Even *Structure* has moments where the intuitive component of science breaks in. Most of ordinary science, Kuhn writes, is about chasing down little clicks, "a fact that makes it no less fascinating to the proper sort of addict" (Kuhn, *Structure*, 37).
68 Lisa F. Barrett, *How Emotions Are Made*, 82.
69 But evolution is also messy, and complicated organisms are never fitted into their world in perfectly tailored boxes (Schaefer, *Religious Affects*, chap. 5).
70 Disraeli, *Church Policy*, 26.
71 See Foucault, *History, Vol. 1*, for this analysis of power as something inherent in relationships rather than, as liberal political theory would have it, an external force invading the sovereignty of subjects.
72 Psychologists call this *affect realism*. Lisa F. Barrett, *How Emotions Are Made*, 74.
73 Aquinas, *Summa*, part I, question 51.
74 Dawkins, *God Delusion*, 395.
75 See Goodenough, *Sacred Depths*; and Levine, "Introduction." See Sideris, *Consecrating Science*, for a comprehensive study and criticism of this approach.
76 Dawkins, *Unweaving*, 8; *God Delusion*, 111.
77 Scheer, Johansen, and Fadil, "Secular Embodiments," 2.
78 Schaefer, "Darwin's Orchids."
79 Nordern, "*Playboy* Interview," 49.
80 Wynter, "Unsettling the Coloniality of Being/Power/Truth/Freedom," 281.
81 Goodall, *Through a Window*, 14.
82 Schaefer, *Religious Affects*, chap. 5.
83 Jakobsen and Pellegrini, "Introduction," 22. See chapter 3 below for further discussion of this question.
84 This is complicated by Weber's suggestion in his late essay "Science as a Vocation" that science is responsible for *disenchantment*, or *Entzauberung* (literally "demagification"). See chapter 3 below for further discussion.
85 See, for instance, Farman, "Mind out of Place," "Re-enchantment Cosmologies," and *On Not Dying*; Ogden, *Credulity*; and Elizabeth A. Wilson, *Affect*. Interesting parallels can also be drawn with recent work on Soviet and post-Soviet secularism, such as Luehrmann, *Secularism Soviet Style*; Pelkmans, *Fragile Conviction*; and Smolkin, *Sacred Space*. An exception is Asad, *Secular Translations*, which directly engages—and attacks—science. See chapter 3 for a discussion.
86 Taylor, *Secular Age*, 12.
87 Hume, *Natural History*, 66; see also M. Sullivan, *Secular Assemblages*.
88 Shelley, "Necessity of Atheism"; Comte, *Positivism*.
89 Barton, *X Club*, 31; Draper, *History of the Conflict*; A. D. White, *History of the Warfare of Science*.
90 Freud, *Future*, 71.
91 Lloyd, "Introduction," 4.
92 See Ferreira da Silva, *Global Idea*; S. J. Gould, *Mismeasure*, 36; and Jaggar, "Love and Knowledge," 158.

93 Ferreira da Silva, *Global Idea*, xl.
94 These are mostly drawn from English-language sources. The handful of exceptions, considered in translation, are Nietzsche, Weber, and Foucault.
95 Shapin and Lawrence, "Introduction," 14.

Chapter 1: The Longing to Believe

1 Hofstadter, "Paranoid Style," 77.
2 See, for instance, Barkun, *Culture of Conspiracy*; Coady, "Are Conspiracy Theorists Irrational?"; Keeley, "Conspiracy Theories"; Lewandowsky and Cook, *Conspiracy Theory Handbook*; Pelkmans and Machold, "Conspiracy Theories"; and Sunstein and Vermeule, "Conspiracy Theories."
3 See Lepselter, *Resonance*; Rice, *Awful Archives*; Sedgwick, *Touching Feeling*; and Stewart, *Ordinary Affects*.
4 Aristotle, *Metaphysics*, 2.
5 Augustine, *Confessions*, 211.
6 Spinoza, *Ethics*, 29.
7 Spinoza, *Ethics*, 29.
8 De Condorcet, *Outlines*, 256. Discussed further in M. Sullivan, *Secular Assemblages*. My thanks to Marek Sullivan for teaching me this material.
9 Popper, *Logic*, 8–9.
10 Colombetti, *Feeling Body*; Maiese, *Embodied Selves*; Protevi, "Adding Deleuze."
11 Nussbaum, *Political Emotions*; *Upheavals of Thought*.
12 In Thagard, *Hot Thought*, 211.
13 Thagard, *Hot Thought*, 21.
14 Huntley, "Hume and Darwin," 465.
15 Browne, *Voyaging*, 364.
16 Hume, *Enquiry*, 19–20.
17 Hume, *Enquiry*, 23, emphasis in original.
18 Hume, *Enquiry*, 22.
19 Hume, *Enquiry*, 151.
20 Kant, *Critique*.
21 Hume, *Enquiry*, 35, emphasis added.
22 Hume, *Enquiry*, 35.
23 Hume, *Enquiry*, 35.
24 Hume, *Treatise*, 416.
25 Hume, *Treatise*, 415.
26 Hume, *Enquiry*, 21.
27 Hume, *Treatise*, 418.
28 Hume, *Treatise*, 437.
29 Harrison, *Territories*, 5.
30 Hume, *Treatise*, 450.
31 Hume, *Treatise*, 423.
32 Hume, *Treatise*, 451.

33 Hume, *Treatise*, 452.
34 Psychologists call this a *variable ratio response pattern*.
35 Hume, *Treatise*, 449.
36 Hume, *Treatise*, 449.
37 See the introduction.
38 Dennett, *Darwin's Dangerous Idea*, 62.
39 Grosz, *Nick of Time*.
40 G. Moore, *Nietzsche, Biology, and Metaphor*, 193. Moore shows, for instance, that Nietzsche's *will to power* concept was derived from the biologist Wilhelm Rolph's theory of the drive of all organisms to expand (47–55.). He argues that Nietzsche's stated hostility to Darwinism was based on misunderstandings—circulated by Darwin's commentators in both England and Germany—including the mistaken claim that Darwin saw evolution as a story of human progress and perfection (55).
41 Lemm, *Nietzsche's Animal Philosophy*, 1.
42 Nietzsche, *Collected Works*, 10:5.
43 Nietzsche, *Collected Works*, 10:47.
44 Grosz, *Volatile Bodies*, 126.
45 Nietzsche, *Collected Works*, 10:146, emphasis added.
46 Nietzsche, *Collected Works*, 10:89.
47 Nietzsche, *Collected Works*, 10:88, emphasis removed.
48 Nietzsche, *Thus Spoke Zarathustra*, 9.
49 Nietzsche, *Untimely Meditations*, 140.
50 This parallels Weber's use of the same German word, discussed in chapter 3.
51 Nietzsche, *Birth of Tragedy*, 73.
52 Nietzsche, *Untimely Meditations*, 169.
53 Nietzsche, *Untimely Meditations*, 169.
54 Nietzsche, *Untimely Meditations*, 169.
55 Nietzsche, *Untimely Meditations*, 169–70.
56 Nietzsche, *Untimely Meditations*, 173.
57 Nietzsche, *Beyond*, 96.
58 Nietzsche, *Beyond*, 96.
59 Nietzsche, *Beyond*, 98.
60 Nietzsche, *Untimely Meditations*, 135.
61 Nietzsche, *Collected Works*, 10:279.
62 Nietzsche, *Collected Works*, 10:279.
63 Nietzsche, *On the Genealogy*, 112, emphasis in original.
64 For further discussion of the inductive method as it was understood in the Victorian scientific context, see Hull, "Darwin's Science."
65 Nietzsche, *Collected Works*, 10:82.
66 Nietzsche, *On the Genealogy*, 114.
67 Tomkins, "Quest," 310. See chapter 4 of this volume for further discussion.
68 James, *Varieties*, 47.
69 Hamner, *American Pragmatism*, 133.

70 James, *Will to Believe*, vii; *Pragmatism*, 27.
71 James, *Will to Believe*, 5.
72 James, *Will to Believe*, 5.
73 James, *Will to Believe*, 5.
74 Another interpretation has it that Pascal already knew all this, and that James missed the fact that Pascal was forwarding the thought experiment as a tool to probe one's own intuitions, not as an apologetic device (Ryrie, *Unbelievers*, 185).
75 James, *Will to Believe*, 40.
76 James, *Varieties*, 338.
77 James, *Varieties*, 30.
78 Rosfort and Stanghellini, "Mood for Thought," 404.
79 James, *Pragmatism*, 8.
80 It's similar to what Antonio Damasio calls the *passion for reason*, discussed further in chapter 4.
81 James, "What Is an Emotion?," 189. See chapter 4 of this volume for further discussion.
82 James, *Will to Believe*, 63.
83 Peirce, "Fixation of Belief," 114.
84 James, *Will to Believe*, 21.
85 James, *Will to Believe*, 18.
86 Shusterman, "Strenuous Mood," 433.
87 Shusterman, "Strenuous Mood," 449.
88 Hamner, *American Pragmatism*, 151.
89 Levine, *Darwin Loves You*, 34.
90 Rice, *Awful Archives*, 154.
91 Mahdawi, "Most Unhinged."
92 Whalen, "Kids Shipped in Armoires?"
93 Kimball, "Wayfair Child Trafficking Conspiracy."
94 See, for instance, Sunstein and Vermeule, "Conspiracy Theories."
95 Hofstadter, "Paranoid Style," 86, emphasis added.
96 Rice, *Awful Archives*, 66.
97 Hofstadter, "Paranoid Style," 86.
98 Barkun, *Culture of Conspiracy*, 3.
99 Lepselter, *Resonance*, 3.
100 Lepselter, *Resonance*, 23–24.
101 Lepselter, *Resonance*, 4.
102 Lewandowsky and Cook, *Conspiracy Theory Handbook*, 3.
103 Stewart, *Ordinary Affects*, 89.
104 Oreskes, *Why Trust Science?*, 139.
105 James, *Pragmatism*, 28.
106 Nietzsche, *Collected Works*, 10:156.
107 LaMothe, "What Bodies Know," 589.
108 See, for instance, Grosz, *Time Travels* and *Becoming Undone*; Lemm, *Nietzsche's Animal Philosophy*; and Schaefer, "Embodied Disbelief."

109 Katherine McKittrick's vision of Black method offers a similar call for a dynamic between intellectual fluidity and disciplined precision (McKittrick, *Dear Science*, 5n12).
110 Kuhn, *Structure*, 5.
111 Daston and Galison, *Objectivity*, 18.
112 Daston and Galison, *Objectivity*, 38.
113 Daston and Galison, *Objectivity*, 39–40. See also Shah, *Who Is the Scientist-Subject?*, chap. 2, for a sustained critique of Daston and Galison for insufficiently attending to the affective strands of science.
114 Harrison, *Territories*, 15, 122.

Chapter 2: Sensualized Epistemology

1 Foucault, *History*, 6, emphasis in original.
2 Foucault, *History*, 7.
3 See Foucault, *Madness and Civilization*; *Order of Things*; and *Archaeology of Knowledge*.
4 Foucault, *Discipline and Punish*, 27.
5 Foucault, *History*, 11.
6 Ricoeur, *Freud and Philosophy*. See further discussion in chapter 3 of this volume.
7 See Schaefer, *Evolution of Affect Theory*, for an overview of affect theory's different dialects.
8 Sedgwick, *Touching Feeling*, 2.
9 Foucault, *Discipline and Punish*, 164.
10 Foucault, *Discipline and Punish*, 138.
11 Ahmed, "Affective Economies," 119.
12 Berlant, *Cruel Optimism*, 53.
13 See Schaefer, *Religious Affects*, chap. 1.
14 Chen, *Animacies*; Cvetkovich, *Depression*; Pellegrini and Puar, "Affect"; Schaefer, *Religious Affects*, chap. 1.
15 Gregg and Seigworth, "Inventory of Shimmers." See also Frank and Wilson, introduction to *A Silvan Tomkins Handbook*.
16 See, for instance, D. Gould, *Moving Politics*, which begins by stating that it will draw on both definitions of *affect* as "becoming" and definitions of *affect* as something like "emotion," before largely abandoning the former and working entirely with theories of emotion.
17 Massumi, *Parables*, 16. I've argued against this position at length elsewhere. See Schaefer, *Religious Affects*, chap. 1, and *Evolution of Affect Theory*. This position is also, in my view, the target of Ruth Leys's critique of affect theory as *antiintentional* (Leys, "Turn to Affect" and *Ascent of Affect*). Although I contend that Leys gets both the affect theory and the science wrong in this assessment, her core point—that a version of affect that is the binary opposite of cognition is a nonstarter—is one I endorse.

18 Ahmed, *Promise*, 13.
19 Cvetkovich, *Depression*, 4; Pellegrini, "'Signaling.'"
20 Ahmed, *Cultural Politics*, 12; see also Ahmed, "Collective Feelings."
21 Austin, *Things with Words*, 149.
22 He calls this an *exercitive*. Austin, *Things with Words*, 150.
23 Austin, *Things with Words*, 148. Austin died within a few years of delivering the lectures.
24 Reddy, *Navigation*, 104. History of emotions is a sort of cousin of affect theory emerging primarily from the field of history. There hasn't been enough work done to knit the two conversations together, but see Scheer, "Are Emotions … ?"; and Schaefer, *Evolution of Affect Theory*.
25 Reddy, *Navigation*, 102.
26 Muñoz, *Sense of Brown*, "Feeling Brown," and "Feeling Brown, Feeling Down"; Cvetkovich, *Depression*, 67.
27 Schaefer, *Religious Affects*, introduction.
28 Tomkins's work is considered dated by psychologists, so I'm addressing him here rather than in chapter 4. Leys is also extremely critical of Tomkins, based on a significant misreading of his work. See Schaefer, *Evolution of Affect Theory*.
29 No commas in the title because, as he told his students, "there isn't any way to separate the three interlocked concepts" (Nathanson, "Prologue," xi).
30 Sedgwick, *Tendencies*, 164.
31 Tomkins, *Affect Imagery Consciousness*, 4. See Frank and Wilson, *A Silvan Tomkins Handbook*, chap. 1, for further discussion.
32 Tomkins, "Quest," 309.
33 Tomkins, *Shame*, 49.
34 Frank and Wilson, *Silvan Tomkins Handbook*, chap. 1.
35 Tomkins, *Shame*, 50.
36 Tomkins, *Shame*, 51.
37 Tomkins, *Shame*, 62.
38 Sedgwick, *Weather in Proust*, 43.
39 Sedgwick, *Touching Feeling*, 19.
40 Tomkins, *Affect Imagery Consciousness*, 12.
41 Berlant, *Cruel Optimism*, 53.
42 Foucault, "Confession of the Flesh," 208.
43 Tomkins, "Quest," 321.
44 Tomkins, *Shame*, 57.
45 Tomkins, "Left and Right," 391.
46 Tomkins, "Left and Right," 391.
47 Tomkins, "Affect and the Psychology of Knowledge," 79.
48 Tomkins, "Left and Right," 393.
49 Tomkins, "Affect and the Psychology of Knowledge," 89.
50 Tomkins, "Affect and the Psychology of Knowledge," 97.
51 See Tomkins, "Affect and the Psychology of Knowledge," 89.
52 Frank and Wilson, *Silvan Tomkins Handbook*, 114.

53 See Lisa F. Barrett, *How Emotions Are Made*; and Leys, *Ascent of Affect*. But Frank and Wilson, *Silvan Tomkins Handbook*, chap. 3, argue that Tomkins's alignment with basic emotions approaches is much less sturdy than is commonly suggested.
54 Barrett, a critic of the basic emotions hypothesis, frames this a bit differently, as discussed in chapter 4 of this volume.
55 Tomkins, *Shame*, 76.
56 Nathanson, prologue, xii.
57 Tomkins, *Shame*, 37; and see chapter 4 of this volume.
58 Tomkins, *Shame*, 78.
59 Tomkins, "Quest," 322.
60 This is similar to Elizabeth Wilson's finding in her study of the emotions driving artificial intelligence researchers, though her focus is more on surprise than interest (*Affect*).
61 Tomkins, *Shame*, 153.
62 Tomkins, *Shame*, 153.
63 Tomkins, *Affect Imagery Consciousness*, 169. This means it's mistaking *one affect among many* for *affect* as such. See Schaefer, *Evolution of Affect Theory*, 53.
64 Sedgwick, *Tendencies*, 3.
65 Ahmed, *Cultural Politics*, 6; *Queer Phenomenology*, 1.
66 Ahmed, *Promise*, 40. See also Heidegger, *Being and Time*; and Ahmed, "Not in the Mood."
67 Ahmed, *Cultural Politics*, 13.
68 Pedwell, "Mood Work," 48.
69 Ngai, *Our Aesthetic Categories*, 5.
70 Sedgwick, *Touching Feeling*, 1.
71 Berlant, *Cruel Optimism*, 64.
72 Berlant, *Cruel Optimism*, 145.
73 Tomkins, "Affect and the Psychology of Knowledge," 73.
74 Baldwin, *Fire Next Time*, 43.
75 Lorde, *Sister Outsider*, 37.
76 Lorde, *Sister Outsider*, 36.
77 Lorde, *Sister Outsider*, 56.
78 Muñoz, *Sense of Brown*, 102.
79 Muñoz, *Sense of Brown*, 101.
80 Muñoz, *Sense of Brown*, 10.
81 Muñoz, "Feeling Brown," 69.
82 Muñoz, "Feeling Brown, Feeling Down."
83 Muñoz, "Feeling Brown," 70; *Sense of Brown*, 11.
84 Puar, *Terrorist Assemblages*, xii.
85 Puar, *Terrorist Assemblages*, 32.
86 Chen, *Animacies*, 3.
87 Chen, *Animacies*, 5.
88 Chen, *Animacies*, 12. See chapter 7 of this volume for further discussion.

89 Perry, *More Beautiful*, 21.
90 Holland, *Erotic Life*, 6.
91 Holland, *Erotic Life*, 5, emphasis added.
92 See Schaefer, *Religious Affects*, 123.
93 Holland, *Erotic Life*, 59. See also Lorde, *Sister Outsider*, 53.
94 Bonilla-Silva, *Racism without Racists*, 4.
95 Bonilla-Silva, *Racism without Racists*, 11.
96 Bonilla-Silva, *Racism without Racists*, 74.
97 Bonilla-Silva, *Racism without Racists*, 7.
98 Bonilla-Silva, "Feeling Race"; "New Political Praxis." He goes so far as to call this new attention to feeling "a revision to my structural theory of racism" ("New Political Praxis," 1779).
99 Bonilla-Silva, "New Political Praxis," 1779. An interesting dynamic emerges here between Bonilla-Silva and Paula Ioanide in their commentaries on each other's work. Ioanide is critical of Bonilla-Silva's lack of attention (in his earlier work) to the way racialized reason is shaped by the force of feeling. Bonilla-Silva, for his part, seems to have taken this concern seriously in reaffirming the importance of feeling as an element of a structural analysis of racism (Ioanide, *Emotional Politics of Racism*, 16). But he also criticizes Ioanide for tending to represent thinking and feeling as binary opposites, as if we needed to supersede emotion and proceed with a strictly rational conversation about race (Bonilla-Silva, "New Political Praxis," 1781).
100 Bonilla-Silva, "New Political Praxis," 1780; "Feeling Race," 8.
101 Bonilla-Silva, "Feeling Race," 2.
102 Holland, *Erotic Life*, 6.
103 Tomkins, "Quest," 307.
104 Hofstadter, "Paranoid Style," 85.
105 In Hofstadter, "Paranoid Style," 79.
106 Hofstadter, "Paranoid Style," 80.
107 Barkun, *Culture of Conspiracy*, 49.
108 Arendt, *Origins of Totalitarianism*, 354.
109 Watson, "Stabbed at the Front."
110 Barkun, *Culture of Conspiracy*, 49.
111 Barkun, *Culture of Conspiracy*, 53.
112 Kundnani, *Muslims Are Coming!*, 242.
113 Kundnani, *Muslims Are Coming!*, 247.
114 O'Donnell, "Islamophobic Conspiracism."
115 Holland, *Erotic Life*, 9.
116 Barkun, *Culture of Conspiracy*, 6.
117 Hughey, "Show Me Your Papers!," 178.
118 Foucault, *History*, 57.
119 Foucault, *History*, 69.
120 Foucault, *History*, 71.
121 Foucault, *History*, 72.

122 Schaefer, *Religious Affects*, chap. 4.
123 Sedgwick, *Touching Feeling*, 124, emphasis removed.
124 Berlant and Stewart, *Hundreds*, 6.

Chapter 3: Science as an Intoxication

1 Jackson, *Church of St. Mary*, 4.
2 Ward, "Preface," xvi.
3 In Jackson, *Church of St. Mary*, 60.
4 Newman, "Architectural Setting," 137.
5 Newman, "Architectural Setting," 172; Tinniswood, *His Invention*, 102.
6 Oxford University Archives, "Register of Convocation," 189.
7 *Oxford University Statutes*, 1:72–73.
8 Ward, "Preface," iv.
9 See Hirschkind, "Secular Body"; Jakobsen and Pellegrini, "Introduction"; Mazzarella, "Mind the Gap!"; Modern, *Secularism*; Pellegrini, "Feeling Secular"; and essays in Scheer, Fadil, and Johansen, *Secular Bodies*.
10 See essays in Kahn and Lloyd, *Race and Secularism*.
11 "Bleak Outlook," *New York Times*, February 25, 1968.
12 Berger, "Secularism in Retreat."
13 Berger, "Secularism in Retreat."
14 Berger, "Secularism in Retreat."
15 Marx, *Critique*, 131.
16 Weber, *Protestant Ethic*, 24.
17 Plamper, *History of Emotions*, 48.
18 Weber, *Protestant Ethic*, 26. Weber is careful to add that he does not see capitalism as *only* an effect of the Reformation (91).
19 Birnbaum, "Conflicting Interpretations," 138. See also Weber, *Protestant Ethic*, 104.
20 Campbell, "Weber's Essay," 212.
21 Weber, *Protestant Ethic*, 79.
22 Weber, *Protestant Ethic*, 83.
23 Weber, *Protestant Ethic*, 51, 154.
24 In Weber, *Protestant Ethic*, 175.
25 Weber, *Protestant Ethic*, 180.
26 Weber, *Protestant Ethic*, 181.
27 Weber, *Protestant Ethic*, 182. See also Josephson-Storm, *Myth of Disenchantment*, 285.
28 See Jason Ā. Josephson-Storm, "A Note on the Dating of Max Weber's 'Science as a Vocation.'" *Absolute Disruption* (blog), October 24, 2017, https://absolute-disruption.com/2017/10/24/a-note-on-the-dating-of-max-webers-science-as-a-vocation/.
29 Weber, *From Max Weber*, 139, emphasis added.
30 Josephson-Storm, *Myth of Disenchantment*, 286.

31 Berger was by no means alone in this line of interpretation. See Pope, Cohen, and Hazelrigg, "Divergence."
32 Taylor, *Secular Age*, 2; Berger, *Sacred Canopy*, 107.
33 Berger, *Sacred Canopy*, 111.
34 Berger goes even further back, musing that the seeds for the disenchanting mission of Protestantism were actually already sown in Christianity by the religious traditions of "Ancient Israel" (*Sacred Canopy*, 113).
35 Berger, *Sacred Canopy*, 113.
36 Taylor, *Secular Age*, 38.
37 Berger, "Secularism in Retreat."
38 Jakobsen and Pellegrini, "Introduction," 2.
39 Berger, *Sacred Canopy*, 51.
40 As Noreen Khawaja has argued, the existentialist vocabulary recirculated by mid-twentieth-century Western intellectuals reflects the concerns of earlier Protestant intellectual and ascetic traditions (Khawaja, *Religion of Existence*).
41 Asad, *Genealogies*, 23.
42 Geertz, *Interpretation*, 5.
43 Asad, *Genealogies*, 27.
44 Asad, *Genealogies*, 28.
45 See Geertz, *Interpretation*, 112.
46 Asad, *Genealogies*, 41.
47 Asad, *Genealogies*, 46.
48 Asad, *Genealogies*, 35.
49 Asad, *Genealogies*, 53.
50 Asad, *Formations*, 2.
51 Asad, *Formations*, 1. Asad reserves the word secular*ism*, as a distinct doctrine of modernity, for this phenomenon.
52 Asad, *Formations*, 8.
53 Jakobsen and Pellegrini, "Introduction," 3.
54 Asad, *Formations*, 14.
55 Asad, *Formations*, 17.
56 Taylor, "Western Secularity," 39.
57 Calhoun, Juergensmeyer, and VanAntwerpen, "Introduction," 11.
58 See, e.g., Agrama, *Questioning Secularism*; Gourgouris, *Lessons*; Habermas, "Post-secular Society"; and Milbank, *Theology*. As Lee points out, even sociologists who are scrupulously careful about not reducing religion to a matter of belief tend to fall back on viewing nonreligion as basically an intellectual position (*Recognizing the Non-religious*, 62; see also Scheer, Johansen, and Fadil, "Secular Embodiments," 1).
59 Asad, *Genealogies*, 77.
60 Asad, *Genealogies*, chap. 2. See also Asad, "Modern Classic." See chapter 2 of this volume for more on embodiment in Foucault's thought.
61 Asad, *Formations*, 17.
62 Asad, *Formations*, 25.

63 Hirschkind hesitates to answer his own question, though. His concern is that the *secular body*, if there is one, must be meaningfully distinguished from, for instance, the *liberal body* or the *modern body*—as built by medicine, law, or scholarship ("Secular Body?," 634). But as Monique Scheer and her colleagues write, "While there might not be *a* secular body, as Hirschkind suggests, there certainly seem to be important understandings and enactments of the body associated with the secular" (Scheer, Johansen, and Fadil, "Secular Embodiments," 7).

64 Jakobsen and Pellegrini, "Introduction," 22. See also Mazzarella, "Mind the Gap!"; Modern, *Secularism*; and Taves and Bender, "Introduction."

65 See Bennett, *Enchantment*; Connolly, *Why I Am Not a Secularist*; and essays in Levine, *Joy of Secularism*.

66 Luehrmann, *Secularism Soviet Style*; Pelkmans, *Fragile Conviction*; Smolkin, *Sacred Space*.

67 Jakobsen and Pellegrini, "Introduction," 28.

68 Scheer, Johansen, and Fadil, "Secular Embodiments," 2. See also Johansen, "Secular Excitement."

69 Scheer, Johansen, and Fadil, "Secular Embodiments," 10. But see M. Sullivan, *Secular Assemblages*, for a full account of how French Enlightenment thinkers sought to corral and coordinate—rather than eliminate—the emotions.

70 B. Robbins, "Enchantment?," 89. Taylor does talk about the affective dimensions of reason elsewhere, but associates them only with thought about existential things or human experience, not science (Taylor, "Reason, Faith, and Meaning").

71 Asad, *Secular Translations*, 150.

72 Josephson-Storm, *Myth of Disenchantment*, 286.

73 B. Robbins, "Enchantment?," 75.

74 B. Robbins, "Enchantment?," 74.

75 That said, neither Robbins nor Josephson-Storm fully arrives at this affective understanding of disenchantment. Robbins's anatomy of the enchantment/disenchantment dynamic is social and ethical, not affective. For Josephson-Storm the story of disenchantment fails because scholars are still looking at things that seem to fall outside the traditional purview of science, like parapsychology. Neither of these get at the point I'm making here: it's not that disenchantment didn't happen, but that disenchantment in Weber has been misunderstood.

76 Weber, *From Max Weber*, 132.

77 Weber, *From Max Weber*, 151.

78 Weber, *From Max Weber*, 156.

79 Weber, *From Max Weber*, 135.

80 Weber, *From Max Weber*, 135, emphasis removed.

81 Weber, *From Max Weber*, 136.

82 Weber, *From Max Weber*, 139.

83 Weber, *From Max Weber*, 139. Weber also writes that disenchantment results in a crisis of *meaning* (140). But a loss of meaning isn't a loss of feeling. What

Weber means by meaning is something more like *the fantasy of ultimate truth* rather than everyday joys, and he clearly looks down on those who are unable to "bear the fate of the times like a man" (155).

84 Asad, for his part, wants to distance himself from the disenchantment thesis, though the resonance between that framework and his thinking is clear (Asad, *Secular Translations*, 150).
85 Weber, *From Max Weber*, 135.
86 Weber, *From Max Weber*, 136.
87 Ghosh, *Max Weber*, 4–5.
88 Josephson-Storm, *Myth of Disenchantment*, 298.
89 Bennett, *Enchantment*, 91.
90 Bennett, *Enchantment*, 5.
91 Bennett, *Enchantment*, 54.
92 Levine, "Introduction," 4.
93 Levine, *Darwin Loves You*, xvi.
94 Levine, *Darwin Loves You*, 40.
95 Farman, *On Not Dying*; Elizabeth A. Wilson, *Affect*; Smolkin, *Sacred Space*.
96 Bennett, *Enchantment*, 6.
97 Taylor, "Western Secularity," 38.
98 Asad et al., *Is Critique Secular?*
99 Mahmood, "Religious Reason," 842.
100 Mahmood, "Religious Reason," 847.
101 Mahmood, "Religious Reason," 848.
102 Amy Hollywood offers an important reminder here: to suggest that religion is opposed to critique is to ignore the depth and complexity of the intellectual repertoires of religion itself (Hollywood, *Acute Melancholia*, 8).
103 Mahmood, "Religious Reason," 848.
104 Asad, "Free Speech," 36.
105 J. Butler, "Sensibility of Critique," 113.
106 Foucault, "What Is Enlightenment?," 35.
107 For an overview and commentary on the historical development of this essay from its first publication in 1996 to its long-form version in 2003, see Wiegman, "Times We're In." In a version of "Religious Reason and Secular Affect" from 2015, Mahmood explicitly connects her work and Sedgwick's (Saba Mahmood, "Moral Injury and Muhammed's Cartoons: Thinking Reparatively with Eve Sedgwick." Fifth Annual Eve Sedgwick Memorial Lecture, Boston University, March 5, 2015, https://www.youtube.com/watch?v=knANfXk-29Q).
108 Sedgwick, *Touching Feeling*, 126.
109 Sedgwick, *Touching Feeling*, 138.
110 Sedgwick, *Touching Feeling*, 130.
111 Sedgwick, *Touching Feeling*, 126.
112 Berlant and Stewart, *Hundreds*, 42.
113 Felski, *Limits*, 1; see also Ricoeur, *Freud and Philosophy*.
114 Felski, *Limits*, 3.

115 Sedgwick, *Touching Feeling*, 149.
116 Felski, *Limits*, 32; see also Berlant and Stewart, *Hundreds*, 42.
117 Best and Marcus, "Surface Reading," 16–17; see also Levinson, "What Is New Formalism?"
118 Felski and Fraiman, "Introduction," vi.
119 Felski and Fraiman, "Introduction," vi.
120 As Robyn Wiegman points out, relocating the genesis of Sedgwick's essay to the early years of queer theory makes it even more clear that she is staking out a particular line of disagreement with Butler (Wiegman, "Times We're In," 12).
121 J. Butler, *Gender Trouble*.
122 Sedgwick, *Touching Feeling*, 149.
123 Sedgwick, *Touching Feeling*, 149.
124 Sedgwick, *Weather in Proust*, 66.
125 Love, *Feeling Backward*, 7.
126 Felski, *Limits*, 18.
127 In Felski, *Limits*, 37.
128 Felski, *Limits*, 10.
129 Felski, *Limits*, 21.
130 Felski, *Limits*, 188.
131 Latour, "Why Has Critique … ?," 238–39.
132 Felski, *Limits*, 87.
133 Felski, *Limits*, 91.
134 Felski, *Limits*, 91.
135 Felski, *Limits*, 87, emphasis in original.
136 Felski, *Limits*, 10.
137 Berlant and Stewart, *Hundreds*, 41.
138 Sedgwick, *Touching Feeling*, 126; Felski, *Limits*, 5.
139 Wiegman, "Times We're In," 11.
140 Wiegman, "Times We're In," 11.
141 Harney and Moten, *Undercommons*, 19.
142 Felski, *Limits*, 5.
143 Hollywood, *Acute Melancholia*, 6.
144 Lloyd, "Introduction," 5.
145 See also Connolly, *Why I Am Not a Secularist*, 5.
146 Joan Wallach Scott, for instance, has argued that secularism, especially in the French context, is not a guarantor of gender equality. She suggests that secular formations often authorize themselves with reference to subordination of women—invoking scientific discourses that reassert the same conservative gender ideology in new packaging (J. W. Scott, *Sex and Secularism*, 15).
147 Asad, *Formations*, 3.
148 W. F. Sullivan, *Impossibility of Religious Freedom*, 8; Calhoun, Juergensmeyer, and VanAntwerpen, "Introduction," 16.
149 Mahmood, *Religious Difference*, 8.
150 Fernando, *Republic Unsettled*.

151 Thomas, *Faking Liberties*.
152 See chapter 7.
153 Scheer, Johansen, and Fadil, "Secular Embodiments," 2.
154 Jackson, *Church of St. Mary*, 66–67.
155 This performance sometimes took place with a related ceremony called the Vesperies. *Oxford University Statutes*, 1:57.
156 *Oxford University Statutes*, 1:58.
157 Shuger, "Birth."
158 Wood, *History*, 795.
159 *Oxford University Statutes*, 1:73.
160 Jackson, *Church of St. Mary*, 66.
161 Oxford University Archives, "Register of Convocation," 189.
162 Oxford University Archives, "Register of Convocation," 189.
163 Geraghty, "Wren's Preliminary Design," 282.
164 Shuger, "St. Mary the Virgin," 316.
165 Shuger, "St. Mary the Virgin," 313.
166 In Shuger, "St. Mary the Virgin," 339.
167 In Shuger, "St. Mary the Virgin," 320.
168 In Shuger, "St. Mary the Virgin," 320.
169 Shuger, "St. Mary the Virgin," 321.
170 James, *Varieties*, 48.
171 Otto, *Idea*, 19.
172 In Jackson, *Church of St. Mary*, 60.
173 Wood, *History*, 795, emphasis added.
174 Lee, "Observing the Atheist"; Lee, *Recognizing the Non-religious*; Blankholm, "Secularism and Secular People."
175 Lee, *Recognizing the Non-religious*, chap. 2.
176 Berger, "Secularism in Retreat."
177 Taves and Bender, "Introduction," 4.
178 Josephson-Storm, *Myth of Disenchantment*, 3.
179 See, e.g., W. F. Sullivan, *Impossibility of Religious Freedom*; and Wenger, *We Have a Religion*.

Chapter 4: Feeling Is Believing

1 Winkielman and Cacioppo, "Mind at Ease," 992.
2 Haggard and Isaacs, "Micro-momentary Facial Expressions." *Lie to Me*, incidentally, was inspired by Paul Ekman, a protégé of Silvan Tomkins.
3 Winkielman and Cacioppo, "Mind at Ease," 990.
4 Reber, Winkielman, and Schwarz, "Perceptual Fluency."
5 Winkielman and Cacioppo, "Mind at Ease," 993.
6 Winkielman and Cacioppo, "Mind at Ease," 989.
7 Leys, *Ascent of Affect*. This debate is the debate around *intentionality*—whether emotions are necessarily attached to concepts. Ultimately, I agree with Leys's

suggestion that emotion and cognition can't be separated, though many of the moves she makes on the way are highly questionable. For a critical overview, see Schaefer, *Evolution of Affect Theory*.

8 The reverse claim, that affect always carries cognitive content, is more controversial; see discussion of Zajonc and Lazarus, below.
9 Latour, *On the Modern Cult*, 111.
10 Darwin, *Descent*, 71.
11 In Darwin, *Expression*, 336.
12 Darwin, *Expression*, 204.
13 Darwin, *Expression*, 208.
14 James, "What Is an Emotion?," 191.
15 James, "What Is an Emotion?," 193.
16 James, "What Is an Emotion?," 201.
17 James, "What Is an Emotion?," 199.
18 James, "What Is an Emotion?," 203.
19 James, *Principles*, 935.
20 Titchener, *Text-Book*, 225.
21 Titchener, *Text-Book*, 408.
22 Titchener, *Text-Book*, 408.
23 Cheney and Seyfarth, *Baboon Metaphysics*, 5.
24 In Miller, "Cognitive Revolution," 142.
25 Cacioppo and Berntson, "Affective Distinctiveness," 1348.
26 For a more favorable reading of Skinner and the behaviorist tradition, though one that still creates little room for emotion, see Louise Barrett, "Why Brains Are Not Computers."
27 Pogliano, "Lucky Triune Brain," 343; see also Holden, "Paul MacLean," 1066.
28 Or *protoreptilian formation*, or *R-complex*.
29 Or *paleomammalian formation*.
30 Holden, "Paul MacLean," 1068.
31 MacLean, *Triune Brain*, 12.
32 Holden, "Paul MacLean," 1067.
33 MacLean, "Putting On Our Thinking Caps."
34 See, e.g., Bulkeley, *Wondering Brain*, 18–21.
35 Lisa F. Barrett, "Zombie Ideas."
36 LeDoux, *Emotional Brain*, 99.
37 A. B. Butler, "Triune Brain Concept," 1189.
38 Damasio and Van Hoesen, "Emotional Disturbances," 87.
39 Damasio and Van Hoesen, "Emotional Disturbances," 92.
40 A. B. Butler, "Triune Brain Concept," 1185.
41 A. B. Butler, "Triune Brain Concept," 1192.
42 Damasio, Tranel, and Damasio, "Somatic Markers," 217–18.
43 Damasio, Tranel, and Damasio, "Somatic Markers," 218.
44 Bechara et al., "Insensitivity to Future Consequences," 8.
45 Later versions of the experiment streamlined this setup by having penalty-only cards.

46 Bechara et al., "Insensitivity to Future Consequences," 13.
47 Bechara et al., "Insensitivity to Future Consequences," 12.
48 Bechara et al., "Insensitivity to Future Consequences," 14.
49 Bechara et al., "Insensitivity to Future Consequences," 14. See also Damasio, Tranel, and Damasio, "Somatic Markers."
50 Damasio, Tranel, and Damasio, "Somatic Markers," 226.
51 Damasio, *Descartes' Error*, xii.
52 Damasio, *Descartes' Error*, xii.
53 Immordino-Yang, *Emotions*, 32.
54 Damasio, *Descartes' Error*, 245.
55 Damasio, *Descartes' Error*, 71. See also Ramirez and Cabanac, "Pleasure."
56 Tomkins, *Shame*, 76.
57 Damasio, *Feeling of What Happens*, 79.
58 Damasio, *Feeling of What Happens*, 58.
59 Damasio, *Feeling of What Happens*, 78.
60 Panksepp, *Affective Neuroscience*, 39.
61 Panksepp, *Affective Neuroscience*, 145.
62 Panksepp, *Affective Neuroscience*, 144.
63 There is substantial methodological debate about the extent to which one can infer how non-neurodamaged brains operate using brain-damaged patients. See Dunn, Dalgleish, and Lawrence, "Somatic Marker Hypothesis," 252.
64 Bechara et al., "Deciding Advantageously before Knowing," 1293.
65 Bechara et al., "Deciding Advantageously before Knowing," 1293.
66 Berlant and Stewart, *Hundreds*, 6.
67 Maia and McClelland, "Reexamination of the Evidence," 16075. In their response, Bechara et al. fall back on their experiments with vmPFC-damaged patients, suggesting that their lack of SCRs and their failure to develop advantageous strategies on the task are the real evidence for the SMH (Bechara et al., "Iowa Gambling Task," 159). See also Fernie and Tunney, "Learning on the IGT"; Simonovic et al., "Pupil Dilation"; and Simonovic et al., "Performance under Stress." See Dunn, Dalgleish, and Lawrence, "Somatic Marker Hypothesis," for a review.
68 Persaud, McLeod, and Cowey, "Post-decision Wagering."
69 Steingroever et al., "Performance of Healthy Participants."
70 Fernie and Tunney, "Learning on the IGT," 13.
71 Dunn, Dalgleish, and Lawrence, "Somatic Marker Hypothesis," 252.
72 Affective neuroscientist Joseph LeDoux is sometimes taken to be a proponent of a programmatic divide between emotion and cognition, what he calls the *low road* and the *high road* of perception (LeDoux, *Emotional Brain*, 163). However, it's clear in LeDoux's writings that he defines these words idiosyncratically. Specifically, he uses *emotion* to refer only to focused and intense felt response to stimuli—big feelings rather than the small pulses identified by Damasio's SMH (299). As Justin Storbeck and Gerald Clore write, there can't possibly be an emotional response without some minimum degree of cognitive discrimina-

tion. "Can the low route sufficiently discriminate a snake from a bunny without cortical involvement?" they ask. "We say No" (Storbeck and Clore, "Interdependence," 1215). LeDoux seems to endorse an understanding of emotion that emphasizes the interplay between feeling and cognition in his more recent work. See LeDoux, "Coming to Terms."

73 Phelps, "Emotion and Cognition," 28.
74 Phelps, "Emotion and Cognition," 29.
75 Phelps, "Emotion and Cognition," 33.
76 Cherry, "Recognition of Speech."
77 Phelps, "Emotion and Cognition," 39.
78 Phelps, "Emotion and Cognition," 46.
79 Duncan and Barrett, "Affect," 1187.
80 Duncan and Barrett, "Affect," 1187.
81 Duncan and Barrett, "Affect," 1185–86.
82 Duncan and Barrett, "Affect," 1186.
83 Duncan and Barrett, "Affect," 1194.
84 Duncan and Barrett, "Affect," 1185.
85 Duncan and Barrett, "Affect," 1202.
86 Pessoa, "Relationship," 148.
87 Pessoa, "Relationship," 151.
88 Pessoa, "Relationship," 154.
89 Pessoa, "Relationship," 155.
90 Pessoa, "Relationship," 148.
91 Pessoa, "Relationship," 149.
92 Pessoa, "Relationship," 153.
93 Davidson, "Seven Sins," 129.
94 See, e.g., Decety, Michalska, and Kinzler, "Developmental Neuroscience"; Frank, "Strategic Role"; Haidt and Graham, "When Morality Opposes Justice"; Horberg, Oveis, and Keltner, "Emotions as Moral Amplifiers"; Paxton and Greene, "Moral Reasoning"; and Singer and Klimecki, "Empathy and Compassion."
95 Haidt, *Righteous Mind*, 52.
96 See, e.g., Asma and Gabriel, *Emotional Mind*; Lisa F. Barrett, "Are Emotions Natural Kinds?" and *How Emotions Are Made*; Lisa F. Barrett et al., "Of Mice and Men"; and Panksepp, "Cognitive Conceptualism" and "Neurologizing."
97 Lisa F. Barrett, *How Emotions Are Made*, 22.
98 Lisa F. Barrett, *How Emotions Are Made*, 72.
99 Lisa F. Barrett, *How Emotions Are Made*, 80.
100 Zajonc, "Attitudinal Effects," 17.
101 Zajonc, "Attitudinal Effects," 14.
102 Zajonc, "Attitudinal Effects," 18.
103 Zajonc, "Attitudinal Effects," 21.
104 Zajonc, "Attitudinal Effects," 18.
105 Zajonc, "Attitudinal Effects," 21.

106 Zajonc, "Attitudinal Effects," 21, emphasis added.
107 Zajonc, "Feeling and Thinking: Preferences," 151.
108 Zajonc, "Feeling and Thinking: Preferences," 154, emphasis original.
109 Zajonc, "Feeling and Thinking: Preferences," 169–70.
110 Zajonc, "Feeling and Thinking: Preferences," 157n9.
111 See 262n72 above for a similar criticism of LeDoux's claim of separate channels for so-called emotion and cognition.
112 Zajonc, "Feeling and Thinking: Preferences," 154, 167; see also Sadalla and Loftness, "Emotional Images as Mediators."
113 Zajonc, "Feeling and Thinking: Preferences," 163.
114 Zajonc, "Feeling and Thinking: Preferences," 154.
115 Lazarus, "Thoughts," 1020.
116 Zajonc, "On the Primacy of Affect"; see also Zajonc, "Feeling and Thinking: Closing the Debate."
117 Zajonc, "On the Primacy of Affect," 119.
118 Lazarus, "Thoughts," 1019. O'Malley, "Feeling without Thinking?," makes a similar point about Zajonc's narrow definition of cognition.
119 Rotteveel and Phaf, "Mere Exposure in Reverse," 1323.
120 Storbeck and Clore, "Interdependence," 1221.
121 Storbeck and Clore, "Interdependence," 1213.
122 Jacoby and Whitehouse, "Illusion of Memory," 130.
123 Jacoby and Whitehouse, "Illusion of Memory," 133.
124 Jacoby and Whitehouse, "Illusion of Memory," 127.
125 Strack, Martin, and Stepper, "Human Smile."
126 Phaf and Rotteveel, "Affective Modulation," 313.
127 Phaf and Rotteveel, "Affective Modulation," 310.
128 Rotteveel and Phaf, "Mere Exposure in Reverse," 1338.
129 Rotteveel and Phaf, "Mere Exposure in Reverse," 1340.
130 Ladd and Gabrieli, "Trait and State Anxiety," 6.
131 Whittlesea, "Illusions of Familiarity," 1235.
132 Whittlesea, "Illusions of Familiarity," 1241.
133 Whittlesea, "Illusions of Familiarity," 1243–44.
134 Whittlesea, "Illusions of Familiarity," 1248.
135 Whittlesea, "Illusions of Familiarity," 1245.
136 Postexperiment interviews confirmed the contour images had not been consciously noticed (Reber, Winkielman, and Schwarz, "Perceptual Fluency," 46).
137 Reber, Winkielman, and Schwarz, "Perceptual Fluency," 46.
138 Reber, Winkielman, and Schwarz, "Perceptual Fluency," 48.
139 Winkielman and Cacioppo, "Mind at Ease," 989.
140 Langlois, Roggman, and Musselman, "Attractive Faces." Monin's innovation was able to show that the distinctiveness index was *not* the reason for the attractiveness-familiarity link.
141 Monin, "Warm Glow Heuristic," 1040.
142 Monin, "Warm Glow Heuristic," 1037.

143 Monin, "Warm Glow Heuristic," 1035.
144 See also Phaf and Rotteveel, "Affective Modulation," 315.
145 Zajonc, "Attitudinal Effects," 2.
146 Zebrowitz, White, and Weineke, "Mere Exposure and Racial Prejudice," 260.
147 Smith, Dijksterhuis, and Chaiken, "Faces and Racial Attitudes."
148 Qian et al., "Perceptual Individuation Training"; Lebrecht et al., "Perceptual Other-Race Training."
149 Qian et al., "Perceptual Individuation Training."
150 Smith, Dijksterhuis, and Chaiken, "Faces and Racial Attitudes," 62.
151 Slaby, "Steps"; Frost, *Biocultural Creatures*.
152 Lisa F. Barrett, *How Emotions Are Made*, 80.

Chapter 5: Only Better Beasts

1   Riskin, "Evolution."
2   E. Darwin, *Temple of Nature*, 35–37.
3   Secord, *Victorian Sensation*, 2.
4   Browne, *Voyaging*, 462; Secord, *Victorian Sensation*, 526.
5   Gordon and Buckland, *Life and Correspondence*, 243.
6   Rusert, *Fugitive Science*, 57. Anticipating one of Darwin's key insights, Smith even drew on Charles Lyell's *Principles of Geology* (Rusert, *Fugitive Science*, 52).
7   Desmond, *Huxley*, 16.
8   Sedgwick, Clark, and Hughes, *Life and Letters*, 84.
9   Sedgwick, Clark, and Hughes, *Life and Letters*, 84.
10 Sedgwick, Clark, and Hughes, *Life and Letters*, 357–58.
11 Sedgwick, Clark, and Hughes, *Life and Letters*, 357.
12 Sedgwick, Clark, and Hughes, *Life and Letters*, 361.
13 Hesketh, *Of Apes and Ancestors*, 99. *Darwinism* and *Darwinian* are, as James Moore and Ian Hesketh have shown, contested words, meaning anything from a rigid and narrow focus on evolution by natural selection (by which terms Darwin himself was often not Darwinian), to evolutionism writ large, to an even more general naturalistic framework for science (J. Moore, "Deconstructing Darwinism"; Hesketh, "First Darwinian"). Recognizing that the word means different things to different factions at different times, my use will refer to an evolutionary biological framework marked by Darwin's emphasis on accident, continuity with animals, and nondirected development. Much as the meaning of the word *Darwinism* changed with time, its influence on the life sciences waxed and waned, reaching its nadir during what some have called the *eclipse of Darwinism* (see Bowler, *Eclipse*).
14 Browne, *Power of Place*, 94.
15 Desmond, *Huxley*, 617. See also Shah, *Who Is the Scientist-Subject?*, 5–6, for a methodological discussion of the use of scientific autobiography.
16 Hodge, "Lifelong Generation Theorist," 211; Marshall, "Erasmus Darwin."
17 Iliffe, *Newton*, 31; Paley, *Natural Theology*, 12–13.

18 Lightman, "Unbelief," 262.
19 Harrison, *Territories*, 149.
20 Pigliucci, "Introduction," 16–17.
21 Darwin Correspondence Project (DCP), letter no. 2532, http://www.darwinproject.ac.uk/letter/DCP-LETT-2532.xml.
22 Darwin, *Autobiography*, 23.
23 Darwin, *Autobiography*, 38.
24 Darwin, *Autobiography*, 38.
25 Browne, *Voyaging*, 124.
26 Browne, *Voyaging*, 188.
27 Darwin, *Works*, 1:25.
28 In Browne, *Voyaging*, 190.
29 Darwin, *Works*, 1:38.
30 DCP, letter no. 171, http://www.darwinproject.ac.uk/letter/DCP-LETT-171.xml.
31 DCP, letter no. 248, http://www.darwinproject.ac.uk/letter/DCP-LETT-248.xml.; see also Browne, *Voyaging*, 228.
32 See, e.g., Levine, *Darwin Loves You*; Stott, "Wetfooted Understory."
33 DCP, letter no. 4061, http://www.darwinproject.ac.uk/letter/DCP-LETT-4061.xml.
34 DCP, letter no. 3176, http://www.darwinproject.ac.uk/letter/DCP-LETT-3176.xml.; letter no. 9481, http://www.darwinproject.ac.uk/letter/DCP-LETT-9481.xml.
35 Browne, *Voyaging*, 294.
36 Darwin, *Autobiography*, 73.
37 Browne, *Voyaging*, 361.
38 Browne, *Voyaging*, 363.
39 Innes, "Recollections."
40 Darwin, *Notebook D*; Browne, *Voyaging*, 363.
41 Browne, *Voyaging*, 143.
42 Browne, *Voyaging*, 446.
43 DCP, letter no. 2436, http://www.darwinproject.ac.uk/letter/DCP-LETT-2436.xml.
44 DCP, letter no. 1174, http://www.darwinproject.ac.uk/letter/DCP-LETT-1174.xml.
45 Darwin, *Life and Letters*, 277.
46 Darwin, *Autobiography*, 79.
47 Browne, *Voyaging*, 396.
48 In Browne, *Voyaging*, 411.
49 Darwin, *Autobiography*, 81.
50 Browne, *Voyaging*, 503.
51 Browne, *Voyaging*, 447.
52 Desmond and Moore, *Darwin*.
53 Browne, *Voyaging*; Ruse, "Origin"; Buchanan and Bradley, "'Darwin's Delay.'"

54 Browne, *Voyaging*, 469. Another approach suggests that Darwin's delay was actually purely accidental—the result of a long list of intervening to-dos (Van Wyhe, "Mind the Gap"). Buchanan and Bradley argue that this is inadequate, based largely on how scrupulous Darwin was about shielding some friends from his line of thinking while furtively back-channeling others ("'Darwin's Delay,'" 535).
55 Buchanan and Bradley, "Darwin's Delay," 531–32.
56 Sponsel, *Darwin's Evolving Identity*, 2.
57 Sponsel, *Darwin's Evolving Identity*, 182.
58 Sponsel, *Darwin's Evolving Identity*, 5.
59 In Sponsel, *Darwin's Evolving Identity*, 223.
60 DCP, letter no. 4910, http://www.darwinproject.ac.uk/letter/DCP-LETT-4910.xml.
61 Browne, *Power of Place*, 27.
62 DCP, letter no. 2285, http://www.darwinproject.ac.uk/letter/DCP-LETT-2285.xml.
63 Browne, *Power of Place*, 39.
64 Browne, *Power of Place*, 53.
65 DCP, letter no. 2298, http://www.darwinproject.ac.uk/letter/DCP-LETT-2298.xml.
66 Browne, *Power of Place*, 60.
67 Hesketh, *Of Apes and Ancestors*, 15.
68 Browne, *Power of Place*, 399; Secord, *Victorian Sensation*, 37.
69 Browne, *Power of Place*, 60.
70 Browne, *Power of Place*, 60.
71 See, e.g., Darwin's obsequious response to Sedgwick's blast (DCP, letter no. 2555, http://www.darwinproject.ac.uk/letter/DCP-LETT-2555.xml.). Nonetheless, this wasn't sheer fulsomeness, as he seems to have held on to sincere affection for his former mentor (DCP, letter no. 2734, http://www.darwinproject.ac.uk/letter/DCP-LETT-2734.xml.).
72 "I ought to have been something larger than I am," she wrote in a poignant assessment late in life (in Wedgwood, "Critical Study," 9).
73 Wedgwood, "Boundaries of Science: A Dialogue" and "Boundaries of Science: A Second Dialogue."
74 DCP, letter no. 3206, http://www.darwinproject.ac.uk/letter/DCP-LETT-3206.xml.
75 DCP, letter no. 2534, http://www.darwinproject.ac.uk/letter/DCP-LETT-2534.xml.
76 Darwin, *Origin*, 422.
77 Browne, *Power of Place*, 95.
78 Browne, *Power of Place*, 155; see also DCP, letter no. 2713, http://www.darwinproject.ac.uk/letter/DCP-LETT-2713.xml.
79 Browne, *Power of Place*, 96.
80 Browne, *Power of Place*, 83.

81 Darwin, *Autobiography*, 45.
82 Browne, *Voyaging*, 213.
83 DCP, letter no. 3176.
84 Darwin, *Descent*, 174–75. See also Keel, *Divine Variations*, 80.
85 Desmond, *Huxley*, 330.
86 DCP, letter no. 3426, http://www.darwinproject.ac.uk/letter/DCP-LETT-3426.xml.
87 DCP, letter no. 3439, http://www.darwinproject.ac.uk/letter/DCP-LETT-3439.xml.
88 Hesketh, "First Darwinian," 4.
89 Darwin, *Descent*, 65–66.
90 Darwin, *Descent*, 117.
91 Keel, *Divine Variations*, 87–88. See also Browne, *Voyaging*, 244.
92 P. White, "Darwin's Emotions," 818.
93 E. Richards, *Darwin*, 33–34.
94 Darwin, *Descent*, 134, 167.
95 See Browne, *Power of Place*, 342–47; Grosz, *Time Travels*; E. Richards, *Darwin*.
96 Darwin, *Descent*, 606.
97 E. Richards, *Darwin*, 6.
98 Levine, *Darwin Loves You*, 182.
99 E. Richards, *Darwin*, 28–29.
100 Browne, *Voyaging*, 508.
101 Desmond, *Huxley*, 219.
102 Desmond, *Huxley*, 163.
103 Desmond, *Huxley*, 181.
104 Desmond, *Huxley*, 203.
105 Desmond, *Huxley*, 176.
106 Desmond, *Huxley*, 200.
107 Huxley, "On the Reception of the 'Origin of Species,'" 197.
108 DCP, letter no. 2544, http://www.darwinproject.ac.uk/letter/DCP-LETT-2544.xml; Huxley, "Origin of Species," 77; Browne, *Power of Place*, 105.
109 Desmond, *Huxley*, 284.
110 Desmond, *Huxley*, 262.
111 L. Huxley, *Life and Letters*, 163; but see van Wyhe, "Why There Was No 'Darwin's Bulldog.'"
112 Desmond, *Huxley*, 197.
113 In Desmond, *Huxley*, xiii.
114 Desmond, *Huxley*, 257.
115 DCP, letter no. 2544.
116 Huxley, "Origin of Species," 22–23.
117 Huxley, "Origin of Species," 23.
118 In Desmond, *Huxley*, 63.
119 In Desmond, *Huxley*, 587.
120 In Desmond, *Huxley*, 587.

121 Desmond, *Huxley*, 610.
122 Darwin, *Autobiography*, 88.
123 Darwin, *Autobiography*, 88.
124 DCP, letter no. 2754, http://www.darwinproject.ac.uk/letter/DCP-LETT-2754.xml.
125 DCP, letter no. 2873, http://www.darwinproject.ac.uk/letter/DCP-LETT-2873.xml.
126 Huxley, "Origin of Species," 52.
127 Huxley, "Origin of Species," 52.
128 Huxley, "Origin of Species," 53.
129 In Browne, *Power of Place*, 138.
130 Desmond, *Huxley*, xvi.
131 Desmond, *Huxley*, 313; Browne, *Power of Place*, 403.
132 Desmond, *Huxley*, 7.
133 Desmond, *Huxley*, 252.
134 Desmond, *Huxley*, 75–76; Lightman, *Origins of Agnosticism*, 15.
135 L. Huxley, *Life and Letters*, 217.
136 L. Huxley, *Life and Letters*, 221, emphasis added.
137 L. Huxley, *Life and Letters*, 221.
138 L. Huxley, *Life and Letters*, 219.
139 L. Huxley, *Life and Letters*, 220.
140 Desmond, *Huxley*, 389.
141 Huxley, *Essays*, 355.
142 Desmond, *Huxley*, 403–4.
143 Desmond, *Huxley*, 365.
144 Huxley, *Essays*, 362.
145 Huxley, *Essays*, 330.
146 J. Moore, "Deconstructing Darwinism," 388; Desmond, *Huxley*, 374. Ruth Barton points out that Huxley, given his layered use of irony and deception in his writings, both public and private, is not necessarily a reliable source about his own motives and intentions. "When Huxley tells posterity that he chose the label 'agnostic' for himself because he felt naked or embarrassed," she writes, "I do not believe him" (Barton, *X Club*, 34).
147 Lightman, *Origins of Agnosticism*, 25.
148 J. Moore, "Deconstructing Darwinism," 355.
149 Barton, *X Club*, 187.
150 Browne, *Power of Place*, 38–39.
151 L. Huxley, *Life and Letters*, 187.
152 Secord, *Victorian Sensation*, 151.
153 In Hesketh, *Of Apes and Ancestors*, 122n2.
154 Chambers was, by this time, a prime suspect for the authorship of *Vestiges*, but the truth was not formally revealed until 1884 (Secord, *Victorian Sensation*, 22).
155 Browne, *Power of Place*, 120.

156 Paul White describes how Huxley rejected the recently coined term *scientist* in favor of the more refined *man of science*, but I will here use the modern term for ease of reading (P. White, *Thomas Huxley*, 5; see also Harrison, *Territories*, 160).
157 DCP, letter no. 2852, http://www.darwinproject.ac.uk/letter/DCP-LETT-2852.xml.
158 Hesketh, *Of Apes and Ancestors*, 80.
159 Hesketh, *Of Apes and Ancestors*, 31.
160 Browne, *Power of Place*, 114.
161 Hesketh, *Of Apes and Ancestors*, 81.
162 Hesketh, *Of Apes and Ancestors*, 103.
163 Huxley Papers, 15.117, letter of September 9, 1860. For a history of this letter's circulation, see Jensen, "Return," n67.
164 Huxley Papers, 15.117, letter of September 9, 1860.
165 Hesketh, *Of Apes and Ancestors*, 82. In Huxley's telling, this was the climax of the show, but Hooker claims that it was his commentary that knocked Wilberforce off his plate, a version of the story corroborated by some contemporary journalism and Darwin himself (DCP, letter no. 2852; letter no. 2863, http://www.darwinproject.ac.uk/letter/DCP-LETT-2863.xml.; letter no. 2881, http://www.darwinproject.ac.uk/letter/DCP-LETT-2881.xml.; see also Hesketh, *Of Apes and Ancestors*, 82). Many of Huxley's enemies—including the bishop himself—interpreted the outcome of the battle differently. They thought they had won, or at least fought to a draw (Hesketh, *Of Apes and Ancestors*, 84).
166 Hesketh, *Of Apes and Ancestors*, 90.
167 DCP, letter no. 2853, http://www.darwinproject.ac.uk/letter/DCP-LETT-2853.xml.; letter no. 2861, http://www.darwinproject.ac.uk/letter/DCP-LETT-2861.xml.; letter no. 2865, http://www.darwinproject.ac.uk/letter/DCP-LETT-2865.xml.
168 Hesketh, *Of Apes and Ancestors*, 91.
169 DCP, letter no. 2864, http://www.darwinproject.ac.uk/letter/DCP-LETT-2864.xml.
170 Browne, *Power of Place*, 118.
171 DCP, letter no. 2802, http://www.darwinproject.ac.uk/letter/DCP-LETT-2802.xml.; letter no. 2830, http://www.darwinproject.ac.uk/letter/DCP-LETT-2830.xml.; Hesketh, *Of Apes and Ancestors*, 29.
172 DCP, letter no. 2853.
173 DCP, letter no. 2854, http://www.darwinproject.ac.uk/letter/DCP-LETT-2854.xml.
174 Browne, *Power of Place*, 194.
175 Barton, *X Club*, 371.
176 Browne, *Power of Place*, 249.
177 DCP, letter no. 2854.
178 Darwin, *Autobiography*, 71.
179 Darwin, *Autobiography*, 71.
180 Darwin, *Autobiography*, 72.

181 In Darwin, *Life and Letters*, 275.
182 Darwin, *Life and Letters*, 276.
183 Darwin, *Life and Letters*, 277.
184 Darwin, *Life and Letters*, 274.
185 Darwin, *Life and Letters*, 275.
186 In Browne, *Power of Place*, 484.
187 Van Wyhe and Pallen, "'Annie Hypothesis,'" 3; cf. Desmond and Moore, *Darwin*.
188 Browne, *Power of Place*, 155.
189 Gray, *Natural Selection Not Inconsistent*, 43.
190 Gray, *Natural Selection Not Inconsistent*, 55.
191 DCP, letter no. 2814, http://www.darwinproject.ac.uk/letter/DCP-LETT-2814.xml.
192 DCP, letter no. 2814.
193 DCP, letter no. 3256, http://www.darwinproject.ac.uk/letter/DCP-LETT-3256.xml.
194 Darwin, *Autobiography*, 81.
195 Darwin, *Autobiography*, 75.
196 Levine, *Darwin Loves You*, 40.
197 Levine, *Darwin Loves You*, 163.
198 DCP, letter no. 2814.
199 DCP, letter no. 3342, http://www.darwinproject.ac.uk/letter/DCP-LETT-3342.xml.
200 Darwin, *Notebook N*, 36.
201 James, *Pragmatism*, 25.
202 Darwin, *Autobiography*, 72.
203 This omission was engineered partly through Emma's influence (Browne, *Power of Place*, 433).
204 In Browne, *Power of Place*, 484.
205 Keel, *Divine Variations*, 88.
206 See chapters 3 and 7.
207 Subramaniam, *Ghost Stories*, 226.
208 Levine, *Darwin Loves You*, 217.
209 See, e.g., Conway Morris, "Darwin Was Right"; and R. Richards, "Darwinian Enchantment."

Chapter 6: The Secular Circus

1 Hitchens, "Smart Set."
2 Rodgers, *Mencken*, 119.
3 Rodgers, *Mencken*, 45. See Mencken, *Treatise*.
4 Larson, *Summer*, 140.
5 Dixon, *Science and Religion*.
6 Livingston, *Religious Thought*, 33.
7 Livingston, *Religious Thought*, 131.
8 Marsden, *Fundamentalism*.

9. Numbers, *Creationists*, 21.
10. Wright, "Passing of Evolution," 20.
11. Laats, *Fundamentalism and Education*, 3.
12. Larson, *Summer*, 24; Moran, "Scopes Trial and Southern Fundamentalism," 118.
13. Israel, *Before Scopes*, 158.
14. Israel, *Before Scopes*, 7.
15. Israel, *Before Scopes*, 66.
16. Israel, *Before Scopes*, 139.
17. Larson, *Summer*, 48.
18. Larson, *Summer*, 60.
19. *Knoxville Journal*, "Test Evolution Law."
20. Larson, *Summer*, 88.
21. Larson, *Summer*, 91.
22. Larson, *Summer*, 92.
23. In Larson, *Summer*, 109.
24. Larson, *Summer*, 96.
25. Larson, *Summer*, 94.
26. Larson, *Summer*, 105.
27. Rodgers, *Mencken*, 231.
28. Larson, *Summer*, 295.
29. Mencken, *On Religion*, 187.
30. Larson, *Summer*, 164.
31. Larson, *Summer*, 134.
32. Larson, *Summer*, 179.
33. Larson, *Summer*, 182.
34. Larson, *Summer*, 187.
35. Shuger, "St. Mary the Virgin," 339; Hesketh, *Of Apes and Ancestors*, 78.
36. Numbers, *Creationists*, x.
37. It is less clear whether the impact of that argument was immediately apparent (Larson, *Summer*, 189).
38. In Larson, *Summer*, 190.
39. Larson, *Summer*, 191.
40. Larson, *Summer*, 220.
41. Shapiro, "Civic Biology," 428.
42. Numbers, "Darwinism, Creationism," 35.
43. Du Bois, *Black Reconstruction*, 106.
44. Larson, *Summer*, 94.
45. Israel, *Before Scopes*, 3.
46. Moran, "Scopes Trial and Southern Fundamentalism," 98.
47. Larson, *Summer*, 221.
48. Rodgers, *Mencken*, 45.
49. In Rodgers, *Mencken*, 46.
50. Mencken, "Sahara," 160.
51. Rodgers, *Mencken*, 354.

52 Mencken, "Sahara," 157.
53 Mencken, "Sahara," 157.
54 Du Bois, *Black Reconstruction*, 41.
55 Mencken, "Sahara," 159.
56 Mencken, "Sahara," 163.
57 Mencken, "Sahara," 163.
58 Mencken, "Sahara," 165.
59 Mencken, "Sahara," 163.
60 S. J. Gould, *Mismeasure*, 101–3.
61 Rodgers, *Mencken*, 224.
62 Larson, *Summer*, 92.
63 Mencken, *On Religion*, 172; Rodgers, *Mencken*, 274.
64 Mencken, *On Religion*, 164.
65 Mencken, *On Religion*, 164.
66 Mencken, *On Religion*, 164.
67 Mencken, *On Religion*, 166.
68 Mencken, *On Religion*, 167.
69 Mencken, *On Religion*, 179.
70 Mencken, *On Religion*, 179.
71 Mencken, *On Religion*, 182–83.
72 McCloud, *Divine Hierarchies*, 35.
73 Mencken, *On Religion*, 213.
74 Mencken, *On Religion*, 197.
75 Mencken, *On Religion*, 189.
76 Mencken, *On Religion*, 221; Rodgers, *Mencken*, 293.
77 Desmond, *Huxley*, 320.
78 Holland, *Erotic Life*, 6. See discussion in chapter 2 of this text.
79 In Rodgers, *Mencken*, 282.
80 Rodgers, *Mencken*, 288.
81 In Rodgers, *Mencken*, 289.
82 In Larson, *Summer*, 221.
83 Larson, *Summer*, 221.
84 Kazin, *Godly Hero*, 4.
85 In Kazin, *Godly Hero*, 92.
86 Kazin, *Godly Hero*, 264. There's even a question as to whether the fundamentalist constituency that rallied around Bryan in Dayton was the same as his voting bloc (Larson, *Summer*, 238).
87 See Schaefer, "Whiteness and Civilization."
88 Kazin, *Godly Hero*, 204.
89 Kazin, *Godly Hero*, 61.
90 Kazin, *Godly Hero*, 263.
91 Larson, *Summer*, 27.
92 Numbers, *Creationists*, 41.
93 S. J. Gould, *Rocks of Ages*, 147.

94 S. J. Gould, *Rocks of Ages*, 154.
95 S. J. Gould, *Rocks of Ages*, 169.
96 Kazin, *Godly Hero*, xiii.
97 Kazin, *Godly Hero*, 170.
98 Kazin, *Godly Hero*, 7.
99 Kazin, *Godly Hero*, 161.
100 Kazin, *Godly Hero*, 278.
101 Kazin, *Godly Hero*, 278.
102 Curtis, *American Religious Freedom*, 64. Kazin describes a forty-six-line unpublished poem found in Bryan's papers offering a sort of theological justification of Jim Crow (Kazin, *Godly Hero*, 228).
103 Baker, "Robes, Fiery Crosses," 333; Larson, *Summer*, 44.
104 Robinson, "Crusader," 12.
105 Moran, "Scopes Trial and Southern Fundamentalism." There were some exceptions. See Larson, *Summer*, 122.
106 Robinson's work effectively disproves Larson's characterization that Black commentators were indifferent to what was taking place ("Crusader"; see Larson, *Summer*, 122).
107 Robinson, "Crusader," 13; Moran, "Reading Race," 892.
108 Moran, "Reading Race," 899.
109 Du Bois, "Scopes," 218.
110 Kazin, *Godly Hero*, 263.
111 Larson, *Summer*, 41.
112 In Larson, *Summer*, 41.
113 Larson, *Summer*, 41.
114 Bryan, "God and Evolution," 1.
115 Bryan, "God and Evolution," 1.
116 Bryan, "God and Evolution," 1.
117 Bryan, "God and Evolution," 1.
118 Bryan, *Seven Questions*, 136.
119 Bryan, *Seven Questions*, 145.
120 Bryan, *Seven Questions*, 146–47.
121 Bryan, *Seven Questions*, 158.
122 In Moran, *Scopes Trial*, 145–46.
123 Moran, *Scopes Trial*, 147.
124 Kazin, *Godly Hero*, 289.
125 Larson, *Summer*, 197.
126 Larson, *Summer*, 198.
127 Larson, *Sex, Race, and Science*, 100.
128 Larson, *Sex, Race, and Science*, 107.
129 Larson, *Sex, Race, and Science*, 157.
130 Shapiro, *Trying Biology*, 128.
131 Shapiro, *Trying Biology*, 134, 141.
132 Shapiro, *Trying Biology*, 64.

133 Anthea D. Butler, *White Evangelical Racism*.
134 Larson, *Summer*, 44.
135 McLean v. Arkansas Documentation Project, "Testimony of Ronald W. Coward."
136 E. Scott, "Creation Science Lite," 78–79.
137 Oreskes and Conway, *Merchants*, 265. I discuss this further in the epilogue.
138 Naomi Oreskes and Erik Conway point out that this "two sides to every story" approach has also been the tactic of antiscience partisans in debates around smoking, acid rain, and climate change (*Merchants*, 268).
139 Derrida, *Animal*, 47.

Chapter 7: The Four Horsemen

1 Zucchino, "North Carolina Triple Slaying."
2 *All In with Chris Hayes*, "Brother Speaks."
3 Safi, "After the UNC Chapel Hill Shootings."
4 Tayler, "Religion's New Atheist Scapegoat." See also Schaefer, *Religious Affects*, chap. 5.
5 Zucchino, "North Carolina Triple Slaying."
6 Zucchino, "North Carolina Triple Slaying."
7 Blumberg, "Atheists React," emphasis added.
8 Wyloge, "Hundreds Gather."
9 Safi, "After the UNC Chapel Hill Shootings."
10 Dawkins, *God Delusion*, 343.
11 Puar, *Terrorist Assemblages*, xii.
12 See chapter 2 for a full discussion of Chen's animacy hierarchies.
13 Angier, "Confessions," 34.
14 McGrath, *Twilight*, 1.
15 Amarasingham, "What Is the New Atheism?"; Cotter, Quadrio, and Tuckett, "Introduction."
16 Dennett, "Bright Stuff."
17 Khalil, *Jihad, Radicalism*, 2.
18 See Cotter, Quadrio, and Tuckett, "Introduction," 3, for an extended list of figures associated with New Atheism, including more works from continental European authors.
19 Wolf, "Church of Non-believers."
20 Wolf, "Church of Non-believers."
21 Dawkins, *Selfish Gene*, x.
22 E. O. Wilson, "What Is Sociobiology?," 11.
23 Dawkins, *Selfish Gene*, 5–6.
24 Hamilton, "Evolution of Social Behaviour," 16.
25 Gould and Lewontin, "Spandrels."
26 See chapter 2. Discussed further in Schaefer, *Religious Affects*, chap. 6.
27 S. J. Gould, *Panda's Thumb*, 20–21.
28 Keller, "Language and Ideology," 99. See also Midgley, *Ethical Primate*.

29 See Schaefer, *Religious Affects*, chap. 6, and "Blessed, Precious Mistakes."
30 The term itself is an abbreviation of *mimeme*, cognate with *mimesis* or *mimicry* (Dawkins, *Selfish Gene*, 206).
31 See, e.g., E. O. Wilson, *Sociobiology*, 561.
32 Dawkins, *Selfish Gene*, 205.
33 Dawkins, *Selfish Gene*, 212–13.
34 Hedges, *I Don't Believe*, 53.
35 Dawkins, *Unweaving*, ix.
36 Dawkins, *Selfish Gene* (40th anniversary ed.), xv.
37 Pigliucci, "New Atheism," 144.
38 S. J. Gould, "Darwinian Fundamentalism."
39 Dennett, *Darwin's Dangerous Idea*, 143.
40 Dennett, *Consciousness Explained*, 173; *Kinds of Minds*, 23; *Darwin's Dangerous Idea*, 135.
41 Dennett, *Breaking the Spell*, chap. 5.
42 Dennett, *Breaking the Spell*, 184–85.
43 Dennett, *Breaking the Spell*, 11; Dawkins, *God Delusion*, 32.
44 Harris, *End of Faith*, 12.
45 Harris, *End of Faith*, 29.
46 Dawkins, *God Delusion*, 345, emphasis original.
47 Vásquez, *More Than Belief*, 5.
48 Vásquez, *More Than Belief*, 12. See also Asad, *On Suicide Bombing*, 40.
49 Pigliucci, "New Atheism," 144.
50 Harris, *Moral Landscape*, 30; see also Pigliucci, "New Atheism," 149.
51 Dennett, *Breaking the Spell*, 38.
52 Dennett, *Breaking the Spell*, 70.
53 Dennett, *Breaking the Spell*, 141.
54 Dawkins, *God Delusion*, 21; Harris, *End of Faith*, 178.
55 Cimino and Smith, *Atheist Awakening*, 29–30.
56 Dawkins, *Selfish Gene*, xi.
57 In Kitcher, *Vaulting Ambition*, 250.
58 Kitcher, *Vaulting Ambition*, 250.
59 Levine, *Darwin Loves You*, 125.
60 S. J. Gould, "Darwinian Fundamentalism," emphasis added.
61 Levine, *Darwin Loves You*, 125.
62 Dawkins, *God Delusion*, 345.
63 Dawkins, *God Delusion*, 23–24.
64 Dawkins, *God Delusion*, 15.
65 Eagleton, "Lunging, Flailing, Mispunching."
66 Hitchens, *God Is Not Great*, 13.
67 Richard Dawkins, Daniel Dennett, Sam Harris, and Christopher Hitchens, *The Four Horsemen*, digital video, 2007, http://www.youtube.com/watch?v=9DKhc1pcDFM and http://www.youtube.com/watch?v=TaeJf-Yia3A&feature=relmfu.

68 Charles, *Religulous*.
69 Charles, *Religulous*.
70 Charles, *Religulous*.
71 Cimino and Smith, *Atheist Awakening*, 83.
72 Stahl, "One-Dimensional Rage," 103.
73 Aslan, "Preface," xiii.
74 Ahmed, "Affective Economies," 132.
75 Hitchens, *God Is Not Great*, 22.
76 Hitchens, *God Is Not Great*, 11.
77 Hitchens, "Images."
78 Mencken, *On Religion*, 164.
79 Hitchens, "Smart Set."
80 Shatz, "Left and 9/11."
81 Dawkins (@RichardDawkins), "@ToddKincannon Haven't read Koran …," Twitter, February 28, 2013, https://twitter.com/RichardDawkins/status/307369895031603200.
82 Dawkins (@RichardDawkins), "Suggest always put …," Twitter, July 25, 2014, https://twitter.com/RichardDawkins/status/492729120418430976.
83 M. Robbins, "Richard Dawkins, 'Islamophobia,' and the Atheist Movement."
84 Dawkins (@RichardDawkins), "Alas, criminal individual killers …," Twitter, February 11, 2015, https://twitter.com/RichardDawkins/status/565651522709901314.
85 Dawkins (@RichardDawkins), "Listening to the lovely bells …," Twitter, July 16, 2018, https://twitter.com/RichardDawkins/status/1018933359978909696.
86 M. Sullivan (@MarekSullivan), "Eating lovely rhubarb crumble …," Twitter, July 17, 2018, https://twitter.com/MarekSullivan/status/1019191080611405826.
87 Dawkins (@RichardDawkins), "The call to prayer …," Twitter, July 18, 2018, https://twitter.com/RichardDawkins/status/1019566464569892866.
88 Dennett, *Breaking the Spell*, 234.
89 In Knapton, "Richard Dawkins."
90 Knapton, "Richard Dawkins"; Slater, "'Smart' People."
91 Dawkins et al., *Four Horsemen*.
92 Harris, *End of Faith*, 108.
93 Harris, *End of Faith*, 109.
94 Dawkins et al., *Four Horsemen*.
95 Dawkins et al., *Four Horsemen*.
96 Khalil, *Jihad, Radicalism*, 4.
97 Khalil, *Jihad, Radicalism*, 4.
98 Harris, *End of Faith*, 123.
99 Khalil, *Jihad, Radicalism*, 100. Khalil has a positive assessment of Harris's more recent work, especially the 2015 volume Harris coauthored with Maajid Nawaz, *Islam and the Future of Tolerance* (Khalil, *Jihad, Radicalism*, 123). But even here, Harris spends much of his time reiterating his points from chapter 4 of *End of Faith* (Harris and Nawaz, *Future of Tolerance*, 5).

100   Nanda, "Trading Faith for Spirituality."
101   Nanda, "Trading Faith for Spirituality."
102   Harris, *End of Faith*, 214.
103   Harris, *End of Faith*, 12.
104   Khalil, *Jihad, Radicalism*, 114.
105   Harris, *End of Faith*, 110.
106   Chen, *Animacies*, 9.
107   Asad, *On Suicide Bombing*.
108   Stephen Bullivant speculates that atheism may have been able to buy its respectability precisely by exhibiting hostility to Muslims in a moment when Islamophobia's stock was soaring as a feature of American and British foreign policy (Bullivant, "New Atheism and Sociology," 120). New Atheism's hand-in-glove fit with global Islamophobia might explain its sudden success—secularism driven by racialized reason rather than the other way around.
109   Eagleton, "Lunging, Flailing, Mispunching"; Hedges, *I Don't Believe*.
110   Cimino and Smith, *Atheist Awakening*; Engelke, "Soft Atheism."
111   See Cameron, *Black Freethinkers*; and Swann, *Black Atheists*. See also Pinn, *By These Hands*.
112   Pinn, *When Colorblindness*, 20.
113   Pinn, *End of God-Talk*, 6, emphasis removed.
114   Pinn, *End of God-Talk*, 4.
115   Pinn, *When Colorblindness*, 20.
116   Pinn, *When Colorblindness*, 21.
117   Pinn, *When Colorblindness*, 23.
118   Pinn, *When Colorblindness*, 31.
119   Hutchinson, *Godless Americana*, 127.
120   Hutchinson, *Godless Americana*, x.
121   Hutchinson, "#AtheismSoWhite."
122   Hutchinson, *Moral Combat*, 204.
123   Hutchinson, "#AtheismSoWhite."
124   Hutchinson, *Moral Combat*, 45.
125   Puar, *Terrorist Assemblages*; Farris, *Rise of Femonationalism*.
126   Hutchinson, *Moral Combat*, 39; *Godless Americana*, 130.
127   Hutchinson, *Moral Combat*, 16.
128   Hutchinson, *Moral Combat*, 16.
129   Pinn, *End of God-Talk*, 6.
130   Pinn, *End of God-Talk*, 9.
131   Quoting historian Kenneth Manning, in Pinn, *End of God-Talk*, 53.
132   Pinn, *End of God-Talk*, 45.
133   Pinn, *End of God-Talk*, 52.
134   Pinn, *End of God-Talk*, 54.
135   Stedman, *Faitheist*, 2.
136   Stedman, *Faitheist*, 14.
137   Stedman, *Faitheist*, 145–46.

138 Stedman (@ChrisDStedman), "Still sick over...," Twitter, February 11, 2015, https://twitter.com/ChrisDStedman/status/565522719333437440.
139 Stedman, personal interview, March 27, 2014.
140 Hutchinson, *Godless Americana*, 147, 133.
141 Stedman, *Faitheist*, 11.
142 Stedman, *Faitheist*, 5.
143 Muñoz, *Sense of Brown*, 17.
144 See Pellegrini, "Feeling Secular," 205.
145 Stedman, personal interview.
146 Stedman, *Faitheist*, 160.
147 Stedman, personal interview.
148 Pinn, *End of God-Talk*, 27; see also Swann, *Black Atheists*.
149 Pinn, *End of God-Talk*, 41.
150 Stedman, *Faitheist*, 88.
151 Stedman, *Faitheist*, 88.
152 Stedman, *Faitheist*, 123.
153 Stedman, *Faitheist*, 86.
154 Asad, "Free Speech," 56–57.
155 Hollywood, *Acute Melancholia*, 12.
156 Pinn, *When Colorblindness*, 47.
157 Safi, "After the UNC Chapel Hill Shootings."
158 Mbembe, *Dark Night*, 41.

Epilogue

1 Pew Research Center, "Public's Views on Evolution."
2 Oreskes, *Why Trust Science?*, 55.
3 Latour, *Down to Earth*, 21.
4 Latour, *Down to Earth*, 23.
5 See Schaefer, *Religious Affects*, chap. 2.
6 Ewing and Grady, *Jesus Camp*.
7 Ewing and Grady, *Jesus Camp*.
8 Derrida, *Resistances*, 6.
9 Freud, *Interpretation of Dreams*, 120.
10 Oreskes and Conway, *Merchants*, 6–7.
11 Oreskes and Conway, *Merchants*, 242.
12 Barkun, *Culture of Conspiracy*, 2.
13 Marx, *Marx-Engels Reader*, 197.
14 Latour, "Why Has Critique...?," 227.

Bibliography

Agrama, Hussein Ali. *Questioning Secularism: Islam, Sovereignty, and the Rule of Law in Modern Egypt*. Chicago: University of Chicago Press, 2012.
Ahmed, Sara. "Affective Economies." *Social Text* 22, no. 2 (2004): 117–39.
Ahmed, Sara. "Collective Feelings, or, The Impressions Left by Others." *Theory, Culture, and Society* 21, no. 2 (2004): 25–42.
Ahmed, Sara. *The Cultural Politics of Emotion*. New York: Routledge, 2004.
Ahmed, Sara. "Not in the Mood." *New Formations* 82 (2014): 13–28. muse.jhu.edu/article/558908.
Ahmed, Sara. *The Promise of Happiness*. Durham, NC: Duke University Press, 2010.
Ahmed, Sara. *Queer Phenomenology: Orientations, Objects, Others*. Durham, NC: Duke University Press, 2006.
Alaimo, Stacy, and Susan Hekman. "Introduction: Emerging Models of Materiality in Feminist Theory." In Alaimo and Hekman, *Material Feminisms*, 1–19.
Alaimo, Stacy, and Susan Hekman, eds. *Material Feminisms*. Bloomington: Indiana University Press, 2008.
All In with Chris Hayes. "Brother of Slain Muslim Student Speaks." MSNBC, February 13, 2015. http://www.msnbc.com/all-in/watch/brother-of-slain-muslim-student-speaks-398402627979.
Amarasingam, Amarnath, ed. *Religion and the New Atheism: A Critical Appraisal*. Leiden, NL: Brill, 2010.
Amarasingam, Amarnath. "What Is the New Atheism?" In Amarasingam, *Religion and the New Atheism*, 1–10.

Angier, Natalie. "Confessions of a Lonely Atheist." *New York Times Magazine*, January 14, 2001. https://www.nytimes.com/2001/01/14/magazine/the-bush-years-confessions-of-a-lonely-atheist.html.

Aquinas, Thomas. *The Summa Theologiae of St. Thomas Aquinas*. 2nd and rev. ed., 1920. Online ed., edited by Kevin Knight, 2017. http://www.newadvent.org/summa/.

Arendt, Hannah. *The Origins of Totalitarianism*. New York: Harcourt Brace Jovanovich, 1973.

Aristotle. *The Metaphysics*. Translated by Hugh Tredennick. London: William Heinemann, 1933.

Asad, Talal. "Autobiographical Reflections on Society and Religion." *Religion and Society: Advances in Research* 11 (2020): 1–6.

Asad, Talal. *Formations of the Secular: Christianity, Islam, Modernity*. Stanford, CA: Stanford University Press, 2003.

Asad, Talal. "Free Speech, Blasphemy, and Secular Criticism." In Asad et al., *Is Critique Secular?*, 20–57.

Asad, Talal. *Genealogies of Religion: Discipline and Reasons of Power in Christianity and Islam*. Baltimore: Johns Hopkins University Press, 1993.

Asad, Talal. *On Suicide Bombing*. New York: Columbia University Press, 2007.

Asad, Talal. "Reading a Modern Classic: W. C. Smith's *The Meaning and End of Religion*." In *Civil Society in Malerkotla, Punjab: Fostering Resilience Through Religion*, edited by Karenjot Bhangoo Randhawa, 205–22. London: Lexington, 2012.

Asad, Talal. "Reply to Judith Butler." In Asad et al., *Is Critique Secular?*, 137–45.

Asad, Talal. *Secular Translations: Nation-State, Modern Self, and Calculative Reason*. New York: Columbia University Press, 2018.

Asad, Talal, Wendy Brown, Judith Butler, and Saba Mahmood. *Is Critique Secular? Blasphemy, Injury, and Free Speech*. Berkeley: University of California Press, 2009.

Aslan, Reza. Preface to Amarasingam, *Religion and the New Atheism*, xiii–xv.

Asma, Stephen T., and Rami Gabriel. *The Emotional Mind: The Affective Roots of Culture and Cognition*. Cambridge, MA: Harvard University Press, 2019.

Augustine. *Confessions*. Translated by Henry Chadwick. Oxford: Oxford University Press, 1991.

Austin, J. L. *How to Do Things with Words: The William James Lectures Delivered at Harvard University in 1955*. Oxford: Oxford University Press, 1962.

Ayer, Alfred. *Hume: A Very Short Introduction*. Oxford: Oxford University Press, 2000.

Baker, Kelly J. "Robes, Fiery Crosses, and the American Flag: The Materiality of the 1920s' Klan's Christianity, Patriotism, and Intolerance." *Material Religion* 7, no. 3 (2011): 312–42.

Baldwin, James. *The Fire Next Time*. New York: Penguin, 1963.

Barad, Karen. *Meeting the Universe Halfway: Quantum Physics and the Entanglement of Matter and Meaning*. Durham, NC: Duke University Press, 2007.

Barkun, Michael. *A Culture of Conspiracy: Apocalyptic Visions in Contemporary America*. Berkeley: University of California Press, 2003.

Barrett, Lisa Feldman. "Are Emotions Natural Kinds?" *Perspectives on Psychological Science* 1 (2006): 28–58.
Barrett, Lisa Feldman. *How Emotions Are Made: The Secret Life of the Brain*. New York: Houghton Mifflin Harcourt, 2017.
Barrett, Lisa Feldman. "Zombie Ideas." *APS Observer*, October 2019. https://www.psychologicalscience.org/observer/zombie-ideas.
Barrett, Lisa Feldman, K. A. Lindquist, E. Bliss-Moreau, S. Duncan, M. Gendron, J. Mize, and L. Brennan. "Of Mice and Men: Natural Kinds of Emotions in the Mammalian Brain? A Response to Panksepp and Izard." *Perspectives on Psychological Science* 2 (2007): 297–312.
Barrett, Louise. "Why Brains Are Not Computers, Why Behaviorism Is Not Satanism, and Why Dolphins Are Not Aquatic Apes." *Behavior Analyst* 39, no. 9 (2016): 9–23.
Barton, Ruth. *The X Club: Power and Authority in Victorian Science*. Chicago: University of Chicago Press, 2018.
Bechara, Antoine, Antonio Damasio, Hanna Damasio, and Steven Anderson. "Insensitivity to Future Consequences Following Damage to Human Prefrontal Cortex." *Cognition* 50 (1994): 7–15.
Bechara, Antoine, Hanna Damasio, Daniel Tranel, and Antonio Damasio. "Deciding Advantageously before Knowing the Advantageous Strategy." *Science* 275 (February 28, 1997): 1293–95.
Bechara, Antoine, Hanna Damasio, Daniel Tranel, and Antonio Damasio. "The Iowa Gambling Task and the Somatic Marker Hypothesis: Some Questions and Answers." *Trends in Cognitive Sciences* 9, no. 4 (2005): 159–62.
Bennett, Jane. *The Enchantment of Modern Life: Attachments, Crossings, and Ethics*. Princeton, NJ: Princeton University Press, 2001.
Bennett, Jane. *Vibrant Matter: A Political Ecology of Things*. Durham, NC: Duke University Press, 2010.
Berger, Peter L. *The Sacred Canopy: Elements of a Sociological Theory of Religion*. New York: Anchor, 1969.
Berger, Peter L. "Secularism in Retreat." *National Interest*, no. 46 (Winter 1996).
Berlant, Lauren. *Cruel Optimism*. Durham, NC: Duke University Press, 2011.
Berlant, Lauren. *The Female Complaint: The Unfinished Business of Sentimentality in American Culture*. Durham, NC: Duke University Press, 2008.
Berlant, Lauren, and Kathleen Stewart. *The Hundreds*. Durham, NC: Duke University Press, 2019.
Best, Stephen, and Sharon Marcus. "Surface Reading: An Introduction." *Representations* 108, no. 1 (Fall 2009): 1–21.
Birnbaum, N. "Conflicting Interpretations of the Rise of Capitalism: Marx and Weber." *British Journal of Sociology* 4, no. 2 (1953): 125–41.
Blackman, Lisa. *Haunted Data: Affect, Transmedia, Weird Science*. London: Bloomsbury Academic, 2019.
Blankholm, Joseph. "Secularism and Secular People." *Public Culture* 30, no. 2 (2018): 245–68.

Bloor, David. *Knowledge and Social Imagery*. 2nd ed. Chicago: University of Chicago Press, 1991.

Blumberg, Antonia. "Atheists React to Chapel Hill Shooting of Muslim Family Members." *Huffington Post*, February 11, 2015. https://www.huffpost.com/entry/atheist-reactions-chapel-shooting_n_6662512.

Bonilla-Silva, Eduardo. "Feeling Race: Theorizing the Racial Economy of Emotions." *American Sociological Review* 84, no. 1 (2019): 1–25.

Bonilla-Silva, Eduardo. *Racism without Racists: Color-Blind Racism and the Persistence of Racial Inequality in the United States*. 4th ed. Plymouth, UK: Rowman and Littlefield, 2014.

Bonilla-Silva, Eduardo. "Toward a New Political Praxis for Trumpamerica: New Directions in Critical Race Theory." *American Behavioral Scientist* 63, no. 13 (2019): 1776–88.

Bowler, Peter. *The Eclipse of Darwinism: Anti-Darwinian Evolutionary Theories in the Decades around 1900*. Baltimore: Johns Hopkins University Press, 1983.

Brown, Wendy. Introduction to Asad et al., *Is Critique Secular?*, 7–19.

Browne, Janet. *Charles Darwin: The Power of Place*. New York: Knopf, 2002.

Browne, Janet. *Charles Darwin: Voyaging. A Biography*. Princeton, NJ: Princeton University Press, 1995.

Bryan, William Jennings. "God and Evolution: Charge That American Teachers of Darwinism 'Make the Bible a Scrap of Paper.'" *New York Times*, February 26, 1922.

Bryan, William Jennings. *Seven Questions in Dispute*. London: Revell, 1924.

Buchanan, Roderick D., and James Bradley. "'Darwin's Delay': A Reassessment of the Evidence." *Isis* 108, no. 3 (2017): 530–52.

Bulkeley, Kelly. *The Wondering Brain: Thinking about Religion with and beyond Cognitive Neuroscience*. New York: Routledge, 2004.

Bullivant, Stephen. "The New Atheism and Sociology: Why Here? Why Now? What Next?" In Amarasingam, *Religion and the New Atheism*, 109–24.

Butler, A. B. "Triune Brain Concept: A Comparative Evolutionary Perspective." In *Encyclopedia of Neuroscience*, edited by Larry Squire, 1185–93. Cambridge: Academic Press, 2009.

Butler, Anthea D. *White Evangelical Racism: The Politics of Morality in America*. Chapel Hill: University of North Carolina Press, 2021.

Butler, Judith. *Gender Trouble*. New York: Routledge, 1990.

Butler, Judith. "The Sensibility of Critique: Response to Asad and Mahmood." In Asad et al., *Is Critique Secular?*, 101–36.

Cacioppo, John, and Gary Berntson. "Affective Distinctiveness: Illusory or Real?" *Cognition and Emotion* 21, no. 6 (2007): 1347–59.

Calhoun, Craig, Mark Juergensmeyer, and Jonathan VanAntwerpen. Introduction to *Rethinking Secularism*, edited by Craig Calhoun, Mark Juergensmeyer, and Jonathan VanAntwerpen, 3–30. New York: Oxford University Press, 2011.

Cameron, Christopher. *Black Freethinkers: A History of African-American Secularism*. Evanston, IL: Northwestern University Press, 2019.

Campbell, Colin. "Do Today's Sociologists Really Appreciate Weber's Essay *The Protestant Ethic and the Spirit of Capitalism?*" *Sociological Review* (2005): 207–25.
Charles, Larry, dir. *Religulous*. Santa Monica, CA: Lions Gate Entertainment, 2008.
Chen, Mel Y. *Animacies: Biopolitics, Racial Mattering, and Queer Affect*. Durham, NC: Duke University Press, 2012.
Cheney, Dorothy, and Robert Seyfarth. *Baboon Metaphysics: The Evolution of a Social Mind*. Chicago: University of Chicago Press, 2007.
Cherry, E. Colin. "Some Experiments on the Recognition of Speech, with One and with Two Ears." *Journal of the Acoustical Society of America* 25, no. 5 (1953): 975–79.
Cimino, Richard, and Christopher Smith. *Atheist Awakening: Secular Activism and Community in America*. Oxford: Oxford University Press, 2014.
Coady, David. "Are Conspiracy Theorists Irrational?" *Episteme: A Journal of Social Epistemology* 4, no. 2 (2007): 193–204.
Coakley, Sarah, ed. *Faith, Rationality, and the Passions*. Malden, MA: Wiley-Blackwell, 2012.
Code, Lorraine. "Taking Subjectivity into Account." In *Feminist Epistemologies*, edited by Linda Martín Alcoff and Elizabeth Potter, 15–48. New York: Routledge, 1993.
Colombetti, Giovanna. *The Feeling Body: Affective Science Meets the Enactive Mind*. Cambridge, MA: MIT Press, 2014.
Comte, Auguste. *A General View of Positivism*. Translated by J. H. Bridges. London: Trübner, 1865.
Connolly, William. *Why I Am Not a Secularist*. Minneapolis: University of Minnesota Press, 1999.
Conway Morris, Simon. "Darwin Was Right. Up to a Point." *Guardian*, February 12, 2009. https://www.theguardian.com/global/2009/feb/12/simon-conway-morris-darwin.
Coole, Diana, and Samantha Frost, eds. *New Materialisms: Ontology, Agency, and Politics*. Durham, NC: Duke University Press, 2010.
Cotter, Christopher, Philip Andrew Quadrio, and Jonathan Tuckett. Introduction to *New Atheism: Critical Perspectives and Contemporary Debates*, edited by Cotter, Quadrio, and Tuckett, 1–13. Cham, Switzerland: Springer International, 2017.
Crawley, Ashon. *The Lonely Letters*. Durham, NC: Duke University Press, 2020.
Curtis, Finbarr. *The Production of American Religious Freedom*. New York: New York University Press, 2016.
Cvetkovich, Ann. *Depression: A Public Feeling*. Durham, NC: Duke University Press, 2012.
Damasio, Antonio. *Descartes' Error: Emotion, Reason, and the Human Brain*. New York: Putnam, 1994.
Damasio, Antonio. *The Feeling of What Happens: Body and Emotion in the Making of Consciousness*. New York: Harcourt, 1999.
Damasio, Antonio. *Looking for Spinoza: Joy, Sorrow, and the Feeling Brain*. New York: Mariner, 2003.

Damasio, Antonio, Daniel Tranel, and Hanna Damasio. "Somatic Markers and the Guidance of Behavior." In *Frontal Lobe Function and Dysfunction*, edited by Harvey Levin, Howard Eisenberg, and Arthur Lester Benton, 217–28. New York: Oxford University Press, 1991.

Damasio, Antonio, and G. W. Van Hoesen. "Emotional Disturbances Associated with Focal Lesions of the Limbic Frontal Lobe." In *Neuropsychology of Human Emotion*, edited by Kenneth Heilman and Paul Satz, 85–110. New York: Guilford, 1983.

Darwin, Charles. *The Autobiography of Charles Darwin*. Edited by Nora Barlow. New York: W. W. Norton, 2005.

Darwin, Charles. *The Descent of Man and Selection in Relation to Sex*. 2nd ed. London: John Murray, 1882.

Darwin, Charles. *The Expression of the Emotions in Man and Animals*. Edited by Joe Cain and Sharon Messenger. London: Penguin, 2009.

Darwin, Charles. *The Life and Letters of Charles Darwin*. Vol. 1. Edited by Francis Darwin. New York: Appleton, 1897.

Darwin, Charles. *Notebook D* [Transmutation of species (7–10.1838)]. CUL-DAR123. Edited by Paul Barrett, transcribed by Kees Rookmaaker. Darwin Online. http://darwin-online.org.uk/.

Darwin, Charles. *Notebook N* [Metaphysics and expression (1838–1839)]. CUL-DAR126. Edited by Paul Barrett, transcribed by Kees Rookmaaker. Darwin Online. http://darwin-online.org.uk/.

Darwin, Charles. *The Origin of Species by Means of Natural Selection, or the Preservation of Favoured Races in the Struggle for Life*. 6th ed. London: John Murray, 1876.

Darwin, Charles. *The Works of Charles Darwin*, vol. 1: *Diary of the Voyage of HMS Beagle*. Edited by Paul Barrett and R. B. Freeman. New York: New York University Press, 1987.

Darwin Correspondence Database. University of Cambridge. http://www.darwinproject.ac.uk/.

Darwin, Erasmus. *Temple of Nature: A Poem, with Philosophical Notes*. Baltimore: Bonsal and Niles, 1804.

Daston, Lorraine, and Peter Galison. *Objectivity*. New York: Zone, 2007.

Davidson, Richard J. "Seven Sins in the Study of Emotion: Correctives from Affective Neuroscience." *Brain and Cognition* 52 (2003): 129–32.

Dawkins, Richard. *The God Delusion*. New York: Mariner, 2008.

Dawkins, Richard. *The Selfish Gene*. Oxford: Oxford University Press, 1976.

Dawkins, Richard. *The Selfish Gene*. 40th anniversary ed. Oxford: Oxford University Press, 2016.

Dawkins, Richard. *Unweaving the Rainbow: Science, Delusion, and the Appetite for Wonder*. Boston: Houghton Mifflin, 1998.

Decety, Jean, Kalina Michalska, and Katherine Kinzler. "The Developmental Neuroscience of Moral Sensitivity." *Emotion Review* 3, no. 3 (July 2011): 305–7.

de Condorcet, Nicolas. *Outlines of an Historical View of the Progress of the Human Mind*. Philadelphia: Lang and Ustick, 1796.

Deleuze, Gilles. *Bergsonism*. Translated by Hugh Tomlinson and Barbara Habberjam. New York: Zone, 1988.
Deleuze, Gilles. *Spinoza: Practical Philosophy*. Translated by Robert Hurley. San Francisco: City Lights, 1988.
Deloria, Vine, Jr. *The Metaphysics of Modern Existence*. Golden, CO: Fulcrum, 2012.
Dennett, Daniel. *Breaking the Spell: Religion as a Natural Phenomenon*. New York: Penguin, 2006.
Dennett, Daniel. "The Bright Stuff." *New York Times*, July 12, 2003.
Dennett, Daniel. *Consciousness Explained*. Boston: Little, Brown, 1991.
Dennett, Daniel. *Darwin's Dangerous Idea: Evolution and the Meanings of Life*. New York: Simon and Schuster, 1995.
Dennett, Daniel. *Kinds of Minds: Toward an Understanding of Consciousness*. New York: Basic Books, 1996.
Derrida, Jacques. *The Animal That Therefore I Am*. Translated by David Wills. New York: Fordham, 2008.
Derrida, Jacques. *Resistances of Psychoanalysis*. Translated by Peggy Kamuf, Pascale-Anne Brault, and Michael Naas. Palo Alto, CA: Stanford University Press, 1998.
Desmond, Adrian. *Huxley: From Devil's Disciple to Evolution's High Priest*. New York: Basic Books, 1997.
Desmond, Adrian, and James Moore. *Darwin*. London: W. W. Norton, 1991.
Dharwadker, Vinay. "Emotion in Motion: The Nāṭyashāstra, Darwin, and Affect Theory." *PMLA* 130, no. 5 (2015): 1381–404.
Disraeli, Benjamin. *Church Policy*. London: Gilbert and Rivington, 1864.
Dixon, Thomas. *From Passions to Emotions: The Creation of a Secular Psychological Category*. Cambridge: Cambridge University Press, 2003.
Dixon, Thomas. *Science and Religion: A Very Short Introduction*. Oxford: Oxford University Press, 2008.
Draper, John William. *History of the Conflict between Religion and Science*. Cambridge: Cambridge University Press, 2009.
Du Bois, W. E. B. *Black Reconstruction in America: An Essay toward a History of the Part Which Black Folk Played in the Attempt to Reconstruct Democracy in America, 1860–1880*. New York: Oxford University Press, 2007.
Du Bois, W. E. B. "Scopes." *Crisis* 30 (September 1925): 218.
Dumler-Winckler, Emily. *On Modern Virtue: Mary Wollstonecraft and a Tradition of Dissent*. Oxford: Oxford University Press, forthcoming.
Duncan, Seth, and Lisa Feldman Barrett. "Affect Is a Form of Cognition: A Neurobiological Analysis." *Cognition and Emotion* 21, no. 6 (2007): 1184–211.
Dunn, Barnaby, Tim Dalgleish, and Andrew Lawrence. "The Somatic Marker Hypothesis: A Critical Evaluation." *Neuroscience and Biobehavioral Reviews* 30 (2006): 239–71.
Eagleton, Terry. "Lunging, Flailing, Mispunching." *London Review of Books*, October 19, 2006.
Einstein, Albert. "Religion and Science." *New York Times Magazine*, November 9, 1930, 1–4.

Eliot, George. *Middlemarch: A Study of Provincial Life*. Edited by David Carroll. New York: Oxford University Press, 2008.

Engelke, Matthew. "Soft Atheism." *Public Books*, February 15, 2015. https://www.publicbooks.org/soft-atheism/.

Ewing, Heidi, and Rachel Grady, dirs. *Jesus Camp*. New York: Magnolia Pictures / Loki Films, 2006.

Fanon, Frantz. *Black Skin, White Masks*. Translated by Charles Lam Markmann. London: Pluto, 1986.

Farman, Abou. "Mind out of Place: Transhuman Spirituality." *Journal of the American Academy of Religion* 87, no. 1 (March 2019): 57–80.

Farman, Abou. *On Not Dying: Secular Immortality in the Age of Technoscience*. Minneapolis: University of Minnesota Press, 2020.

Farman, Abou. "Re-enchantment Cosmologies: Mastery and Obsolescence in an Intelligent Universe." *Anthropological Quarterly* 85, no. 4 (2012): 1069–88.

Farris, Sara. *In the Name of Women's Rights: The Rise of Femonationalism*. Durham, NC: Duke University Press, 2017.

Felski, Rita. *The Limits of Critique*. Chicago: University of Chicago Press, 2015.

Felski, Rita, and Susan Fraiman. "Introduction: In the Mood." *New Literary History* 43, no. 3 (2012): v–xii.

Fernando, Mayanthi. *The Republic Unsettled: Muslim French and the Contradictions of Secularism*. Durham, NC: Duke University Press, 2014.

Fernie, Gordon, and Richard Tunney. "Learning on the IGT Follows Emergence of Knowledge but Not Differential Somatic Activity." *Frontiers in Psychology* 4 (October 2013): 1–14.

Ferreira da Silva, Denise. *Toward a Global Idea of Race*. Minneapolis: University of Minnesota Press, 2007.

Feyerabend, Paul. *Against Method*. 3rd ed. London: Verso, 1993.

Fleck, Ludwik. *Genesis and Development of a Scientific Fact*. Translated by Frederik Bradley and Thaddeus Trenn. Chicago: University of Chicago Press, 1979.

Foucault, Michel. *The Archaeology of Knowledge*. Translated by A. M. Smith. London: Routledge, 2002.

Foucault, Michel. "Confession of the Flesh." In *Power/Knowledge: Selected Interviews and Other Writings, 1972–1977*, edited by Colin Gordon, 194–228. New York: Pantheon Books: 1980.

Foucault, Michel. *Discipline and Punish: The Birth of the Prison*. Translated by Alan Sheridan. New York: Vintage, 1977.

Foucault, Michel. *The History of Sexuality*. Vol. 1, *An Introduction*. Translated by Robert Hurley. New York: Vintage, 1990.

Foucault, Michel. *Madness and Civilization: A History of Insanity in the Age of Reason*. Translated by Richard Howard. New York: Vintage, 1973.

Foucault, Michel. *The Order of Things: An Archaeology of the Human Sciences*. New York: Routledge, 1989.

Foucault, Michel. "What Is Enlightenment?" Translated by Catherine Porter. In *The Foucault Reader*, edited by Paul Rabinow, 32–50. New York: Pantheon, 1984.

Frank, Adam, and Elizabeth A. Wilson. *A Silvan Tomkins Handbook: Foundations for Affect Theory*. Minneapolis: University of Minnesota Press, 2020.
Frank, Robert H. "The Strategic Role of the Emotions." *Emotion Review* 3, no. 3 (2011): 252–54.
Freud, Sigmund. *The Future of an Illusion*. Edited by James Strachey. New York: W. W. Norton, 1989.
Freud, Sigmund. *The Interpretation of Dreams*. In *The Standard Edition of the Complete Psychological Works of Sigmund Freud*, vol. 4, edited by James Strachey. London: Hogarth, 1958.
Frost, Samantha. *Biocultural Creatures: Toward a New Theory of the Human*. Durham, NC: Duke University Press, 2016.
Geertz, Clifford. *The Interpretation of Cultures: Selected Essays*. New York: Perseus, 1973.
Geraghty, Anthony. "Wren's Preliminary Design for the Sheldonian Theatre." *Architectural History* 45 (2002): 275–88.
Ghosh, Peter. *Max Weber and the Protestant Ethic: Twin Histories*. Oxford: Oxford University Press, 2014.
Goodall, Jane. *Through a Window: My Thirty Years with the Chimpanzees of Gombe*. Boston: Houghton Mifflin, 1990.
Goodenough, Ursula. *The Sacred Depths of Nature*. Oxford: Oxford University Press, 1998.
Gordon, Elizabeth Oke, and William Buckland. *The Life and Correspondence of William Buckland, D.D., F.R.S.* Edited by Elizabeth Oke Gordon. Cambridge: Cambridge University Press, 2010.
Gould, Deborah. *Moving Politics: Emotion and ACT UP's Fight against AIDS*. Chicago: University of Chicago Press, 2009.
Gould, Stephen Jay. "Darwinian Fundamentalism." *New York Review of Books*, June 12, 1997, 34–38.
Gould, Stephen Jay. *The Mismeasure of Man*. Rev. and expanded ed. New York: W. W. Norton, 1996.
Gould, Stephen Jay. *The Panda's Thumb: More Reflections in Natural History*. New York: W. W. Norton, 1980.
Gould, Stephen Jay. *Rocks of Ages: Science and Religion in the Fullness of Life*. New York: Ballantine, 1999.
Gould, Stephen Jay, and Richard C. Lewontin. "The Spandrels of San Marco and the Panglossian Paradigm: A Critique of the Adaptationist Programme." *Proceedings of the Royal Society of London* B 205 (1979): 581–98.
Gourgouris, Stathis. *Lessons in Secular Criticism*. New York: Fordham University Press, 2013.
Gray, Asa. *Natural Selection Not Inconsistent with Natural Theology*. Cambridge, MA: Welch, Bigelow, 1861.
Gregg, Melissa, and Gregory Seigworth. "An Inventory of Shimmers." In *The Affect Theory Reader*, edited by Melissa Gregg and Gregory Seigworth, 1–28. Durham, NC: Duke University Press, 2010.

Grosz, Elizabeth. *Becoming Undone: Darwinian Reflections on Life, Politics, and Art.* Durham, NC: Duke University Press, 2011.

Grosz, Elizabeth. *Time Travels: Feminism, Nature, Power.* Durham, NC: Duke University Press, 2005.

Grosz, Elizabeth. *Volatile Bodies: Toward a Corporeal Feminism.* Bloomington: Indiana University Press, 1994.

Habermas, Jürgen. "Notes on Post-secular Society." *New Perspectives Quarterly* 25, no. 4 (October 2008): 17–29.

Haggard, E. A., and K. S. Isaacs. "Micro-momentary Facial Expressions as Indicators of Ego Mechanisms in Psychotherapy." In *Methods of Research in Psychotherapy,* edited by L. A. Gottschalk and A. H. Auerbach, 154–65. New York: Appleton-Century-Crofts, 1966.

Haidt, Jonathan. *The Righteous Mind: Why Good People Are Divided by Politics and Religion.* London: Penguin, 2012.

Haidt, Jonathan, and J. Graham. "When Morality Opposes Justice: Conservatives Have Moral Intuitions That Liberals May Not Recognize." *Social Justice Research* 20 (2007): 98–116.

Hamilton, W. D. "The Genetical Evolution of Social Behaviour." *Journal of Theoretical Biology* 7 (1964): 1–16.

Hamner, M. Gail. "Affect Theory as a Tool for Examining Religion Documentaries." In *Feeling Religion,* edited by John Corrigan, 93–117. Durham, NC: Duke University Press, 2018.

Hamner, M. Gail. *American Pragmatism: A Religious Genealogy.* Oxford: Oxford University Press, 2003.

Haraway, Donna J. *Simians, Cyborgs, and Women.* New York: Routledge, 1991.

Harding, Susan. *The Science Question in Feminism.* Ithaca, NY: Cornell University Press, 1986.

Harjo, Laura. *Spiral to the Stars: Mvskoke Tools of Futurity.* Tucson: University of Arizona Press, 2019.

Harney, Stefano, and Fred Moten. *The Undercommons: Fugitive Planning and Black Study.* New York: Autonomedia, 2013.

Harris, Sam. *The End of Faith: Religion, Terror, and the Future of Reason.* New York: W. W. Norton, 2004.

Harris, Sam. *Letter to a Christian Nation.* New York: Knopf, 2006.

Harris, Sam. *The Moral Landscape: How Science Can Determine Human Values.* New York: Free Press, 2010.

Harris, Sam, and Maajid Nawaz. *Islam and the Future of Tolerance: A Dialogue.* Cambridge, MA: Harvard University Press, 2015.

Harrison, Peter. *The Territories of Science and Religion.* Chicago: University of Chicago Press, 2015.

Hedges, Chris. *I Don't Believe in Atheists.* New York: Free Press, 2008.

Heidegger, Martin. *Being and Time.* Translated by John Macquarrie and E. Robinson. Malden, MA: Blackwell, 1962.

Hesketh, Ian. "The First Darwinian: Alfred Russel Wallace and the Meaning of Darwinism." *Journal of Victorian Culture* 20, no. 20 (2019): 1–15.

Hesketh, Ian. *Of Apes and Ancestors: Evolution, Christianity, and the Oxford Debate*. Toronto: University of Toronto Press, 2009.

Hirschkind, Charles. "Is There a Secular Body?" *Cultural Anthropology* 26, no. 4 (2011): 633–47.

Hitchens, Christopher. *God Is Not Great: How Religion Poisons Everything*. New York: Twelve/Hachette Book Group, 2007.

Hitchens, Christopher. "Images in a Rearview Mirror." *Nation*, November 15, 2001. https://www.thenation.com/article/images-rearview-mirror/.

Hitchens, Christopher. "A Smart Set of One." *New York Times*, November 17, 2002.

Hodge, M. J. S. "Darwin as a Lifelong Generation Theorist." In *The Darwinian Heritage*, edited by David Kohn, 207–43. Princeton, NJ: Princeton University Press, 1985.

Hofstadter, Richard. "The Paranoid Style in American Politics." *Harper's Magazine*, November 1964, 77–86.

Holden, Constance. "Paul MacLean and the Triune Brain." *Science* 204, no. 4397 (June 8, 1979): 1066–68.

Holland, Sharon Patricia. *The Erotic Life of Racism*. Durham, NC: Duke University Press, 2012.

Hollywood, Amy. *Acute Melancholia and Other Essays: Mysticism, History, and the Study of Religion*. New York: Columbia University Press, 2016.

hooks, bell. "Theory as Liberatory Practice." *Yale Journal of Law and Feminism* 4, no. 1 (1991): 1–12.

Horberg, Elizabeth, Christopher Oveis, and Dacher Keltner. "Emotions as Moral Amplifiers: An Appraisal Tendency Approach to the Influences of Distinct Emotions upon Moral Judgment." *Emotion Review* 3, no. 3 (2011): 237–44.

Hughey, Matthew W. "Show Me Your Papers! Obama's Birth and the Whiteness of Belonging." *Qualitative Sociology* 35 (2012): 163–81.

Hull, David L. "Darwin's Science and Victorian Philosophy of Science." In *The Cambridge Companion to Darwin*, 2nd ed., edited by Jonathan Hodge and Gregory Radick, 173–96. Cambridge: Cambridge University Press, 2009.

Hume, David. *An Enquiry concerning Human Understanding*. Edited by P. Milligan. Oxford: Oxford University Press, 2007.

Hume, David. *The Natural History of Religion and Dialogues concerning Natural Religion*. Edited by A. Wayne Colver and John Valdimir Price. Oxford: Oxford University Press, 2014.

Hume, David. *A Treatise of Human Nature*. Edited by L. A. Selby-Bigge. Oxford: Oxford University Press, 1960.

Huntley, William. "David Hume and Charles Darwin." *Journal of the History of Ideas* 33, no. 3 (1972): 457–70.

Hutchinson, Sikivu. "#AtheismSoWhite: Atheists of Color Rock Social Justice." *Huffington Post*, January 26, 2016. https://www.huffpost.com/entry/atheismsowhite-atheists-o_b_9078736.

Hutchinson, Sikivu. *Godless Americana: Race and Religious Rebels*. Los Angeles: Infidel, 2013.

Hutchinson, Sikivu. *Moral Combat: Black Atheists, Gender Politics, and the Values Wars*. Los Angeles: Infidel, 2011.

Huxley, Leonard, ed. *The Life and Letters of Thomas Henry Huxley*. Vol. 1. London: Macmillan, 1900.

Huxley, Thomas Henry. *Essays upon Some Controverted Questions*. London: Macmillan, 1892.

Huxley, Thomas Henry. "On the Reception of the 'Origin of Species.'" In *The Life and Letters of Charles Darwin*, vol. 2, edited by Francis Darwin, 179–204. New York: D. Appleton and Co., 1897.

Huxley, Thomas Henry. "The Origin of Species." In *Collected Essays*, vol. 2, 23–80. London: Macmillan, 1896.

The Huxley Papers. Preserved in the Imperial College of Science and Technology, London, by Warren R. Dawson. The Huxley File. Edited by Charles Blinderman and David Joyce. https://mathcs.clarku.edu/huxley/letters/60.html.

Iliffe, Robert. *Newton: A Very Short Introduction*. Oxford: Oxford University Press, 2006.

Immordino-Yang, Mary Helen. *Emotions, Learning, and the Brain: Exploring the Educational Implications of Affective Neuroscience*. New York: W. W. Norton, 2016.

Innes, John Brodie. "Recollections of Charles Darwin." Darwin Online, n.d. http://darwin-online.org.uk/content/frameset?pageseq=1&itemID=CUL-DAR112.B85-B92&viewtype=side. Accessed March 24, 2021.

Ioanide, Paula. *The Emotional Politics of Racism: How Feelings Trump Facts in an Era of Colorblindness*. Stanford, CA: Stanford University Press, 2015.

Israel, Charles A. *Before Scopes: Evangelicalism, Education, and Evolution in Tennessee 1870–1925*. Athens: University of Georgia Press, 2004.

Jackson, Thomas Graham. *The Church of St. Mary the Virgin, Oxford*. Oxford: Clarendon, 1897.

Jacobs, Struan. "Polanyi and Kuhn: Priority and Credit." *Tradition and Discovery* 33, no. 2 (2006): 25–36.

Jacoby, Larry, and Kevin Whitehouse. "An Illusion of Memory: False Recognition Influenced by Unconscious Perception." *Journal of Experimental Psychology: General* 118, no. 2 (1989): 126–35.

Jaggar, Alison M. "Love and Knowledge: Emotion in Feminist Epistemology." In *Gender/Body/Knowledge: Feminist Reconstructions of Being and Knowing*, edited by Alison M. Jaggar and Susan R. Bordo, 145–71. New Brunswick, NJ: Rutgers University Press, 1989.

Jakobsen, Janet R., and Ann Pellegrini. "Introduction: Times like These." In Jakobsen and Pellegrini, *Secularisms*, 1–35.

Jakobsen, Janet R., and Ann Pellegrini, eds. *Secularisms*. Durham, NC: Duke University Press, 2008.

James, William. *Pragmatism: A New Name for Some Old Ways of Thinking*. Edited by Bruce Kuklick. Indianapolis: Hackett, 1981.

James, William. *The Principles of Psychology*. Cambridge, MA: Harvard University Press, 1983.
James, William. *The Varieties of Religious Experience: A Study in Human Nature*. New York: Collier, 1961.
James, William. "What Is an Emotion?" *Mind* 9, no. 34 (1884): 188–205.
James, William. *The Will to Believe and Other Essays in Popular Philosophy*. New York, London: Longmans Green, 1907.
Jammer, Max. *Einstein and Religion*. Princeton, NJ: Princeton University Press, 1999.
Jensen, J. Vernon. "Return to the Huxley-Wilberforce Debate." *British Journal for the History of Science* 21, no. 2 (1988): 161–79.
Johansen, Birgitte Schepelern. "Secular Excitement and Academic Practice." In *Affect and Emotion in Multi-Religious Secular Societies*, edited by Christian von Scheve, Anna Lea Berg, Meike Haken, and Nur Yasemin Ural, 194–210. London: Routledge, 2020.
Jordan-Young, Rebecca, and Katrina Karzakis. *Testosterone: An Unauthorized Biography*. Cambridge, MA: Harvard University Press, 2019.
Josephson-Storm, Jason Ā. *The Myth of Disenchantment: Magic, Modernity, and the Birth of the Human Sciences*. Chicago: University of Chicago Press, 2017.
Kahn, Jonathon S., and Vincent W. Lloyd, eds. *Race and Secularism in America*. New York: Columbia University Press, 2016.
Kant, Immanuel. *Critique of Pure Reason*. Translated and edited by Mary Gregor. Cambridge: Cambridge University Press, 2015.
Kazin, Michael. *A Godly Hero: The Life of William Jennings Bryan*. New York: Knopf, 2006.
Keel, Terence. *Divine Variations: How Christian Thought Became Racial Science*. Stanford, CA: Stanford University Press, 2018.
Keeley, Brian L. "Of Conspiracy Theories." *Journal of Philosophy* 96, no. 3 (1999): 109–26.
Keller, Evelyn Fox. *A Feeling for the Organism: The Life and Work of Barbara McClintock*. 10th anniv. ed. New York: Owl, 1993.
Keller, Evelyn Fox. "Language and Ideology in Evolutionary Theory: Reading Cultural Norms into Natural Law." In *The Boundaries of Humanity: Humans, Animals, Machines*, edited by James J. Sheehan and Morton Sosna, 85–102. Berkeley: University of California Press, 1991.
Khalil, Mohammad Hassan. *Jihad, Radicalism, and the New Atheism*. Cambridge: Cambridge University Press, 2018.
Khawaja, Noreen. *The Religion of Existence: Asceticism in Philosophy from Kierkegaard to Sartre*. Chicago: University of Chicago Press, 2016.
Kimball, Whitney. "About the Wayfair Child Trafficking Conspiracy." *Gizmodo*, July 10, 2020. https://gizmodo.com/about-the-wayfair-child-trafficking-conspiracy-1844342713.
Kimmerer, Robin Wall. *Braiding Sweetgrass: Indigenous Wisdom, Scientific Knowledge, and the Teachings of Plants*. Minneapolis: Milkweed, 2013.
Kitcher, Philip. *Vaulting Ambition: Sociobiology and the Quest for Human Nature*. Cambridge, MA: MIT Press, 1985.

Knapton, Sarah. "Richard Dawkins: Religious Education Is Crucial for British Schoolchildren." *Telegraph*, June 11, 2017. https://www.telegraph.co.uk/science/2017/06/11/richard-dawkins-religious-education-crucial-british-schoolchildren/.

Knoxville Journal. "Test Evolution Law Is Brewing." May 3, 1925.

Kochan, Jeff. *Science as Social Existence: Heidegger and the Sociology of Scientific Knowledge*. Cambridge: Open Book, 2017.

Kubrick, Stanley, dir. *2001: A Space Odyssey*. Beverly Hills, CA: Metro-Goldwyn-Mayer. 1968.

Kuhn, Thomas. *The Structure of Scientific Revolutions*. 3rd ed. Chicago: University of Chicago Press, 1996.

Kundnani, Arun. *The Muslims Are Coming! Islamophobia, Extremism, and the Domestic War on Terror*. London: Verso, 2014.

Laats, Adam. *Fundamentalism and Education in the Scopes Era: God, Darwin, and the Roots of America's Culture Wars*. New York: Palgrave Macmillan, 2010.

Ladd, Sandra, and John Gabrieli. "Trait and State Anxiety Reduce the Mere Exposure Effect." *Frontiers in Psychology* 6 (2015): 1–9.

LaMothe, Kimerer. "What Bodies Know about Religion and the Study of It." *Journal of the American Academy of Religion* 76, no. 3 (2008): 573–601.

Langlois, J. H., L. A. Roggman, and L. Musselman. "What Is Average and What Is Not Average about Attractive Faces?" *Psychological Science* 5 (1994): 214–20.

Larson, Edward J. *Sex, Race, and Science: Eugenics in the Deep South*. Baltimore: Johns Hopkins University Press, 1996.

Larson, Edward J. *Summer for the Gods: The Scopes Trial and America's Continuing Debate over Science and Religion*. New York: Basic Books, 2006.

Latour, Bruno. *Down to Earth: Politics in the New Climatic Regime*. Translated by Catherine Porter. Cambridge: Polity, 2018.

Latour, Bruno. *On the Modern Cult of the Factish Gods*. Durham, NC: Duke University Press, 2010.

Latour, Bruno. *Pandora's Hope: Essays on the Reality of Science Studies*. Cambridge, MA: Harvard University Press, 1999.

Latour, Bruno. "Why Has Critique Run Out of Steam? From Matters of Fact to Matters of Concern." *Critical Inquiry* 30, no. 2 (2004): 225–48.

Latour, Bruno, and Steve Woolgar. *Laboratory Life: The Construction of Scientific Facts*. 2nd ed. Princeton, NJ: Princeton University Press, 1986.

Lazarus, Richard. "Thoughts on the Relations between Emotion and Cognition." *American Psychologist* 37, no. 9 (1982): 1019–24.

Lebrecht, Sophie, Lara Pierce, Michael Tarr, and James Tanaka. "Perceptual Other-Race Training Reduces Implicit Racial Bias." *PLoS ONE* 4, no. 1 (2009): e4215.

LeDoux, Joseph. "Coming to Terms with Fear." *PNAS* 111, no. 8 (February 25, 2014): 2871–78.

LeDoux, Joseph. *The Emotional Brain: The Mysterious Underpinnings of Emotional Life*. New York: Simon and Schuster, 1996.

Lee, Lois. "Observing the Atheist at Worship: Ways of Seeing the Secular Body." In Scheer et al., *Secular Bodies, Affects and Emotions: European Configurations*, 43–60.

Lee, Lois. *Recognizing the Non-religious: Reimagining the Secular*. Oxford: Oxford University Press, 2015.

Lemm, Vanessa. *Nietzsche's Animal Philosophy: Culture, Politics, and the Animality of the Human Being*. New York: Fordham University Press, 2009.

Lepselter, Susan. *The Resonance of Unseen Things: Poetics, Power, Captivity, and UFOs in the American Uncanny*. Ann Arbor: University of Michigan Press, 2016.

Levine, George. *Darwin Loves You: Natural Selection and the Reenchantment of the World*. Princeton, NJ: Princeton University Press, 2006.

Levine, George. Introduction. In Levine, *Joy of Secularism*, 1–23.

Levine, George, ed. *Joy of Secularism: 11 Essays for How We Live Now*. Princeton, NJ: Princeton University Press, 2011.

Levinson, Marjorie. "What Is New Formalism?" *PMLA* 122, no. 2 (2007): 558–69.

Lewandowsky, Stephan, and John Cook. *The Conspiracy Theory Handbook*. Fairfax, VA: Center for Climate Change Communication, 2020. http://sks.to/conspiracy.

Leys, Ruth. *The Ascent of Affect: Genealogy and Critique*. Chicago: University of Chicago Press, 2017.

Leys, Ruth. "The Turn to Affect: A Critique." *Critical Inquiry* 37, no. 3 (2011): 434–72.

Lightman, Bernard. *The Origins of Agnosticism: Victorian Unbelief and the Limits of Knowledge*. Baltimore: Johns Hopkins University Press, 1987.

Lightman, Bernard. "Unbelief." In *Science and Religion around the World*, edited by John Hedley Brooke and Ronald L. Numbers, 252–77. Oxford: Oxford University Press, 2011.

Livingston, James. *Religious Thought in the Victorian Age: Challenges and Reconceptions*. New York: Continuum, 2007.

Lloyd, Vincent W. "Introduction: Managing Race, Managing Religion." In Kahn and Lloyd, *Race and Secularism in America*, 1–22.

Longino, Helen. *Science as Social Knowledge: Values and Objectivity in Scientific Inquiry*. Princeton, NJ: Princeton University Press, 1990.

Lorde, Audre. *Sister Outsider: Essays and Speeches*. Berkeley: Crossing, 1984.

Love, Heather. *Feeling Backward: Loss and the Politics of Queer History*. Cambridge, MA: Harvard University Press, 2007.

Luehrmann, Sonja. *Secularism Soviet Style: Teaching Atheism and Religion in a Volga Republic*. Bloomington: University of Indiana Press, 2011.

Lyell, Charles. *Principles of Geology*. Edited by James Secord. New York: Penguin, 1997.

MacLean, Paul. "Putting On Our Thinking Caps." *New York Times*, January 1, 1971.

MacLean, Paul. *The Triune Brain in Evolution: Role in Paleocerebral Functions*. New York: Plenum, 1990.

Mahdawi, Arwa. "The Most Unhinged Trump Conspiracy Theory Comes from—Who Else?—QAnon Followers." *Guardian*, October 3, 2020. https://www

.theguardian.com/commentisfree/2020/oct/03/trump-coronavirus-conspiracy-theory-qanon.

Mahmood, Saba. *Religious Difference in a Secular Age: A Minority Report*. Princeton, NJ: Princeton University Press, 2016.

Mahmood, Saba. "Religious Reason and Secular Affect: An Incommensurable Divide?" *Critical Inquiry* 35 (Summer 2009): 836–62.

Maia, Tiago V., and James L. McClelland. "A Reexamination of the Evidence for the Somatic Marker Hypothesis: What Participants Really Know in the Iowa Gambling Task." *PNAS* 101, no. 45 (2004): 16075–80.

Maiese, Michelle. *Embodied Selves and Divided Minds*. Oxford: Oxford University Press, 2016.

Manning, Erin. *Always More Than One: Individuation's Dance*. Durham, NC: Duke University Press, 2013.

Manning, Erin, and Brian Massumi. *Thought in the Act: Passages in the Ecology of Experience*. Minneapolis: University of Minnesota Press, 2014.

Marsden, George. *Fundamentalism and American Culture: The Shaping of Twentieth-Century Evangelicalism, 1870–1925*. New York: Oxford University Press, 1982.

Marshall, Ashley. "Erasmus Darwin *contra* David Hume." *Journal for Eighteenth-Century Studies* 30, no. 1 (2007): 89–111.

Marx, Karl. *Critique of Hegel's "Philosophy of Right."* Edited and translated by Joseph O'Malley. Cambridge: Cambridge University Press, 1977.

Marx, Karl. *The Marx-Engels Reader*. 2nd ed., edited by Robert C. Tucker. London: W. W. Norton, 1978.

Massumi, Brian. *Parables for the Virtual: Movement, Affect, Sensation*. Durham, NC: Duke University Press, 2002.

Mazzarella, William. "Mind the Gap! or, What Does Secularism Feel Like?" In *The Sahmat Collective: Art and Activism in India since 1989*, edited by Jessica Moss and Ram Rahman, 258–65. Chicago: Smart Museum of Art, 2013.

Mbembe, Achille. *Out of the Dark Night: Essays on Decolonization*. New York: Columbia University Press, 2021.

McCloud, Sean. *Divine Hierarchies: Class in American Religion and Religious Studies*. Chapel Hill: University of North Carolina Press, 2007.

McGrath, Alister. *The Twilight of Atheism: The Rise and Fall of Disbelief in the Modern World*. New York: Doubleday, 2004.

McKittrick, Katherine. *Dear Science and Other Stories*. Durham, NC: Duke University Press, 2021.

McLean v. Arkansas Documentation Project. "Testimony of Ronald W. Coward, Biology/Psychology Teacher, Pulaski Co. Special School District (Plaintiffs Witness)—Transcript Paragraph Formatted Version." http://www.antievolution.org/projects/mclean/new_site/pf_trans/mva_tt_p_coward.html.

Mencken, H. L. *H. L. Mencken on Religion*. Edited by S. T. Joshi. Amherst, MA: Prometheus Books, 2002.

Mencken, H. L. "The Sahara of the Bozart." In *The American Scene: A Reader*, edited by Huntington Cairns, 157–68. New York: Knopf, 1977.

Mencken, H. L. *Treatise on the Gods.* New York: Knopf, 1930.
Midgley, Mary. *The Ethical Primate: Humans, Freedom, Morality.* London: Routledge, 1994.
Milbank, John. *Theology and Social Theory: Beyond Secular Reason.* 2nd ed. Malden, MA: Blackwell, 2006.
Miller, George A. "The Cognitive Revolution: A Historical Perspective." *Trends in Cognitive Science* 7, no. 3 (2003): 141–44.
Modern, John Lardas. *Secularism in Antebellum America.* Chicago: University of Chicago Press, 2011.
Moleski, Martin. "Polanyi vs. Kuhn: Worldviews Apart." *Tradition and Discovery: The Polanyi Society Periodical* 33, no. 2 (2006): 8–24.
Monin, Benoît. "The Warm Glow Heuristic: When Liking Leads to Familiarity." *Journal of Personality and Social Psychology* 85, no. 6 (2003): 1035–48.
Moore, Gregory. *Nietzsche, Biology, and Metaphor.* Cambridge: Cambridge University Press, 2002.
Moore, James. "Deconstructing Darwinism: The Politics of Evolution in the 1860s." *Journal of the History of Biology* 24, no. 3 (1991): 353–408.
Moran, Jeffrey. "Reading Race into the Scopes Trial: African American Elites, Science, and Fundamentalism." *Journal of American History* 70, no. 1 (2004): 891–911.
Moran, Jeffrey. *The Scopes Trial: A Brief History with Documents.* Boston: Bedford/St. Martin's, 2002.
Moran, Jeffrey. "The Scopes Trial and Southern Fundamentalism in Black and White: Race, Region, and Religion." *Journal of Southern History* 70 (2004): 95–120.
Muñoz, José Esteban. "Feeling Brown: Ethnicity and Affect in Ricardo Bracho's 'The Sweetest Hangover (and Other STDs).'" *Theatre Journal* 52, no. 1 (March 2000): 67–79.
Muñoz, José Esteban. "Feeling Brown, Feeling Down: Latina Affect, the Performativity of Race, and the Depressive Position." *Signs* 31, no. 3 (2006): 675–88.
Muñoz, José Esteban. *The Sense of Brown.* Edited by Joshua Chambers-Letson and Tavia Nyong'o. Durham, NC: Duke University Press, 2020.
Nanda, Meera. "Trading Faith for Spirituality: The Mystifications of Sam Harris." Butterflies and Wheels, December 9, 2015. http://www.butterfliesandwheels.org/2005/trading-faith-for-spirituality-the-mystifications-of-sam-harris/.
Nathanson, Donald L. "Prologue: Affect Imagery Consciousness." In *Affect Imagery Consciousness: The Complete Edition*, edited by Silvan S. Tomkins and Bertram P. Karon, xi–xxvi. New York: Springer, 2008.
Newman, John. "The Architectural Setting." In *The History of the University of Oxford*, vol. 4: *Seventeenth-Century Oxford*, edited by Nicholas Tyacke, 135–78. Oxford: Oxford University Press, 1997.
New York Times. "A Bleak Outlook Is Seen for Religion." February 25, 1968.
Ngai, Sianne. *Our Aesthetic Categories: Zany, Cute, Interesting.* Cambridge, MA: Harvard University Press, 2012.

Nietzsche, Friedrich. *Beyond Good and Evil*. Edited by Rolf-Peter Horstmann and Judith Norman, translated by Judith Norman. Cambridge: Cambridge University Press, 2002.

Nietzsche, Friedrich. *The Birth of Tragedy*. Translated by Ronald Speirs. Cambridge: Cambridge University Press, 1999.

Nietzsche, Friedrich. *The Collected Works of Friedrich Nietzsche*, vol. 10, *The Joyful Wisdom*. Edited by Oscar Levy, translated by Thomas Common. Edinburgh: T. N. Foulis, 1910.

Nietzsche, Friedrich. *On the Genealogy of Morality*. Edited by Keith Ansell-Pearson, translated by Carol Diethe. Cambridge: Cambridge University Press, 2006.

Nietzsche, Friedrich. *Thus Spoke Zarathustra*. Translated by Graham Parkes. New York: Oxford University Press, 2005.

Nietzsche, Friedrich. *Untimely Meditations*. Edited by Daniel Breazeale, translated by R. J. Hollingdale. Cambridge: Cambridge University Press, 1997.

Nordern, Eric. "*Playboy* Interview: Stanley Kubrick." In *Stanley Kubrick: Interviews*, edited by Gene D. Phillips, 47–74. Jackson: University Press of Mississippi, 2001.

Numbers, Ronald L. *The Creationists*. Berkeley: University of California Press, 1992.

Numbers, Ronald L. "Darwinism, Creationism, and 'Intelligent Design.'" In *Scientists Confront Creationism: Intelligent Design and Beyond*, edited by Andrew J. Petto and Laurie R. Godfrey, 31–58. New York: W. W. Norton, 2008.

Nussbaum, Martha. *Political Emotions: Why Love Matters for Justice*. Cambridge, MA: Belknap Press of Harvard University Press, 2013.

Nussbaum, Martha. *Upheavals of Thought: The Intelligence of Emotions*. Cambridge: Cambridge University Press, 2001.

O'Donnell, S. Jonathon. "Islamophobic Conspiracism and Neoliberal Subjectivity: The Inassimilable Society." *Patterns of Prejudice* (2017): 1–23.

Ogden, Emily. *Credulity: A Cultural History of US Mesmerism*. Chicago: University of Chicago Press, 2018.

O'Malley, Michael. "Feeling without Thinking? Reply to Zajonc." *Journal of Psychology* 108, no. 1 (1981): 11–15.

Oreskes, Naomi. *Why Trust Science?* Princeton, NJ: Princeton University Press, 2019.

Oreskes, Naomi, and Erik M. Conway. *Merchants of Doubt: How a Handful of Scientists Obscured the Truth on Issues from Tobacco Smoke to Global Warming*. New York: Bloomsbury, 2010.

Otto, Rudolf. *The Idea of the Holy: An Inquiry into the Non-rational Factor in the Idea of the Divine and Its Relation to the Rational*. Translated by John Harvey. New York: Pelican, 1959.

Oxford University Statutes, vol. 1, *Containing the Caroline Code, or Laudian Statutes, Promulgated A.D. 1636*. Translated by G. R. M. Ward. London: William Pickering, 1845.

Paley, William. *Natural Theology: or, Evidences of the Existence and Attributes of the Deity Collected from the Appearances of Nature*. New York: Sheldon, 1879.

Panksepp, Jaak. *Affective Neuroscience: The Foundations of Human and Animal Emotions*. Oxford: Oxford University Press, 1998.

Panksepp, Jaak. "Cognitive Conceptualism: Where Have All the Affects Gone? Additional Corrections for Barrett et al. (2007)." *Perspectives on Psychological Science* 3, no. 4 (2008): 305–8.

Panksepp, Jaak. "Neurologizing the Psychology of Affects: How Appraisal-Based Constructivism and Basic Emotion Theory Can Coexist." *Perspectives on Psychological Science* 2 (2007): 281–96.

Pascal, Blaise. *Thoughts and Minor Works*. Translated by W. F. Trotter, M. L. Booth, and O. W. Wight. New York: P. F. Collier and Son, 1910.

Paxton, Joseph M., and Joshua D. Greene. "Moral Reasoning: Hints and Allegations." *Topics in Cognitive Science* 2 (2010): 511–27.

Pedwell, Carolyn. "Cultural Theory as Mood Work." *New Formations* 82 (2014): 47–63.

Peirce, Charles. "The Fixation of Belief." In *The Essential Peirce: Selected Philosophical Writings, Vol. 1 (1867–1893)*, edited by Nathan Houser and Christian Kloesel, 109–23. Bloomington: Indiana University Press, 1992.

Pelkmans, Mathijs. *Fragile Conviction: Changing Ideological Landscapes in Urban Kyrgyzstan*. Ithaca, NY: Cornell University Press, 2017.

Pelkmans, Mathijs, and Rhys Machold. "Conspiracy Theories and Their Truth Trajectories." *Journal of Global and Historical Anthropology* 59 (2011): 66–80.

Pellegrini, Ann. "Feeling Secular." *Women and Performance: A Journal of Feminist Theory* 19, no. 2 (2009): 205–18.

Pellegrini, Ann. "'Signaling through the Flames': Hell House Performance and Structures of Religious Feeling." *American Quarterly* 59, no. 3 (2007): 911–35.

Pellegrini, Ann, and Jasbir Puar. "Affect." *Social Text* 27, no. 3 (2009): 35–38.

Perry, Imani. *More Beautiful and More Terrible: The Embrace and Transcendence of Racial Inequality in the United States*. New York: New York University Press, 2011.

Persaud, Navindra, Peter McLeod, and Alan Cowey. "Post-decision Wagering Objectively Measures Awareness." *Nature Neuroscience* 10, no. 2 (February 2007): 257–61.

Pessoa, Luiz. "On the Relationship between Emotion and Cognition." *Nature Reviews Neuroscience* 9 (February 2008): 148–58.

Pew Research Center. "Public's Views on Human Evolution." Pewforum.org, December 30, 2013. https://www.pewforum.org/2013/12/30/publics-views-on-human-evolution/.

Phaf, R. Hans, and Mark Rotteveel. "Affective Modulation of Recognition Bias." *Emotion* 5, no. 3 (2005): 309–18.

Phelps, Elizabeth A. "Emotion and Cognition: Insights from Studies of the Human Amygdala." *Annual Review of Psychology* 57 (2006): 27–53.

Pigliucci, Massimo. "Introduction: The Problems with Creationism." In *Scientists Confront Creationism: Intelligent Design and Beyond*, edited by Andrew J. Petto and Laurie R. Godfrey, 16–24. New York: W. W. Norton, 2008.

Pigliucci, Massimo. "New Atheism and the Scientistic Turn in the Atheism Movement." *Midwest Studies in Philosophy* 37 (2013): 142–53.

Pinn, Anthony B. *By These Hands: A Documentary History of African American Humanism*. New York: New York University Press, 2002.

Pinn, Anthony B. *The End of God-Talk: An African American Humanist Theology*. Oxford: Oxford University Press, 2012.

Pinn, Anthony B. *When Colorblindness Isn't the Answer: Humanism and the Challenge of Race*. Durham, NC: Pitchstone, 2017.

Plamper, Jan. *The History of Emotions: An Introduction*. Translated by Keith Tribe. Oxford: Oxford University Press, 2015.

Pogliano, Claudio. "Lucky Triune Brain: Chronicles of Paul D. MacLean's Neuro-Catchword." *Nuncius* 32 (2017): 330–75.

Poirier, Maben Walter. "A Comment on Polanyi and Kuhn." *Thomist: A Speculative Quarterly Review* 53, no. 2 (1989): 259–79.

Polanyi, Michael. *Personal Knowledge: Towards a Post-critical Philosophy*. London: Routledge, 1962.

Pope, Whitney, Jere Cohen, and Lawrence Hazelrigg. "On the Divergence of Weber and Durkheim: A Critique of Parsons' Convergence Thesis." *American Sociological Review* 40, no. 4 (1975): 417–27.

Popper, Karl. *The Logic of Scientific Discovery*. New York: Routledge, 2002.

Prakash, Gyan. *Another Reason: Science and the Imagination of Modern India*. Princeton, NJ: Princeton University Press, 1999.

Prescod-Weinstein, Chanda. *The Disordered Cosmos: A Journey into Dark Matter, Spacetime, and Dreams Deferred*. New York: Bold Type, 2021.

Protevi, John. "Adding Deleuze to the Mix." *Phenomenology and the Cognitive Sciences* 9 (2010): 417–36.

Puar, Jasbir. *Terrorist Assemblages: Homonationalism in Queer Times*. Durham, NC: Duke University Press, 2007.

Qian, Miao, Paul Quinn, Gail Heyman, Olivier Pascalis, Genyue Fu, and Kang Lee. "Perceptual Individuation Training (but Not Mere Exposure) Reduces Implicit Racial Bias in Preschool Children." *Developmental Psychology* 53, no. 5 (2017): 845–59.

Quashie, Kevin. *Black Aliveness, or a Poetics of Being*. Durham, NC: Duke University Press, 2021.

Rabinow, Paul. *Essays on the Anthropology of Reason*. Princeton, NJ: Princeton University Press, 1996.

Ramirez, Martin, and Michel Cabanac. "Pleasure, the Common Currency of Emotions." In *Emotions Inside Out: 130 Years after Darwin's "The Expression of the Emotions in Man and Animals,"* edited by Paul Ekman, Joseph J. Campos, Richard J. Davidson, and Frans B. M. de Waal, 293–95. New York: New York Academy of Sciences, 2003.

Ranganathan, Siyali Ramamrita. *Ramanujan: The Man and the Mathematician*. Bombay: Asia Publishing House, 1967.

Reber, Rolf, Piotr Winkielman, and Norbert Schwarz. "Effects of Perceptual Fluency on Affective Judgments." *Psychological Science* 9, no. 1 (1998): 45–48.

Reddy, William M. *The Navigation of Feeling: A Framework for the History of Emotions*. Cambridge: Cambridge University Press, 2004.

"Register of Convocation 1659–1671 NEP/*supra*/27, register Ta." Translated by Scheherazade Khan. Oxford University Archives. Bodleian Libraries, University of Oxford.

Rice, Jenny. *Awful Archives: Conspiracy Theory, Rhetoric, and Acts of Evidence*. Columbus: Ohio State University Press, 2020.

Richards, Evelleen. *Darwin and the Making of Sexual Selection*. Chicago: University of Chicago Press, 2017.

Richards, Robert. "Darwinian Enchantment." In Levine, *Joy of Secularism*, 185–204.

Ricoeur, Paul. *Freud and Philosophy: An Essay on Interpretation*. New Haven, CT: Yale University Press, 1977.

Riskin, Jessica. "Evolution: The Science Napoleon Hated." *Republics of Letters* 6, no. 1 (2018): 1–10.

Riskin, Jessica. *Science in the Age of Sensibility: The Sentimental Empiricists of the French Enlightenment*. Chicago: University of Chicago Press, 2002.

Robbins, Bruce. "Enchantment? No, Thank You!" In Levine, *Joy of Secularism*, 74–94.

Robbins, Martin. "Richard Dawkins, 'Islamophobia,' and the Atheist Movement." *Guardian*, May 3, 2013. https://www.theguardian.com/science/the-lay-scientist/2013/may/03/atheism-dawkins.

Robinson, Shantá R. "A Crusader and an Advocate: The Black Press, the Scopes Trial, and Educational Progress." *Journal of Negro Education* 87, no. 1 (2018): 5–21.

Rodgers, Marion Elizabeth. *Mencken: The American Iconoclast*. Oxford: Oxford University Press, 2005.

Rose, Steven. *Lifelines: Biology beyond Determinism*. New York: Oxford University Press, 1998.

Rosfort, René, and Giovanni Stanghellini. "In the Mood for Thought: Feeling and Thinking in Philosophy." *New Literary History* 43, no. 3 (2012): 395–417.

Rotteveel, Mark, and R. Hans Phaf. "Mere Exposure in Reverse: Mood and Motion Modulate Memory Bias." *Cognition and Emotion* 21, no. 6 (2007): 1323–46.

Rubenstein, Mary-Jane. *Strange Wonder: The Closure of Metaphysics and the Opening of Awe*. New York: Columbia University Press, 2009.

Ruse, Michael. "The Origin of the Origin." In *The Cambridge Companion to the "Origin of Species,"* edited by Michael Ruse and Robert J. Richards, 1–13. Cambridge: Cambridge University Press, 2008.

Rusert, Britt. *Fugitive Science: Empiricism and Freedom in Early African American Culture*. New York: New York University Press, 2017.

Ryrie, Alec. *Unbelievers: An Emotional History of Doubt*. Cambridge, MA: Harvard University Press, 2019.

Sadalla, E. K., and S. Loftness. "Emotional Images as Mediators, in One-Trial Paired-Associates Learning." *Journal of Experimental Psychology* 95 (1972): 295–98.

Safi, Omid. "After the UNC Chapel Hill Shootings, We Hope for Justice. And Love." *Guardian*, February 13, 2015. https://www.theguardian.com/commentisfree/2015/feb/13/unc-chapel-hill-hope-justice-love.

Schaefer, Donovan O. "Blessed, Precious Mistakes: Evolution, Deconstruction, and the American New Atheism." *International Journal for Philosophy of Religion* 76 (2014): 75–94.

Schaefer, Donovan O. "Darwin's Orchids: Evolution, Natural Law, and the Diversity of Desire." *GLQ: A Journal of Lesbian and Gay Studies* 27, no. 4 (2021): 525–50.

Schaefer, Donovan O. "Embodied Disbelief: Poststructural Feminist Atheism." *Hypatia* 29, no. 2 (2014): 371–87.

Schaefer, Donovan O. *The Evolution of Affect Theory: The Humanities, the Sciences, and the Study of Power*. Cambridge: Cambridge University Press, 2019.

Schaefer, Donovan O. *Religious Affects: Animality, Evolution, and Power*. Durham, NC: Duke University Press, 2015.

Schaefer, Donovan O. "Whiteness and Civilization: Shame, Race, and the Rhetoric of Donald Trump." *Journal of Communication and Critical/Cultural Studies* 17, no. 1 (2020): 1–18.

Scheer, Monique. "Are Emotions a Kind of Practice (And Is That What Makes Them Have a History)? A Bourdieuian Approach to Understanding Emotion." *History and Theory* 51 (May 2012): 193–220.

Scheer, Monique, Nadia Fadil, and Birgitte Schepelern Johansen, eds. *Secular Bodies, Affects, and Emotions: European Configurations*. London: Bloomsbury Academic, 2019.

Scheer, Monique, Birgitte Schepelern Johansen, and Nadia Fadil. "Secular Embodiments: Mapping an Emergent Field." In Scheer et al., *Secular Bodies, Affects, and Emotions: European Configurations*, 1–14.

Scott, Eugenie. "Creation Science Lite: 'Intelligent Design' as the New Antievolutionism." In *Scientists Confront Creationism: Intelligent Design and Beyond*, edited by Andrew J. Petto and Laurie R. Godfrey, 59–109. New York: W. W. Norton, 2008.

Scott, Joan Wallach. *Sex and Secularism*. Princeton, NJ: Princeton University Press, 2018.

Secord, James. *Victorian Sensation: The Extraordinary Publication, Reception, and Secret Authorship of "Vestiges of the Natural History of Creation."* Chicago: University of Chicago Press, 2000.

Sedgwick, Adam, John Willis Clark, and Thomas McKenny Hughes. *Life and Letters of the Reverend Adam Sedgwick*. Vol. 2. Cambridge: Cambridge University Press, 1890.

Sedgwick, Eve Kosofsky. *Tendencies*. Durham, NC: Duke University Press, 1993.

Sedgwick, Eve Kosofsky. *Touching Feeling: Affect, Pedagogy, Performativity*. Durham, NC: Duke University Press, 2003.

Sedgwick, Eve Kosofsky. *The Weather in Proust*. Edited by Jonathan Goldberg. Durham, NC: Duke University Press, 2011.

Shah, Esha. *Who Is the Scientist-Subject? Affective History of the Gene*. New York: Routledge, 2018.

Shapin, Steven, and Christopher Lawrence. "Introduction: The Body of Knowledge." In *Science Incarnate: Historical Embodiments of Natural Knowledge*, edited by

Christopher Lawrence and Steven Shapin, 1–19. Chicago: University of Chicago Press, 1998.

Shapiro, Adam R. "Civic Biology and the Origin of the School Antievolution Movement." *Journal of the History of Biology* 41 (2008): 409–33.

Shapiro, Adam R. *Trying Biology: The Scopes Trial, Textbooks, and the Antievolution Movement in American Schools*. Chicago: University of Chicago Press, 2013.

Shatz, Adam. "The Left and 9/11." *Nation*, September 5, 2002. https://www.thenation.com/article/left-and-911/.

Shaviro, Steven. *Discognition*. London: Repeater, 2015.

Shelley, Percy Bysshe. "The Necessity of Atheism." In *Selected Prose Works of Shelley*, edited by Henry Salt, 1–14. London: Watts and Co., 1915.

Shuger, Deborah. "St. Mary the Virgin and the Birth of the Public Sphere." *Huntington Library Quarterly* 72, no. 3 (2009): 313–46.

Shusterman, Richard. "Thought in the Strenuous Mood: Pragmatism as a Philosophy of Feeling." *New Literary History* 43, no. 3 (2012): 433–54.

Sideris, Lisa H. *Consecrating Science: Wonder, Knowledge, and the Natural World*. Oakland: University of California Press, 2017.

Simonovic, Boban, Edward J. N. Stupple, Maggie Gale, and David Sheffield. "Performance under Stress: An Eye-Tracking Investigation of the Iowa Gambling Task (IGT)." *Frontiers in Behavioral Neuroscience* 12 (2018): 1–10.

Simonovic, Boban, Edward J. N. Stupple, Maggie Gale, and David Sheffield. "Pupil Dilation and Cognitive Reflection as Predictors of Performance on the Iowa Gambling Task." In *Proceedings of the 39th Annual Conference of the Cognitive Science Society*, edited by G. Gunzelmann, A. Howes, T. Tenbrink, and E. J. Davelaar, 3180–85. Cambridge, MA: Cognitive Science Society, 2017.

Singer, Tania, and Olga M. Klimecki. "Empathy and Compassion." *Current Biology* 24, no. 18 (2014): R875–78.

Slaby, Jan. "Steps towards a *Critical Neuroscience*." *Phenomenology and the Cognitive Sciences* 9 (2010): 397–416.

Slater, Nick. "'Smart' People Are Often Dumber Than You Think." CurrentAffairs.org, April 9, 2019. https://www.currentaffairs.org/2019/04/smart-people-are-often-dumber-than-you-think.

Smith, Pamela, Ap Dijksterhuis, and Shelly Chaiken. "Subliminal Exposure to Faces and Racial Attitudes: Exposure to Whites Makes Whites Like Blacks Less." *Journal of Experimental Social Psychology* 44 (2008): 50–64.

Smolkin, Victoria. *A Sacred Space Is Never Empty: A History of Soviet Atheism*. Princeton, NJ: Princeton University Press, 2018.

Sorabji, Richard. *Emotion and Peace of Mind: From Stoic Agitation to Christian Temptation*. Oxford: Oxford University Press, 2003.

Spinoza, Benedict de. *Ethics*. Edited and translated by Edwin Curley. New York: Penguin, 1996.

Sponsel, Alistair. *Darwin's Evolving Identity: Adventure, Ambition, and the Sin of Speculation*. Chicago: University of Chicago Press, 2018.

Stahl, William A. "One-Dimensional Rage: The Social Epistemology of the New Atheism and Fundamentalism." In Amarasingam, *Religion and the New Atheism*, 97–108.

Stedman, Chris. *Faitheist: How an Atheist Found Common Ground with the Religious*. Boston: Beacon, 2012.

Steingroever, Helen, Ruud Wetzels, Annette Horstmann, Jane Neumann, and Eric-Jan Wagenmakers. "Performance of Healthy Participants on the Iowa Gambling Task." *Psychological Assessment* 25 (2013): 180–93.

Stengers, Isabelle. *Cosmopolitics I*. Translated by Robert Bononno. Minneapolis: University of Minnesota Press, 2010.

Stewart, Kathleen. *Ordinary Affects*. Durham, NC: Duke University Press, 2007.

Storbeck, Justin, and Gerald L. Clore. "On the Interdependence of Cognition and Emotion." *Cognition and Emotion* 21, no. 6 (2007): 1212–37.

Stott, Rebecca. "The Wetfooted Understory: Darwinian Immersions." In Levine, *Joy of Secularism*, 205–24.

Strack, F., L. L. Martin, and S. Stepper. "Inhibiting and Facilitating Conditions of the Human Smile: A Nonobtrusive Test of the Facial Feedback Hypothesis." *Journal of Personality and Social Psychology* 54 (1988): 768–77.

Subramaniam, Banu. *Ghost Stories for Darwin: The Science of Variation and the Politics of Diversity*. Urbana: University of Illinois Press, 2014.

Sullivan, Marek. *Secular Assemblages: Affect, Orientalism, and Power*. London: Bloomsbury, 2020.

Sullivan, Winnifred Fallers. *The Impossibility of Religious Freedom*. Princeton, NJ: Princeton University Press, 2005.

Sunstein, Cass, and Adrian Vermeule. "Conspiracy Theories: Causes and Cures." *Journal of Political Philosophy* 17, no. 2 (2009): 202–27.

Svendsen, Lars. "Moods and the Meaning of Philosophy." *New Literary History* 43, no. 3 (2012): 419–31.

Swann, Daniel. *A Qualitative Portrait of Black Atheists: Don't Tell Me You're One of Those!* Lanham, MD: Lexington, 2020.

Taves, Ann, and Courtney Bender. "Introduction: Things of Value." In *What Matters? Ethnographies of Value in a Not-So-Secular Age*, edited by Ann Taves and Courtney Bender, 1–33. New York: Columbia University Press, 2012.

Tayler, Jeffrey. "Religion's New Atheist Scapegoat: Why the Chapel Hill Shootings Weren't about Islamophobia." Salon, March 1, 2015. https://www.salon.com/2015/03/01/religions_new_atheist_scapegoat_why_the_chapel_hill_shootings_werent_about_islamophobia/.

Taylor, Charles. "Reason, Faith, and Meaning." In *Faith, Rationality, and the Passions*, edited by Sarah Coakley, 13–28. Malden, MA: Wiley-Blackwell, 2012.

Taylor, Charles. *A Secular Age*. Cambridge, MA: Belknap Press of Harvard University Press, 2007.

Taylor, Charles. "Western Secularity." In *Rethinking Secularism*, edited by Craig Calhoun, Mark Juergensmeyer, and Jonathan VanAntwerpen, 31–53. New York: Oxford University Press, 2011.

Thagard, Paul. *Hot Thought: Mechanisms and Applications of Emotional Cognition.* Cambridge, MA: MIT Press, 2006.

Thomas, Jolyon Baraka. *Faking Liberties: Religious Freedom in American-Occupied Japan.* Chicago: University of Chicago Press, 2019.

Timmins, Adam. "Why Was Kuhn's *Structure* More Successful Than Polanyi's *Personal Knowledge*?" HOPOS 3 (2013): 306–17.

Tinniswood, Adrian. *His Invention So Fertile: A Life of Christopher Wren.* Oxford: Oxford University Press, 2001.

Titchener, Edward Bradford. *A Text-Book of Psychology.* New York: Macmillan, 1919.

Tomkins, Silvan. "Affect and the Psychology of Knowledge." *Affect, Cognition, and Personality: Empirical Studies* (1965): 72–97.

Tomkins, Silvan. *Affect Imagery Consciousness: The Complete Edition.* New York: Springer, 2008.

Tomkins, Silvan. "Left and Right: A Basic Dimension of Ideology and Personality." In *The Study of Lives: Essays on Personality in Honor of Henry A. Murray*, edited by R. W. White, 389–411. New York: Atherton, 1963.

Tomkins, Silvan. "The Quest for Primary Motives: Biography and Autobiography of an Idea." *Journal of Personality and Social Psychology* 41, no. 2 (1981): 306–29.

Tomkins, Silvan. *Shame and Its Sisters: A Silvan Tomkins Reader.* Edited by Eve Kosofsky Sedgwick and Adam Frank. Durham, NC: Duke University Press, 1995.

van Wyhe, John. "Mind the Gap: Did Darwin Avoid Publishing His Theory for Many Years?" *Notes and Records of the Royal Society of London* 61 (2007): 177–205.

van Wyhe, John. "Why There Was No 'Darwin's Bulldog': Thomas Henry Huxley's Famous Nickname." *Linnean* 35, no. 1 (2019): 26–30.

van Wyhe, John, and Mark Pallen. "The 'Annie Hypothesis': Did the Death of His Daughter Cause Darwin to 'Give up Christianity'?" *Centaurus* 54, no. 2 (2012): 1–19.

Vásquez, Manuel. *More Than Belief: A Materialist Theory of Religion.* New York: Oxford University Press, 2011.

Ward, G. R. M. "Preface by the Translator." In *Oxford University Statutes*, vol. 1, edited and translated by G. R. M. Ward, iii–xxix. London: William Pickering, 1845.

Ward, Graham. *Unbelievable: Why We Believe and Why We Don't.* London: I. B. Tauris, 2014.

Watson, Alexander. "Stabbed at the Front: After 1918 the Myth Was Created That the German Army Only Lost the War Because It Had Been 'Stabbed in the Back' by Defeatists and Revolutionaries on the Home Front." *History Today* 58, no. 11 (2008): 21–27.

Weber, Max. *The Protestant Ethic and the Spirit of Capitalism.* Translated by Talcott Parsons. New York: Scribner, 1958.

Weber, Max. "Science as a Vocation." In *From Max Weber: Essays in Sociology*, edited by H. H. Gerth and C. Wright Mills, 129–56. New York: Oxford University Press.

Weber, Max. *The Sociology of Religion.* Translated by Ephraim Fischoff. Boston: Beacon, 1991.

Wedgwood, Barbara Lee. "A Critical Study of the Life and Works of Julia Wedgwood." PhD diss., University College London, 1983.

Wedgwood, Frances Julia. "The Boundaries of Science: A Dialogue." *Macmillan's Magazine* 2, no. 8 (1860): 134–38.

Wedgwood, Frances Julia. "The Boundaries of Science: A Second Dialogue." *Macmillan's Magazine* 4, no. 21 (1861): 237–47.

Wenger, Tisa. *We Have a Religion: The 1920s Pueblo Indian Dance Controversy and American Religious Freedom*. Chapel Hill: University of North Carolina Press, 2009.

Whalen, Andrew. "Kids Shipped in Armoires? The Person Who Started the Wayfair Conspiracy Speaks." *Newsweek*, July 10, 2020. https://www.newsweek.com/wayfair-child-trafficking-conspiracy-theory-cabinets-scandal-1517013.

White, Andrew Dickson. *A History of the Warfare of Science with Theology in Christendom*. Vol. 1. Cambridge: Cambridge University Press, 2009.

White, Paul. "Darwin's Emotions: The Scientific Self and the Sentiment of Objectivity." *Isis* 100 (2009): 811–26.

White, Paul. "Introduction." *Isis* 100 (2009): 792–97.

White, Paul. *Thomas Huxley: Making the "Man of Science."* Cambridge: Cambridge University Press, 2003.

Whitehead, Alfred North. *Process and Reality: An Essay in Cosmology*. Corrected ed., edited by David Ray Griffin and Donald W. Sherburne. New York: Free Press, 1978.

Whitehead, Alfred North. *Science and the Modern World*. New York: Pelican, 1948.

Whittlesea, Bruce. "Illusions of Familiarity." *Journal of Experimental Psychology: Learning, Memory, and Cognition* 19, no. 6 (1993): 1235–53.

Wiegman, Robyn. "The Times We're In: Queer Feminist Criticism and the Reparative 'Turn.'" *Feminist Theory* 15, no. 1 (2014): 4–25.

Wilson, Elizabeth A. *Affect and Artificial Intelligence*. Seattle: University of Washington Press, 2010.

Wilson, Elizabeth A. *Gut Feminism*. Durham, NC: Duke University Press, 2015.

Wilson, E. O. *Sociobiology: The New Synthesis*. 25th anniv. ed. Cambridge, MA: Belknap Press of Harvard University Press, 2000.

Wilson, E. O. "What Is Sociobiology?" *Social Science and Modern Society* 15, no. 5 (1978): 10–14.

Wilson, Shawn. *Research Is Ceremony: Indigenous Research Methods*. Winnipeg, Manitoba: Fernwood, 2008.

Winkielman, Piotr, and John T. Cacioppo. "Mind at Ease Puts a Smile on the Face: Psychophysiological Evidence That Processing Facilitation Elicits Positive Affect." *Journal of Personality and Social Psychology* 81, no. 6 (2001): 989–1000.

Wolf, Gary. "The Church of Non-believers." *Wired*, November 1, 2006. https://www.wired.com/2006/11/atheism/.

Wood, Anthony À. *The History and Antiquities of the University of Oxford. Volume the Second. Part the Second*. Edited by John Gutch. Oxford: Printed for the Author, 1796.

Wood, William. *Blaise Pascal on Duplicity, Sin, and the Fall: The Secret Instinct*. Oxford: Oxford University Press, 2013.

Wright, George Frederick. "The Passing of Evolution." In *The Fundamentals: A Testimony to the Truth*, vol. 7, 5–20. Chicago: Testimony, 1915.
Wyloge, Evan. "Hundreds Gather in Arizona for Armed Anti-Muslim Protest." *Washington Post*, May 30, 2015.
Wynter, Sylvia. "Disenchanting Discourse: 'Minority' Literary Criticism and Beyond." *Cultural Critique* 7 (1987): 207–44.
Wynter, Sylvia. "Unsettling the Coloniality of Being/Power/Truth/Freedom: Towards the Human, After Man, Its Overrepresentation—An Argument." *CR: The New Centennial Review* 3, no. 3 (2003): 257–337.
Zahl, Simeon. *The Holy Spirit and Christian Experience*. Oxford: Oxford University Press, 2020.
Zahl, Simeon. "On the Affective Salience of Doctrines." *Modern Theology* 31, no. 3 (2015): 428–44.
Zajonc, Robert. "Attitudinal Effects of Mere Exposure." *Journal of Personality and Social Psychology Monograph Supplement* 9, no. 2, part 2 (1968): 1–27.
Zajonc, Robert. "Feeling and Thinking: Closing the Debate over the Independence of Affect." In *Feeling and Thinking: The Role of Affect in Social Cognition*, edited by Joseph P. Forgas, 31–58. Cambridge: Cambridge University Press, 2001.
Zajonc, Robert. "Feeling and Thinking: Preferences Need No Inferences." *American Psychologist* 35, no. 2 (1980): 151–75.
Zajonc, Robert. "On the Primacy of Affect." *American Psychologist* 39, no. 2 (1984): 117–23.
Zebrowitz, Leslie, Benjamin White, and Kristin Wieneke. "Mere Exposure and Racial Prejudice: Exposure to Other-Race Faces Increases Liking for Strangers of That Race." *Social Cognition* 26, no. 3 (2008): 259–75.
Zucchino, David. "North Carolina Triple Slaying Arouses Fear of Hate Crimes against Muslims." *Los Angeles Times*, February 11, 2015. https://www.latimes.com/nation/nationnow/la-na-north-carolina-shooting-deaths-20150211-story.html.

Index

Abu-Salha, Razan Mohammad, 200, 227
Abu-Salha, Yusor Mohammad, 200, 227
Act, the (Oxford ceremony), 82, 102–3
adaptationism, 205–6, 209–10
affect: affective economies, 60, 72–73; agonism and, 48–51, 63; as becoming, 61; cognition and, 9, 11, 17–18, 61, 111–33; in conspiracy theory, 51–52; critique and, 95–96; emotion and, 5–6; epistemology and, 34; Foucault and, 60–61; language and, 61–65; postcritical turn and, 96–100; power and, 19–21, 58; racialized reason and, 70–77, 172, 186, 195, 227–29; racism and, 24–26, 28, 36, 59; science and, 34–35, 49, 54–55; secularism and, 83–92, 102, 105–6, 202–4; susceptibility as, 5. *See also* feeling
affective neuroscience, 112–14, 119
affect theory: cogency theory and, 5, 11, 17–18, 25, 78–79, 108, 232–33; Deleuzian, 4–5, 61, 69; experimental psychology and, 108–12, 122–33; feminist approaches, 5–6, 60–61, 69–71, 212–13; neuroscience and, 108–9, 112–22, 132–33; phenomenological, 19–21, 58–61; secularism and, 26–28; Tomkins on, 59, 61, 63–69
African American humanism, 219–22
agnosticism: Darwin and, 21, 140, 156, 163, 165–67; Huxley and, 157, 269n146; Scopes Trial and, 180, 191
agonism: affect theory and, 63, 65–66, 68–69; in cogency theory, 9, 12, 36, 59, 78, 147, 231–32, 236; knowledge-making and, 52, 54, 56; New Atheism and, 227; power and, 19; science and, 23, 41, 45–46, 48, 179, 229; thinking/feeling binary and, 116, 120, 124. *See also* sense of science
Ahmed, Sara, 60–61, 69, 71–72, 74, 212, 244n18
American Civil Liberties Union (ACLU), 174–78
anger, 65, 98, 201, 224
animacy hierarchy, 72, 203, 212–14, 228
apophenia, 51–52
Aquinas, Thomas, 20
Aristotle, 35, 46

Asad, Talal: on critique, 26, 95–96, 101–2, 226; on disenchantment, 92–93, 258n84; feeling/thinking binary and, 245n22; on formations of the secular, 83, 89–91, 218, 256n51; on religion as a category, 88–89, 208; science and, 247n85; secular embodiment and, 26, 91, 92
Asma, Stephen T., 245n20, 263n96
atheism: Darwin and, 163, 166; decline of, 204, 278n108; fear of, 173, 190; racialization in, 224, 229; Soviet, 91; *See also* New Atheism; New New Atheism
Augustine, 35
Austin, J. L., 59, 61–63, 65
awe, 18, 54, 69, 82, 95, 104–6, 188

Baldwin, James, 71
Barakat, Deah Shaddy, 200, 227
Barkun, Michael, 51, 76, 248n2
Barrett, Lisa Feldman: on arousal, 68, 122; on behaviorism, 261n26; on cognition/emotion binary, 17, 27, 120, 133; on the triune brain, 113
basic emotions hypothesis, 67, 122, 253nn53–54
behaviorism, 111–13, 261n26
Bennett, Jane, 91, 94–95, 245n24
Berger, Peter, 84–91, 93, 105
Berlant, Lauren: on affect theory, 60, 65; click and, 3; on cognition, 79; on critique, 97; sensualized epistemology of, 26, 70
Beruf. See vocation
Best, Stephen, 97
black monolith myth: *2001: A Space Odyssey* (Kubrick) and, 21–22; affect theory and, 70, 78, 108; cogency theory and, 139; Darwin and, 110, 165; knowledge-making and, 45, 95; New Atheism and, 226; rationality and, 15, 37; secularism and, 25, 92, 222; triune brain and, 113
Black studies, 5, 110
Bonilla-Silva, Eduardo, 74, 78, 254n98, 254n99
boredom, 63, 159, 165–66

Breaking the Spell (Dennett), 204, 207, 209
British Association for the Advancement of Science (BAAS), 158–59, 161, 175
Browne, Janet, 1, 142–45, 148, 161
Bryan, William Jennings: cogency theory and, 172, 189; eugenics and, 192–93; in *Inherit the Wind*, 173–74, 188; Mencken and, 183–86; populism, 187–88; racialized reason of, 28, 189–91, 194–95, 203, 274n102; Scopes Trial and, 176–79, 273n86
Buckland, William, 138, 156
Butler, Anthea, 194
Butler, Judith, 96, 98, 259n120
Butler Act, 174–76, 178, 186

Cacioppo, John, 107–8, 126, 128, 130. *See also* mere exposure effect
Chambers, Robert (Mr. Vestiges), 137–39, 148, 153, 158–59, 168, 269n154
Chapel Hill murders, 203, 220, 223, 228
Chen, Mel Y., 59, 72, 203, 213–14, 217. *See also* animacy hierarchy
Civic Biology (Hunter), 188, 192–93
click: affect theory and, 69; cogency theory and, 6, 20, 48, 78, 231, 235; conspiracy theory and, 34, 36, 49–53, 75; Darwin and, 143–44, 153, 165–66; feeling of, 2–3, 15–18, 99, 104; knowledge-making and, 15–18, 24, 39–40, 55–56, 247n67; mere exposure effect and, 108–10, 122, 129–30, 132; New Atheism and, 203, 208–10, 218, 227; racialized reason and, 184–85, 195
climate change, 7, 52, 209, 235–37, 275n138; science of, 13, 231, 232, 234
climate denialism, 3, 7, 28, 52, 232, 235
Clinton, Hillary, 50–51
cogency theory: affect theory and, 20, 59–61, 67–70, 77–79; conspiracy theory and, 24, 34–35, 75; definition of, 4, 9–10, 231–32; experimental psychology and, 108–9, 126–27, 132–33; feminism and, 246n42; knowledge-making and, 21, 45, 167; liberalism and, 197; neuroscience and, 108–9, 114, 122, 132–33;

racialization and, 73–75, 171–72, 195, 217–18; science and technology studies (STS) and, 11, 14; secularism and, 25–26, 95, 202–3; theology and, 244n14

cognition: affect theory and, 19, 25, 61, 67–70, 251n17, 261n7, 262–63n72; cogency theory and, 5–7, 10–11, 20, 132–33; Darwin on, 21; experimental psychology and, 27, 108–12, 122–33; Hume on, 38; neuroscience and, 27, 108–9, 112–22, 132–33

Colombetti, Giovanna, 35, 244n15

Comitia (Oxford ceremony). *See* Act, the

Comte, Auguste, 23, 85

Connolly, William, 91

conspiracy theory: cogency theory and, 23–25, 35–36, 231; feelings of, 8, 52; Jewish-Communist, 189, 195; New Atheism and, 28, 202–3, 210, 214, 224, 227; pedophilia, 34; Pizzagate, 50; QAnon, 50; racialized reason and, 75–77; Satanism, 34; Wayfair, 50, 52. *See also* climate denialism; McCarthyism

core affect, 120

cosmic religious feeling, 2, 207

creationism, 178–79, 188, 194, 196–97, 230, 233

critical neuroscience, 132

critique: disenchantment and, 104–6; Marxist, 65, 220; postcritical turn and, 97–100; secularism and, 26, 84, 95–96, 101–2, 226. *See also* postcritical turn

Cvetkovich, Ann, 62

Damasio, Antonio, 114–19; on *Descartes' Error*, 18, 108; Iowa Gambling Task (IGT), 117–18; passion for reason, 18–19, 117, 119, 122, 250n80; somatic marker hypothesis, 109, 113–14, 116

Darrow, Clarence, 173, 175–78, 186, 189, 192–93

Darwin, Charles: charm offensive, 147–50, 154; in contemporary atheism, 202, 206, 210, 212, 225–27; correspondence with Gray, 164–65; Darwin's delay, 144–47, 267n54; Darwin-Wedgwood clan, 149–50; on emotion and cognition, 21, 36–37, 110–11; instinct for truth, 145; passion for reason of, 140, 225; relationship to Huxley, 152–58, 160–62; scientific nervousness of, 144, 146; views on race, 150–52; views on religion, 145, 162–66, 172, 191; views on William Paley, 141–44

Darwin, Emma (née Wedgwood), 144–45, 162, 271n203

Darwin, Erasmus, 37, 137, 141

Darwin, Francis, 1, 162–63

Daston, Lorraine, 11, 55, 251n113

Dawkins, Richard, 20, 204–7; feeling and, 20–21, 40; Islamophobia of, 201; on memes, 206–8, 226, 276n30; racialized reason of, 214–16, 219–221; on religion, 204–7, 210–12; scientific views of, 202, 208–10

day-age theory, 177

Deleuze, Gilles, 25, 61, 244n12

Dennett, Daniel: on Nietzsche, 41; racialized reason and, 215; on religion, 204, 207–9, 211; scientific views of, 28, 202, 210

Derrida, Jacques, 197

Descartes, René, 9–10, 157

Descartes' Error (Damasio), 27, 108, 116. *See also* Damasio, Antonio

Descent of Man, and Selection in Relation to Sex, The (Darwin), 107, 110, 151–52, 162

Desmond, Adrian, 138, 141, 146, 152–53, 155

Discipline and Punish (Foucault), 60

disenchantment: feelings of, 82–84, 104–6; secularism studies and, 26, 257n84; Weber on, 26, 85–88, 92–95, 247n84, 257n75, 257–58n83

disputations, 102–4, 106, 177

Disraeli, Benjamin, 19–20

Dixon, Thomas, 244n14, 245n24

drives: cogency theory and, 75; cogitation and 9–10; Damasio on, 116; Freud on, 63; Nietzsche on, 249n40; racialized reason and, 132; Tomkins on, 63–65, 68

Du Bois, W. E. B., 179, 182, 189–90

Edwards v. Aguillard, 179
Einstein, Albert, 2, 35, 207, 237
Eliot, George (Mary Ann Evans), 8, 137, 200
embodiment, 11, 26, 41, 54, 60–61, 91, 256n60, 257n63
emotion. *See* feeling
emotion/reason binary. *See* thinking/feeling binary
empiricism, 11, 13–14, 37, 46, 246n40
End of Faith, The (Harris), 204, 207, 215, 217, 277n99
English Civil War, 81
Enlightenment, the, 89, 96. *See also philosophes*
Enquiry Concerning Human Understanding, An (Hume), 37
Entzauberung. See disenchantment
Epperson v. Arkansas, 178
equal-time laws, 178–79, 195–96
eugenics: in antievolution discourse, 192–94; *Bell v. Buck*, 193; Bryan and, 188; Darwin and, 151, 167; Mencken and, 170–72, 181, 183, 185; religion and, 185; in the South, 183, 185–86, 193–94; sterilization campaigns, 193; in textbooks, 188, 192–93
evolution: Darwin and, 37, 110, 138–39; denialism of, 230–31, 32–33; Lamarck and, 137; by natural selection, 139, 144–45, 147, 153, 164–65, 206, 265n13; neuroscience and, 114; New Atheism and, 28, 206–7; Nietzsche on, 41; racialized reason and, 140, 150–52, 186, 193–94; religion and, 149, 168, 170–74, 190–91; secularization and, 27
E.V.R. (patient), 114–16
Expression of the Emotions in Man and Animals, The (Darwin), 110–11, 162

Fadil, Nadia, 91, 257n63
Fanon, Frantz, 7, 244n19
feeling: clarification of usage, 4–5; climate denialism and, 234–35; power and, 19–21, 63; racialized reason and, 25, 59, 75, 213; religion and, 104, 162; secularism and, 29, 91–92, 94, 223–25; structures of, 8, 133; of truth, 9, 235–37. *See also* affect; anger; awe; boredom; click; disenchantment; humiliation; interest
Felski, Rita, 26, 97–101
feminism: affect and, 25, 59, 61; science and, 13; secularism and, 221
femonationalism, 221
Ferreira da Silva, Denise, 24, 244n19
formations of the secular, 83, 140, 259n146
Formations of the Secular (Asad), 89–91
Foucault, Michel: affect theory and, 25, 60, 63, 65, 77–78, 96; Asad and, 91; on power, 19, 58–60, 247n71; on psychology, 57–58; on scientific progress, 6–7, 12
Frank, Adam, 64, 253n53
Freud, Sigmund, 23, 58, 63, 234
Frost, Samantha, 132
fundamentalism, 171, 173, 179, 184–85, 211, 224

Gabriel, Rami, 245n20, 263n96
Galison, Peter, 11, 55, 251n113
Geertz, Clifford, 88–89, 91
Goodall, Jane, 22
Gould, Stephen Jay: on adaptationism, 202, 205, 209–10; African American humanism and, 222; on Bryan, 188, 193; *Rocks of Ages*, 188; on teaching, 195
Gray, Asa, 149–50, 162, 164–65

Haidt, Jonathan, 121–22, 245n20, 263n94
Hamner, M. Gail, 46, 245n33
Harris, Sam: on belief, 207; relationship to Hinduism, 217; Islamophobia of, 215–17, 221, 277n99; on morality, 208–9
Harrison, Peter, 39, 55
hedonic fluency, 108, 130
hedonicity of hate, 73, 181, 213
Heidegger, Martin, 69
hermeneutic of suspicion, 58, 97
Hicks, Craig Stephens, 200–202, 214, 228. *See also* Chapel Hill murders

Hirschkind, Charles, 91, 257n63
history of emotions, 252n24
History of Sexuality, Vol. I, The (Foucault), 57–58, 60
Hitchens, Christopher: criticism of religion, 211; Islamophobia of, 213–14
Hofstadter, Richard, 33–34, 51, 75
Holland, Sharon Patricia, 26, 59, 73–75, 77–78, 186
Hollywood, Amy, 101, 226, 258n102
homonationalism, 221
Hooker, Joseph Dalton: correspondence with Darwin, 143, 145, 147, 161; on the Huxley-Wilberforce debate, 270n165
Hume, David, 36–41; on calm passions, 36, 39–40, 45, 53–54; influence on Darwin, 25, 36–37, 41, 46, 141; influence on James, 46; passion for philosophy of, 2, 39; on reason and emotion, 37–38, 40, 116; religion and, 157, 164; theory of agonism, 54, 68, 120; on violent passions, 40
humiliation, 65, 179, 214
Hutchinson, Sikivu, 28, 219–22, 227; on racialization, 221–22; radical humanism, 220
Huxley, Thomas Henry: agnosticism of, 157–58; cogency theory and, 140–41; as Darwin's bulldog, 23, 152–55; difficulty of interpretation, 269n146; love of fight, 27–28, 140, 153–54; Mencken and, 170, 180–81, 195; passion for reason of, 152–53; on religion, 23, 155–58, 212, 219. *See also* Huxley-Wilberforce debate
Huxley-Wilberforce debate, 140, 158–62, 171, 177, 270n165

illocutionary force, 61–63, 65, 78
Indian philosophy, 5, 245n22
Indigenous philosophy, 5
Inherit the Wind, 170, 173–74, 178, 187–88
intellectual passions: agonism and, 49, 55, 167; cogency theory and, 78; in critique, 98; for Polanyi, 14–18, 141; secularism and, 84; for Sedgwick, 69

Intelligent Design (ID), 170, 196, 223
interest: cogency theory and, 78, 253n60; Damasio and, 117; Hume and, 40; James and, 48; New New Atheism and, 223, 225; Nietzsche and, 53; Polanyi and, 16, 141; postcritical turn and, 100; Tomkins and, 18, 25, 65, 67–70, 75, 119
Iowa Gambling Task, (IGT) 115–18, 262n67
iron cage of modernity, 23, 86–87. *See also* disenchantment; rationalization; Weber, Max
Islamic philosophy, 5, 245n22
Islamophobia, 76, 102, 203, 213, 278n108

Jacoby, Larry, 126–28, 130
Jaggar, Alison, 14
James, William, 36, 45–49; academic training, 45; feelings and, 25, 46, 104; on nervousness, 36, 53–54, 141, 144, 212; on Pascal's wager, 46–47, 250n74; sentiment of rationality, 18, 36, 46–48, 111; tough-mindedness, 49, 141
Jesus Camp (Ewing and Grady), 232
Jim Crow, 181, 183, 189, 199, 274n102
Johansen, Birgitte Schepelern, 91, 257n63
Josephson-Storm, Jason, 87, 92, 94, 106, 257n75

Kant, Immanuel, 37, 45, 157
Kazin, Michael, 187–89, 274n102
kettle logic (Freud), 234
Khalil, Mohammad Hassan, 216–17, 277n99
Kingsley, Charles, 149–50, 156, 172–73
Kitzmiller v. Dover, 170
knowledge-making: affect theory and, 58–59, 66, 78; cogency theory and, 3–6, 9, 17–18, 29, 231; feeling and, 29, 58–59, 95–96; New Atheism and, 202, 218; racialized reason and, 11, 102, 180, 186; secularism and, 83, 167
Kuhn, Thomas, 10; click and, 247n67; Kuhn-Polanyi relationship, 14, 17, 245n56; on paradigms, 12; on scientific progress, 13, 55, 245n40; on theory, 10
Ku Klux Klan (KKK), 174, 181, 184, 189, 195

Lamarck, Jean-Baptiste, 37, 137, 141, 148
LaMothe, Kimerer, 54
Larson, Edward, 179, 186, 188, 190, 193, 274n106
Latour, Bruno: on climate change, 231–32; cogency theory and, 231–32, 236; on feeling, 4; postcritical turn and, 13, 26, 99; STS and, 11, 13
Laud, William, 81–82, 103–4, 106
Lazarus, Richard, 124–25, 261n8, 264n118. *See also* Zajonc-Lazarus Debate
Ledoux, Joseph, 262–263n72, 264n111
Lepselter, Susan, 51–52
Levine, George, 49, 91, 94–95, 152, 165, 167, 210
Leys, Ruth, 109, 244n12, 251n17, 252n28, 253n53, 260n7
liberal Christianity, 158–59, 172–73
liberalism: embodiment and, 257n63; feelings and, 29, 196–97; Hicks and, 201–2, 228; philosophy of, 66, 247n71
Life and Letters (Darwin), 142, 162–63, 166
limbic system, 109, 113–14, 125. *See also* triune brain
linguistic fallacy, 19, 63, 203, 207–8, 228
Lorde, Audre, 71, 73
Lyell, Charles, 138, 142, 144, 147, 265n6

MacLean, Paul, 27, 112–14
Maher, Bill, 211
Mahmood, Saba, 26, 95–96, 101, 258n107
Maiese, Michelle, 35
Marcus, Sharon, 97
Marx, Karl, 22, 58, 85–86, 156, 235
Mbembe, Achille, 229
McCarthy, Joseph, 51, 188
McCarthyism, 171
McClintock, Barbara, 1–2, 35
McKittrick, Katherine, 11, 244n19, 251n109
McLean v. Arkansas, 188, 195
meme (Dawkins's concept), 206–8, 226, 276n30
Mencken, H. L.: Bryan and, 171, 179, 185–86, 188, 203; eugenics and, 28, 170, 172, 181–83; Huxley and, 28, 180; in *Inherit the Wind*, 170, 173; New Atheism and, 213, 224; racialized reason and, 183–86, 195, 233
mere exposure effect (MEE), 27, 107–10, 122–33
methodological symmetry, 5–6, 48
microexpressions, 107
Monin, Benoît, 128, 130, 264n140
Moore, James, 41, 146, 158, 265n13
moral psychology, 121
movement atheism. *See* New Atheism
Mr. Vestiges. *See* Chambers, Robert
Muñoz, José Esteban, 224; national affect and, 62, 71–72; on racialized reason, 59, 71
mysterium tremendum, 104

Natural Theology (Paley), 142. *See also* Paley, William
New Atheism: anger and, 223; critique of religion, 207–9; individuals associated with, 204, 275n18; Islamophobia of, 212–18; Nietzsche and, 53; parallels to conspiracy theory, 28, 203, 209–12, 227, 229; racialized reason, 202, 217–18, 220–21; relationship to sociobiology, 28, 202, 204–7
new materialisms, 246n42
New New Atheism, 219
Ngai, Sianne, 70
Nietzsche, Friedrich, 25, 33, 41–45; on Darwin, 41, 249n40; on embodiment, 33, 41–42, 54; Foucault and, 58–59; Mencken and, 181; views on science, 36, 42–45, 48, 55
nontheistic religion, 222. *See also* Pinn, Anthony
Nussbaum, Martha, 35, 244n13

Obama, Barack, 77, 214, 230
objectivity, 11–12, 54–55, 72, 102, 218, 221
Oreskes, Naomi, 53, 196, 231, 234, 275n138
Origin of Species, On the (Darwin), 138–39, 148–49, 151, 153–54, 162–64
Otto, Rudolf, 104
Oxford University, 80; secular feelings and, 102, 104; secularization of, 81–82, 106

Paley, William, 140–42, 144, 155–56
Panksepp, Jaak, 68, 117, 122, 245n20
panopticon, 60
paradigm, 12–13, 15–16, 53, 55, 111–12, 121–22, 139
paranoid reading, 96–97, 100, 205
Pascal, Blaise, 46, 49, 244n14, 250n74
Pascal's Wager, 46–47
passions: cool, 36, 39, 53, 54; intellectual, 14–17, 18, 49, 55, 141; for knowledge, 41; persuasive, 16, 42; for reason, 18, 56, 109, 116–17, 122, 196, 202, 218, 220, 250n80; for truth, 145, 149, 158, 168, 234; violent, 40
Pellegrini, Ann, 22, 88–91
performatives, 59, 61–62
Perry, Imani, 8, 24, 72, 74
persuasion: act of, 5, 62, 167, 234, 236; passion for, 186; persuasion zone, 232, 235
Pessoa, Luiz, 27, 120–21
Phaf, Hans, 125–28
Phelps, Elizabeth, 27, 119
phenomenology, 244n18
philosophes, 5, 35, 257n69
Pigliucci, Massimo, 208
Pinn, Anthony, 28, 219–22, 227; African American humanism of, 219–22; feelings and, 224–25; nontheistic religion, 222; on racialized reason, 220, 228
Polanyi, Michael, 14–18; Kuhn and, 14, 17, 246n56; on passion in science, 2, 14–18, 141; on persuasive passion, 16, 42, 186
Popper, Karl, 35
populism, 187–88
postcritical turn, 5, 13, 26, 96, 100, 205.
  See also critique; paranoid reading
postmodernism: hatred of, 209–10
poststructuralism, 13, 59, 66, 97
power: in affect theory, 19–20, 60–62, 64, 74; Asad and, 89; Foucault's theory of, 58, 60, 247n71; postcritical turn and, 95, 98–100; power-knowledge-affect, 58–59, 78; racialized reason and, 78, 224
pragmatism, 46–47, 49

Protestant Ethic and the Spirit of Capitalism, The (Weber), 85, 87, 93, 255n18
Protestant Reformation, 23, 81, 87, 157, 255n18
Protevi, John, 35
Protocols of the Elders of Zion, 76
psychoanalysis, 25, 57, 59, 63–64, 77
psychology of knowledge, 25, 66, 70
Puar, Jasbir, 72, 221

queer theory: affect theory and, 25–26, 59, 61–64, 70–71; postcritical turn and, 98, 100, 259n120

race science, 4, 150–51, 183, 185–86, 212.
  See also eugenics; scientific racism
racialization: conspiracy theory and, 76; definition of, 218; feelings and, 77–78, 110, 180; secularism and, 24, 28, 84, 219, 224, 227; theories of, 26–27, 70–75, 132
racialized reason, 4, 23, 56; affect theory and, 25–26, 59, 70–75, 78–79, 102, 254n99; atheism and, 202, 210, 212–13, 217–18, 221, 226–27; conspiracy theory and, 24–25, 75–77; Darwin and, 150, 152; neuroscience and, 126, 132–33; in Scopes Trial, 28, 171–72, 180–81, 186, 189, 194–95
Ramanujan, Srinivasa, 2
rationalization, 86–87, 90, 92
Reber, Rolf, 128–30
Reddy, William, 62, 252n24
relativism, 15, 17, 209–10
Religious Affects (Schaefer), 19–20, 251n17
Religulous. *See* Maher, Bill
reparative reading, 96–98, 100
repressive hypothesis, 57–58
reptilian brain, 112–13. *See also* triune brain
Rice, Jenny, 50–51
Richards, Evelleen, 151–52
Ricoeur, Paul, 58
Rogers, Leslie, 197–99
Ryrie, Alec, 244n14, 250n74

Safi, Omid, 201, 228
Scheer, Monique, 91, 102, 252n24, 257n63

science and technology studies (STS): beginnings of, 12–13; conspiracy theory and, 231; feelings and, 4, 11, 78; feminist, 8, 13, 167; methodological symmetry and, 5–6; secularism studies and, 23
science-religion conflict thesis, 23
scientific racism, 6, 167, 223. *See also* eugenics; race science
scientific rationality: cogency theory and, 10–13, 21, 27, 36, 55–56, 75; humanities and, 6; secularism and, 21, 27, 167
scientism, 207–10
Scopes Trial of 1925: cogency theory and, 171–72; in *Inherit the Wind*, 170–72, 173–74; political context of, 179, 188; racism in, 28, 171–72, 180–83, 186, 189–99; science teaching and, 195–96
Scopes, John T., 170, 173–74, 176–78, 180, 188–89
secular body, 26, 91, 257n63
secularism: affect theory and, 84; anthropology of, 90–92, 105, 256n51; belief and, 88–89; in cogency theory, 20, 22, 25–29, 202; feelings of, 84, 91–92, 95–96, 106, 167–68, 219, 226–27; myth of objectivity, 95, 101; New Atheism and, 204, 219; New New Atheism and, 220–26; racialized reason and, 24, 227–29, 278n108; scientific, 140, 170–71, 179, 195; Soviet, 247n85; and thinking/feeling binary, 4, 8
secularism studies: feelings and, 26, 84, 91–92; on New Atheism, 95; overview of, 22–23, 83–84, 90, 105; STS and, 25
secularization: Asad on, 88–91; Berger on, 84–85, 88; classical theory of, 4, 22, 26, 84–85, 229–30; disenchantment and, 83, 92; of Oxford, 82, 106; racialization and, 229; Taylor on, 90–91; Weber on, 85–88
Sedgwick, Adam, 138–39, 148, 152, 168
Sedgwick, Eve Kosofsky: affect theory of, 26, 59, 69–71, 79, 140; postcritical turn and, 26, 69, 96–100; queer theory and, 64, 70; on thinking/feeling binary, 9–10; Tomkins and, 63–64
Selfish Gene, The (Dawkins), 204–8
sense of science, 1, 4, 12; of Darwin, 27, 140, 144, 146, 150, 165; definition of, 23–25; within cogency theory, 34–36; conspiracy theory and, 23–24, 49–54; of Huxley, 153–54, 157–58, 181; in New New Atheism, 219, 227; Nietzsche and, 45; in the Scopes Trial, 171, 179, 195–97; Tomkins and, 68
sentiment of rationality, 17–18, 36, 45–49, 54, 111
shame: Bryan and, 187; in cogency theory, 232; in critique, 99; for Darwin, 147; for Huxley, 157; persuasion and, 233–34; for sense of science, 24, 49, 54–55; for Tomkins, 63, 65, 68–69
Shapin, Steven, 10, 29
Sheldonian Theatre, 19–20, 26, 82–84, 103
Sideris, Lisa, 247n75
simplex system: conspiracy theory as, 24, 50, 56, 75; fundamentalism as, 184; New Atheism as, 28, 202–3, 208, 210; Spinoza and, 35
Slaby, Jan, 132
sociobiology, 28, 202, 204–5
soft atheism. *See* New New Atheism
somatic marker hypothesis (SMH), 109, 114–16, 262n63, 262n67
Spinoza, Benedict de, 2, 5, 8, 35, 245n24
Stedman, Chris, 28, 222–26, 227; criticism of New Atheism, 222–23; on feeling, 224; within New New Atheism, 28, 219, 227; views on science, 223, 225–26
Stengers, Isabelle, 244n10
Stewart, Kathleen, 52, 79, 97
St. Mary the Virgin (SMV). *See* University Church of St. Mary the Virgin (SMV)
strong programme, 13
Structure of Scientific Revolutions, The (Kuhn), 12, 14
subjectivity: in affect theory, 19–20, 60, 64–66, 69, 229; for New Atheism, 208, 216; for poststructuralism, 66
subtraction story, 90

surprise, 40, 70, 96–97, 213, 253n60
suspicion: masters of, 58–59; postcritical turn and, 53, 97–98, 100, 205; of scientific rationality, 6–7; of self, 181, 229

tacit knowledge, 14, 17, 246n56
Taylor, Charles: on disenchantment, 88, 92–93, 95, 257n70; embodiment and, 91–92; theory of secularism, 2, 23, 87, 105, 202
Tennessee v. Scopes. *See* Scopes Trial of 1925
textualism, 203, 208, 216, 218, 221
Thagard, Paul, 35, 245n22
thinking/feeling binary, 4–5, 8, 10, 17, 38–41, 54, 78, 108–9, 226, 231
Titchener, Edward Bradford, 111, 117, 126, 131
Tomkins, Silvan, 63–70; affect theory of, 59, 63–65, 253n63; criticism of, 252n28, 253n53; engagements with, 63, 69, 100; on knowledge-making, 18, 25, 66–70, 117, 119; on racism, 70; on religion, 18
Treatise of Human Nature, A (Hume), 38–39
triune brain: criticism of, 113–14, 119, 121–22, 132; structure of, 112–13, 125; and thinking/feeling, 27, 109, 113, 132
Trump, Donald, 50, 169, 215

University Church of St. Mary the Virgin (SMV), 80–82, 84, 102–4, 177
US Civil War, 150, 164

Vásquez, Manuel, 203, 208
Vestiges of the Natural History of Creation (Chambers): authorship of, 159, 269n154; political significance of, 148–49, 153; popularity of, 139, 146; responses to, 138–39, 152–53; scientific rigor of, 153, 156, 158, 212
vocation: for Darwin, 142; for Huxley, 153; for Weber, 26, 80, 86, 93, 247n84

Wallace, Alfred Russel, 147, 151
warm glow heuristic, 131
Weber, Max, 22; on capitalism, 85, 255n18; on disenchantment, 26, 87–88, 92–95, 106, 210, 247n84, 257n75, 257–58n83; misinterpretations of, 87–89; on secularization, 22–23; theory of rationalization, 85–86, 90
Wedgwood, Julia Frances "Snow," 149, 172
Whitehead, Alfred North, 5, 244n15, 245n24
Whitehouse, Kevin, 126–28, 130
white supremacy, 4, 140, 194, 210, 212, 228
Whittlesea, Bruce, 128–30
Wiegman, Robyn, 100, 258n107, 259n120
Wilberforce, Samuel, 140, 159–60, 177, 270n165
Wilson, Elizabeth A., 64, 247n85, 253n53, 253n60
Wilson, E. O., 205, 209
Winkielman, Piotr, 107–8, 126, 130, 264n136. *See also* mere exposure effect
Wynter, Sylvia, 22, 244n19

X Club, the, 23, 158, 161

Zahl, Simeon, 244n14
Zajonc, Robert: on mere exposure effect, 27, 107, 123, 130, 233; racialized reason and, 131, 133; theory of affect, 68, 124–25
Zajonc-Lazarus Debate, 124–26, 261n18, 264n118

www.ingramcontent.com/pod-product-compliance
Lightning Source LLC
Chambersburg PA
CBHW051048230426
43666CB00012B/2615